THE PACIFIC ISLANDS

THE
PACIFIC ISLANDS

REVISED EDITION

DOUGLAS L. OLIVER

ILLUSTRATIONS BY SHEILA MITCHELL OLIVER

Foreword by Harry L. Shapiro

THE UNIVERSITY PRESS OF HAWAII
HONOLULU

The Pacific Islands was originally published by Harvard University Press in 1951. The revised edition was copublished in 1961 by The American Museum of Natural History and Doubleday & Company, Inc., as a Doubleday Anchor Book; and in 1962 by Harvard University Press.

First printing by
The University Press of Hawaii 1975
Second printing 1977

Maps on pages 21 and 158 drawn by
RAFAEL PALACIOS

Foreword Copyright © 1961 by The American Museum of Natural History

Copyright © 1951, 1961 by Douglas L. Oliver

Library of Congress Catalog Card Number 75-19352
ISBN 0-8248-0397-3
Manufactured in the United States of America

TO RUTH AND PHIL PHILLIPS

ACKNOWLEDGMENT

Many institutions and individuals have contributed financially to my studies in and about the Pacific Islands during the last twenty-five years: Harvard's Department of Anthropology and Peabody Museum; Messrs. Cornelius Crane, Pierre Ledoux, and Donald Scott; the Office of Naval Research; the Rockefeller Foundation; the Howard Foundation; the National Science Foundation; the Tri-Institutional Pacific Research Program; the American Academy of Arts and Sciences. To all these I express appreciation.

Particular thanks are due Dr. Reo Fortune and Routledge and Kegan Paul, Ltd., for permission to abstract parts of *Sorcerers of Dobu,* and the Cambridge University Press for permission to abstract parts of Gregory Bateson's *Naven.* I also wish to thank Dr. J. O. Brew for permission to utilize objects in the Peabody Museum in preparation of the book's illustration.

To the following I owe special kinds of debts for having made my long preoccupation with Oceania something far more valuable than a mere academic interest: Eleanor McClennen, Pierre Ledoux, Knowles Ryerson, Philip Phillips, Howry Warner, H. G. MacMillan, Richard Black, John Useem, J. K. Howard, Harold Coolidge, G. P. Murdock, Alex Spoehr, Leonard Mason, Kenneth Emory, Felix Keesing, Paul Kay, Roger Green, Richard Moench, Robert Jay, Alice Dewey, and Robert Levy, all of the United States; Ian Hogbin, Mervyn Scales, Harry Maude, Jim Davidson, John Barnes, Bill Geddes, and W. E. Stanner, all of Australia; Ernest Beaglehole, Ralph Piddington, and V. D. Stace, of New Zealand;

Raymond Firth, of Great Britain; Jean Guiart and Jacques Barrau, of France and New Caledonia; and Henri Jacquier, Mlle. Aurora Natua, Raoul Tessier, Ralph White, Michel Jullien, Dr. Emile Massal, Mr. and Mrs. Bengt Danielsson, and Mr. and Mrs. Kellam, all of Tahiti; G. A. V. Stanley, Dr. A. V. Price, Bishop Thomas Wade, and Manao, of New Guinea; and John Van Beueskom of the Netherlands.

To my wife, Sheila Oliver (of Cockatoo Island!), I can only say that I wish that the text of this book lived up to her illustrations.

I specially wish to thank Professor Ernest Beaglehole of the University of New Zealand at Wellington, and Mr. Harry Maude of the Australian National University at Canberra, for their suggestions concerning revision of the original edition. The latter particularly, drawing on his unequaled knowledge of past and present happenings in the Islands, went through the text line by line.

March 1961   DOUGLAS L. OLIVER
Cambridge, Massachusetts

POSTSCRIPT

Since this is a reprinting and not a revision of the 1961 (revised) edition of this book, no effort has been made to bring the text up to date to reflect such events as the new political status of West New Guinea, et cetera. The opportunity provided by reprinting has however been seized to correct certain factual errors which some careful readers have called to my attention. To these latter, including Professor A. P. Elkin, Mr. R. C. Schmitt, and Dr. J. N. Warner, I am most grateful.

December 1962   D.L.O.

FOREWORD

The Pacific Islands and the waters that surround them have occupied a rather special place in the imagination of the western world. What they mean to other people, particularly the Chinese, the Japanese, and the Indians, who also have variously exploited and settled on them, is difficult to say since they have not expressed themselves in the form of a special Pacific Island literature as the westerners have. To us, at any rate, these are the islands of adventure and glamor, the delectable havens of escape, the scenes of fantastic and exotic beauty, and the seats of earthly paradises. And recently they have acquired an additional appeal as the theaters of suffering and heroism in World War II.

One would think that any region as overexposed to literary and cinematic clichés would inevitably disappoint in the reality. But the extraordinary thing is how often it exceeds expectation in its charm. Indeed, from one point of view, this is its danger in the immediate future, for as modern communications and travel facilities improve, more and more of these lovely spots may be inundated by the tourism that destroys what attracts it.

But beneath the charm, real for all its superficiality, lies another world, all too little known but far more significant. It is a world, intricate, varied, and subtle, with traditions and a history of its own. It is a world isolated from the currents of continental life but developing through thousands of years of fascinating multiplicity of cultures adapted to varying environments. For the past two or three centuries, and recently with quick-

ened tempo, all this has been undergoing profound
modifications introduced mainly but not exclusively
by western civilization. Missionaries, traders, whalers,
planters, and many another have brought extinction to
some, ruin and despair to others, and change to virtually
all these cultures and the people who were their in-
heritors. It is both a sad and a fascinating story that has
much to teach us if we have the wit to understand it.

For that we can have no better mentor than Professor
Oliver, whose own investigations have taken him to
many of the islands of the Pacific and have introduced
him firsthand to the fundamental aspects of the life of
the people. But what makes him unique among the
students of the native cultures of the Pacific is a deep
concern with the way in which the people of this vast
area have been affected by the sudden, almost cataclys-
mic introduction of modern civilization. This part of his
account of the Pacific Islands, written with compassion
and insight, is a major contribution. Here he has assembled data not readily accessible and organized them
in a cogent and meaningful way. To be a Polynesian, a
Melanesian, or any other native Pacific Islander in these
difficult and troublesome times is something the casual
visitor or reader knows nothing about. It is high time he
did. And here is Douglas Oliver to do the job.

HARRY L. SHAPIRO
*Chairman, Department
of Anthropology*

March 1961
*The American Museum
of Natural History*

CONTENTS

CATACLYSM AND AFTERMATH

ILLUSTRATIONS AND MAPS

Unless otherwise indicated, the illustrations were
sketched from objects in collections at the
Peabody Museum, Harvard University

THE PACIFIC ISLANDS

INTRODUCTION

During World War II, at the cost of immeasurable suffering and of severe loss of life and materials, the United States captured scores of dead volcanoes and sterile atolls scattered between Hawaii and the Philippines. Certainly no bargain, even in this era of inflated land values! But there is something irresistible about an island, and, with strategy to sustain whim, our admirals and generals and statesmen decided to hold on to these Pacific outposts.

America first went in for South Sea Island real estate in 1888, when Eastern Samoa was acquired for a naval station. A few more acres and palms were added in 1898, when Guam was taken from Spain. (In 1898 Hawaii also was annexed, but by then there was precious little South Sea Island look about Honolulu and the cane fields.) Neither Samoa nor Guam aroused much popular interest at the time, and it was really not until 1941 that island-winning became a national goal. With memories of Kwajalein and Peleliu and Saipan no longer fresh, it probably requires reminding that the United States won these bits of land, along with a hundred other inhabited islands, from the Japanese and then assumed responsibility for them under terms of a United Nations Trusteeship.

Now they are in our care for better or for worse. And whether we like it or not, satisfying our strategists has imposed upon our government the awful responsibility of preserving and guiding some sixty-five thousand brown-skinned islanders most Americans had not even heard of twenty years ago. In numbers, of course, these new wards of ours are hardly enough to fill a decent-sized stadium; but they happen to dwell scattered over an ocean area as large as the United States itself, and in some respects their ways of life are as different from ours as stone ax is from atom bomb. As things now stand, so few Americans know about these matters that the destinies of our island wards remain in the hands of a small number of administrators—which *may* be all right but *could* be all wrong, and in any case is hardly a democratic procedure for handling a national problem. One reason, therefore, for writing this book was to provide the nonspecialist American with some background for understanding the historical consequences of westernization and for exercising the responsibilities of trusteeship.

But there is another, more urgent reason for issuing one more book about the Pacific Islands at this time. While American administration extends only to a few of these islands, the United States cannot remain indifferent to any part of the larger Oceanic area in which Hawaii, Guam, Eastern Samoa, and the Trust Territory Islands are fixed by geography and history. In 1939 the vast region of Oceania—Australia and all the South Pacific Islands east of Indonesia and the Philippines—

was a land of Never-Never to most of us. Then, suddenly, we had to learn its features in minute detail, so that for a while the Guadalcanals and Tarawas were all too well known and their importance to American security grimly recognized. Furthermore, many Americans even became interested in the lives of Oceania's native inhabitants, realized our accountability for some of their tragic plights, and acknowledged our obligation to contribute to their welfare. A victorious nation, however, is a forgetful one, and our awareness of Oceania quickly faded. First, with our wishful thinking directed to peace and home, and later, with our anxieties riveted elsewhere, nothing seemed more remote than the peoples and problems of those faraway islands. Then came Korea, and with it some realization that what has happened and is likely to happen in Oceania is not so remote from our lives after all. Other books, including some excellent recent ones, have covered various phases of Oceania's history, but the whole story in its vast span of time and space has never been made readily available in a single book. Therefore, it seemed at least worth trying and this book is the outcome—written not for the anthropologist or the historian or the romanticist but for those nonspecialists who wish to look beyond Melville's entertainments and Maugham's ironies to learn what took place to change these innumerable Edens into what they are today and may become tomorrow. Here is the outline of the story:

Beginning many thousands of years ago, dark-skinned Stone Age peoples from Asia began venturing across the watery immensities of the Pacific. Sometimes drifting eastward in small bands, sometimes exploring in organized migrations, they eventually colonized nearly every one of the South Pacific's vast number of habitable islands—from continent-sized Australia to isolated Easter Island some nine thousand miles distant from the Asiatic mainland. In time these black and brown pioneers man-

XXINTRODUCTION

aged with the crudest of artifacts to overcome sea and swamp and sand and fashion satisfying lives for themselves. Manners of speech and ways of life differed from island to island, and even from valley to valley, but each of these cultures represented a balanced complex of techniques and ideas and institutions skillfully adjusted to its own physical setting.

Then, a few centuries ago, Occidentals and westernized Orientals "discovered" these islands and, with the aid of their superior technologies and their efficiently directed greed, transformed them into pastures, plantations, mines, and Sunday schools. Whatever these aliens touched they altered or destroyed. Even the humanitarians among them, with their selfless brand of avarice, helped to wreck the institutions and beliefs which kept the islanders in delicate balance with their specialized Oceanic environments and lent meaning to their lives. Moreover, each kind of alien enterprise left its characteristic mark. Missions needed converts, so savage exuberance was reduced to drab sobriety. Grazing required land, so the inhabitants were pushed off it. Copra required labor, so villages were ransacked for semislaves. Cane growing demanded more monotonous efficiency than the masters could inculcate, so natives were shoved aside and Asiatics brought in in such numbers that they overwhelmed what was left of island life.

On a few islands favored by their poverty in alien-prized things, natives continued to live out their lives with pride in their doings and certainty in their reasoning. Elsewhere, existing on the fringes of a civilization they could not escape or wholly embrace, most islanders lost far more than they gained.

Colonial regimes finally bestirred themselves to soften the shock of westernism upon their native wards, and for a while it appeared that islanders would work out satisfying compromises between the old and the new. But then the cataclysm of World War II broke upon them, further upsetting their lives and confusing their newly acquired values. For a short time after the end of this conflict it seemed that these islands would again be reclaimed by blissful obscurity. It appeared inevitable that islanders would become more and more western- ized, but the wishful fancy of most South Seas govern- ments was that this change would take place slowly, at a "healthy evolutionary" pace. Even events in Southeast Asia and elsewhere did not shake the faith that "it can't happen here"—or rather, "it won't happen soon." But, as we have come to expect in this midcentury, the clocks of the islanders now run faster. One island population (Western Samoa) has already pressed for and received its autonomy. In others, New Caledonia and French Polynesia, local self-government is fast becoming a real- ity, although at this writing they are still linked with France. Even the loyal Fijians, those most British of all islanders, are beginning to upset the comfortable expec- tations of their rulers. And the pace of such develop- ments can only accelerate as more and more ship- and jetloads of tourists serve to remind islanders of things to be wished for in the world outside.

But even the pace of 1961 may well seem too meas- ured when the increasing numbers of islanders who can read learn what impatience can bring about in Africa, that other great reserve of "primitive" mankind.

THE ISLANDERS

I

OCEANIC EDEN

Ten thousand islands lie scattered over the face of Oceania, ranging from tiny atoll islets barely visible above pounding surf to continental Australia, three million square miles large. Every conceivable kind of physical setting is to be found. Almost within sight of the snow fields which cap New Guinea's central mountains are sweltering equatorial swamps. And the traveler need not voyage from Australia's desert to rain-soaked Hawaii to compare climatic extremes: he can find nearly as great contrast on single islands.

Physical environment does not necessarily shape man's culture, but it does provide limits beyond which he cannot easily go; and the epic of Oceania can be understood only against its geographic setting. To go back still another step: this setting was shaped by certain events in the history of the earth, certain phenomena of climate, and certain dispersals of plant and animal life.

One hundred million years ago the western rim of the true Pacific Basin extended from Japan south to the Caroline Islands and then swung east and southeast to culminate in Fiji and New Zealand. West of the Basin

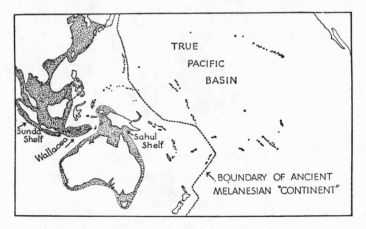

and its deep floor of heavy basalt was the continental Australasiatic Platform, a shelf of lighter granitic materials reaching all the way to Asia itself. To complicate this simple pattern, both Platform and Basin were traversed by long faults, lines of structural weakness, extending generally west to east and northwest to southeast. When earth pressures and tensions developed beyond the holding point, intense folding and faulting thrust up great ridges along these lines, and the mountains thus raised became the backbones of future islands in the Platform area. In the Basin itself, the earth pressures which rent the crust along the faults caused basaltic magma to erupt and form lines and clusters of huge volcanoes. At the close of this early epoch of mountain building, the exposed islands were very extensive throughout both Platform and Basin. Later the Basin floor gradually submerged thousands of feet, leaving only the tops of the volcanic archipelagoes exposed. This action, geologists believe, was caused by the weight of the great masses of volcanic materials resting upon the crust and was accompanied by a compensatory rise of the Platform area plus formidable uplifting and tilting along its eastern borders.

During those remote epochs much of the region now known as Malaysia consisted of larger islands separated from one another by only shallow seas and periodically united with Asia itself. East of this ancient Sundaland lay Papualand, a united Australia and New Guinea; while separating Sundaland from Papualand was Wallacea, an area of unstable islands and deeper, wider ocean troughs, which constituted a barrier to the eastward migration of most plants and land animals, and in a sense has been Oceania's western moat.

As the volcanic islands of the Basin submerged, thick coral reefs formed around their shores, and today low coral atolls and islands are the only visible remains of former volcanoes. Coral reefs are made up of the skeletons of marine plants and animals which fasten onto land surfaces in shallow warm water. Among these is the familiar coral polyp, a small marine animal which attaches itself to the skeletons of preceding generations of plants and animals and extracts lime from seawater to build its own shell. Coral-forming life will thrive only in water, and only to a depth of about 150 feet. As the solid surfaces to which the coral is attached submerge or emerge, the growth of the coral extends upward or downward. Too rapid submergence or emergence will cause the reef-forming organisms to die; hence today there are "dead" coral limestone areas on most exposed islands, either high up above sea level or on their deeply submerged flanks.

During early Pleistocene times the Basin floor rose about a thousand feet, again exposing many islands which had become encrusted with thick layers of coral. The Pleistocene glaciations which devastated such large areas of the Northern Hemisphere also affected the Pacific Islands. Ocean water was alternately impounded and released from the northern ice sheets, causing a series of fluctuations in shore lines of the islands and resulting in variations in coral reef developments. During these epochs earthquakes and new volcanic eruptions took place along younger fault lines of Basin and Platform; and these changes, added to the plodding formation of new coral reefs, continue into the present, producing unstable shore lines throughout the islands.

Although some of the earliest human wanderers into Oceania found more exposed dry land and shallower waters in the Platform area than exist at present, there still were many channels and gulfs to cross. And at no time within mankind's short span have the Basin islands been interconnected.

To anyone who has sweltered in the summer heat of the cities and plains of the so-called "temperate" zone, the climates of most of Oceania are delightful. The temperatures, while never very cold in the inhabited regions, seldom become excessively hot except in continental Australia and in the windless parts of the largest islands. The Pacific waters covering most of Oceania store up heat but radiate it more slowly than do large land areas, and consequently the Oceanic climate is more even the year round.

Winds contribute to this general temperateness and uniformity. Eastern and central Oceania are affected by steady brisk trade winds throughout most of the year—islands north of the equator by winds from the northeast and east, and southern islands by winds from the southeast and east. In between, where the two trade winds meet, there are limited areas of calm; and, as every newspaper reader and movie-goer knows, particularly violent hurricanes now and then disturb the Pacific's usual calm. But more important than hurricanes for mankind's story

in Oceania are the short seasonal shifts in winds, marked
by reversal in direction, from west to east, permitting sailing canoes to run rather than beat toward the east. Trade
winds precipitate much rain on most of the islands in
their paths, and particularly on the windward sides of
the islands. There are, however, some areas of slight
precipitation even in the paths of the trades.

Seasonal winds, or monsoons, take the place of trade
winds in western Oceania. The periodic heating and
cooling of Asia's great land mass, augmented by seasonal
changes in Australia, influences wind directions as far
east as the Solomons: during summer in the Southern
Hemisphere, warm winds blow from Australia and New
Guinea toward Asia, creating the southeast monsoon;
then during the southern winter the winds blow from the
opposite direction, becoming the northwest monsoon. In
the islands the northwest monsoon is accompanied by
increased rainfall, but nearer the equator such seasonal
variation is less marked and rainfall is great the year
round.

Ocean currents, as well as temperature, rainfall, and
winds, affect man's existence in Oceania. Two gigantic
whorls dominate water movements in the Pacific: the
one north of the equator circles clockwise, the one south
counterclockwise. The equatorial limb of the northern
whorl flows without major obstructions from the American side to the Philippines before turning north. Its
southern counterpart is deflected southward by the numerous large islands in its path. Between these two currents, and changing in latitude along with changes in
position of the thermal equator, is the narrow equatorial countercurrent.

Ancestors of most Oceanic plants and animals came
from Australia and Asia, and the nearer an island is to
these large land masses the more varied are its forms of
life. Wind, water, birds, and man himself carried plants

from the homeland, but many genera and species dropped out along the way, so that the eastern islands have very limited botanical inventories. The plant associations most important to the economy of the islands are listed below:

Seacoast or strand: large trees, such as casuarinas, Indian almonds, Barringtonias; smaller trees and shrubs, such as pandanus, hibiscus, xylocarps; woody vines; grasses; sedges; and nipa palms. Common to all these plants is an ability to thrive in unfavorable environments, for example, in brackish and salt water; in addition, their seed or fruit can be borne long distances in salt water without losing viability. The coconut palm also thrives along seacoasts and strands, but usually occurs only where it has been planted by man.

Mangrove forests: true mangroves, terrestrial ferns, epiphytes (air plants); highly specialized plants adapted to growth in mud flats partly or totally covered by salt or brackish water. Any traveler in the islands will recognize these forests growing out from shores protected from wind and wave and along the swampy banks of tidal creeks. Mangrove trees grow close together, their numerous prop roots interlaced and emerging from the slime to provide nearly impassable barriers. (Veterans of the costly assault on Munda airfield will painfully recall this lesson in botany.) Since the seeds and fruits of mangrove forest plants resemble strand flora in their capacity for long salt-water immersion, mangrove forests have become established along the shores of even the most distant islands.

Primary, virgin forests: plant communities of tropical forest giants occurring throughout Oceania where sufficient rainfall and rich soil permit the growth of large trees and where man has not disturbed the growth. Such primary forests are made up of different complexes of plants, according to whether they are located near brackish tidal streams, fresh-water swamps, well-drained valleys, steep or gentle slopes. In these forests the plant population is extremely varied.

Secondary forests and open grasslands: smaller trees and shrubs tangled together so that they are difficult to traverse. These secondary forests occur throughout the islands where the original primary forest has been destroyed and not permitted to return to its normal state. Primitive, shifting, slash-and-burn gardening has been one important factor in the destruction of primary forests, and forest fires another. The native practice of periodically firing scrub and grass in connection with hunting has helped obstruct the natural recuperation of forests. Open grasslands occur on the sites of destroyed primary forests as well as in areas of poor soil and scant rainfall. They are common on the lee side of some of the larger islands, and very extensive on the high plateaus of New Guinea.

All these and many other plant associations are found on continental Australia; and before white men shoved the aborigines back into the deserts and mountains and fens, the early inhabitants had their choice of many environments but lacked the technologies to exploit them fully.

Except in Australia agriculture was practiced throughout Oceania, but islanders also made use of wild plants for food and construction, ornaments and dyes, medicine and magic. Chief among the wild plant foods were the starchy, pithy center of the sago palm; the terminal buds, seeds, and fruit of the pandanus; shoots and flower buds of wild bananas; shoots of the bamboo; and the leaves or fronds and tender stems of numerous other plants. Wild taro and yams were also eaten in some communities. Islanders have been supplementing their diets with these wild foods for thousands of years, and, of course, before husbandry was introduced, the collection of wild things was the basis of survival. Even

recently countless canoeloads of travelers cast up on un-
populated islands have staved off starvation by dependence on wild foods until their gardens began to bear
fruit. (One of the most intriguing and useful little projects of the Pacific war was organized by some Honolulu
ethnologists who taught servicemen how to utilize wild
plants and animals on uninhabited Pacific islands and
thereby assured survival for many castaways.)

Eastward-migrating birds were not greatly impeded
by the sea barriers which separated Oceania from Asia,
but few mammals got through without man's help.
Marsupials, rats, and bats managed to reach the western islands, but only rats and bats went as far as the
central and eastern islands. Forest birds kept mainly to
the western islands; only the sea birds, like the strand
and shore plants, migrated as far as the easternmost
specks of land and made their homes on even the most
isolated and desolate atolls. These gracefully wheeling,
far-flying fish-eaters—frigates, albatrosses, petrels, terns,
curlews, plovers—caught the imagination of shore-dwelling islanders and were immortalized in their myths and
their art. These same birds helped to vegetate remote
islands by carrying plant seeds during their flights, and
in certain islands their accumulated droppings, mixed
with other phosphorus-rich organic materials, today are
a source of valuable fertilizer.

The living things on the land and in the air are perhaps the lesser part of Oceania's organic resources. Inlanders on the larger islands were able to subsist by
gardening and collecting wild things; but shore dwellers
had to depend largely upon the sea for much of their
food. Lagoons and reefs supplied fish for everyday eating, as well as shell for ornaments and artifacts. Turtles,
crabs, lobsters, shrimp, bivalves, and sea cucumbers
added variety to diets, and outside the reefs schools of
tuna and bonito were there for the catching. Whales

were present, too, but they were left for aliens to capture.

From man's point of view, physical setting consists of several elements: the form of the land and the nature of the soil, the quality of the climate, the types and dispositions of plants, and the presence of animal life. In Oceania these components are variously combined to produce seven major types of islands, differentiated according to the limits they imposed upon the islanders and their primitive technologies:

Treeless atolls or coral islands (typical examples are Canton, Johnston, and Howland Islands). Grass and herbs provide survival food for castaways and small parties of fishermen, but the lack of good soil and drinking water renders these land specks unsuitable for permanent native settlements. Sea birds and fish abound and, if drinking water were present, human life could be sustained indefinitely on these islands; but for the most part the vegetation-loving Oceanic natives have avoided them. On the other hand, the very conditions which discouraged native settlers and made these islands bird refuges resulted in the deposit of valuable guano fertilizer and produced ready-made runways for twentieth-century aircraft.

Dry-forest atolls or coral islands (typical are most of the Marshall and Ellice Islands, and many of the Tuamotus and northern Cooks). Strand flora, together with some arable soil and fresh water, make these islands habitable for limited numbers of people; rich marine resources supplement the scanty vegetable and fruit diets. However, overpopulation is a constant threat, and crowded native communities have sought solutions in mass emigration and in infanticide. Yet despite the paucity of resources on these islands, some communities have developed intricate and aesthetically pleasing arts and crafts, utilizing every material at their disposal. They have, moreover, appeared to compensate for the

limitations imposed upon their economies by evolving
exceedingly complex institutional relations.

Luxuriant, moist atolls or coral islands (typical examples are the Gilbert and Tokelau Islands, Swains Island, Fanning, Ebon, Ulithi, and Nissan). These are the
lush and beautiful "tropical isles" of romantic novel and
motion picture. They have sufficient soil to support cultivation of taro and bananas, in addition to the coconut
palms and breadfruit grown also on the dry islands.

Raised-coral islands (typical examples are Makatéa,
Niue, Ocean, Nauru, Angaur, Peleliu, and Fais). These
islands were formed out of successive elevations of old
coral reef and are composed of limestone covered by
thin layers of soil which support low and dense stands
of dry-land flora (medium-sized trees, small trees,
shrubs, vines, ferns, and so forth). Rough pitted limestone surfaces and tangled growth make these islands
difficult to cross. Fresh water in the form of springs and
streams is usually lacking, and cave pools or rain-catch-
ment basins provide drinking water. Coconuts and other
food plants grow fairly well in the scattered pockets of
soil, but frequent droughts are a menace to native agriculture. Since many of these islands contain rich phosphate deposits, they have assumed an economic value
far surpassing that of any other kind of island of comparable size.

Unweathered volcanic islands (typical examples are
the northern Marianas and Niuafoo). Because the
weathering of these islands has not progressed far, there
is considerably less soil on them, and hence less vegetation, than on the "older" weathered volcanic islands.
Most forest growth is limited to the valleys, and the
ridges are covered with grasses and smaller plants. Native populations can and do thrive in moderate numbers
on these islands; usually the little soil present is rich and
supports luxuriant growths of coconuts and other food
plants.

Weathered volcanic islands (typical examples are the Hawaiian, Society, and Samoan Islands). These islands, some of them rising thousands of feet above sea level, contain many kinds of environment: wide strands, brackish and fresh-water swamps, gentle and steep slopes, extensive lava fields, and so forth. They are subjected to great variation in rainfall. Plant life is extremely varied. Nearly every kind of growing thing or growing condition needed by man to develop complex technologies is to be found. Minerals alone are lacking.

Certain "mixed" islands, including Guam, Saipan, Rota, and Mangaia, possess characteristics of both weathered volcanic and raised-coral settings.

"Continental" islands: New Guinea, Viti Levu, New Caledonia, Espíritu Santo, Guadalcanal, Bougainville, New Britain, New Ireland, and most other large islands in the Melanesian archipelagoes. These islands are formed of continental rocks complicated by volcanic intrusions and possess even wider varieties in environment and plant life than the volcanic islands. Their richer, mineral-bearing soils support nearly every kind of vegetation. Their high mountains, dense forests, and broad swamps have encouraged the existence of numerous isolated native communities, favoring the development of cultural and even racial diversity.

If, to this inventory of settings, vast Australia itself is added, with its continental diversities in terrain, climate, plants, and animals, then some conception may be gained of the physical conditions faced by black and brown men when they began their treks into Oceania many thousand years ago.

II

THE COMING OF THE ISLANDERS

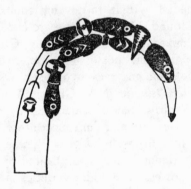

When white men first sailed their puny vessels across the face of Oceania, they found nearly every island inhabited by dark-skinned peoples whom they called "Indians." But this ethnological misnomer did not persist long, for every traveler learned soon to distinguish between the copper-skinned, straight-haired, nearly amphibious canoe-men living in the eastern islands and the brown or black, frizzly-haired savages in the west. And even the most incurious white visitors began to pose the questions that have intrigued travelers ever since: Who are these islanders? Where did they come from? How did they manage to reach these far-flung shores, to survive and develop complex institutions, intricate and pleasing arts, impressive monuments?

Guesses have been as numerous as the islands themselves, and nearly as varied. Some guessers have by ingenious logic raised civilized "Lost Continents" out of the Pacific depths and then partly submerged them again, to account for man's existence on the islands. Other writers have preferred to bring in culture-bearers from outside—from Egypt or Greece or Peru. Even the travel-worn Lost Tribes of Israel have been arrayed in outrigger canoes and sent to join the Oceanic regatta to suit the tastes of some "historians." But while these fanciful scholars were marketing their colorful theories, their more pedestrian colleagues were plodding along, applying their calipers, recording languages, exploring institutions; and from their labors have begun to take form the outlines of an epic much more plausible and not a whit less intriguing than the Sunday-supplement accounts.

The story that has emerged has a grander human perspective than any of the time-shallow reconstructions built up around the imagined exploits of a few fabulous adventurers. The real story of Oceania goes back many thousands of years and principally concerns the gradual spreading out of poorly equipped little bands, ousted from their homelands by pressures they could not contend with.

The story's unfolding has progressed only since anthropologists have been guided in their researches by the distinctions that must be drawn between race, culture, and language in an attempt to reconstruct mankind's history. *Race* refers to biological factors, to color of skin, texture of hair, shape of head and body, and to the many other inherited physical traits which persuade us to classify mankind into several more or less separate categories. *Culture* includes the material things man possesses, the techniques he utilizes, the institutions he participates in—his goals, his rituals, his beliefs. *Language* is the system of verbal symbols used by man for communication, and as such is, of course, an aspect of culture. But just as race is not necessarily linked with culture—say, a brown skin with a shell-barbed spear—so a particular word or sentence structure is not linked with a particular culture. The anthropological students of Oceania know, for example, that an item of culture—a tool, a practice, a belief—may disseminate far beyond the physical travels of its inventors and even without carrying its original language label. Likewise, anthropologists have ample evidence of the mixing of races unaccompanied by an equivalent mixing of cultures. Without these methodological cautions little headway could have been made toward reconstructing the history of Oceania; but even greater cautions have been required. Traits—cultural, linguistic, or racial—may appear similar without necessarily signifying historical relationship. An ax form, or a belief in kinship with an animal species, found to be similar in two widely distant islands, may conceivably be the result either of historical relationship or of independent invention; careful investigation has to rule out the second alternative before the anthropologist can begin to trace historical connections and generalize about the migrations of peoples and cultures and languages. Some specialists, in fact, see so many difficulties in interpreting the data that they look upon attempts at historical reconstruction as fruitless, academic sport. There is much to be said for the principles of these purists, but it is none the less intriguing to play at the game—and so much the merrier because no two experts agree on all details of the rules. Many do agree, however, on some broad outlines, which can now be drawn.

Among the earliest human beings to occupy Oceania were Negritos—short-statured, dark-skinned, frizzly-haired Negroids, probably pushed out of southern Asia during the last glacial period and ultimately related to the short-statured Negroid peoples of Africa. Both the African and the Asiatic pygmy Negroids are believed to have been preagricultural hunters and food gatherers, adapted to life in equatorial rain forests. The climatic changes which probably brought about their original dispersal may also have caused some bands of them to straggle southeast down the Malay Peninsula. Or, stronger neighbors may have shoved them along. Whatever the cause, they occupied parts of Malaysia and some of them eventually crossed the succession of straits separating Malaysia from Oceania and so came to populate, probably very sparsely, many forest regions in New Guinea and Australia and the near-by islands.

The straits between land masses may well have been narrower in those days, for northern ice sheets locked up quantities of the oceans' waters and extended the shore lines outward; but the migrating Negritos would have required craft of some sort. As for their other possessions, we can only guess what they did not have: they had neither agriculture nor domesticated animals nor polished stone tools. Their islands were ultimately overrun by later migrants out of Asia, so there remain only a few isolated pockets of fairly "pure" Oceanic Negritos hidden away in inaccessible mountain areas of New Guinea and the other large islands of Melanesia; and even these racially intact Negrito survivors have adopted the artifacts and the agricultural technology of their more advanced neighbors.

The Negrito migration into Oceania must have required many hundreds or even thousands of years and represented an unorganized trickle of families and small bands rather than any concerted large-scale movement. The scarcity of game alone would have limited the numbers of people traveling together, just as it kept their population density thin once they settled down.

When Europeans discovered Australia they found there a native population quite unlike any encountered elsewhere in the Pacific Islands. They were dark-skinned like the islanders, but their hair was wavy rather than frizzly and their bodies were more hirsute. In time the newcomers learned to distinguish several regional varieties of the aborigines: in the north, bodies were slimmer and skins darker; in the south, bodies were bulkier, skin color lighter, and hair straighter; while in the rain forests of Queensland and on Tasmania were found people of shorter stature and frizzlier hair, recalling in many respects the Negritos. There were also many regional differences in the ways of life of these aborigines, but they were all alike in that they did not garden or keep animals for food.

There can be little doubt about the great antiquity of man in Australia; evidence of human existence goes back ten to fourteen thousand years, and skeletal remains link some of the earliest inhabitants with an early type of man living on Java (*i.e., Wadjak* man). Disagreement arises, however, concerning reasons for the regional variations in physical types. Some experts believe that three separate racial stocks have migrated to Australia—Ainoid, Veddoid, and Negrito. Here are the outlines of this theory:

During the fourth glacial epoch, possibly even prior to the migration of the Negritos, bands of a different kind of human hunters and food gatherers moved from Malaysia out into New Guinea and Australia. Physically these people were totally unlike the Negritos; their skin color was lighter, their hair wavy rather than frizzly, and their bodies very hirsute. In fact, they were members of a very old basic white stock called Ainoids because of their partial resemblance to the Ainu, the non-Japanese aborigines of Hokkaido. These hirsute whites spread through the larger islands of western Oceania and blended with the Negritos they met. In the islands of Melanesia the Negrito component was predominant and the product more Negroid than Ainoid, but in Australia the Ainoids were relatively more numerous and retained most of their original racial features; this was particularly true in southern Australia.

The Ainoids were followed by other preagricultural hunters and food gatherers during early postglacial times. These Veddoids, so named because of their physical affinities with the aboriginal Vedda population of India, were dark skinned, wavy haired, and linear in build; in Australia they survived in purest form in the tropical north.

Throughout New Guinea and its neighboring islands, Negritos, Ainoids, and Veddoids intermixed in such varying proportions that the products were exceedingly complicated, but the Negrito element was everywhere dominant. In Australia there was also some racial intermixing, but the Ainoid racial component remained dominant in the south and the Veddoid in the north, with surviving elements of the Negritos confined to tropical forests in Queensland or pushed off into Tasmania.

This explanation also attempts to account for some differences in the customs of Australian aborigines. According to this view, Negritos, Ainoids, and Veddoids were roving bands of hunters and food gatherers, lacking polished stone and the other tools and arts of the New Stone Age. There is some evidence that the Negritos, like their racial cousins left behind in the Andaman Islands, in Malaya, and in the Philippines, were most at home in forests. On the other hand, Ainoids and Veddoids appear to have been better adapted to open country, to chase-hunting with spears and boomerangs rather than with the bow-and-arrow forest methods employed by Negritos. Further, it is likely that either Ainoids or Veddoids were the first to bring in the domesticated dog—the well-known dingo of the Australian bush.

An alternative explanation for the racial and cultural variation which existed in Australia when Europeans

arrived focuses on the antiquity of the aborigines. In the
view of some experts the hundreds of generations during which humans have lived in Australia would, through
regular processes of biological selection and cultural adjustment, be adequate to account for such variation,
without introducing the notion of originally separate
racial stocks. For these specialists the aborigines are all
descended from the same Wadjak-related race—with
perhaps some minor additions of Negrito genes.

Some specialists also believe that the many physical variations to be found among the Melanesian
Negroids can only be explained by positing the immigration of full-statured, as well as short-statured,
Negroids; but this difference of opinion—like the one
concerning the Australian aborigines—will only be settled
by further research, especially in archaeology.

Four to five thousand years ago the neolithic revolution, the New Stone Age, began to spread into Oceania,
manifesting itself in the practice of gardening and animal husbandry and in the technique of making tools by
grinding and polishing stone into desired shapes—a considerable improvement over the older methods of chipping and flaking. Most of these new technologies did
not spread into Australia, whose inhabitants remained
nomadic hunters and food gatherers up to the time of
their recent "discovery"; but the Negroid islanders in
Oceania were all transformed into more or less sedentary
farmers. It is possible that this transformation may have
come about through a chain-borrowing of ideas from one
community to another, beginning in southeast Asia and
disseminating as far as Fiji. On the other hand, later
waves of immigrants may have had some direct influence in the spread of the new culture traits.

Millennia before the Christian era, so-called "Indonesian"[1] racial types began moving down into Malaysia

[1] Not to be confused with the term now being applied in a
political sense to citizens of the new Republic of Indonesia.

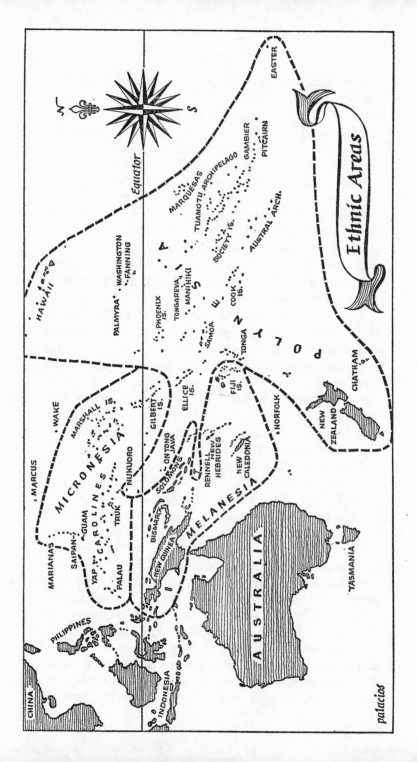

out of southeast Asia. They are thought to have been a composite race, made up of Mongoloid and white components (the Mediterranean variant of the white race may have extended through northern India to southeast Asia); even at that early time southeast Asia was a meeting place of Indian and east Asiatic influences. Physically these Indonesians (or proto-Malays, as some specialists name them) were light brown in skin color, medium to short in stature, hair black and straight or wavy, and broad in cheekbone. They differed from the classic Mongoloid type with lighter skin, straighter hair, and very flat, moon-round face, familiarly associated with peoples living today in north China, Manchuria, and eastern Siberia.

Indonesians practiced the neolithic arts developed in the forests of southeast Asia—the cultivation of root crops and domestication of pig and fowl. With their better tools they constructed sturdy, far-sailing canoes, which enabled them to undertake bolder sea voyages than earlier migrants, who had had to hug the shores in their crude craft. As more and more Indonesians pressed down into Malaysia, they absorbed most of their predecessors, producing complex hybrid types.

Starting at an early period, at least four thousand years ago, hybridized Indonesians began scouting and settling along the coasts of New Guinea and the other islands of Melanesia. Others populated many of the Micronesian islands north and northeast of New Guinea. Some of these migrations must have been undertaken by small family groups; later ones may have been large, well-organized colonizing expeditions. While they were mixing their blood, their languages, and their cultures with those of the Negroids met along the coasts of Melanesia, Malaysia became filled with more and more Asiatics, and these more recent immigrants were progressively more Mongoloid. The process is still going on today, and modern Malays continue to drift in small numbers toward the east into the domain of the Oceanic

Negroids, so that there is still taking place a gradual, scarcely perceptible "Malayization" of western Oceania.

At some points in this long slow process, several of the more adventurous bands struck out beyond the island outposts in central Melanesia. Few migrations in world history have excited so much interest and admiration as these. Using islands for steppingstones and extending the laps of the journeys over many centuries, some of these people eventually colonized islands as far as eight thousand miles distant from the embarking points of their ancestors in Malaysia. Some went north to populate eastern Micronesia; Palau, Yap, and the Marianas had already been settled directly from farther southwest. Others went southeast to Fiji, and then on to Tonga and Samoa, where they arrived more than twenty centuries ago and where they and their descendants developed the somewhat distinctive ways of life now known as "Polynesian."

As everyone now knows, the Polynesians did not stop there. In fact, during the next millennia they reached every habitable island in the vast triangle created by Hawaii in the north, New Zealand in the south, and Easter Island in the east. Some probably reached the shores of the Americas; and a few of these latter may have returned, carrying with them the sweet potato, the only distinctively New World trait in their predominantly Southeast Asian cultures. Other Polynesians were carried back into the heart of Melanesia or northwest into the southern Carolines.

Formerly anthropologists classified the peoples of Oceania into four great divisions: Australia, Melanesia ("Black Islands": New Guinea to New Caledonia and Fiji), Micronesia ("Small Islands": the Marianas, Palaus, Carolines, Marshalls, and Gilberts), and Polynesia. It is still feasible to distinguish Australia as a separate unit—racially, culturally, and linguistically; and Polynesia also remains distinctive in some respects; but "Melanesia" and "Micronesia" are now useful mainly as names for geographic regions.

In terms of race, for example, it is not possible to draw sharp boundaries among the Pacific Island populations. Several racial stocks have gone into the racial composition of Island Oceania: Negritoid (and possibly full-statured Negroid), Australoid (including, possibly, Ainoid and Veddoid variants), and southern Mongoloid (with, possibly, some white elements as well). There remain some pockets of relatively "pure" Negritoids in parts of New Guinea and in other large Melanesian islands, and some populations in the western Carolines appear almost wholly Mongoloid. Elsewhere race mixture seems to have taken place on a large scale, and with widely varying proportions of racial components from population to population. This somewhat random kind of hybridization, along with widespread population movements, has resulted in a regular patchwork of physical types. Except for a few enclaves, most of the populations of Melanesia have frizzlier hair and darker skins than those of Micronesia and Polynesia; but Negroid types can be found among Polynesian-speaking peoples, and "Polynesian" types as far west as New Guinea.

In terms of language it is also no longer possible to make a neat division into *Melanesian, Micronesian,* and *Polynesian.* Within this vast area there are two types of language: one consisting of scores of tongues known to belong to a single great family of *Austronesian* languages, the other consisting of tongues which share only the characteristic of *not* being Austronesian—a catchall, residual category which has been given the label *Papuan* —owing to the fact that most of them are to be found on New Guinea and neighboring islands—*i.e.,* in the domain of the *Papuans* ("frizzly hairs"). Progress has been made in recent years toward establishing relationships among some of the Papuan tongues, but they remain, at present writing, distinct from Austronesian and all other languages with which they have been compared.

Recent research on Austronesian languages has taken some dramatic turns. Until lately linguists divided this great family of languages into four parallel major subdivisions: *Indonesian* (including Malay, Javanese, and all other languages spoken throughout Indonesia, British Borneo, and the Philippines, along with the languages of Formosa's aborigines, and some tongues spoken on faraway Madagascar); *Micronesian* (from the Marianas and Palau through the Gilberts); *Polynesian;* and *Melanesian* (spoken from coastal New Guinea to New Caledonia and Fiji). This fourfold division no longer stands. Instead, linguists divide the family into a much larger number of major subdivisions. And what is of great interest to scholars attempting to reconstruct the histories of Pacific Island cultures, is the fact that one subdivision of one of these divisions includes the languages of Fiji, of Polynesia, and of East Micronesia, along with some languages spoken in central Melanesia as well, demonstrating very close relationships among all these tongues and indicating that they developed from a common language within a relatively short period of time. The second important discovery made in recent years was one that linked Austronesian with certain languages spoken by some aborigines of southern China, thus lending weight to other theories that the later migrants into the Pacific and much of their culture derived ultimately from shore-dwelling sailors living along the coast of the South China Sea.

Such are the bare outlines. Working from them, it is possible to sketch with a fair degree of accuracy the kinds of native existences white men found when they timidly entered Oceania scores of millennia after its first true discovery and settlement by brown and black men.

III

THE AUSTRALIAN ABORIGINES

European discoverers of Australia found the island-continent inhabited by some 300,000 natives subsisting by means of one of the simplest, most primitive technologies ever recorded. In many respects a look at their life affords an opportunity to see a chapter of the Old Stone Age carried down into the present.

The aborigines have inhabited Australia for more than ten thousand years. Their extraordinary conservatism in economic techniques is certainly not due to any inherent biological limitations—science has yet to prove any correlation between cultural attainments and race. Rather it is due partly to the nature of the physical environment, partly to the simplicity of their artifacts, and in some measure to the infrequency of contacts with peoples possessing superior technologies. Furthermore, although the aborigines have not advanced very far technologically, they have succeeded in adjusting and stabilizing human relations, including intertribal relations, to degrees apparently unattainable in our modern world of individual insecurity, family instability, interclass strife, and nationalistic wars. These facts should be recalled before adjudging one culture "inferior" to another.

Some of the physical conditions that restrict population in present-day Australia also served to limit the number of aborigines in ages past. The eastern and southeastern coasts are temperate and well drained and their immediate hinterlands today support intensive agriculture and stock raising; and on a much smaller scale this is also true of the extreme southwest corner. But most of the remainder of the continent is unproductive bushland or even sterile desert.

Some experts assert that three racial stocks were responsible for the peopling of Australia: Negritoid, Ainoid, and Veddoid. To most laymen, however, all aborigines appear to be alike throughout the continent. This is in some sense an accurate observation, because in most parts of the land Negritoid, Ainoid, and Veddoid strains have been merged into a composite "Australoid" stock.

Students of culture, like the specialists in race, can also detect cultural differences from one part of Australia to another. But in many important fundamentals there is remarkable homogeneity in culture throughout the continent. This may have come about through similarities of original technologies, through the equalizing effect of the environment, through diffusion, or through all three. Even in languages, which are known to be strongly resistant to fundamental change, specialists are beginning to discern many similarities among the some three hundred aboriginal tongues, even going so far as to place them into the same family.

Ethnic reconstruction is a fascinating but highly speculative pastime; at this stage it is not possible to know what cultural differences there were among the first immigrant groups, although it is highly probable that they were all hunters and food gatherers, that one at least of them owned dogs, used canoes or rafts, and worked and hunted with wooden and stone artifacts. Beyond that, ethnologists cannot go.

In recent centuries there have been episodic visits to the northwest coasts by travelers from Malaysia, together with some two-way traffic across the Torres Strait, connecting Australia and New Guinea; but for most of the continent the millennia have passed in isolation from the rest of the world. Elsewhere in the world the Old Stone Age evolved into the New, bringing agriculture and pottery; and successive ages of metal developed and passed into obsolescence, with not even a faint echo of these great cultural revolutions reaching or becoming established in Australia.

Much imaginative theory has been written about the native inhabitants of the island of Tasmania, separated by the narrow Bass Strait from the extreme southeast tip of Australia. This has been a rich field for surmise, for those miserable people were annihilated by the European settlers on that island. With troublesome factual evidence thus conveniently destroyed, theorists have had a field day; but it is highly unlikely that the extinct Tasmanians were other than a group of Australian aborigines who were pushed, or elected to go, farther than their cousins. It is likely that they contained more of the Negritoid element than the general population now contains, since early writers described them as having been short and woolly haired.

For many thousands of years, indeed, since the invention of husbandry, mankind has lived chiefly by manipulating the environment, by actively and practically entering into the business of producing the essentials of survival. Not so the Australian aborigine. He took what nature provided and co-operated only to the extent of attempting to stimulate natural processes by ritual acts. He gathered and ate seeds, but did not go the further step and sow those seeds; in fact, it is said that he did not even comprehend that the plant and its fruit develop from seed. Similarly he hunted for animal food with spear or boomerang or club or trap, but made no attempt to capture animals and then breed them for increase. Actually the aborigine's lack of progress in husbandry is not surprising: even the modern British inhabitants of Australia have not succeeded in developing any indigenous species to practical food uses.

Nowhere in Australia was the food supply plentiful enough to permit the natives to live wholly sedentary lives; they had to hunt and gather their food over wide areas, temporarily exhausting resources in one place and moving on to the next. But this nomadism was somewhat circumscribed: groups usually returned to the same places year after year, and the wide territory over which each group moved was identified with it alone. In more fertile regions this territory may be thought of as having been continuous; but in desert regions it consisted of several fertile places connected by paths, with all the intervening economically useless country ignored and not identified with any group.

The aborigine's tools were made from stone and wood; spears, boomerangs, clubs, knives, axes, and pointed sticks were used to capture and kill game, to gather grubs and edible plants. Wooden bowls served for cooking and eating. Body covering was limited to ornamental or ritually important pendants or pubic tassels. Some tribes constructed temporary huts of twigs and leaves and mud, mainly for protection against mosquitoes; others built only the sketchiest of lean-tos and preferred to sleep in the open, close to small fires if it was cold. Carrying their few possessions with them, the aborigines moved from one water-hole campsite to another. In such poor country it was imperative that hunters and gatherers of food know every feature of the environment, the habit and habitat of every edible plant and animal, the site of every moist place, every sign of weather change. It is no wonder then that nature meant more than mere scenery to the aborigines. To them all its varied aspects were animated by spirits not unlike those which animate persons—more powerful, perhaps, but members of the same animate and personalized universe. Their dependence upon that universe of animals and plants and places and forces was complete, since they harvested only what was produced naturally. According to their beliefs, nature moved along in its accustomed way—changing seasons, reproducing animals, and growing plants—but this natural progression had to be stimulated by ritual acts carried out by human beings. These acts were introduced by the spirit Heroes who wandered about the world in the Dream Time past, creating all features of the universe. Accounts of their wanderings and actions were retained in myths; the countryside was filled with water holes where they drank, cairns where they established spirit homes for preincarnate humans and animals, and caves where they became transformed into rocks. Learning these myths and acting out those happenings were as important for human survival as was manual skill in throwing a spear, for unless proper ritual was carried out to encourage kangaroo spirits to become incarnate, there would be no kangaroo to toss a spear at; and unless the spear itself possessed some animus, it could not hit its mark.

Aboriginal Australia was divided into some three hundred tribes, each associated with a separate area. Tribal unity was based on common language and common mythology, but not usually upon group action. For the individual native, membership in a local group or *horde* was much more important than tribal membership. Each horde was identified with a subdivision of the tribal area and consisted of a number of families related to one another through various kinship ties. Males usually dwelt throughout their lives in the territory where they were born; wives were selected from other parts of the tribe and moved to their husbands' places at marriage. But although residence was more commonly based upon father relationships, ties with the mother were also emphasized through important totemic means. Yet more important than either of these social groupings was the biological family unit.

We call it the biological family, but the aborigines, while obviously aware that children issue from the mother's womb, did not emphasize the connection between copulation and procreation, a logical parallel to their ignorance of the principles of plant and animal husbandry. In the view of some tribes all human spirits were preexistent, brought into being by the great Heroes during the Dream Time and left by them in the spirit homes scattered about the local group's territory. These spirits entered women's wombs and were subsequently born as human infants; at death the spirits returned to their incorporeal existence in the same territory. The term "father" had a unique meaning: he was the kinsman whose spirit had previously issued from the child's own spirit home; as husband of the child's mother, he may have helped ritually to induce the child's unborn spirit to enter his spouse's womb. "Mother" provided the womb receptacle in which the infant spirit lodged and formed into flesh and bone, but a "mother's" true childhood and spirit home was far removed from that of her child.

These beliefs did not rule out the development of strong family ties as we know them, for nurture and training of the child was carried out by its mother and father at least until puberty was reached. The ties with brothers and sisters were also intimate; their spirits came from the same spirit homes and their "flesh" was formed in the same womb. Brothers commonly dwelt together in the same horde throughout life, and assisted one another in economic and ritual enterprises. Sisters usually left their own communities at marriage and went to live in the territory of their husbands, but their kinship ties with parents and siblings were maintained throughout life by visits and exchanges, by social and ceremonial activities.

The family unit has been aptly called the group of orientation. For, in Australia as in most other primitive cultures, an individual's family relationships determined the kinship terms and behavior he used toward every other person in his social universe. Brothers were generally regarded as equivalent, and so were sisters. Thus, for example, an aborigine might call his mother's sister *mother*, not "aunt," as in our language, and his father's brother *father* rather than "uncle." Accordingly, the son of one's paternal uncle might be *brother* and not "cousin." Like ourselves, the aborigine had a separate relationship name and a conventional manner of behavior for each relative in his own family; but by extending these names, by calling his mother's clan "sister" *mother*, his grandson's clan "brother" *grandson*, and so forth, the aborigine could determine his relationship and expected behavior toward every person in his tribe. This is known as the classificatory system of kinship terminology, as contrasted with our own more denotative system, which in some respects describes more precisely the actual biological relationships but does not distinguish as many "relatives." Nearly all Oceanic cultures have some form of classificatory kinship systems, but it is nowhere the case that natives do not discriminate—if not in name, then at least in some forms of behavior and in sentiment—between, say, biological and classificatory mothers.

The male aborigine commonly spent most of his life with his wife and children (except his daughters, who eventually married and moved away), and with families related to him through his father and his sons. All these males were inseparably bound to the territories from which their spirits issued and in which they would remain after physical death. Physical survival depended upon knowledge of all the local resources, and upon revitalizing ceremonially the local spiritual powers that ensured plenty. All the males in a local group constituted a kind of lodge, dedicated to keep alive the sacred lore and practices essential for survival, and to train youngsters in these matters.

Some of those rites were historical in that the lodge members acted out episodes in the sagas of the Dream Time Heroes. Other rites were performed to ensure the increase of specific plant and animal items essential for existence. Women were not permitted to join in these sacred affairs; they were mere females and their spirit homes were located in other territories. Nor were young boys admitted to the mysteries until they demonstrated their worthiness. The influential members of the lodge and consequently of the horde, since the lodge constituted the privileged nucleus of the horde, were those men old enough to have mastered all the mysteries but not yet senile enough to have become useless as food providers and warriors. To become fierce warriors, good providers, and knowledgeable experts in the mysteries, males had to undergo a series of initiation rites, which began with some form of bodily mutilation: circumcision, subincision, bloodletting, tooth removing, and the like. The novice underwent all manner of privation and abuse before he was permitted to see and whirl the sacred bull-roarer—the "voice" of a local supernatural—or to perform the kangaroo "increase" rite, and so eventually qualify as a full-fledged lodge member.

In everyday life males did most of the hunting and

females most of the plant gathering, but they did very few things co-operatively. This together with the more common practice of virilocality, of women being up-rooted from their own homes and spending their lives in their husbands' communities, had the effect of separat-ing males from females socially even more than is usual for most Oceanic cultures. Add to this the fact that social maturity among males was reached only after a long slow process of accumulating practical knowledge and mastering sacred lore, and it comes as no surprise to learn that influence and authority in the horde was mo-nopolized by the older males, and that much emphasis was placed upon age differences. In some tribes this took an extreme form, with very old men marrying very young girls—a custom upon which Dr. Freud based one of his most entertainingly erroneous theories.

In spite of the everyday importance of the male-oriented local group, the aborigines also respected and developed institutions around the matrilineal ties. These were particularly important to a woman, who was not allowed to remain with her own local group after marriage or to enter into the mysteries of either her own or her husband's local group.

The basic form of matrilineal grouping was made up of people who regarded themselves formed of the same flesh—their bodies, as contrasted with their spirits, hav-ing been formed through the same line of mothers. Most of these groups were totemic: members of each such group considered themselves to be related with specific natural phenomena (plants, animals, and so forth), toward which they showed the respect befitting kinsmen.

In some tribes this principle of matrilineal grouping was complicated by the development of sections or sub-sections, all relatives of an individual being divided into four or eight groups, with choice of a spouse limited to one of the groups. For example, in one tribe possessing the section system, a man, his brothers and sisters, his mother's mother's brother's son's daughter, his father's father's sister's daughter's daughter, his father's mother's brother's daughter's daughter, etc., belong to one section; his wife (and all his potential wives), his wife's brother, his sister's husband, his cross-cousins, etc., etc., to another section; his mother, his mother's brother, his wife's father, his son's wife, his daughter's husband, his sister's children, etc., to a third section; and his father, his father's sister, his wife's mother, his own children, etc., to a fourth section. The subsection system appears even more complicated.

The analysis and elaboration of these specialized forms of social groupings have provided anthropologists with a façade frightening enough to discourage any non-specialist; it is every bit as effective as the priestly symbols of higher mathematics. Behind this façade, however, the section and subsection systems are simple institutions and accomplish useful social ends. In describing the classificatory kinship principle it was pointed out how a few kinship terms may be extended to include many "relatives," a useful device for determining how one should act toward distant relatives and acquaintances. Even a stranger from another tribe is immediately "located" in this way, and consequently one knows how to behave toward him. In the section and subsection systems this process evolves a further step: by lumping several real and classificatory kinspeople into a single section or subsection, and by adopting more or less the same kind of conventional behavior to all those in the same group, social etiquette becomes greatly simplified and relationships further stabilized. In many tribes these groups are even extended to include certain plants, animals, natural objects, and forces, in the totemic sense that these things are members of particular groups along with human kinsmen. In this manner not only are all human beings interrelated in a system of family-social groups, but all things and aspects of nature have their places in the all-inclusive social universe.

In addition to territorial and matrilineal groupings, many tribes had a moiety ("half") organization, either paralleling or cutting across lines created by local, group, matrilineal, section, or subsection ties. Moiety organization usually functioned only on ceremonial occasions, when members of each one of the two moieties carried out certain duties or enjoyed certain privileges. And here again, all elements of the natural universe were assigned to one or the other of the moieties.

Thus through practice and belief the aborigine rationalized and stabilized his relationship with all other human beings and with the environment upon which he was so directly dependent.

IV

THE MELANESIANS

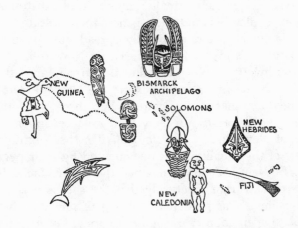

Melanesia, the dwelling place mainly of Oceanic Negroids, is a region of sharp contrasts. Islands vary in size from massive New Guinea, fifteen hundred miles long, to tiny artificial islets built by natives on reefs. Some inhabitants of Melanesia may spend their nights shivering from the damp coolness in high mountain villages, while others a hundred miles away swelter in swamps. Mossy mountain forests, grassland plateaus, tangled jungles, sago and mangrove swamps, parched treeless plains, and palm-covered strands: all these are to be found, sometimes on single islands that could be flown across in minutes. Active volcanoes, frequent earthquakes, monsoonal storms, and typhoons add violence to the environmental variety. Plagues of insect pests and their attendant ills—malaria, dengue, and filariasis—along with dysentery, blackwater fever, leprosy, and all man-

ner of bacteria and parasites that deface the skin, glaze
the eyes, destroy the lungs, and poison the blood: with
all these added to the physical setting, it is little wonder
that Melanesia long remained a refuge area for primitive
man.

To recapitulate the story of its peopling: short-
statured Negroids were perhaps the first to drift in from
Malaysia; then came smaller numbers of Australoids.
These peoples blended their genes, their cultures, and
their languages, and eventually spread out to occupy
the larger islands as far northeast as New Ireland, as
far southwest as New Caledonia, and as far east as
Fiji. In the resulting racial mixture the Negroid element
strongly dominated everywhere, but there was otherwise little uniformity. In the virtually inaccessible mountains of New Guinea and Bougainville, the Negrito an-
cestry of the inhabitants is documented by their pygmy
size. In New Caledonia, on the other hand, facial features demonstrate practically that the southern Australoid element was particularly strong. Elsewhere, in the
desolate open country of southern Papua, facial features
and the lean body types bear witness to the presence of
the northern Australoid element.

Culturally it may be assumed that the first settlers
were hunters and food gatherers, and that even in the
early period segregation and isolation must have led to
considerable differentiation in institutions and practices
from one tribe to the next. The hybrid languages that
resulted from the blending of peoples and cultures have
been referred to as "Papuan" in type, to differentiate
them from other languages rather than to imply any
linguistic affinities among them.

Later on, to this amalgam was added the predominantly Mongoloid racial types, Austronesian languages,
and New Stone Age cultural traits of husbandry, polished stone artifacts, and pottery making. The cultural
traits may have preceded, by trade and chain-borrowing,
the actual migrations of their bearers. In any event,

there resulted a cultural revolution throughout Melanesia, and the seminomadic Negroids became sedentary agriculturists, their principal cultivated plants being taro, yams, bananas, breadfruit, and coconuts—all Asiatic in origin.

Taro, a member of the Araceae family to which the calla lily also belongs, is so widespread, has become differentiated into so many local varieties, and is so fundamental in many very isolated and conservative native cultures, that it may well have been the first cultivated food plant introduced into the islands. It requires rich and fairly moist soil, and matures four to six months after planting. When ripe, its thick starchy root, the edible portion, is cut off below the stalk, which is then replanted. Its tender leaves are eaten as greens after thorough cooking. Cultivated yams are grown almost as widely as taro. Yams vary greatly in size, some weighing thirty to forty pounds; and in contrast to taro they spoil only slowly after harvesting. This factor has led many communities to grow them in excess of daily food needs and utilize them as symbols of wealth and prestige. On some islands breadfruit (*Artocarpus communis*) grows wild, but more often it is cultivated and when in season constitutes the staple food. Either roasted or baked, the breadfruit tastes much like a chestnut. Bananas, or rather plantains, the cooking type, are widely cultivated, usually as a supplement to the more staple taro, yams, breadfruit, and sago.

The sago palm, from whose pith a tapiocalike flour is extracted, grows semiwild in swampy areas; but there is a possibility that it may have been introduced by human agents. It is used throughout wide areas of Oceania and is the principal food in the river regions of New Guinea. The coconut palm provides supplemental food, drink, and construction materials for islanders from one end of the Pacific to the other; it was probably carried by human agents to all but the western islands, since its seed nut does not retain viability after long immersions in salt water.

Rice cultivation did not spread past Malaysia and the Marianas into Melanesia or Polynesia in pre-European times; and although it is now imported and eaten by islanders with great relish, most modern attempts to cultivate it in the islands have had scant success, owing mainly to the islanders' impatience with the kind of plodding, sustained labor its production requires.

When Europeans first visited Melanesia and Polynesia, they noted many communities cultivating sweet potatoes, the single instance of a native American cultivated food plant found in pre-European Oceania.[1]

Along with gardening and other neolithic traits, the Oceanic Negroids also adopted the practice of raising pigs and fowl. Pig raising, in fact, became a major preoccupation, but little attention was paid to the few scrawny fowl that haunted villages in search of overlooked crumbs.

Racially the earlier "Indonesians" who drifted into Melanesia may have been as much Negroid as Mongoloid, as a result of having absorbed Negroid remnants surviving up to that time in Malaysia; but later migrants were progressively more Mongoloid in racial features, and altered accordingly the Negroid aboriginals with whom they mixed. In like manner, those Papuan tongues strongly influenced by the newer immigrants came to resemble Austronesian languages in many respects and have come to be known as Melanesian languages to differentiate them from the more conservative, less influenced Papuan languages. Melanesian languages are now spoken along the coasts of eastern New Guinea and throughout most of the rest of Melanesia. They vary a great deal among themselves, but share certain features of syntax and vocabulary which link them with other

[1] See page 66.

members of the very widespread Austronesian family of
languages.

As the centuries passed, the later immigrants and their
hybrid descendants occupied and retained most of the
shore areas throughout Melanesia, pushing the more
Negroid aboriginals back into the forests and mountains
and swamps. Travel was easier by water than by land,
so that shore dwellers moved about freely and culture
traits were passed along for hundreds of miles. Entirely
different was the fate of inland communities, isolated
and insulated against outside influences. Isolation, however, did not result in simplification: some communities
cut off from all outside contacts for centuries developed
exceedingly complex languages and religious concepts
even though their tools and technologies remained
simple.

Quite apart from the infiltrations into Melanesia direct from Malaysia, there have occurred innumerable
drifts back into the region from Polynesia and Micronesia, in addition to more casual continuing contact along
the borders. On Rennell, Bellona, Sikiana, Tikopia,
Anuda, Duff, Ndai, and Ontong Java, to mention the
most important islands, dwell colonies from Polynesia
and Micronesia. And Polynesian influence is also apparent in Negroid communities in Fiji and the eastern
Solomons, as is influence from Micronesia in the Admiralties and in the small islands north and east of New
Ireland. Nor have native migrations entirely ceased.
Even within the memory of living men, seagoing Austronesian-speaking groups from Shortland Island settled on the east coast of Bougainville; and this process
is occurring elsewhere.

Cultural similarities and differences throughout the
numerous Papuan- and Austronesian-speaking communities are almost impossible to appraise, much less account for, on the basis of theoretical migrations and
contacts. One investigator may come along and observe
that certain communities possess similar traits, say, bull-

roarers, fiber hats, and eel worship, and conclude that
the cultures in question are related. But then more careful investigation may establish that bull-roarers are
sacred objects used in religious rites in one culture and
mere children's toys in another, or that the eel is respected as a totemic forebear in one community while
being regarded as a sorcerer's evil genius in another.

There are nevertheless some generalizations that may
be made. For one thing, there is in most places throughout Melanesia a distinction between "beach" natives and
"bush" natives: the former usually have wider contacts,
more advanced technologies, richer diets, and consequently better physiques. This is not invariably the case,
but it is generally so. Islanders themselves reflect this
distinction when they call interior "bush" natives the
pidgin equivalent of "yokels." In the sense that most
Papuan-speakers are "bush" dwellers, whereas most
coast dwellers speak Austronesian, one might say that
Papuan-speakers are culturally the more primitive of the
two. This characterization is, however, not universally
valid, any more than is the characterization that Papuan-
speakers are racially more Negroid.

Bougainville Island constitutes a fair sample of the
problems confronting the anthropologist in Melanesia.
The island is over a hundred miles long and thirty to
forty miles wide; it contains two mountain ranges culminating in volcanoes eight to ten thousand feet high.
In the southern and western parts of the island the strand
is separated from habitable land by wide swamps; elsewhere the precipitous mountains plunge directly to the
sea. A native population of thirty-five thousand lives in
small hamlets scattered over the whole island. Papuan-
speakers (eight different language groups) dwell inland
in the central and southern regions; Austronesian-
speakers (seven distinct language groups) inhabit the
coasts and the northern interior. Along the east coast a
recently immigrant colony of Austronesian-speakers
from Shortland Island is gradually succeeding in "Aus-

tronesianizing" the neighboring inland Papuan communities; but in the southwest the coastal natives are
gradually forsaking their unhealthy beach villages and
moving inland, where they are becoming "Papuanized"
in language and in culture by the dynamic Papuan-
speakers of that region.

In southern Bougainville natives are taller along the
coast and nearly pygmylike in the mountainous interior,
but in the northern Bougainville mountains live Papuan-
speaking natives who are quite tall and husky.

Adding further complication to any attempt to reduce
ethnic history to a neat outline is the fact that all natives
on Bougainville—Austronesian- and Papuan-speakers,
coastal or interior, large or small—are coal black, being
far darker than any other inhabitants of Melanesia, including even the most isolated Papuan-speakers of New
Guinea.

Although Melanesia may offer nothing but frustration
to the tidy-minded ethnologist, it provides a unique
laboratory for the student of living cultures. In no other
place in the world is there such a wide variety of cultures, developed in so many kinds of environments. A
few refrains run through most of them: polished stone
artifacts, bows and arrows, root-crop agriculture, domestication of pigs, dogs, and fowl, some hunting and
fishing and gathering of wild plants, unilaterally organized groups, animism, and so forth, but there the similarities end. To gain even a superficial impression of
cultural variation in Melanesia, three groups will be described: Dobu, Sepik, and Siuai.

Dobu[2]

Off the southeast tip of New Guinea stretches Massim,
an area of tranquil seas studded with large and small

[2] This brief account of Dobu culture has been adapted
from Reo Fortune's *Sorcerers of Dobu* (London: George
Routledge and Sons, Ltd., 1932).

islands, some of them high, rocky, and forbidding, others
flat and barely emerging above the reefs, yet covered
with luxuriant vegetation. Nearly every island is inhabited or occasionally visited by far-traveling Austronesian-speaking islanders who are brown skinned and
medium statured, skillful gardeners and lively traders,
gifted artists and ritualists. For Melanesia, the Massim
area is unusually homogeneous: cultures and languages
are similar from the tip of New Guinea and Rossel Island in the southwest and southeast to the Trobriand
Islands and Woodlark Island in the northwest and northeast.

Near the middle of Massim dwell the Dobu Islanders,
a few hundred natives inhabiting the mountainous remnants of volcanoes, a setting of rough topography, dense
forests, steep hillsides, and deep bays—spectacular and
beautiful, but not very favorable for farming or fishing,
and consequently a poor place for people having to eke
out their living with primitive tools. In spite of these
discouraging limitations, Dobuans grow enough yams
for survival and manage to vary their meager diet with
occasional coconuts, sago, a few fowl and pigs, and what
few fish they are able to obtain near their shores. Their
structures are mediocre by most Melanesian standards,
and their villages are small affairs: ten to twenty pile
dwellings arranged in a rough circle around a clearing.
Short grass skirts for women and loin coverings for men
constitute their clothing.

The limited physical resources of their environment
may account for the Dobuans' jealous regard for property, just as their precarious existence may have led to
their exceedingly elaborate rites and beliefs concerned
with gaining supernatural assistance. To the Dobuans
the universe and its events have aspects both mundane
and sacred; people have not only solid material bodies
but also immortal spirits, which are often manifested in
shadows and which frequently leave the body during

sleep, resulting in dreams. The universe is filled with supernatural essences which may be impressed into service of the individual who is fortunate enough to own and use the specific rituals. Objects, like persons, have spiritual personalities and can be caused to do man's bidding provided he commands with the appropriate incantation.

There is a limited supply of desirable things in these islands, and a limited supply of magic power to help acquire them; consequently there is a fierce and endless competition, with the race going to the strongest, to the one who owns and uses effectively the largest collection of magic designed to secure supernatural aid. The successful gardener must plant and cultivate skillfully, but in addition his yam seed must have the correct magical properties and be induced to grow by his performance of the appropriate rite. A youth must enlist supernatural aid in order to create desire and acquiescence in the girl he wants; the very fact that he may be a comely lad is due to his magical powers over beauty-making spirits. A person with many magical powers which result in his personal beauty, his success in love affairs and gardening and trading, is a "good" person. Persons poor in magical powers, as manifested in personal ugliness and failure in affairs, are "bad." "Good" individuals inspire consuming envy in their less fortunate fellows, who are believed to attack them with sorcery. Men who acquire knowledge of sorcery steal a thing identified with an enemy and charm it so that the enemy sickens or dies. Women practicing witchcraft can leave their sleeping bodies and strike their foes, or they can extract the spirits of enemies and leave them inanimate. Some persons, diviners, possess powers to counteract sorcery and witchcraft.

In this atmosphere of envy and misanthropy the Dobuans live out their lives, following conventional standards of behavior and participating in four kinds of formally organized groups: the nuclear family, the *susu*, the village, and the locality.

The nuclear family unit consists of a man and his wife and their unmarried children; members of this group dwell together in their own separate house and garden together in their separate plot. Husband and wife usually come from different villages; the family dwells one year in the husband's village and the next in the wife's—a circumstance that has important effects upon all of Dobu. Within house or garden the family enjoys absolute privacy, except at times of critical illness or when a daughter's lover steals inside. Family ties are cemented not only by the marital relations between husband and wife, but by the fact of producing and consuming food together and by reason of the great amount of time spent together. Parents exercise a moderate authority over their offspring, and the older children mildly dominate their younger siblings. Under these conditions the nuclear family might develop indissoluble strength and strong sentimental ties were it not for interference of the *susu* institution.

Dobu society places great emphasis upon the matrilineal relationship: upon kinship grouping based upon ties with the mother. A woman and her children, together with her brothers and sisters and the latters' children, comprise a *susu* ("mother's milk"). Many other societies in Melanesia emphasize this kind of grouping, but in Dobu it has a particular significance. Nearly all property, including house sites, land and the trees growing on it, viable yam seed, canoes, potent magical formulas, burial sites, and even the corpses of members, in fact, most items of value, pass down through the *susu*. A child may dwell alternate years in a house built on a site belonging to his father in his father's home village, but he may not inherit that site or any of his father's property; instead, he inherits house site, arable land, and so forth, from his maternal uncle. And when he dies his prop-

erty will go to his sister's son, and his corpse will remain
with his maternal relative and be interred in his *susu*
burial place. Thus families form as a result of marriage
and continue until divorce or death of one of the parents,
but the *susu* goes on forever, or until all the lineage dies
out.

The core of each village consists of several *susu* interrelated through somewhat distant matrilineal ties. Frequently it happens that the exact genealogy of such ties
cannot be recalled by these Dobuans, who have very
shallow memories; in such cases the several *susu* in a
village base their claims of kinship upon totemic grounds,
upon descent from a supernatural bird ancestress. All
these matrilineally related individuals are "Owners" of
the village; their spouses and, in the case of male owners, their children are "Strangers," or "those-resulting-
from-marriage." It happens then that each Dobuan has
two villages and lives in them alternate years: in one
village he is an Owner and in the other he is a Stranger
and will permanently leave it when his marriage is dissolved by divorce or death of his spouse. From this it is
evident that the whole village is not a very stable social
unit; it is a fixed enough base for its Owners (although
even these dwell in their own village only one year out
of two), but for Strangers it is an alien community in
which they may never sink roots. Further, its population
is continually shifting—one set of Owners and Strangers
one year and another the next.

The Stranger does not have a comfortable life in the
village. Chances are that, aside from spouse and children, he will have no kinsmen there other than in-laws:
convention rules that Owners will not mate with more
than one individual from any one neighboring village.
The Stranger must address most Owners by formal relationship terms; calling by personal name is the privilege of matrilineal kinsmen. Owners do not fail to impress
upon a Stranger that he (or she) has few rights and no

property in their village. They back up the Stranger's spouse in the event of a domestic quarrel, and, if trouble of any sort occurs, they are quick to blame the Stranger —for why would an Owner wish to harm his own kinsmen?

A Stranger's patience may be tried on another score: his spouse is usually not above enjoying a casual "incestuous" affair with a fellow Owner, but the Stranger is in no position to object vigorously. In such cases the Stranger might attempt suicide, counting on his own village Owner kinsmen to redress his wrongs. Or he may resort to divorce, usually against the objections of those of his kinsmen who have made a property investment in his marriage.

It is little wonder, then, that these circumstances generate an unusual amount of jealousy and hatred and insecurity, and with these there is the ever-present anxiety born of the belief that all enemies are potential sorcerers or witches, possessing the magical means of inflicting sickness or ruin or death. One's own in-laws are specially suspect, and the suspicion extends even to one's spouse. Villages are thus aligned against neighboring villages. Indeed, the excessive preoccupation with envy, malice, and black magic has singled out Dobu even in Melanesia where such conditions are very common.

In Dobu there is little in the way of leadership that might serve to counter some of these disruptive factors. Some individuals gain local influence through strong personalities and through success in economic and love affairs, which in Dobu is tantamount to possession of a large store of effective magic, but such "leaders" are not influential beyond their own villages. In fact, they are dangerously vulnerable outside their own villages, since they are objects of malicious attacks of sorcery by less fortunate persons.

Several neighboring villages, separated as they may be by domestic feuds and fear of black magic, will nevertheless band together to wage war against distant villages. Fearing the distant unknown dangers more than the known ones at home, people rarely go outside their loose confederation or locality for lovers or spouses. Except for an occasional overseas trading voyage, the Dobuan rarely goes beyond the limits of his locality, unless he is a diviner.

As a child the Dobuan will learn to know two homes, one belonging to his father and one to his mother. Although he lives alternate years in his father's village, he will soon·be impressed with the circumstance that this is not his real home, and that things belonging to his father will ultimately pass into the hands of his cousin, his father's sister's son. On the other hand, in his mother's village—his own true home and the place where he will someday be buried—he is surrounded by close kinsmen. One of these latter, his mother's brother, will be his special benefactor, teaching him his private stock of success-producing magic and bequeathing to him his land and other valuables.

When he is no longer a child, he will leave off sleeping at night in his parents' houses and will remain with other youths in some vacant house or will sneak into the house of his sweetheart of the moment and spend the night in surreptitious love-making. A Dobuan youth woos many maidens before he settles upon one for spouse. When that takes place he simply remains past dawn in her house, to be discovered by her parents and impressed into marriage. At that point the youth's close maternal kin—all the Owners of his *susu* village—have to pool their resources to present a gift to Owners of the bride's *susu* village, little being given to reciprocate. In a sense, marriage is a contract between villages, with mutual liabilities at its establishment and at its dissolution by death or divorce. This factor serves in some measure, but not sufficiently, as statistics show, to keep marriages intact.

The bridegroom establishes his own home on land provided by his maternal uncle, and he and his wife settle down to the most important business of Dobuan life, the growing of yams.

The Negroids of Oceania have earned fame as gifted craftsmen and notoriety as fierce savages, but above all else they are skillful gardeners. Most of their food comes from their gardens or groves. Some of them depend mainly on starch pounded out of the heart of sago palms. Others concentrate upon the cultivation of taro, others upon yams, still others upon plantains, and some of these people combine two or three of these food plants. When available, coconuts, wild foods, manioc, recently introduced sweet potatoes, fish, pork, fowl, opossum (phalanger), flying fox, and other dainties supplement these basic foods, but in each community there is usually an excessive dependence upon one of the four starchy staples. In Dobu the yam is most important. Yams have the quality of good preservation, so that in some yam-eating places, like the near-by Trobriands, the surpluses may be stored and accumulated and hence constitute a kind of capital goods, serving to enhance the prestige of their owners. Dobu, however, produces barely enough yams to satisfy hunger, and even this requires continual effort on the part of gardeners.

On Dobu neighbors assist a family to do the initial clearing of land, but thereafter each family cultivates its own garden. Man and wife must both supply seed yams for their family garden, and each must save seed produced from his separate stock for the following year's planting. No distinction is made between husband's and wife's yams in the eating, but it is essential to maintain separate seed stocks for this reason: yams have personality like many other growing things, and they will grow only if proper rituals are performed during their growth period. Further, by the nature of things, all viable seeds and their associated magic are *susu* property, passed down from mother to daughter and from uncle to nephew. It is understandable then why both partners to a marriage must belong to *susu* possessing adequate stocks of yam seed plus magic to induce growth, and prospective in-laws insist upon this lest they become burdened with feeding a nonproductive son- or daughter-in-law.

Not only must gardeners remain constantly with their growing yams to induce them by magic and by tender care to grow in the poor marginal Dobuan land, but they must stay near by to guard magically against their theft by envious neighbors. For unless they are properly cared for and protected, yams, being living creatures, may be persuaded to leave their owner's garden and thereby reduce his possessions to less enviable proportions.

The Dobuan's life plods on in a succession of moves from his own village to his wife's and back again; in a continuous round of planting, cultivating, and harvesting his precious yams; in occasional extramarital sex adventures; and in intermittent strife with in-laws, sometimes terminating in divorce and usually fraught with anxieties manifested in fear of sorcery and witchcraft. Now and then there is the diversion of an overseas trading voyage to the near-by Trobriands or to Tubetube.

These expeditions, known as *kula*, link the whole Massim area in a vast complex institution of ritual exchange. The basis of it lies in the movements of two kinds of valuable ornamental objects from one island to another around the whole area. Trochus-shell armbands are made in the northeastern islands and circulate counterclockwise, going from a man in one place to his trade ally in another. Spondylus-shell necklaces originate in the south and circulate clockwise. Dobu is a midpoint in the exchange circle. About once a year natives from Tubetube visit Dobu bringing necklaces which they leave with their Dobu trade partners. Later on these latter carry the necklaces north to the Trobriands and leave them there with their trade partners. Trobrianders

then reciprocate by taking armbands to their trade partners in Dobu, who in turn carry the armbands to their
Tubetube partners as repayment for the necklaces previously received. Several years elapse before armbands
and necklaces complete a cycle. Conventional commercial trading of pottery, greenstone for making adzes,
sago, wooden bowls, and so forth, also takes place during these *kula* exchanges, but this aspect is subsidiary
to the main ceremonial exchange of necklaces and armbands. An Occidental businessman observing the *kula* in
operation might well be puzzled at the absence of profit
motive involved in this energy-consuming swapping of
economically useless ornaments just for the pleasure of
exchanging. Yet that is what it adds up to. These islanders love trading for trading's sake; in this respect they
constitute classic exceptions to the Western concept of
economic man.[3]

One explanation of the *kula* describes it as an elaborate peace-keeping mechanism. It does have that effect,
but it is primarily just another manifestation of these
natives' emphasis upon reciprocity and their love of
exchange itself along with the ritual paraphernalia surrounding it. Among other things, it is a diversion from
the continual round of gardening and domesticity; even
Dobuans know boredom.

Sepik[4]

Out of New Guinea's high central mountain ranges
flows the great Sepik River system, which curls around

[3] This fascinating institution has been described in great
detail and with consummate skill by the late Professor Bronislaw Malinowski in *Argonauts of the Western Pacific* (London: George Routledge and Sons, Ltd., 1932), one of the
monumental works on Oceania (now also in a Dutton Every-
man Paperback).

[4] This section is a summary of an account by Gregory
Bateson in *Naven* (Cambridge, England: University Press,
1936; Stanford University Press, Stanford, ed. 2, 1958).

in a broad elbow and after countless meanders finally reaches the sea halfway along the north coast of the island. Along its middle and lower reaches it is hundreds of yards wide and fathoms deep. Seasonally flooding its banks, it creates a broad area of fens, a region of sago swamps and marshy grassland, with localized forests growing only on the few spots of higher, drier ground. Crocodiles lurk along the water's edge and plagues of insects, including the dread anopheles, fill the air. The climate is hot and humid and breezeless to an oppressive extreme. Altogether, it is a place to be avoided. Yet here along the Sepik dwell thousands and thousands of Negroids who have developed some of the most complex and artistic cultures in Oceania.

Sepik natives dwell in large villages, some of them a thousand strong, and base their lives on the products and moods of the river. Their houses are built on high piles to keep their floors above the periodic flooding of the river. Their nights are spent in huge baskets, tightly woven to keep out mosquitoes. The river furnishes them with firewood and with protein food (prawns, fish, crocodiles); in river swamps grow the sago palms from which they obtain their staple food; in river mud flats they plant their yams and tobacco. Venicelike, wherever they go they pole or paddle their way in their long, slender dugouts. Dwelling in a harsh and dramatic, ever-changing environment they live lives filled with drama, climaxed by their fierce head-hunting forays and by cruel but artistic pain-inflicting ceremonials—a sharp contrast to plodding, brooding Dobu.

In Dobu, village houses are grouped around central burial places; Sepik rivermen build their dwellings in two long parallel lines facing a huge dancing ground on which are built impressive clubhouses for men. Sepik dwellings are large, housing two or three families of brothers and their wives and offspring, each occupying a separate portion. Each half or moiety of the village—

that is, each one of the two lines of houses—belongs to male householders related to one another through the male line. Members of one of these patrilineal moieties have the sun for their chief totem and believe themselves to be descended from a line of mythical ancestors associated with heavenly entities—stars, clouds, sky-canoes, and the like. The opposite moiety has for its chief totems the vulva and things of the earth. Children belong to the moiety of the father, and after marriage a woman dwells in her husband's community.

Each moiety is subdivided into a great number of small patrilineal totemic groups, and loyalty among members is probably a firmer tie than any other among Sepiks. Identified with each group are scores of totems, ranging from mythical beings (invoked for magical services) to natural objects and sacred places. Sepik rivermen enjoy hour-long debates over group cosmologies and attach much importance to erudition in these matters. Nearly all objects they use, including artifacts and structures, are richly decorated with totemic representations.

Women share these activities much less than men; they are usually too preoccupied with the everyday business of providing food, running households, and tending children. Women's work is to produce and prepare most of the staple foods; men go in for the more spectacular activities. Men fell sago palms, but women remove the sago and cook it. Men band together to hunt crocodiles; women spend the early hours of each day wading in chill water for prawns. While men are lazing or debating in their clubhouses, women are searching for firewood or doing monotonous chores in gardens and dwellings.

In Dobu, emphasis is upon the distinction between husbands' and wives' groups of matrilineal relatives; in Sepik villages emphasis is upon differences between males and females as such, and upon the progress of individuals from infancy to adult status. Men are thought to be the active element in sex, women the despised passive. Men should be aggressive, "hot," killers, and debaters; women should be meek, "cold," domestic. Women may not enter men's clubhouses, those enormous gabled structures, over a hundred feet long and fifty feet high, containing large wooden slit-gongs, panpipes, bullroarers, ancestor masks, and relics of head-hunting raids. Nor may youths enter the clubhouses, nor learn the secret of producing spirit voices, nor participate in men's exciting activities, until they have undergone a series of initiation rites involving painful and harrowing treatment. Usually a youth's initiators belong to the opposite moiety; and in some villages, initiation consists of a series of stages so spaced that only the eldest men attain to the highest grade and thereby become familiar with the ultimate mysteries.

Underlying most of the beliefs and practices connected with initiation throughout the Sepik area is the concept that fertility, of people and of the earth and its creatures, is associated with the active male element, with totems and ancestors linked to people through the male line. Many of these totems and ancestors reside in men's clubhouses; their voices are manifested in the sounds of the gongs and pipes and bull-roarers. When these spirits speak—which they must, occasionally, for life and fertility to be maintained—all females and uninitiated boys become terrified by this awful display of supernaturalism; at this and all other times females and boys must keep away from the clubhouses under penalty of death.

Before an initiate is shown these mysteries, his back is ornamentally scarified, he is cruelly beaten, subjected to foul acts, and thoroughly frightened. Then he may participate in men's affairs and contemptuously shun the activities of females and uninitiated boys. He will attempt to add to his own and his group's prestige by killing an enemy—any "foreigner" from another village and group—and he will undertake to secure his relatives' material assistance in finding a wife for himself. Proscriptions connected with the choice of a spouse are complex to an extreme seldom found outside Australia. There are certain relatives whom one must not marry, and others singled out as preferred mates. Ties with one's own group-mates, with mother's group, with special ritual friends, and a number of other considerations, complicate choice of a mate to such a degree that some inquiring anthropologists despair of making any "sense" of Sepik marriage sociology.

Men rise to influence by their aggressiveness in warfare, their skill in histrionics and in magic, and their good judgment in selecting wives industrious enough to help assemble food and wealth for giving lavish, prestige-bringing feasts. As men progress in the men's clubs, adding more human skulls to their trophies and thereby adding vigor to their villages, becoming more erudite in the mythology of their groups, and gaining intimacy with totemic beings, they secure power for themselves on earth and continuity for their spirits after death, possibly even reincarnation in a group descendant.

Siuai[5]

Bougainville Island has provided an ideal refuge for its Stone Age head-hunting occupants. One hundred and ten miles long and averaging thirty miles wide, it is formed of two great mountain ranges culminating in volcanoes eight to ten thousand feet high and divided by gorges and swamps into many virtually inaccessible regions. Rain forests cover the land except in the few isolated areas which have been carved out for native set-

[5] This account is based on my field work in Bougainville during 1938–39: *A Solomon Island Society*, (Cambridge, Mass.: Harvard University Press, 1955).

tlements and gardens. Natural obstacles and human hostilities have kept Bougainville broken up into more than a dozen separate language and culture areas, with Papuan-speakers confined mainly to the interior.[6]

In the southwest a wide alluvial plain slopes away from the central mountains to the shores. On this plain, between mountains and the broad moat of coastal swamp, live the Siuai people, about five thousand strong, speaking a common Papuan language but otherwise not tribally united. Fast-flowing mountain streams have cut the plain into fan-shaped strips of land; along these the Siuai have cleared away forests and planted their taro and plantains. Their hamlets of three to ten homes are located near garden sites. Around the hamlets domesticated fowl and pigs forage for food; wild pigs keep to the deep forests where men go with their spears and dogs to hunt them. Men sometimes hunt for opossums, flying foxes, and edible birds, but seldom get any. As fishermen the Siuai are likewise ineffective; except for an occasional large-scale drive for fish, men leave the streams to be harvested by their womenfolk, who wade along the banks to collect prawns. Women also know where to search in the forests for grubs, mushrooms, greens, and other wild tidbits to enliven the day-in, day-out fare of taro, plantains, and coconuts. Once a year, when almonds ripen, nutting parties lay in stores for feasts. Sago is saved for times of famine or for fancy puddings consumed at feasts. Pigs are tenderly cared for against the time when they will be consumed at a feast or used to fulfill social or religious obligations.

To these black peasants life is a monotonous round of clearing land, planting and harvesting, of feeding their pigs and gossiping about their neighbors. The seasons vary little; planting is continuous. Breaks occur only when a neighbor dies or gives a feast, or when vengeance drives one to kill an enemy.

[6] See also page 42.

The Siuai man practices a little sorcery and has his troubles with in-laws, but to nothing like the extent of his Dobu counterpart. Also, he likes to frequent the neighborhood men's club and engage in a little head-hunting now and then, but much less than Sepik river-men.[7] The Siuai is essentially a loyal family man, an efficient farmer, and an ambitious trader and capitalist.

Like the Dobuan, he belongs to a matrilineal group and should not marry any of his "sisters." Further, he inherits automatically the land belonging to his small segment of the group and shares many sacred heirlooms with group-mates. Yet he is in no sense a "stranger" to his father's people; in fact, since wives frequently dwell all the while in their husbands' communities, children may become as intimately associated with their father's relatives as with their mother's. It is quite usual for them to inherit their father's land upon payment of a token to his group-mates. In Siuai the symbolic aspects of kinship stress ties with the mother and her matrilineal kin, but strong allegiances are often built up with father's kin, and there is little of the intergroup hostility re-ported in Dobu. Nor in Siuai is there more than a faint echo of the violent male-versus-female drama enacted throughout the daily lives of the Sepiks.

There being little scope for the magician or sorcerer or for the sage or the overaggressive killer, Siuai men apply their surplus energies to competitive striving after power. Leadership cannot be inherited; it is based upon the influence which a man secures for himself. The leader, or *mumi*, reaches that position by means of social

[7] The present tense used throughout this account of Siuai accurately reflects conditions as they were during 1938–39, except with regard to head-hunting, which was effectively outlawed during the first few years of Australian control. The same circumstance probably obtains for the Sepik area, al-though there was reported to have been a recrudescence of head-hunting along the Sepik during World War II.

climbing. He builds his prestige by providing his neighbors with feasts, so that they come to admire him and respect his wishes. In order to become a *mumi,* a man must first own or control material resources. He can either acquire these by his own hard labor or he can persuade kinsmen and friends to extend him loans. One customary method of accumulating wealth is to cultivate large gardens and use the surplus taro to fatten pigs which can then be sold for shell money. Another method is to make pottery and sell that. Still another is to practice for fees as a professional shaman or diviner.

The mere accumulation of wealth does not, however, bring prestige; wealth has to be distributed effectively —which, in this region, is another way of saying that it must be used to provide feasts. It is useful to have had a *mumi* father, to have started off in life with some of his reflected prestige together with what remains of his wealth after most of it has been used up for mortuary distributions. Such an initial advantage prompts many Siuai to say that "only the son of a *mumi* can become a *mumi.*" Actually the *mumi*'s son is only slightly better off than the orphan; he has to increase his inheritance manyfold, or have very liberal financial backers, before he can begin serious social climbing.

It is no wonder that the feast giver is a highly honored man. Feast food (roasted and steamed pork, boiled eel and opossum, tasty vegetable and nut puddings) provides a welcome break in the day-to-day monotony of a vegetarian diet. Then, too, natives keenly enjoy the excitement of milling crowds and the pleasure of panpiping and dancing. However, the ambitious social climber does not merely invite a few of his friends and treat them to a banquet: that would be gratifying but not very efficient. He generally makes the feast the occasion for a house-raising or some other kind of workbee, and no one respects him any less for being practical.

The ambitious man nearly always begins his career

by building a clubhouse. The clubhouse is a rectangular, shedlike structure built directly on the ground and without walls; occasionally an apse is added to the rear or to both front and rear. Large wooden slit-gongs occupy most of the floor space; these are drummed in order to convene workers, to announce feasts, and so forth, and serve as benches for the men who gather in the clubhouse to gossip and sleep. In Siuai house-to-house visiting is not popular, so that the clubhouse is virtually the only important gathering place; accordingly, the man who wishes to increase his prestige must first provide himself with a clubhouse. The most effective way to do this is to invite as many helpers as possible, draw out the work for as long a time as possible, and compensate the workers with such a bountiful feast that they will ever afterward remember the occasion and the clubhouse with pleasure.

Clubhouses are at no great premium in Siuai; there is an average of one for every eight adult males, so that mere possession of one does not assure the owner lasting renown. To serve as an effective symbol of the owner's growing prestige, the clubhouse must in addition be the scene of constant activity; and since nothing draws crowds like a feast, the ambitious owner exploits every opportunity for entertaining in this way. He causes men to cut down trees, fashion them into slit-gongs, and install them in the clubhouse; then in return he rewards them with a meal of pork. When no more slit-gongs can be crowded into his clubhouse, he contrives to have the roof repaired or the floor swept, and provides food for each occasion. After a while natives will say of him: "He is a true *mumi:* he gives large feasts." And when they stroll about they never fail to say: "Let's drop in at so-and-so's clubhouse; there's usually something going on there." They are at pains to ingratiate themselves with the feast giver, to defer to his judgment, to fetch coconuts for him, and laugh at his sallies of wit. In this fashion the ambitious social climber assures himself of a following and at the same time extends his prestige beyond his immediate village.

Some *mumis* stop there; others are driven on by their ambitions to seek wider acclaim and fuller authority. Their careers turn into continual rivalries for prestige and power. *Mumis* in neighboring villages seek to outdo one another in largess, and the adherents of each *mumi* line up behind him with patriotic fervor in order to assert the superiority of "our place" and "our *mumi*." These rivalries culminate in a *mumi*-honoring feast at which the host presents his guest of honor—his chief rival—with large quantities of shell money and numerous pigs. The guest of honor then redistributes these gifts among his own following and sets about to accumulate an equivalent, or more than an equivalent, supply in order to reciprocate. If he cannot repay within one or two years, he loses prestige and is forced to forego social climbing. If he returns an equivalent gift, it is a sign that he is a resourceful man, a true *mumi*, but that he does not wish to compete further. If, however, he returns more than an equivalent, the rivalry continues until one of the two bankrupts himself and all his followers and retires in defeat. A supernatural sanction is added to the affair through the co-operation of the spirits: ancestral spirits of the creditor *mumi* accompany the "gift" and remain with the debtor-guest until he repays; if he does not repay, these spirits tear out his soul—render him "near-death." Thus, a man defeated in a feast rivalry is said to be in a fatal predicament. Of course, he does not die right away (to a western observer there is no evidence of any mentally stimulated wasting away of physical powers); he might, in fact, linger on for years in good health. But, his neighbors claim, his fate catches up with him sooner or later. All metaphor aside, the defeated man is certainly "dead" insofar as further social aspirations are concerned.

A successful social climber is fortunate for a number of reasons. He has little difficulty about securing loans; hangers-on take care not to offend him; and by withholding his favor and patronage he can usually bend followers to his will. Nevertheless, no matter how great his prestige, his political authority is not absolute and rarely extends beyond his own village. Fines constitute the extent of the *mumi's* ability to penalize; and there is little to stop a follower from moving away to another village.

A *mumi's* influence derives some support from the demon world. Haunting every large community is a powerful kind of spirit called a *horomorun,* materializing sometimes as a large snake and roaring like thunder. *Horomoruns* are nourished on the spirit-essence of blood, human or pigs', and they identify themselves only with men who can assure them plenty to eat, that is, with *mumi.* When a *horomorun* has located a likely human candidate for his support, he visits a sickness upon him which can only be removed by a blood sacrifice. Thereafter he dwells in his *mumi's* clubhouse and adds to the *mumi's* power by protecting his property and weakening his enemies. As the *mumi* gives more feasts and gains more prestige, his *horomorun* increases in vigor by fattening on the blood essence of pigs supplied for the feasts. Thus the *horomorun* advances with the *mumi,* and, for every human follower of the *mumi,* there is a demon follower of the *horomorun.* Conversely, the *horomorun* may become a liability, for he will kill his *mumi* if he slows down in feast giving and fails to provide enough blood.

When actual death overtakes a *mumi,* he, like all his fellow Siuai, exits with a flourish. His body is placed in a log bier and cremated when the morning star appears over the horizon. Relatives and friends crowd close to the flames and sing his praises as his ghost trudges to the mountains, where it will either roast in everlasting

volcanic fires or while away eternity in feasting and social climbing, depending on whether his surviving kin
are niggardly or generous in the mortuary feast they
provide in his honor.

Dobu, Sepik, and Siuai are only three out of hundreds
of different cultures in Melanesia. They are not typical,
for no cultures in Melanesia can be called typical. No
primitive region in the world contains such cultural variety as these islands. Huge agricultural settlements sprawl
over the central plateaus of New Guinea, while a few
miles away dwell short-statured hunters, dependent
mainly upon sago and wild things. Along some coasts
live skillful sailors who travel about in enormous and
delicately carved canoes; inland a few miles may live
land-bound peasants who have never seen salt water.
Settlements vary from minute affairs of two or three
houses to large, crowded trade centers.

Every conceivable manner of aligning kin, of choosing
mates, of winning acclaim can be found. Communities
are to be found in the New Hebrides, for instance,
wherein male adult life consists of a single-minded progression through a series of secret orders so complex and
energy-demanding that men spend virtually all their
time in savage protocol. In some other areas ceremonialism hardly exists, so preoccupied are people with winning bare subsistence from harsh environments.

It is almost a relief to leave this bewildering complexity and move into Polynesia, whose native peoples
are spread over a far vaster area and yet appear, speak,
and live nearly alike.

V

THE POLYNESIANS

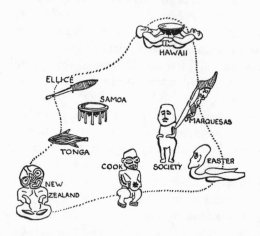

When the pride of Europe, the intrepid captains and navigators of the seventeenth and eighteenth centuries, dared the great Unknown and "discovered" Oceania, they found dwelling on nearly every habitable island from New Zealand and Hawaii, in the south and north, to Easter Island, in the extreme east, a people similar in appearance and language and culture. These people had no separate name for themselves, nor were they universally aware of their homogeneity. It was left to white men to class them together as Polynesians, after the name applied to their numerous island archipelagoes (Gr. *polys*, many + *nēsos*, island).

These handsome brown-skinned islanders greatly excited the admiration of their first white visitors, just as they continue to do today; and unraveling their history has been one of the continuously fascinating problems

of historians of primitive man. Many intriguing theories
about their origins and wanderings have had to be given
up as a result of serious study by geologists and anthropologists. Polynesia has been a happy hunting ground
for proponents of the Lost Continent school of writers,
some seeing survivals of the continent of Mu, the Pacific
analogue of Atlantis. Geologists, however, have shown
conclusively that this area has always been an island
world, a region of volcanic peaks thrust up out of the
floor of the Pacific Basin. It is true that the Polynesian
archipelagoes have been in the past alternately larger
and smaller than at present, as a result of periodic up-
thrusts and sinkings of the islands themselves or of
changes in ocean level. But there have been only slight
local changes since the advent of man, and chances are
that the first human arrivals there found these Basin islands pretty much as they are today.

Another theory that has been widely entertained but
proved erroneous by research is that which links Polynesia with America, deriving the high culture developments of one of them from the other. Some writers have
believed that the high cultures of Central and South
America were brought by Asiatics through Polynesia;
others that the developments in Polynesia were introduced from America. Proponents of the former theory
based their reasoning on their opinion that "civilizations"
do not develop independently, that complex traits are
usually invented in only one place, and that the Old
World—particularly Egypt and the Middle East—was the
source of all complex civilization.

Writers who would derive Polynesian cultures from
the New World point to the circumstances that prevailing winds blow from east to west in the eastern and central Pacific; but these theorists lose sight of the fact that
there are seasons when westerlies blow, and that it has
been repeatedly demonstrated that Polynesians made
many very long voyages from west to east. On the cul-

tural side, the case for New World origins is extremely weak; in only one instance has pre-Columbian cultural contact between Oceania and the New World been established: the presence of the South American sweet potato throughout Polynesia.[1]

The story of Polynesia has only partly unfolded, even after long and careful study of languages, material culture, myths, genealogies, and physical types, carried out by scores of experts, including a few highly skilled Polynesian scientists themselves. However, this research has at least demonstrated that Polynesia was the last great world area to be settled, and that its people, possessing quite advanced cultures, came from the direction of Asia. Beyond this point unanimity among the authorities disappears and a number of different theories have been advanced to account for the dates and the routes of the migrations into Polynesia.

Until recently one of the most favored theories—and certainly one of the most romantic ones—conceived of Polynesians as a homogeneous people with a distinctive culture developed in Malaysia and brought by them to their present islands by means of extraordinary feats of navigation and of endurance. According to this reconstruction the Polynesians were a stable mixture of south-

[1] The spectacular voyage of the Kon-Tiki raft from Peru to Tuamotu (see *The Kon-Tiki Expedition* by Thor Heyerdahl, translated by F. H. Lyon [London: George Allen and Unwin, Ltd., 1950]) demonstrated what no sensible anthropologist has ever denied: that hardy people *could*, accidentally or purposefully, have traveled from the New World to Oceania in ages past. It did not demonstrate, however, that any significant portion of the Polynesian population or culture *did* derive from the New World. Moreover, in 1957 the sixty-eight-year-old French explorer Eric de Bisschop demonstrated the feasibility of a west-east voyage by sailing the raft *Tahiti Nui* from Tahiti to within a few hundred miles of Chile—and then back as far as the Cook Islands (see *From Raft to Raft,* by Bengt Danielsson [New York: Doubleday & Company, Inc., 1960]).

ern Mongoloids and whites, and their original culture was a variant of the Southeast Asian neolithic, with elements—particularly ideological and ritual ones—from the higher civilizations of India and China. Moved by population pressure, perhaps defeat in war, and even exploratory zeal, they set out on organized expeditions in the direction of the rising sun in search of new homes. Avoiding the malarial coasts of New Guinea, with their hostile black savages, they moved through the Micronesian archipelagoes and after a few generations reached two magnificent and uninhabited landfalls—Samoa in the west and the Society Islands in the east. During the decades spent in the austere Micronesian atolls they had to give up food plants that grow only in deeper soils, and they "lost" the art of pottery making. On the other hand, this atoll stay had the effect of developing and tightening their social organization, for—the reasoning goes—large numbers of people cannot survive in restricted environments without some such organization.

To continue this view of Polynesian history: after a few centuries in their new high-island homes some of them began again to move on. Meanwhile they had reacquired through Fiji some of the food plants and other items lost during their atoll sojourn, and the two branches, western and eastern, had begun to differentiate somewhat—in dialect and in other aspects of life. The westerners populated Tonga and other near-by islands, some of them establishing colonies as far west and north as the New Hebrides and the Solomons. The easterners traveled even farther, eventually colonizing the Tuamotus, Marquesas, Hawaii, Easter Island, Australs, Cooks, and New Zealand. For some time most of these far-flung places—except perhaps Easter Island—remained in communication with one another, or at least with Tahiti, by means of deliberate two-way voyaging. Then interest in these hazardous undertakings subsided and sailing and navigational skills deteriorated, so that by the time Europeans arrived, two-way voyaging had been reduced to short distances, and the various archipelagoes remained isolated, with only legendary memories of their former connections.

In a variant of this colorful theory of Polynesian origins, there was not one but two "waves" of immigrants responsible for the peopling of Polynesia: an earlier darker-pigmented population entering through Melanesia, and a later, more "civilized" one coming through Micronesia. In one scholar's view,[2] the former shared a culture which contained elements deriving from Hinduistic India, while the latter had many cultural links with China, including worship of the god Tangaloa (*i.e.*, Tan-kah-lo), along with a kind of elaborate drinking ceremony (of *kava*) strongly reminiscent of the Chinese tea ritual. According to this reconstruction the "tangaloans" conquered their predecessors nearly everywhere they found them, and in this way founded castelike societies, with themselves at the top and the despised, inland-dwelling "commoners" (*Manahune*) below.

There is much to commend itself in these interrelated theories of Polynesian origins. When Europeans first discovered these societies many of them were indeed constructed on aristocratic castelike lines; and their genealogies contained many references to identical events and persons—real and legendary—in their common pasts. Moreover, advent through Micronesia would account for the absence of pottery among a people clearly "neolithic" in all other respects; and many other local variations in race, in language, and in culture would be neatly accommodated by the postulate of separate immigration "waves."

Alas, like many tidy theories about mankind's past, these have not wholly survived the discovery of new facts. First of all, with the application of modern archae-

[2] E. S. C. Handy, *Polynesian Religion*. Honolulu: Bernice P. Bishop Museum Bulletin, no. 34, 1927.

ological investigation potsherds have been found not only on Tonga and Samoa, which are adjacent to pottery-making Fiji, but also in a very old stratum on the far-away Marquesas, indicating that the earliest settlers there once had pottery but abandoned the art of manufacturing it.

The picture of Polynesians voyaging back and forth between their distant archipelagoes has also had to be revised. No one can question that Polynesians did voyage to all these far-flung islands—for they *are* there! The question concerns how they got there, and once there how any of them ever got back to the starting-off places. That Polynesians had large and seaworthy craft no one can doubt; reliable eyewitnesses like Captain Cook report having seen sail-rigged double canoes capable of carrying a hundred and more adults and stocks of food. Such canoes were unwieldy beating against the wind but performed well enough with the wind astern or abeam. Polynesians were also keen navigators: they set courses from familiar landmarks and steered by sun and stars and by direction of wind and wave. Within short ranges and familiar seascapes such skills were adequate—at least in some fortunate instances. But the proposal that these neolithic sailors, however hardy and fearless, could have followed prearranged courses over a thousand or two miles of open sea, without more precise means for locating their destinations or fixing their positions at sea, is beginning to tax the credulity of their warmest admirers. (In this connection it is well to recall that in ancient times sailors may have been very much at home in landlocked seas, but that before the use of instruments for navigation no small oceanic island isolated more than three hundred miles off the Atlantic coasts of Europe and Africa was in two-way communication with the mainland.)

It is not claimed that deliberate long voyaging did *not* take place in Polynesia: in many instances well-equipped

fleets may have set out, for destinations suspected or
merely hoped for, and some of these canoes may indeed
have made lucky landfalls—or returned towards the set-
ting-out point when the wind itself changed direction.
What is *unlikely* is that travelers having once arrived,
say, at Hawaii or New Zealand would have the navigational skills to get them back home. In fact, it now appears most likely that many islands were first populated
—and subsequently added to—not by expeditions of deliberate colonizers but by canoeloads of travelers swept
off course while on short voyages between known points
of land. This kind of accidental migration is still going
on. One couple capable of reproduction is all that is
needed to start a population; and the somewhat random
variation in racial types found throughout Polynesia sug-
gests that many island populations started in this way.
For that matter, *all* Polynesia could, in terms of normal
rates of population increase, be descended from a single
canoeload of men and women separated from their
people about three thousand years ago—the time which
some linguists and archaeologists suggest for the beginning of divergence of Polynesian from related languages
and cultures.

Whoever they were, the forebears of the peoples we
call Polynesians were hardy and resourceful farmers and
fishermen.

Their principal cutting tools were sharpened bamboo
blades and polished adzes made out of stone, where it
was available, and elsewhere out of shell. Weapons were
spears and axes and clubs; bows and arrows were used
only for sport. Their principal gardening implement was
the simple digging stick, with which they formed holes
in the earth to plant taro, yams, sweet potatoes, and
bananas. Strips of the inner bark of the paper mulberry
tree were beaten into thin, pliable sheets for use as mats
and cloaks and aprons. Heavy cordage they made out
of coconut fibers.

Pigs, dogs, and fowl were kept wherever there was enough food for them, and these animals were used to supplement the vegetable diet. Fishing was a regular vocation as well as a sport. Most fish, including shellfish of all kinds, were obtained in streams and lagoons and along the reefs, but the adventurous Polynesians also liked to take their canoes far offshore to capture tuna and bonito.

By comparing the various Polynesian communities as they were before they began to be changed by European influences it is possible to reconstruct a plausible prototype of their common, "ancestral" social institutions—just as linguists have reconstructed some features of a proto-Polynesian language ancestral to all the living languages and dialects.

To begin with, the ancestral Polynesians were "collectivists" rather than "individualists"—they formed groups to carry out most activities, and their more valued possessions were corporately owned. Their most important kind of grouping was one of consanguineal kinfolk, of persons tracing descent from a common ancestor; such groups owned the territories into which their islands and the surrounding lagoons were divided. The individual could belong to any such group to which he could trace genealogical ties, through either parent. Moreover, choice of spouse was governed by the criterion of kinship distance—usually anyone closer than third cousin was tabued—rather than by group membership itself. These arrangements contrast with the kinds of strictly unilineal and exogamous kin groupings that predominate elsewhere in Oceania. Under favorable circumstances, however, patrilineal ties carried more social weight—succession to statuses of privilege and responsibility usually going from father to eldest son. In this sense, all members of the group were ranked according to their "distance" from the real or legendary group founder, with the eldest son of a line of eldest sons at the top, and the youngest sons of youngest sons at the bottom. Consistent with this arrangement, upon marriage women tended to move to their husband's home and their offspring usually identified more closely with their father's kin—although there were social devices for protecting a woman's rights in her father's group, in keeping with the bilateral kin flexibility noted above.

The highest-ranking member of the kin group was not only its leader in secular affairs but its principal communicant with the group's ancestral deities—he was, after all, the closest lineal descendant of the latter. Each group had an open-air temple, consisting usually of terrace and of stone uprights, where ancestral and other group divinities were worshiped. When a segment of a group broke away and established a settlement elsewhere, a stone from the "parent" temple was sometimes placed in the new temple, to preserve social and spiritual ties with the parental group.

Except in a few very restrictive environments, Polynesians did not have to labor too hard for their livelihood, and in general their technologies and economies remained simple. Compared with the Oceanic Negroids, they were much less preoccupied with material things, such as accumulating riches for the sake of gaining prestige. Most of their creative energies went into nonmaterial activities, into elaborating their mythologies, their religious rites, and their political interrelationships, as well as into memorizing lengthy genealogies and developing intricate patterns of conduct.

Social and political relationships among families and other segments of the kinship group were based upon these kinship ties; consequently genealogies were highly important, and knowledge of them carefully preserved. The concepts of *mana* and *tabu* served to sanctify and strengthen the social and political relationships.

Mana was supernatural power. Objects and individuals might possess it in varying degrees. The tool which invariably turned out fine production had *mana*, as had the skilled craftsman—his "skill" and *mana* being the same thing. Gods, of course, had *mana* to a superlative degree, and their direct human descendants, the chiefs and their high-ranking families, partook of that concentration of power. Associated with the *mana* concept was the belief that it was contagious: contact between objects or individuals possessing different amounts of *mana* could be dangerous to the weaker, something like contact with a highly charged electric wire. From this developed the concept of *tabu* (a Polynesian word, by the way): highly "charged" objects and individuals must be kept out of contact with weaker.

In some respects, then, the structure of Polynesian society was fixed, with status ascribed by birth. But there is also evidence of some mobility. People possessing social and technical skills—artisans, warriors, seers, etc.—were highly esteemed; and some of the favorite myth characters were heroes who contended successfully against the conservative order.

The elements of flexibility in Tahitian social institutions—the possibility of aligning oneself with the group of either parent, and the opportunity of achieving high status through skill—must have been considerable assets during the centuries of colonization, when it became necessary to adjust to different kinds of physical environment and to the hazards of under- as well as overpopulation.

The kind of society just postulated may still be found on small isolated islands like Tikopia (northwest of Fiji) not yet radically changed by European influences, where resources were adequate for one or two thousand people and where kinship remained the most important kind of social tie. Elsewhere, on larger and physically richer islands, the principle of *rank* became generalized throughout the populations, with all the highest-ranking members of all descent groups constituting a distinct upper caste. In such instances the ideology of kinship was apt to be superseded by that of *class*.

In places like Hawaii, Tonga, and Tahiti these beliefs became so highly institutionalized that the top-ranking chiefs—direct descendants of powerful deities and hence infused with very potent *mana*—were so *tabu* and their persons so surrounded with restrictions that they became almost immobilized, somewhat like the sacred Japanese Mikado. Marriages in such cases could take place only between persons of nearly equal *mana*, and that accounted for the brother-sister marriages that occasionally occurred.

Another tendency that developed with increasing size of population was the supplanting of kinship ties by those based on place of residence, *i.e.*, *tribal* membership became dominant over kin-group membership, and leadership passed from the highborn aristocrat to the skillful politician and executive. One accompaniment of this was increased warfare, through rivalry for valued but scarce statuses and goods. Another was a separation of chiefly roles, with the ritual priestly jobs remaining in the hands of a highborn figurehead, and the secular power passing into the hands of capable leaders.

And finally, one of the aspects of Polynesian cultures that make them so interesting to anthropologists—and so valuable as laboratories for studying culture change—is the extent to which some of them have seized upon distinctive features of their more or less common cultural inventories and elaborated these into complex institutions. On Samoa, for example, the preparation and drinking of *kava*, a mildly narcotic beverage made from the root of a cultivated pepper plant, was developed into an esthetically complex and extravagantly punctilious ceremony of great social and political significance. Tahiti, on the other hand, carried religious ritualism to an extraordinary degree of elaboration; while on Easter Island the preoccupation with birds became a ritual obsession, and political rivalry became channeled into a kind of deadly game.

Had Oceania remained "undiscovered" by Europeans for a few more centuries, it is not unlikely that the more highly organized Polynesians would have exerted more and more influence upon Melanesia; particularly might this have been the case with places like Tonga, which were evolving strong, aggressive central regimes. On the other hand, there were some Polynesian communities where the aristocracies were already beginning to disintegrate under the dead hand of excessive formalism and immobilizing *tabu*. Some of these weakening dynasties were maintained only through the support of monarchy-minded Europeans—but that is another story.

VI

THE MICRONESIANS

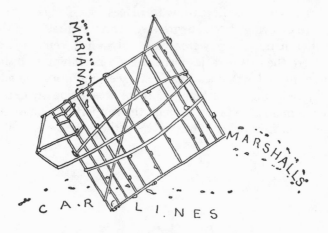

The hundreds of islands of Micronesia (Gr. "Small Islands") are scattered over an ocean area larger than the
United States but contain all together only 1260 square
miles of land area. Farthest north in Micronesia and
nearest to Asia are the Mariana Islands, the culmination
of a vast submerged mountain chain extending south
from Japan. Most southern and largest of the Marianas is
Guam, composed of terraces of coral limestone laid down
on top of a submerged volcanic base. North of Guam lie
Rota, Saipan, and Tinian, all similarly formed and all
large and moderately fertile. Further north are numerous smaller islands whose volcanic histories have been
too recent to permit weathering and soil formation sufficient to support large populations.

South of the Marianas lie the several Caroline Island
archipelagoes: complex volcanic and limestone Palau and

its smaller neighbors in the west; flat limestone Yap in the north; great Truk in the center; Ponape and Kusaie in the east; and a scattering of atolls and volcanic islands in between all these larger island centers.

After Ponape and Kusaie, the high islands peter out and the island universe consists of low-lying atolls all the way south and east to Samoa and Fiji. The northern atolls, the Marshalls and Gilberts, belong ethnically with Micronesia. The southern ones, the Ellice and Phoenix groups, are classed with Polynesia because of the cultural and linguistic relationships of their inhabitants.

To modern man Micronesia has come to be known for its strategic location, for phosphate and bauxite, for sugar-growing soils and fish-productive waters. For primitive man these same islands provided permanent, malaria-free homes.

Throughout Micronesia there were enough local differences in language, technology, social organization, and religious beliefs to make it possible to distinguish eight culture areas: the Mariana Islanders, or Chamorro; the Gilbertese; the Marshallese; the eastern Carolinians (on Ponape, Kusaie, and neighboring islands); the central Carolinians (on Truk, Nomoi, Hall, Puluwat, Pulusuk); the Yap Islanders; the Palau Islanders; and the southwest islanders (on Tobi, Sonsorol, Pul, Meri). While local differences existed even within a single culture area, in each of them there were one or two main islands, usually the largest and richest (for example, Truk, Yap, and Babelthuap), which exercised a kind of cultural suzerainty over surrounding islands. Truk, for instance, was the center of refuge for neighboring low islanders who had to flee occasionally from the devastations of hurricanes; Yap chiefs exacted tribute from surrounding peoples; and Guam was a trade center for all the Marianas.

Although less homogeneous than Polynesians, Micronesians were alike in many fundamentals. They were all

gardeners, living mostly in scattered farmsteads or hamlets rather than in large concentrated villages. Extended
families or lineages were the basic residential and subsistence units. Lineages were an important feature of their
social and religious lives; these lineages were usually
exogamous and, except in the Gilberts and the southwest islands, matrilineal. Some form of caste organization was prevalent except in the central Carolines; leadership, as in Polynesia, depended more upon inheritance
than upon the kind of social climbing typical of Melanesia. In religion, on the other hand, nothing developed
quite comparable to the elaborate and formalized poly-
theisms of Polynesia.

The pre-European population of Micronesia was undoubtedly more numerous than it is today, but there is
no evidence to support the theory of a fabulous "Lost
Civilization." Construction of the massive stone fortifications found on Ponape required engineering skill and
well-organized group work, but nothing beyond the capacities of the Ponapeans living at the time of the first
European contacts. Also, the impressive rows of stone
columns (*latte*) found by the Spaniards in the Marianas
—some of which are still standing beside abandoned
B-29 runways—were probably nothing more mysterious
than substantial house pillars.

Throughout Micronesia all but the leisured families of
high chiefs earned their living by farming and fishing.
The staple plant foods on the high islands were taro or
breadfruit or yams, plus coconuts and pandanus kernels.
On the infertile atolls, however, plant foods were scarce.
In general, atoll dwellers were better fishermen than were
the high islanders: they had to be to survive; some high
islands like Ponape supported such wide varieties of
foods that the inhabitants seldom had to fish beyond
their reefs. The Marianas differed from the rest of Micro-

nesia, and of all Oceania, for that matter, in counting rice among its staples.

Although each inhabited island or the waters around it produced the bare essentials for living, overseas trading was a feature of Micronesian life. Nearly every place produced a specialty—fine mats or unique dyes or special shell ornaments—and exchanged it for something unusual from another place. Yap Islanders used to sail to Palau to quarry and carry back home the large discs of stone used for a special kind of money. Fleets of atoll dwellers from the islands between Yap and Truk undertook regular voyages to Guam, and similar enterprises went on throughout Micronesia. Out of these experiences many Micronesians became daring sailors and skilled navigators; they mastered many intricacies of season, current, and wind, and even developed a kind of chart to guide them on long voyages.

Throughout most of Micronesia monogamy was usual, but in some places affluent individuals took more than one woman into their households; generally, however, only one was the "true" wife, and the others had the status of concubines. A feature common to most of Micronesia was the strong authority exercised by the principal wife over family affairs.

On most islands fidelity was expected of married women, except for a few privileged high-ranking ones; but no such restrictions prevailed before marriage. At Guam, in fact, unmarried girls underwent a period of sex apprenticeship by living at men's clubhouses and remaining available to all; the experience enhanced, if anything, their prestige in the eyes of suitors. Similar institutions existed on Yap and elsewhere.

Extended families or lineages were generally identified with tracts of land, and in some places all lands were thus owned. Furthermore, it was usual for some kin groups to rank higher than others, to own larger and better tracts of land, and to possess special ritual and economic prerogatives. These features were frequently tied in directly with concepts of rank and caste.

Except in the central Carolines, rank and caste were important social and political determinants. In the Marianas members of the nobility avoided marriage with commoners, dwelt in fine houses, monopolized fighting and overseas sailing, and demanded tribute and obeisance. Their chiefs, who belonged only to the most noble kin groups, had autocratic powers, as did chiefs in the other rank-conscious areas. Political chiefs on Palau were somewhat limited in power, but their equivalents in the Marshalls had absolute authority over all life and lands. Ponape was divided into five fairly equal districts, each headed by a paramount chief and a number-two chief; the former was hedged about with sacred restrictions, while the latter actually ruled—a system strongly reminiscent of western Polynesia. Yap's system was extraordinarily complex for Oceania: instead of the usual division into noble and commoner, or noble and debased noble and commoner, Yap's people were segregated into nine classes, with authority pyramiding down from a few leaders whose influence and power extended to tributary islands hundreds of miles away.

Individual competence was not totally ruled out in Micronesia, and there were opportunities for ambitious men to gain some prominence by exercise of specialized skills or by success in competitive feasting, but the main features of status were derived from membership in high-ranking kinship groups. It was not unusual for leaders in some high-ranking groups to extend their individual and group power, and even their land holdings, by successful warfare; this was especially the case in the Marshalls and Gilberts. But in general Micronesian society was based on fixed relationships between groups and resources, and on status determined by birth rather than by individual effort.

THE ALIENS

VII

EXPLORERS: 1520-1780

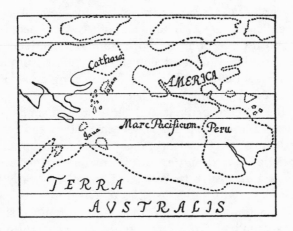

To hail westerners as discoverers of the Pacific Islands
is inaccurate as well as ungracious. While Europeans
were still paddling around in their small, landlocked
Mediterranean Sea or timidly venturing a few miles past
the Pillars of Hercules, the Oceania "primitives" were
moving about the wide Pacific in their fragile canoes and
populating all its far-flung islands.

Nevertheless, it is an accepted western conceit to describe the sixteenth, seventeenth, and eighteenth centuries as the "Era of Discovery" in the Pacific. This era
divides conveniently into three periods: the sixteenth century was the Spanish and Portuguese period, the seventeenth the Dutch, and the eighteenth the English. The
era was brought to a close by the voyages of Captain
James Cook, who did such a thorough job of it that, in

the words of a Frenchman, "he left his successors with little to do but admire."

Many factors led or forced the black and brown islanders to fan out over the Pacific Islands: refuge from stronger enemies, search for more elbowroom, even adventurous curiosity, and perhaps most importantly, loss of way at sea. In contrast one central driving force behind white voyagers was the search for Terra Australis Incognita—the great Unknown Southern Continent.

The existence of an unknown southern continent had been postulated for fourteen centuries before Europeans actually set out to find it. The Roman geographer Pomponius Mela assumed its existence as early as 50 A.D., and the astronomer Ptolemy later expressed similar conjectures. But with the split between Eastern and Roman Christianity, Greek science, including the conceptions of a spherical world and an unknown southern continent, became inaccessible to Western Europe. The early theories, along with other legacies of Greek science, were again made available to the West through Islamic scholars, and Marco Polo's reports also gave substance to them, so that learned men of Europe, including Albertus Magnus and Roger Bacon, began to speak of a southern continent with certitude. Many reasons were adduced to support the belief; Mercator, for example, held that symmetry and stability *demanded* a large and heavy southern land mass: without that for balance, a top-heavy world would topple!

These theories excited men's curiosity and led to endless scholarly controversies about the precise location, the size, the shape, and the nature of the place. Imagination made up for the absence of fact, and the fabled land was generously supplied with great quantities of gold and silks and spices and populated with highly civilized but miserably heathen races.

After the Turks shut off Europe's direct overland access to the silks and spices of the Far East, practical men began to search for alternative routes, thereby raising another incentive to explore in the direction of the theoretical south land. Portugal's Prince Henry the Navigator pressed his countrymen into this enterprise, and by 1498, Portuguese captains had rounded the Cape of Good Hope and arrived at India. By 1511 Portugal's empire was extended to the East Indies, Malacca having been conquered and set up as a colony.

Meanwhile Spain was contesting Portugal's rights to the Spice Islands, and was moving westward toward the Pacific. In the New World, twenty-one years after Columbus' discovery, Balboa sighted the Pacific from his well-publicized peak in Darien, and claimed it, along with all the shores washed by it, for his master, the King of Spain. This action of his, a standard gesture for explorers in those days, was the second claim asserted by Europeans over Oceania. It unwittingly ran counter to the earlier treaty, the famed Tordesillas *Capitulación* of 1494, which divided the world into a western half for Spain and an eastern half for Portugal, with the dividing line running longitudinally 370 leagues west of the Cape Verde Islands, and which consequently placed the western part of the Pacific within the Portuguese sphere.

In these modern days of exploring task forces, geographic societies, and well-heeled gentlemen-travelers, it seems strange that a conjecture as exciting and probably profitable as the existence of Terra Australis Incognita should have been talked about for so many centuries with so little attempt made to locate it. But good reasons there were. In the first place, ships were poor things, unsuited for long voyages. It was not until the single-masted vessels and oared galleys were replaced by three-masted vessels that long ocean voyages were feasible. Another obstacle was the crude state of navigation. Rough compasses and astrolabes helped fix directions and latitude, but the technique for estimating longitude was not perfected until the invention of the sextant in 1731 and the chronometer in 1735. Thus, early voyaging westward and eastward by dead reckoning was an uncertain, perilous adventure, and cartography was a matter of guesswork.

To these technical difficulties was added the problem of supply. Small ships had neither space nor facilities for carrying the right quantities and kinds of food and water and fuel required on long voyages. Nor does it appear that the gallant captains provisioned their ships very intelligently, even within the limits of their ships' capacities. Inevitably, on nearly every long voyage recorded, there came the day when "the few drops of remaining water became loathsome and stank, and biscuits disintegrated to crawling powder," producing scurvy, mutiny, and death for all but the hardiest. Little wonder that the usual ship's company was made up of waterfront dregs and men of little consequence; no other classes of men could be induced—or impressed—to gamble on such certain deprivations for such uncertain rewards.

Yet what ships and crews lacked in fitness, their captain-leaders usually made up for in courage or zeal. The history of Pacific exploration during most of this era of discovery is less of a chronicle of concerted national efforts than an account of the heroic attempts of a few dedicated individuals carrying out their personal missions against official inertia at home and terrible hardships at sea.

Spanish and Portuguese Period

The discovery of the Americas was only an incident to the many men of the period of exploration who held steadfast to their prime goal, the Great East. Many of them, in fact, considered America an obstacle and sought ways to pierce it with a canal. Others were obsessed with the idea of a natural passage through or around America, if it could be found. Among these latter was Ferdinand Magellan.

Magellan was born in Portugal about 1480 and, like many of his countrymen, spent his youth in the service of the Portuguese fleet then opening up a way to the East Indies. After his return to Portugal, a friend who remained in the Indies fired his ambition with accounts of the vast new riches to be found there. The court of Portugal would have none of Magellan or his plans, so he left his country and traveled to Spain. There his plan received royal support: he was to seek out a shorter western passage to the disputed Spice Islands and thus prove that they belonged in Spain's rather than in Portugal's half of the world. Magellan's fleet left Spain in September 1519; thirteen months later, after the mishaps and mutinies usual for such enterprises, its remnants discovered and sailed through the strait that bears its discoverer's name. Following upon this remarkable feat, Magellan accomplished another by sailing across the entire island-strewn Pacific without encountering a single inhabited island until he reached the Marianas in March 1521. After a short stay there he pushed on and discovered the Philippines, where he was killed by natives. The survivors of his expedition proceeded to the Moluccas, and thirty-one of them eventually reached Spain in September 1522, thereby completing the first circumnavigation. Of the two goals of the enterprise, the western passage was thus found, but proof of Spanish rights to the Moluccas was not demonstrated, and these Spice Islands were ultimately acknowledged to belong to the Portuguese half of the world.

Few ships followed Magellan's track out of Spain; most of the later expeditions to the East set out from the new Spanish ports in Mexico and Peru. After 1565, galleons established a regular route from Mexico to the Philippines and return, sailing westward in the latitude of Guam and eastward in a wide sweep to the north,

taking advantage of the prevailing winds in those latitudes. Along this regular course there were no islands
except Guam, which thereby became a thoroughly
Spanish colony, two hundred years earlier than any other
Oceanic island was annexed by a European power. Until 1898 Guam and its neighboring islands remained
Spanish and altogether separate from the influences that
shaped events elsewhere in Oceania.

Meanwhile the great mass of New Guinea had been
sighted and claimed by both Portugal and Spain while
they were engaged in their rivalry for the trade of the
near-by Spice Islands. Some cartographers thought New
Guinea to be the northern tip of the fabled Terra Australis Incognita, which continued to intrigue imaginative
men, including Alvaro de Mendaña.

In 1567 the Viceroy of Peru outfitted two ships and
placed them under the command of his young nephew,
Mendaña, with instructions to search out the unknown
continent, establish a settlement there, and convert all
the natives to Christianity. The expedition sailed between
the Marquesas and Tuamotus without sighting either
and, after the usual sequence of thirst, starvation, scurvy,
loss of life, and near mutiny, finally reached Santa Isabel
in the Solomon archipelago. Mendaña and his crews remained for six months in the Solomons, touching at most
of the southern islands of the group and leaving a trail
of pillage and blood; then they returned to Peru to gather
reinforcements for a new try. The charts that they drew
of their discoveries were so inaccurate that no European
was able to find and identify the Solomon Islands for
two hundred years.

For twenty-five years Mendaña haunted the courts of
Spain and Peru, trying to secure support for a return to
the Solomons, which he considered to be outposts of the
unknown continent. In the end he succeeded in enlisting
lukewarm support and again set out, the company including the wives of his officers and several friars, to es-

tablish a colony and save infidel souls from purgatory.

These strangely assorted adventurers discovered the Marquesas, tarried there long enough to raise their crosses and slay two hundred natives, and then sailed on westward. The expedition eventually reached Santa Cruz Island and prepared to settle down. Fever, mutiny, and death, including that of Mendaña himself, led to the speedy abandonment of the settlement, and the miserable survivors finally limped into Manila. Even this wretched experience did not discourage Mendaña's pious lieutenant, Pedro Fernandes de Quirós, from undertaking another voyage to search out the fabled continent and. save its unknown heathen millions from everlasting damnation by converting them to the true Catholic faith. Quirós' zeal was finally rewarded by royal support, and in 1605 he departed from Peru with three ships. His fleet discovered several islands along the route and reached what was believed to be its destination four and a half months after setting out. The name Australia del Espíritu Santo was given to the new discovery, in the belief that it was the long-sought continent. A great religious thanksgiving was held on the site of this New Jerusalem, but, hardly before the palm garlands had dried out, disillusionment, native hostility, and mutiny caused the settlement to be abandoned. Quirós' ships returned to Mexico, while that of his chief lieutenant, Luis Vaez de Torres, made for Manila. In the course of Torres' voyage he passed through the strait that now bears his name and skirted along the southern shores of New Guinea, thereby demonstrating that New Guinea was in fact an island and not a northern projection of the still unsighted southern continent.

Quirós' zeal to discover new souls to save drove him to continue his petitioning for a new expedition until his death in 1614; and with him Spanish ambition for lands and converts in the South Seas subsided for a century and a half.

Dutch Period

A greater contrast than that between the Spanish and Dutch South Sea adventures is hard to imagine. Spaniards, and their Portuguese agents, were visionaries seeking new lands and souls for the glory of King and Church; the Dutch were businessmen searching for new trade routes and markets.

Spain's maritime supremacy was beginning to wane when the Netherlands won their independence in 1581, and it was hastened by the defeat of the Armada in 1588. After this, Dutch merchants lost little time in forcing their advantage against the weakened Spanish and Portuguese Asiatic outposts, and by 1602 the East Indies were theirs.

The Dutch wasted no energies on winning souls; they demanded more tangible profits in the form of spices and gold. The strength and weakness of Dutch enterprises lay in the monopoly over Far Eastern trade enjoyed by one group, the united Dutch East India Company. Financed by wealthy merchants and backed by the Netherlands Crown, this company had exclusive rights to Dutch trade in the Indies, along with sole access to the area by way of the Strait of Magellan and the Cape of Good Hope—a formidable advantage, since these were the only known routes to the East.

By the second decade of the seventeenth century, Java-bound vessels were rounding the Cape of Good Hope and, taking advantage of favorable winds, sailing northeast for four thousand miles before turning north to Batavia. It was in the course of these voyages that Dutch ships first touched at the western coast of unknown Australia. Moved by the prospects of new commerce, the company directors in the Netherlands and their agents in the Indies authorized several exploratory voyages which helped to chart the northern and western

coast lines of Australia, without, however, establishing
the fact that it was a single continent.

Only twice during this period was the company monopoly violated: the first time by the Le Maires, the
second by Jacob Roggeveen. Isaac Le Maire, an independent Dutch merchant, succeeded after many remon-
strances in obtaining permission to trade in the Pacific
provided, of course, he did not trespass upon the routes
of access of the company. Confident of finding new
routes, Le Maire's son, Jacob, and a famous navigator,
William Schouten, set out from Holland in 1615, discovered and passed through Le Maire Strait, and sailed
around the southernmost cape of South America, which
they named Hoorn after Schouten's birthplace in Holland. They then proceeded to sail across the Pacific with
few mishaps, "discovering" en route several islands in the
northern Tuamotus, two small islands north of Tonga,
and Alofi and Futuna (Hoorn Islands). They finally
reached Batavia by way of the northern coast of New
Ireland and New Guinea. In port their ship was confiscated by company officials, who disbelieved their account of having come by a new route. Years later, the
energetic Isaac Le Maire succeeded in having the route
of the voyage accepted and his property returned—and
the latter, rather than South Seas discoveries, seems to
have been the more important issue to him and to others
who were concerned.

The Dutch were far too preoccupied in their new Indies empire and too incurious about geography to follow
up Le Maire's island discoveries, but twenty-five years
later an energetic governor-general, Anthony Van Die-
men, secured approval for a search for the still elusive
Terra Australis Incognita. Abel Tasman, a sea captain
in the service of the company, was commissioned to
carry out the mission. Tasman provisioned his ships with
plentiful stores and goods and set about on his voyage
in a workmanlike manner. His instructions from his su-

periors bore little resemblance to the inspired Catholic
exhortations which sent Quirós upon his mission; Tasman's orders read: ". . . find out what commodities
their country yields, likewise inquiring after gold and
silver, whether the latter are by them held in high es-
teem; making them believe that you are by no means
eager for precious metals, so as to leave them ignorant
of the value of same; and if they shall offer you gold or
silver in exchange for your articles, you will pretend to
hold the same in slight regard, showing them copper,
pewter, or lead and giving them an impression as if the
minerals last mentioned were by us set greater value
on."[1]

Tasman's voyage was a failure in the judgment of his
employers since he discovered no populous cities or rich
treasures. He was censured for having been "remiss," in
spite of his having sailed around the south of Australia
and having discovered New Zealand and southern
Tonga.

For the remainder of the century the Dutch merchants and administrators kept to their factories and
plantations in the Indies. From time to time shorter voyages were dispatched to near-by New Guinea and western Australia, but the ruling policy of the company directors was reflected in an answer they gave to a report
on some promising new lands: "It were to be wished
that the said land continued still unknown and never
explored, so as not to tell foreigners the way to the Company's overthrow."

Only once more did a Dutchman sight and name new
islands in Oceania. In 1722 Jacob Roggeveen, unaffili-
ated with the all-powerful company, entered the Pacific
from the east and subsequently discovered Easter Island
and the eastern part of present American Samoa. Upon
reaching Java, Roggeveen was punished for his temerity

[1] J. C. Beaglehole, *The Exploration of the Pacific* (London: A. C. Black, Ltd., 1934), p. 174.

in trespassing on the company area by having his ships confiscated.

English Period

During the first half of the eighteenth century most exploration of Oceania was carried out by armchair geographers writing from their academies in Europe. The works and charts of the great discoverers of preceding centuries were pored over and argued about in learned circles. Some scholars persisted in the dream of a great south continent, others weighed the prospects of finding a northwest passage to the Orient; and the controversies fed on ignorance about the true extent and content of the Pacific. Knowledge about the area was so deficient that Jonathan Swift quite logically located his Lilliput and Brobdingnag there.

Almost the only actual explorations carried out at that time were by-products of the highly practical occupation of buccaneering. The greatest English privateer, Sir Francis Drake, had long before concluded that real loot from Spanish ships and settlements was better than the theoretical treasures of the south continent. His royally sponsored voyage of piracy to the Pacific between 1578 and 1580 did not solve many geographic mysteries in Oceania, but it set a noble precedent which Englishmen were still following a century and a quarter later.

Another English navigator, William Dampier, was an accomplished buccaneer with a flair for reportorial writing. Between 1699 and 1711 he made three circumnavigations, during the course of which he learned much that was new about the coast of New Guinea and harried the Spanish galleons carrying gold and silver from Manila to Mexico. After Dampier, English activity in the Pacific ceased temporarily during the period of the Seven Years' War. Then, within a short time, there took place a series of voyages, by four Englishmen and one

Frenchman, that transformed Oceanic geography from a speculative into an exact science. The men responsible for this major accomplishment were Byron, Wallis, Carteret, Bougainville, and Cook.

By 1764 England and France began again to concern themselves with national honor and opened up their treasuries to promote projects designed to aid science and gain prestige—and incidentally to pick up any unattached land masses that happened to be found in the process. Interest was revived in the possibility of discovering the south continent, and the hope of locating a northwest passage to the Orient added strong commercial motivation to Pacific explorations. England sent out Commodore John Byron, who blithely ignored his official directive to locate the northwest passage and sailed instead through Polynesia to the Marianas and thence home. While in Oceania he discovered several islands in the northern Tuamotus, Cooks, and Tokelaus.

Immediately afterward, the Admiralty sent Samuel Wallis and Philip Carteret to search for the south continent. Their two ships parted during a storm, and Wallis sailed on to discover Tahiti and Uvéa (Wallis Island), while Carteret made several discoveries in Melanesia.

Next came Louis Antoine de Bougainville, sent by France to surrender the Falkland Islands to Spain and to sail through the South Seas and regain for France some of the prestige recently lost in her wars with England. Bougainville followed approximately in Wallis' path; then after Tahiti he sailed west to Samoa, the New Hebrides, and on to the Great Barrier Reef. Turning northeast he threaded his way through the dangerous Louisiade Archipelago, past Choiseul and Bougainville, around New Ireland, and thence homeward via Java.

All these voyages were truly remarkable feats of endurance, and reports of them filled many gaps in the Pacific charts. They would excite much greater wonder than they do had they not been followed by other voyages that far surpassed in accomplishment all those previously undertaken: the expeditions of Captain James Cook. It is not possible to speak of Captain Cook in words less than superlatives.

Born in Yorkshire in 1728, the son of a day laborer, Cook escaped the shopkeeper's life which lay before him and went to sea. While in the navy he established a reputation as an outstanding navigator and hydrographer. At the age of forty he was commissioned by the Admiralty and the Royal Society to lead an expedition to Tahiti in order to observe from that point the forthcoming transit of Venus, an event of importance to navigation and astronomy. In addition, Cook received secret instructions to search for the south continent and to stake out English claims to any lands he might discover.

The log of Cook's first voyage, extending from 1768 to 1771, has now become such a classic that it is almost impertinent to attempt a summary. Nevertheless, for the continuity of this chronicle it will be useful to repeat once more his list of discoveries, after he had successfully completed his mission at Tahiti; they included the Leeward Islands, Rurutu, and a survey of the coasts of New Zealand and of almost the entire eastern coast of Australia.

During his second voyage (1772–1775) Cook circumnavigated the globe, going close to the Antarctic in a vain search for the fabled southern continent that continued to engage imaginations. On the same voyage he revisited many islands seen during his first expedition and made many new Oceanic discoveries, including islands in the Tuamotus, the Southern Cooks, Fatu-huku (Marquesas), Palmerston, Niue, New Caledonia, and Norfolk. During his third voyage (1776–1779), undertaken partly to seek a northern passage from the Pacific to the Atlantic, Cook discovered Mangaia, Atiu, Tubuaï, and Christmas Island; he is also credited with the discovery of the Hawaiian Islands, although some historians ascribe that feat to Juan Gaetano, in 1555. In any event, it was the hospitable Hawaiians who finally put an end to his fabulous career by cutting him to pieces in one of the most beautiful settings in the South Seas.

Cook's voyages left little to be discovered in Oceania, and his observations, maps, and charts have not had to be too radically revised. But he was not only an expert navigator and hydrographer; by outstanding administrative ability he kept his officers and crews in good health and spirits throughout the hard, year-long voyages. And so skillful was he in his relations with most islanders that among many Polynesians his name ("Toote") was remembered and respected for generations.

The era of discovery ended with Cook. A few other explorers and navigators came after him and added an island or two to the charts, but by 1780 the stage had been set for the traders, the whalers, and the missionaries.

VIII

WHALERS, TRADERS, AND
MISSIONARIES: 1780-1850

By the end of the eighteenth century most of the Pacific
Islands had been "discovered" by Europeans, and events
were taking place in the civilized world that were des-
tined to transform Oceania. From this time onward the
islands were pawns in the great game of international
rivalries; the main moves were made in Europe and
America and, to a lesser degree, in Australia and the
Far East.

The Napoleonic Wars gave Oceania some respite;
Great Britain and France were too preoccupied in Europe to bother about a few islands on the other side of
the world. France, more than Great Britain, was barred
from Oceanic enterprises, since the Royal Navy block-
aded France and literally ruled the seas. In fact, the
Royal Navy played an important role in Oceania's history throughout the nineteenth century, since it com-

manded the main entrances to the Pacific from stations
in the Falklands, India, and the Cape of Good Hope.
The Royal Navy was also a factor during the War of
1812 in driving American whalers into the Pacific, unwittingly forcing the United States into a scene of fishing
operations in which her vessels quickly captured and
retained paramountcy.

Yet even with her naval ascendancy Great Britain did
not exploit her opportunities to extend her empire to
Oceania. Her one planned accession during this period
was Australia, which she chose as a site for a penal settlement, motivated more by a desire to rid herself of
undesirables than to acquire new territory. True, later
on Great Britain took vigorous steps to consolidate her
position in Australia, as much to keep France out as anything else; and the mother country was pushed into doing this mainly by the clamors of her Australian colonists. For very much the same reasons, Great Britain
finally but most reluctantly agreed to establish sovereignty in New Zealand.

Back of Great Britain's reluctance to extend sovereignty over islands in Oceania was a cultural condition
prevailing in England at that time: "Victorianism," as
it became known, was compounded of a number of
things. It began before Victoria ascended the throne and
prevailed with unusual staying power for ten decades.
An important component was the Evangelical revival,
which comprised an entire system of religio-moral philosophy based upon a reaction against the Regency and
"Popery" and upon a Protestant middle-class standard
of values. The typical Victorian has been characterized
as a hard, commercial-minded tradesman who scrupu-
lously went to church and vigorously supported good
causes. At the government level Victorianism consisted
of an economic-minded bureaucracy which supported
industrialism at home, bringing large profits for a few
but creating stark misery for the English working class,

while paradoxically backing the abolition of slavery abroad and supporting the formation of mission societies to wipe out heathenism.

Nowhere in English public life were these policies stronger than in the Colonial Office. With few exceptions Her Majesty's colonial ministers were supporters of the idea of foreign missions, many of them holding high offices in missionary societies. It has even been claimed that England's colonial policy was formulated out of resolutions coming from Essex Hall, the site of the annual meeting of mission societies. The effect of this on British colonial policy was to support missions, morally and with naval force if necessary, though rarely with money, but to stay clear of other kinds of colonial adventures, including annexation; the general argument was that colonies cost money and must be guarded, and that natives should be allowed to develop their own governments, aided by advice from missionaries. The only counters to this policy were the importunities of nonmissionary colonials and the threats of annexation from other powers, chiefly France.

Sometime after her humiliating defeat at Waterloo, France experienced a resurgence of nationalism which persisted until the middle of the nineteenth century and which was aimed at restoring national honor, mainly by outdoing her archrival, Great Britain. This movement reached its apotheosis with the July Monarchy, and throughout its history was strongly wedded to Roman Catholicism. France sought to bring about this revival of first-rank prestige by restoring her position as an enlightened nation through scientific expeditions and by supporting the spread of the state religion throughout the uncivilized world, especially in those areas in which English Protestantism was attempting to gain a foothold. Along with these cultural strategies, France supported a policy of establishing a world-wide system of "steppingstone" naval bases to counteract British Singapores and Gibraltars. In this endeavor Science, State, Navy, and Church were inseparable. Trade also became a partner, although a very weak one. France's principal objective during this period seems to have been to surpass and frustrate England.

Elsewhere in Europe nothing much of a political nature occurred to shape events in Oceania. Spain was preoccupied with domestic and American affairs and hardly bothered about her Oceanic possessions. Holland's activities in her Indonesian empire were concentrated in Java, leaving her little energy or interest for Oceanic adventures. Germany was still split into several states and hence did not possess a unified "policy" toward Oceania; but, on the other hand, several powerful merchants in the Hanseatic League cities vigorously went after a share of the world's water-borne trade, including the new trade developing in the South Pacific.

Economic more than political events had their repercussions in Oceania. One was the revival of the English whaling industry, stimulated by a generous bounty system designed to increase national income and develop a reserve navy. Another economic stimulus was Europe's high regard for sea animal furs of fine quality: Russian court circles were particularly extravagant in their demands. The first situation led to a vigorous commerce in whale oil, and the second to Russian, British, and American fur-trading activities along the western coast of North America. Russians were especially active, and trading stations of the Russian-American Fur Company extended from Alaska as far south as San Francisco. Their principal rivals were agents of the Hudson's Bay Company and, to a less extent, the representatives of such enterprising American promoters as John Jacob Astor.

Meanwhile the vigorous young United States was pushing its frontiers westward in pursuit of new lands, new treasures, and its "Manifest Destiny" to establish republicanism from the Atlantic to the Pacific and share in the opulent trade of the Far East. By treaty Russia was contained within the present southeastern limb of Alaska, and British Canada was pushed back to Vancouver Island and the adjacent mainland. Spain was cleared out of California during the Mexican War, leaving the port of San Francisco to Americans as a base from which to expand the rich China trade. But by no means was the United States dependent upon West Coast bases from which to exploit this trade. Long before San Francisco, Yankee traders were carrying China silks and teas and porcelains around Africa or South America and back to the fine ladies of Boston and New York and Philadelphia, and this trade had a decisive effect upon Oceania. When the Chinese began to demand more than "Yankee notions" for their wares, European and American traders had to scout the seas for items more to Oriental tastes—for furs, for sweet-smelling sandalwood, for pearl shell, and for gourmets' delicacies. These enterprises brought traders to the shores and islands of the Pacific, and many an American fortune was made by trading cheap Yankee knickknacks to islanders for sandalwood and trepang, which would then be carried to Canton and bartered for silks and tea for ultimate sale back home, with a fine profit at each turnover. But surpassing all these undertakings in commercial importance was whaling, involving hundreds of vessels and thousands of men engaged in the most hazardous, the most practical sport of all, to supply western lamps with oil and western fashions with properly corseted silhouettes.

British whalers hunted in Pacific waters as early as 1776, and within a few decades Oceania became the whalers' bonanza. One after another rich new schooling grounds would be discovered and exhausted, and the fleets move on to another. First was the sperm-whale fishing off the coast of Chile and Peru; then came the dangerous game of hunting in the fruitful but exceedingly rough waters between New Zealand and the young colony of New South Wales. This was followed by "country whaling" through the waters surrounding the Oceanic islands. In 1819, new grounds were found off Japan, and in 1833 those of Kodiak.

During the peak years, during the 1850's, many hundreds of whaling vessels roamed the Pacific. Americans led the field, then the British, and—far behind—the French. A few Prussian whalers appeared now and then, but not until after the middle of the century did German enterprise really expand in the Pacific.

Americans, from Nantucket and New Bedford, far outdistanced their rivals in numbers and energy. The Revolution drove American whalers off the Atlantic, but scarcely was the ink dried on treaties before they were at it again and delivering their catches to London. British naval supremacy again drove Americans from the Atlantic during the War of 1812, but this time the tough Yankees moved into the South Pacific and were soon predominant there. The American government offered no special incentives to maintain this industry; it didn't have to. On the other hand, the British paid liberal bounties to its whalers until 1824, and held out attractive inducements to Americans to join the British fleets.

France went even further in trying to build up a whaling fleet to rival Britain's and bring national prestige. Five vessels were fitted out with the help of generous government subsidies, bounties were paid on catches, and no chances were missed to acquire good personnel, even to securing Americans and Britons to captain the vessels. The French Navy was assigned to provide assistance to French whalers by maintaining discipline abroad and by supplying new replacements and naval stores. It was not unusual for a French man-of-war to stand-to near whaling grounds where French whalers were active.

The French government sent several naval scientific expeditions into Oceania to assist France regain her role as the fair handmaiden of Science and to help French whaling enterprises in the process. Expedition captains were specifically instructed to remain on the lookout for new whaling grounds and to assist any compatriots they met. The voyages and discoveries of such distinguished navigators as Bougainville (1767–1769) and La Pérouse (1785–1788) did indeed reflect great credit upon their government, but these and subsequent efforts were not sufficient to bolster up French whaling to first rank. Their shortcomings in skilled manpower limited the French to hunting the less strenuous right whale in the safer waters of bays, while their American and British rivals were roaming the open seas fishing for the ocean-ranging cachalot or sperm whale.

Whales do not usually appear in tropical lagoons, so that most of the time the whaling fleets kept to the open seas. But even whalers put ashore sometimes, and when this happened in the islands the effect must have been quite stupefying. Picture the scene of a thousand or so lusty fellows suddenly turned loose on a Polynesian settlement after months of poor rations, hard discipline, and body-breaking work away from the sight of women and the smell of rum. The pen of a Melville would be required to describe it, and the science of the geneticist needed to appraise its lasting consequences.

Hawaii, Tahiti, and the Marquesas were the first to receive the full impact. Vessels called at these islands during the off season in whaling to replenish their supplies, to recover health and morale, and frequently to render and dispose of their oil. It would be intriguing to learn how many kegs of rum were drained, how many New England wedding vows broken, and what manner of smell resulted from the mixture of delicate frangipani and cooking whale carcass.

When the fleets sailed again they usually took with

them many of the local natives, who had come aboard
in response to various forms of "invitation" to replace
seamen lost to the sea, to scurvy, or to native belles.

New Zealand and Hawaii eventually replaced eastern
Polynesia in the dubious honor of entertaining the whaling fleets, and at New Zealand there developed a lively
industry in oil rendering. Few islands escaped altogether
the visits of whalers. Some, such as Tahiti, Samoa, the
Marquesas, and Ponape, were especially popular, because of the beauty and hospitality of their women. On
the other hand, most of the Melanesian islands were
avoided because of their inhabitants' inhospitable practice of killing and sometimes eating all white visitors to
their shores.

Aside from the more intangible commerce that went
on during visits of whalers to the islands, their captains
bartered calico, knives, trinkets, rum, and muskets for
the fresh vegetables and fruits and pork needed by their
scorbutic seamen, continuing without much change the
kind of commerce initiated by the explorer-navigators of
the preceding century. Meanwhile a new type of trading
activity was beginning to leave its imprint on Oceania.

Long before the white man appeared, there were organized trading enterprises in Oceania. Among islanders
themselves intervillage barter was universal. Products of
the beach were bartered for those of the forests, and
trade lines usually cut across lines of intertribal hostility.
The natives of many seafaring communities became
trade specialists, acting as middlemen in carrying goods
from one island to another. Foods, stone artifacts, elaborate weapons, shell money, mats, ornaments, cosmetics,
and even human beings were the merchandise of this
commerce. There may have been a few Chinese trading
junks touching at the northwestern islands, but even
without this influence most Oceanians were trade con-
scious and eager for new goods. Nevertheless, they were

hardly prepared for the kind of commerce introduced by the white masters of the China trade.

The silks and teas and porcelains of China were highly treasured in the fine houses of America and Europe, and the China trade vied with whaling in attracting maritime-minded financiers and adventurers. After a while, however, it became increasingly difficult to find European and American goods to tempt the mandarins and at the same time secure the 1000 per cent returns regarded as reasonable profit for such hazardous enterprises. The shores of America supplied one answer to this problem, the Pacific Islands and waters around them another.

The luxuriously soft, warm fur of the North Pacific sea otter found early favor in Russian court circles, and agents of the Russian-American Company were established as far afield as California by about 1780. Beginning in 1785, vessels of the English East India Company visited these coasts and stocked up with furs for the China trade. Boston merchantmen soon followed suit, and until sea otters, ermines, bears, and even seals were almost wiped out, this trade was vigorously pursued. These traders were accustomed to calling in at Hawaii to rest and replenish supplies, and on one of these visits a shrewd Yankee spotted sweet-smelling sandalwood and took some along to China. There it was accepted so eagerly that the trade grew, and a half century later there was hardly a stick of sandalwood left in Oceania.

In the meantime other Oceanic products were discovered to be marketable in China: trepang, the exotic sea slug used by Chinese gourmets in their soups; pearls; nacre; tortoise shell; arrowroot. Coconut oil was more acceptable in western than in Oriental markets.

In addition, there developed a demand for more prosaic Oceanic products in the new colonies growing up in New South Wales and California. The penal settlement near Sydney was so far from self-sufficiency that the governor sent his agents to Tahiti to procure salt pork. And in Hawaii there was carried on a lively trade in potatoes to feed the fur-trading and gold-mining set-tlements on the West Coast. There also developed in New Zealand a trade for timber and flax to supply the New South Wales market; in fact, New Zealand pro-duced goods to suit almost any taste, including that of curio hunters. The Polynesian inhabitants of New Zea-land used to preserve human heads by a painstaking smoking and drying process, and the product was ex-ceptionally valuable if the deceased's face had been finely tattooed. White visitors paid high prices for these shriveled specimens, thereby causing the head-taking and head-curing "industry" to increase alarmingly. It is reported that some Maori chieftains would allow spe-cially favored white visitors to pick out heads from among the living, and these would be ready, tattooed and cured, for the customers upon their return.

Throughout the first half of the nineteenth century Oceanic trade was principally in the hands of British and American merchants. The former predominated in and around New Zealand, the latter in Hawaii, and both shared in the trade of Samoa and of Tahiti as well until French acquisition of that island. Fiji trade was at the beginning mostly controlled by Salem merchantmen; in fact, men of Salem, along with some from Sydney and Melbourne, dominated the trade of southern and central Melanesia. During the first two decades of the century French traders had no share in Oceanic trade, and even later on, though backed by their government, they did not rival the leaders.

At the beginning of the century the trader had his own way with the islander, exchanging calico, mouth organs, dogs, knives, muskets, rum, and the like, for car-goes that brought fortunes in Canton. Gradually this one-sidedness gave way as more traders began to com-pete and as islanders lost their first awe for anything brought in by the white demigods. The reaction went so far in places like Hawaii that full-rigged ships had to be given to island chiefs in exchange for precious sandalwood. Of course, the progress toward fair exchange did not proceed everywhere at the same rate, and even today in places like New Guinea one can hear traders complaining that natives are being "spoiled" by too openhanded whites.

On larger islands like Oahu, Tahiti, Upolu (Samoa), Ovalau (Fiji), and North Island (New Zealand), trading centers were established ashore and served as focal points for native suppliers and visiting merchantmen. In time, the presence of competing white traders and the increasing enlightenment of islanders resulted in more regular and peaceful commerce at these centers. But elsewhere visiting traders chalked up a record of chicanery, violence, and evil to equal the blackest chapter of colonial history. One record[1] related how a sandalwood trader held a native chieftain as hostage while the latter's subjects filled the ship's holds with wood; then, to render the district unhealthy for competing traders who might venture there in the future, the sandalwooder murdered the chief and his family and generally demolished the village before sailing away. Multiply this incident many times and add various refinements of mayhem possible only to members of a superior technical civilization, and it is hardly to be wondered at that natives of some islands were described by contemporary historians as having become "inhospitable" after visits of traders. At least, natives were usually less wasteful of those white victims who ended up on their shores: they ate them and turned the by-products into pretty trophies.

Blessings of another sort were showered upon the islanders during this period. For a variety of reasons white travelers from many parts of the globe landed or

[1] Tom Harrison, *Savage Civilization* (New York: Alfred A. Knopf, Inc., 1937).

were wrecked upon island shores and survived long enough to leave their marks. Subsequent generations of settlers refer to these beachcombers as "pioneers" or "founding fathers," provided, of course, they left affluent progeny or chivvied enough wealth to set up respectable establishments.

The beachcombers were a nondescript lot. Some escaped to the islands from the penal settlements of New South Wales, or from the slightly easier servitude of whaler and merchantman forecastles. A few were cast on the shores from shipwrecks. But there were many who went to the islands purposefully—to seek their fortunes or to solve personal problems occasioned by some little indiscretion with another man's wife or money.

A few islands with hungrier inhabitants managed to escape this infestation by assimilating the beachcombers, quite literally. In many places, however, the beachcombers managed to survive and either settled down peaceably and became second-rate "natives"—being treated as curiosities or allies or slaves—or they turned to commerce and politics and eventually became the founders of dynasties and the bane of missions, governments, and more conventional colonists. Many of them were adopted as "advisers" by local chiefs, who proceeded to pattern their habits and politics on the rather bizarre tastes and concepts of their beachcomber privy counselors.

Now and then tales got back to Sydney or London about the more sordid deeds of beachcombers, traders, and whalers; and such reports managed to stir up some popular and official indignation. There was even good sense enough to attribute ferocity among the natives to revenge for misdeeds of alien white men. It was impossible to do much about it, however, since most of the islands were not yet under the authority of any government. On occasion British and French warships cruising in the area would step in and mete out a little quarter-

deck justice, and as early as 1817 the British Parliament
passed a Police Act which enabled naval officers to take
apprehended mischief-makers to British territory for
trial and punishment.

Meanwhile an entirely new influence was at work in
Oceania—for better or for worse, depending upon the
point of view. Protestant activity began in the islands
with the arrival in Tahiti, in 1797, of the ship *Duff*
carrying a band of London Missionary Society evangelists and craftsmen. Back of this enterprise was the proselyting fervor of the English Evangelical revival and the
tacit support of the Colonial Ministry. The *Duff* pioneers
first applied their persuasions and good works to the top
of the Tahitian hierachy, shrewdly recognizing that conversions would spread quicker *downward*. The strategy
worked, and within twenty years one of the strongest
chiefs and all his followers were gathered into the fold.

It has been periodically fashionable for historians to
deprecate the motives and works of South Seas missionaries, but there are really no grounds for disbelieving
the sincerity of the *Duff* pioneers. And it is certainly no
wonder that they were successful: what a delightful
shock it must have been to the Tahitians to meet for the
first time white settlers who took neither their women
nor their goods, and who by words and acts were obviously there to help them. Along with their lessons in
dogma and morality, the missionaries were able to teach
many practically valuable crafts, since there were several artisans among them.

This progress was interrupted from time to time by
local strife but by the 1830's members of the London
Missionary Society had built up very strong positions
for themselves and their faith in Tahiti and had
branched out to the Leeward, the Cook, and the Samoan Islands. One of their leaders got as far as the New
Hebrides, where he was promptly killed.

It is a tribute to missionary zeal that these dedicated people were able to fill so many heathen minds with parables and cover so many brown bodies with Mother Hubbards. For, from their sponsors back home, they received little other than exhortation. Financial support was probably regarded as too sordid a consideration for such noble work; consequently most missionaries had to become farmers or traders to gain livelihoods. This led many of them to acquire substantial interests in island affairs and even caused some of them to turn trader or planter altogether.

In the course of their proselyting, many of them also gained local political power by means of their influence over converted chieftains. It would have been surprising indeed if they had failed to use their influence to frustrate mischievous traders or beachcombers and rival religious sects. But some of them went so far that they regarded *any* other whites as inimical to their status—and, they rationalized, to the interests of the islanders —so that they and their sponsors maintained constant pressure upon the home government not to permit secular colonization and not to establish secular colonial authority.

In 1799 the Church Missionary Society was organized in England, whence it moved to New South Wales and, in 1814, to New Zealand. The early phase of its history in New Zealand was marked by the zeal of its missionaries to acquire land from the Maoris and to agitate against secular colonization and annexation on the part of all powers, including England.

The Wesleyan Missionary Society was founded in England in 1814 and five years later set up a station in New Zealand. Soon it extended its activities to Tonga, and thence to Fiji and the Loyalty Islands.

Protestant missionary work in the New Hebrides was pioneered by hardy Presbyterians, who encountered fierce opposition from the inhabitants and succeeded in maintaining stations only at the expense of numerous particularly sticky martyrdoms.

A clerical error in the letters patent of an Anglican bishop in New Zealand defined his diocese as being from 50° south latitude to 34° *north*, and directed him to extend the Gospel to "the Isles of the Pacific." This might have daunted most men, but not the daring young Bishop George A. Selwyn. He rallied support in New Zealand and Australia and, from headquarters on Norfolk Island, sent courageous missionaries to the New Hebrides and the Solomons, thereby founding the famed Melanesian Mission.

In Hawaii, Protestantism was established in 1820 by Yankee missionaries from the Boston Mission (American Board of Commissioners for Foreign Missions). This group ultimately converted most of the population and secured great influence over native affairs; it spread to the Marshalls, the eastern Carolines, and the Gilberts, and even made an unsuccessful attempt to work in the Marquesas.

Considering the way such affairs usually run, there was a gratifying absence of rivalry among the various Protestant missions engaged in winning souls and covering bodies in the South Seas. Each kept to its own bailiwick and respected the staked-out claims of others. The London Missionary Society, for example, disavowed responsibility for Hawaii when it was learned that the Boston Mission was already urging these sheep into its fold. But all this quickly changed when the Pope's emissaries appeared on the scene.

In actual fact, Catholic missionaries preceded the Protestants in Oceania by centuries. Spanish priests accompanied the earlier explorers, and they were active in the Marianas as early as the sixteenth century. This mission endeavor was thoroughgoing in the Marianas, nearest to the Spanish Philippines, but was not very energetically pushed to the islands south and east of there, and was felt not at all south of the Line. Later, in 1776, the Viceroy of Peru sent two priests to Tahiti, but they so disliked the life that they did not remain.

The nineteenth-century rebirth of Catholic interest in missions in the islands came about largely as a result of the Restoration in France. Monarch and Church were united in their desire to combat British influence and Protestant heresy, and the arrangement was mutually helpful. Catholic missionaries carried the French language and accounts of the glories of France along with the dogma of the Roman faith. In return, they received the substantive support of an ambitious government and its naval power. There was good reason to hope that France would succeed by missionary work where she had failed by whaling efforts.

A band of Roman Catholics landed in Hawaii in 1827. They could hardly have chosen a more inhospitable site for their pioneering—for, the granite-willed Boston missionaries who had preceded them by seven years had won over the Polynesian rulers to Protestantism and, one can be quite certain, had fully warned their flock against the perils of Popery. The outcome was not surprising: the priests were expelled and the Catholic Church was not able to establish its mission firmly in Hawaii for many years, until French agents and naval officers had threatened, fined, and actually seized the local government. The almost symbiotic relationship between French influence and the Church became evident in the French demands of that era, for it was insisted that priests *and wine* be allowed entry into Hawaii.

Shortly after the initial Catholic attack on Hawaii, the Church broadened her strategy and Pope Pius conceived the grander program of a whole "Mission d'Océanie," designating two French orders as instruments: the Société de Picpus for the islands in the east, and the Société de Marie for those in the west.

Laying out his campaign like a seasoned admiral, His

Excellency the Vicar Apostolic of Eastern Polynesia established a beachhead in the Gambier Islands and, after learning the language, invaded Protestant Tahiti in 1836. History repeated itself, with the difference that the French government ratified the actions of the men-of-war which subsequently seized the native government while interceding on behalf of French priests. In the end, Catholicism won out in Tahiti over the greatly handicapped English Protestant missionaries, and Tahiti became the center from which Catholicism and French sovereignty spread to the Marquesas, the Tuamotus, Tubuaï, and eventually the Leeward Islands.

Meanwhile the Marist bishop, after being repulsed at Tonga, set up a station in the Hoorn Islands and proceeded to establish his base in New Zealand. By mid-century a new start had been made by Catholics in Tonga, and stations had been established in New Caledonia, Fiji, Samoa, Rotuma, and Woodlark. Daring but unsuccessful attempts were made even at faraway Rooke Island off New Guinea and at Isabel in the savage Solomons. The Marists played particularly active roles in helping to bring about the French annexation of New Caledonia in 1853.

The rivalry between the Protestantism and Catholicism of that era may be gauged by the fact that, on Bougainville Island, Methodist and Catholic native converts were burning down each other's chapels as late as 1930—to the considerable embarrassment of their spiritual mentors. How much higher feelings must have run a century ago when Protestant and Catholic missionaries represented rival nations and were sometimes backed by rival naval forces! Of the two, the Catholic missionaries had the stronger support and the closer identity with national (French) interests, but that advantage was perhaps offset by the circumstance that they had to struggle against entrenched Protestantism on many of the islands. In general, Great Britain was on the side of Protestantism, but this moral support was not usually translated into official assistance. The home government had no appetite for more colonial adventures at that time and occasionally slapped the wrists of British missionaries who demanded a show of forceful aid. The correspondence from London to Paris frequently contained stern phrases, but Britain did not assert her "natural" sovereign rights in Oceania except in New Zealand, where the value of the prize and the urgent need for authority in that growing outpost of British subjects led her to annex the island in 1840, just in time to frustrate the French.

Britain's policy aimed at maintaining the independence of the islands, particularly independence from other powers. Influential mission sponsors at home, as well as missionaries in the field, urged the maintenance of this policy, claiming that native leaders, given proper instruction by Protestant ministers, could eventually order their own lives and affairs, provided, of course, they could be shielded from less altruistic influences. Among these influences missionaries included not only Catholics and beachcombers and rogues off merchantmen and whalers, but also any traders or colonists or officials, including English officials. (Later, when the foreign communities became larger and more unruly, the missionaries in the field came around to the view that government authority might be beneficial after all.) Throughout this period the Colonial Ministry preserved its aloofness against pressure at home and abroad. A group of influential English financiers tried to secure official support for colonization schemes, but the missionary point of view was too well entrenched. Also, officials in the Australian colonies and in New Zealand were beginning to assert British "Monroeism" for the South Seas, and urged the home government to begin taking over "what God has willed to be British"—thereby voicing an appeal which was to continue to be a clan wail for colonial governors for several decades to come.

The extent of Britain's intervention, beyond the New Zealand annexation, was to maintain naval vessels among the islands, to quell serious disturbances, and, if possible, to apprehend British culprits. Consuls were appointed at some places, and it was not unusual for these officials to be missionaries.

The United States, with no navy to spare, displayed official concern only for Hawaii, where her citizens were consolidating their spiritual and commercial conquests. The Federal government did, however, on one occasion devote attention to the rest of Oceania by sponsoring the scientific expedition of Commodore Charles Wilkes.

A popular South Seas pastime started during this era as a by-product of international rivalries. It developed out of the plight of bewildered native leaders. To begin with, whites—missionaries, traders, and consuls alike—could not assimilate the fact that the islands were divided into small, separate, political entities, each with its own community or clan chief about equal in power and influence to all neighboring chiefs. To the white subjects of kings and presidents there was something politically indecent and even inconceivable about such arrangements. Consequently a native "king" was caused to emerge, factionally supported by resident subjects of the first great power represented. In time the subjects of another great power would appear and suffer real or imagined wrongs at the hands of the "king." Insults would fly, warships appear, ultimatums be sent, and the pitifully confused "king," cajoled into a partisan role and forced to accept responsibilities beyond his knowledge or capacities, would petition a power—*any* power—to protect or even annex his unruly and unhappy realm. Usually these petitions would be accepted gleefully by the forthright but politically naïve naval officers or consuls on the spot, only to be disavowed by their more scrupulous superiors at home. Or, if the petitions appeared to be receiving favorable consideration in the home capitals, then correspondence would increase between Paris and London and Washington, and the island "king" would end up by having his offer—whether it had been wrung by threats or sent voluntarily and hopefully—politely refused.

By the middle of the nineteenth century the era of missionary kingdoms and warship diplomacy was about over, and a new era of annexation and colonialism ushered in. Haphazard plunder of island resources by whalers and itinerant traders began to be supplanted by the more systematic exploitation of planter and resident trader.

IX

PLANTERS, BLACKBIRDERS, AND MERCHANTS: 1850-1914

During the sixty-five years preceding the First World War political events in the outside world continued to dominate happenings in Oceania. Throughout the first half of this era Great Britain's policies toward Oceania remained unchanged despite the decline in influence of Essex Hall. The Royal Navy continued to play a decisive role, but the home government maintained its reluctance to undertake new and costly colonial adventures in Oceania; in fact, its disposition was to barter South Pacific advantages for satisfactory settlements in areas nearer home. Ministers like Derby and Carnarvon appeared to know little and care less for the "cannibal isles." This indifference was dropped later on, in response to more articulate criticism from Australia and New Zealand and, more important, in reaction to the growing imperialistic threat of a rising Germany.

France continued to assert some influence in Oceanic affairs through her position in Tahiti and New Caledonia, and the missionary zeal of her priests did not abate. For the most part, however, France's role was that of a balance in the game of power politics between wealthy Britain and covetous Germany.

Germany entered the Oceanic arena with a flourish. Her unifier, Bismarck, did not at first favor colonial adventures, preferring to concentrate efforts in building up industrial power in the fatherland; but proponents of world commerce and naval might and colonialism had their way after 1880, resulting in an about-face of imperial policy and culminating finally in World War I.

Elsewhere in Europe, Russia's earlier slight influence on island affairs was wholly reduced by the disastrous Crimean and Russo-Japanese wars. The Dutch were still preoccupied with their East Indies empire and paid scant attention to New Guinea or the rest of Oceania. Spain, aroused by German encroachments, awoke long enough to reassert her rights over the Marianas and the Carolines, but was later liquated as a Pacific power as a result of the Spanish-American War.

During this period America's drive toward power and influence in the Pacific was interrupted by the Civil War and by the periodic ascendancy of the Democratic Party, which was against expansion (a reversal of pre-Civil War party policy; before the war Democratic leaders had been anxious to add new and slavery-minded territories to the Union). In the end, however, the Manifest Destiny of Seward, McKinley, and Roosevelt won out against the nonexpansionism of Cleveland and his party, and this era witnessed Perry's opening up of Japan, the purchase of Alaska, and the battle of Manila—all symptomatic of Washington's growing interest in the Pacific and, to some degree at least, in Oceania.

Developments in Oceania were also affected during this era by events that transpired in the Far East. Japan's entry upon the world scene, exemplified by her victory over Russia and her seizure of Formosa, was particularly ominous for Oceania; it could be inferred that her leaders began plotting their South Seas plans even before World War I. At the same time, China was opened wide to foreign trade and attracted increasing numbers of foreign devils, particularly of the predatory commercial variety, so that the Pacific was crossed with increasing frequency by European, American, and Australian ships, and all of the great powers took pains to acquire fixed way stations along the routes. Traffic also flowed out of the Open Door: Chinese coolies and small traders emigrated by the thousands to every land that would accept them, to escape the more dismal poverty at home.

Perhaps the greatest influence on Oceania was exerted by Australia and New Zealand. During this era those colonies increased many times in population and wealth and matured to dominion status. Their citizens went forth to the islands in large numbers, as adventurers, missionaries, traders, and planters; Sydney and Auckland became the capitals of most of Oceania, in practice if not in political rank. It was with pardonable presumption that Australians and New Zealanders considered most of Oceania as a British, and particularly *their* British, sphere; and it was quite understandable that they should have serious misgivings about German and French designs on the islands.

Economic as well as political factors in the outside world also exercised great influence upon events in Oceania. The rise of steam navigation led to a clamor for coaling stations located at strategic points along the Pacific trade routes. Also, for years before its actual construction, the plan for a canal across Panama increased the interests of major powers in ports of call in Hawaii, Tahiti, and Fiji; and the laying of telegraph cables across the Pacific necessitated the establishment of cable stations along the routes.

Whaling, which had been so important for Oceania during the first half of the nineteenth century, reached its peak shortly after the middle of the century and then rapidly declined owing to the supplanting of whale and sperm oil by Pennsylvania oil and of baleen by steel. Moreover, rival industries including textile manufacturing in New England and gold mining in California, drained away manpower from whaling, and the Civil War thinned out the American whaling fleets. When the Norwegian and Japanese whalers eventually took over leadership from the Americans, they generally by-passed Oceania for the Antarctic.

While whaling declined, however, the copra industry expanded, to supply soap and edible oils for Europe's growing population. Other tropical products became increasingly popular during this era; of these, sugar, coffee, cocoa, fruit, vanilla, fibers, and rubber, all adaptable to Oceania's soil and climate, were in special demand. For a short period, during the American Civil War, there was a stimulus to the production of cotton in Oceania. The developing science of agriculture in the western world also created a demand for fertilizers, leading to a vigorous exploitation of guano reserves throughout the islands. Trepang continued in favor among Chinese gourmets, and pearls and nacre fetched good prices in all civilized markets. Until the pearl beds were depleted, island divers lived active and dangerous lives. Steel manufacture raised nickel, chromium, cobalt, and manganese to high value, and created a thriving mining industry on New Caledonia, where these minerals were found in quantity.

The most important effect of all these outside influences was to introduce upon the Oceanic scene the planter, the blackbirder, and the big trading company. Of these, the planter was perhaps the star actor, supplanting the whaler, itinerant trader, beachcomber, and missionary of the preceding half century.

The planter was a new kind of man: unlike the whaler

and trader he was not drawn to the islands as places of refreshment and ports of call; and he was less interested in native souls than in native labor. He was a colonist —there to stay, at least until he could return in style to his home in Sydney or Liverpool, Bordeaux or Hamburg.

There were, to be sure, some planters already established in Hawaii, Samoa, and Fiji during the first half of the century, but such pedestrian money-making did not appeal to most visitors of that period. It was too slow and monotonous, and the returns though adequate were not excitingly so. Men of that earlier era preferred taking things already available and making fast turn-arounds— large profits derived from quick exchanges. But in time sandalwood gave out, and competition increased for the remaining pearls and nacre and other island produce. More white traders moved in and islanders became less eager to sell out to the first bidder. Also, the increased world demand for tropical agricultural products led businessmen of Paris, Hamburg, Manchester, and Melbourne to plan the ambitious South Seas development schemes which became such a fad and led to so many romantic bankruptcies. Some of the large ventures did actually materialize, but most of the pioneer planting was done by individuals with more hope than capital.

Nearly every known tropical plant of economic value was tried out in Oceania at one time or another, but only copra, sugar, coffee, cocoa, vanilla, fruit, cotton, and rubber have had any real significance.

Copra, the dried meat of the coconut, a source of oil for soap, margarine, and nitroglycerine, has affected the lives of more native islanders than all the other Oceanic products put together. Its production is admirably suited to South Seas conditions: land and climate are ideal for its growth, and even the rudest savage can be quickly trained to process it for commercial markets. There has been, and continues to be, every conceivable kind of production enterprise. Village natives dry their

surplus coconut meat and sell it to small traders; in some
places natives have themselves set up joint plantations.
Probably most of the production has come from "in-
pendent" white planters, employing native labor. "Independent" is put in quotation marks because few of the
planters have managed to remain financially so for very
long, having mortgaged their enterprises if not their use
of invective to the large trading firms which came into
the islands later and which have played an increasingly
important role in commerce and production.

The heyday of South Seas cotton came about as a result of the American Civil War. Desultory plantings were
tried prior to that, but large, organized enterprises developed only after English textile manufacturers began
looking around for substitutes for the American supplies
that were cut off by the Union blockade. Fiji became
the Oceanic center for this boom, and while it lasted
scores of white merchants flocked there. Australians were
particularly active, and there were even a few Dixie adventurers attracted to the islands by cheap labor and un-
obstructed markets. South Seas cotton was excellent in
quality, and the industry prospered until Southern cotton became plentiful again.

Coffee and cocoa also prospered for a while, and still
do so in some islands. Before South Seas coffee temporarily lost out to Brazilian competition and to local pests, it
was produced in quantity by white planters who wished
to spread out their risks beyond copra. New Caledonia,
Tahiti and parts of the New Hebrides continue to produce some; the *Kona* variety is well known, however
marginal a role it plays in Hawaiian economy today; and
the New Guinea highlands are the scene of a flourishing
new coffeegrowing development. Cocoa continues to be
grown mainly in British Samoa and in the New Hebrides.
Coffee and cocoa have both become *planter* rather than
islander crops, but in Hawaii Orientals have replaced
whites as producers.

Sugar has become the most alien industry in Oceania. It was apparent from the beginning of its development that islanders were not suited to the kind of organized industriousness required for efficient production, and planters had to seek laborers elsewhere. Also, in Hawaii and Fiji, the only places where sugar growing became important during this era, the industry was monopolized by large companies of Americans and Britons, so that islanders shared neither in its operation nor its profits. This is not to say, however, that islanders were not affected by the sugar industry; the immigration of tens of thousands of Asiatic sugar laborers to the islands—East Indians to Fiji; Chinese, Japanese, and Filipinos to Hawaii —had a profound effect upon island life. Copra has been a stabilizing influence, with slow evolutionary effects on island life. Even mining has utilized islander labor; in New Caledonia, where this has been less the case, the effects of Asiatic immigration are local and perhaps more temporary. Sugar, on the other hand, has produced revolutionary changes in Oceania probably more than any other single factor.

The expanding populations of Australia and New Zealand stimulated the production and export of citrus fruits and bananas in Fiji, Samoa, and the Cook Islands. Fruit-growing was principally in the hands of islanders although white officials and merchants handled the marketing. In Samoa and in the southern Cooks these enterprises continued throughout the era to provide islanders with funds for purchasing the trade goods which by then had become necessities; but in Fiji banana production almost ceased after Australia erected import barriers at the insistence of her own citizen fruitgrowers in tropical Queensland.

Accompanying the development of copra, cotton, and sugar, numbers of land speculators were attracted to the islands, therewith completing the inventory of rogues inevitable in the annals of any colonial region. On paper

their land deals appear more respectable than those of
the slavers because the murder of a handful of natives
looks more culpable than the alienation of a few thousand acres of land. (One most reputable Melbourne firm
almost succeeded in chiseling a bewildered Fijian "king"
out of 200,000 acres, and there are only about four and
a half million acres in the entire archipelago.) But in the
longer-range view nothing has been so fateful to islanders
as their loss of land. There was not much to begin with,
and by the end of the era this essential resource, this
basis of all islanders' existence, had become alienated to
an alarming degree.

Whaling did not figure as largely in Oceania's history
during this era as it had during the first half of the nineteenth century, but there were booms in other marine
industries. Diving, both for pearls and for shell, became
the economic mainstay of many an island group. In the
atolls of the eastern Pacific, pearling was about the only
income enterprise, until the shell beds were exhausted
by greedy diving. Then, the center shifted to the extreme
west, to the Torres Strait, where the beds were also systematically plundered and would have been cleaned out
completely but for the onset of the First World War and
the temporary abandonment of shell diving.

The world-wide search for fertilizers sent prospectors
to every corner of Oceania. American and British companies cleaned out the guano deposits from the Line Islands and then abandoned these islands to their sea bird
residents. Of much greater economic value were the
phosphate deposits discovered on Ocean, Nauru, Makatéa, and Angaur Islands. Although a few natives were
used in connection with guano digging, this enterprise
otherwise had little lasting effect upon the course of
Oceanic history; but phosphate mining was a different
matter. The permanent native population on each of the
phosphate islands became parasitic upon the mining
community and quickly abandoned the old form of life.

Phosphate operations also affected neighboring islands, since their populations had to be drawn upon for mining labor.

Meanwhile the eternal search for gold went on in the larger islands of Melanesia, and now and then some tough old prospector would strike it just rich enough to keep up the hopes of all his fellows. British New Guinea, particularly, became a graveyard for gold-mining enterprises.

On New Caledonia the mining of nickel, chrome, manganese, and cobalt transformed the island into a most un-Oceanic kind of place, as tens of thousands of GI's learned years later.

Compared with planters, the pearlers and miners had only local significance in Oceania during this era, but there was another species of exploiter that deserves a special niche in the South Seas rogues' gallery: the blackbirder.

A delightful rationalization that has alternately eased or increased the master race's burden in Oceania is that White Men Can Do No Physical Work in the Island Tropics. This might be termed the pre-Seabee concept, and it is weak in logic. Calling the South Seas climate "unbearable" is likely to draw guffaws from any Pacific-ribboned veteran who has lived and worked through a Washington summer. Furthermore, as numerous airfields attest, white men have worked in Oceania most effectively. Nevertheless, the early South Seas planters and their modern successors have always regarded large throngs of native or Asiatic labor an indispensable ingredient to agricultural enterprise. (To the white entrepreneur in the tropics there seems to be something indecently wasteful about an unemployed native!)

The early South Seas plantations did indeed require large numbers of laborers, and this posed a problem for the pioneer planters. In the eastern islands, where plantations were first established, the local Polynesians proved entirely unsatisfactory as laborers. In the first place, their life routines had not conditioned them to the relentlessness of organized work under a foreign master, producing things they did not use and for purposes they did not comprehend. In the second place, the Polynesians' easier subsistence economy satisfied all but the few needs acquired after the arrival of the white man, and the incentive to work for these extras was not strong enough to overcome their general reluctance for wage labor. So, at an early stage, white planters began to look beyond Polynesia for labor.

At Fiji the Negroid peoples were not quite so reluctant to work as were their Polynesian neighbors; and besides, the Fijians were more eager for material rewards and not yet so disillusioned about white men's affairs. But even in Fiji the supply of more tractable laborers gave out, and the inland hill tribes still showed more preference for white man's blood than for his wages; so the planters had to turn to other islands for the labor to cut their copra and pick their cotton.

Meanwhile white farmers and stockmen in Australia were reaching similar conclusions. The ending of the convict transportation system created a need for some other source of cheap labor for herding and farming. Early efforts to introduce East Indian laborers were unsuccessful, so that employers turned to the islands. History reserves for a Mr. Benjamin Boyd the distinction of introducing the first indentured islanders into Australia, the first shipment in 1847 consisting of some sixty-five natives from the Loyalty Islands and the New Hebrides.

Various euphemisms have been applied to this business, but most honest observers agree that it was nothing better than slave trading. It worked like this: masters of vessels so engaged would drop anchor in some bay or lagoon at one of the less frequented islands and "induce" islanders to sign contracts committing them to work hard

and faithfully at a distant island or mainland plantation;
in return for this labor they were to be fed, paid, and
eventually sent home again to dwell in power and prestige brought about by their acquired wealth and sophistication. A simple and straightforward commercial arrangement, ensuring mutual benefits and spreading
civilization at a somewhat accelerated pace!

Unhappily, a few tiresome complications developed.
A peaceful trader or missionary, returning to some normally hospitable village one fine day, would be murdered without warning. Inquiries would turn up the fact
that labor recruiters had just been there inducing islanders to sign on. It soon became common knowledge
that the Pacific blackbirders were as proficient a band of
slavers as ever shocked an abolition society. They captured savage chiefs and their families and held them hostages until enough able-bodied followers had signed on.
In a few cases they even delivered the hostages to the
sharks and scattered shot at the village to make the
place unhealthy for rival recruiters. It is of course possible that many islanders signed on willingly, with no
more coercion than a few misrepresentations about the rewards for laboring in civilization's golden vineyards, not
a difficult negotiation for the contractors since the con-
tractees could not read what they "signed." In any event,
the procedures developed many novel variants, but the
pattern was the same.

Having been delivered to their new masters, who paid
the recruiters handsome fees, the islanders experienced
fates varying according to the characters of their employers. Arguing statistically (of *all* the masters, there
must have been *some* who were not so bad as some
others), many laborers were treated decently, rewarded
justly, and returned to their homes on schedule, all the
better for their foretaste of the culture which eventually
was to change their lives anyway. On the other hand,
many natives did not fare so well, there having been little

in the shape of authority to enforce contract observance upon employers. Particularly did planters become casual about repatriating their laborers upon expiration of contract.

A source of much mischief was the practice of paying off laborers in muskets and ammunition, assisting the islanders to decimate themselves much more efficiently than was possible when they had to depend upon mere clubs and spears. The promise of firearms was in fact the only one that induced many islanders to sign on voluntarily. Through these humble beginnings the arms trade developed until it became a leading feature of island commerce. Sandalwooders, temperamentally well suited to this kind of sport, became especially proficient; they were able to supplement their decreasing profits from the dwindling sandalwood supply by blackbirding and by the arms and rum trade. In the Solomons these harbingers of civilization even joined with some of their favored clients in head-hunting forays: good customer relations.

Most blackbirding took place in the western islands, but the central and eastern islands did not escape altogether. Shiploads of Micronesians and Polynesians were taken to Peru and sold at so much a head to the planters and guano-deposit owners. The islanders proved unsuited to the work and large numbers of them died. The Peruvian guano mines achieved a particularly evil notoriety in this regard, even to the extent of scandalizing the ambassadors of the great powers, whose governments acted with a characteristic alacrity when presented with an opportunity to call attention to scandal in another's house. The result was that blackbirding for guano digging was duly prohibited, and the miserable handful of survivors shipped back to the islands—not, however, to their *home* islands.

A solution was not so simple in the western islands, despite popular indignation and the protests of missionaries. The strongest opponent of blackbirding was the

British Admiralty; naval vessels had to go in and quell uprisings which their officers knew had been caused by the conduct of blackbirders. But the Admiralty alone could not stop the trade; and the Colonial and Foreign Offices appeared unable or unwilling to act, stating that it was not *slavery*—hadn't the natives signed proper contracts? Moreover, they argued, the islands chiefly involved were not under British authority, nor would it be fair to penalize British planters and recruiters while not controlling foreign nationals engaged in the same practices.

Despite this inertia, there were a few attempts made to stamp out the abuses. The British Consul at Fiji went through the motions of "certifying" that landed laborers had in fact undertaken their contracts voluntarily, obtaining this critical intelligence by means of interviews carried out in pantomime; certifications of 2300 natives were thus recorded in 1870, one of the peak years. More effective was the practical work done by the Royal Navy, the Australian squadron having been enlarged to combat slave-running. British Orders in Council, including the famed Kidnapping Act of 1872, gave authority to naval officers to track down British mischief-makers in the islands and carry them to Australia for trial and punishment. This "government by commodore" was about the only organized authority represented in most of the islands at that time, and although it did much practical police work, it was limited by the fact that in Fiji the home government could not, and in Queensland would not, prohibit altogether the commerce in human beings and thereby wipe out the causes for the outrages.

In Fiji the situation was ultimately improved by Britain's annexation of these islands, after many petitions and counterpetitions. Simultaneously with annexation, the British established a high commissioner in Fiji, with deputies in all the island groups lying outside areas under recognized jurisdiction by great powers; these deputies had authority granted to them over British subjects in the no man's lands and were thus able to create some semblance of order. The worst abuses were not wiped out until all the islands had been annexed by one or the other of the great powers, and until Queensland legislated against the importation of island laborers.

Throughout the whole sordid blackbirding period, Queensland remained an embarrassment to Great Britain. Any suggestions from London or Sydney or Melbourne that the colony discontinue the use of island labor were testily answered to the effect that abuses did not occur in Queensland, thank you, and that islanders not only profited by their sojourn but insisted on undertaking new terms of indenture rather than return to the barbarism of their home islands! Such a policy was not surprising to find in a colony where some of the most influential men were the chief employers of island labor. Finally, however, even Queensland saw the light, and as a result of "White Australia" agitations outlawed the importation of island labor in 1902.

The British were the chief characters in the rise and decline of blackbirding, but other nationalities participated to some extent. German planters imported laborers from Micronesia for their Samoan enterprises. The United States assumed a self-righteous tone and deplored the practice, but failed to do anything about it. French colonial officials discouraged recruiting in their own territories, but were glad enough to obtain laborers from other islands. Even the Hawaiian kingdom imported a few Gilbertese to work on the sugar plantations and bolster the declining native population; but this experiment failed on both counts.

The final chapter is not yet written. In some parts of Melanesia labor recruiting and indenture remain even today, but they are hedged about with governmental controls so that it now requires more ingenuity and finesse and higher wages for the white masters to inculcate the gospel of work upon reluctant islanders.

Following in the wake of the pioneer planters and the blackbirders, there appeared in Oceania during this era several large mercantile firms, supplanting the itinerant trader and the small storekeeper in all but the most out-of-the-way places. By World War I these big companies not only dominated commerce but also, by purchase or mortgage, controlled nearly all other economic activity in Oceania; company agents and boards of directors replaced missionaries as the extenders and consolidators of national interest.

At nearly every island port one or two traders, more enterprising and better capitalized than others, emerged as business leaders and absorbed most of their competitors. The next step was to acquire fleets of schooners to bring in produce from outstation trading centers. Then, frequently, the leading traders would obtain land and start their own plantations, or, as in Hawaii, they would acquire capital interests in the plantations for which they served as factors. Some of these mercantile firms evolved from modest local beginnings; others were new ventures planned and financed by outside interests. Among the latter was the firm of Godeffroy and Son, which quickly pulled out ahead of all rivals and constituted Germany's spearhead of imperialism in Oceania.

Johann Caesar Godeffroy was a wealthy merchant and shipowner of Hamburg. His agents established their South Seas headquarters at Apia (Samoa) in 1856; before that Godeffroy ships were carrying passengers to Australia, and Godeffroy branches were established in Hong Kong and Valparaiso. Within a few years agents and affiliates were thriving all over Oceania. In the Marshalls, the eastern Carolines, the Gilberts, and the Ellice Islands, they and their successors constituted not only the sole traders but also practically the only Europeans in these island groups. In more settled places like Fiji and Tonga, they outdid most of their competitors. At Apia, their principal station, they were supreme. Their agents were the first traders to brave the dangers of wild New Britain and became the forerunners of German sovereignty there.

Back of the Godeffroy field agents were aggressive German financiers, intent upon building up a trade empire to surpass Britain's. In addition to their British employees they sent out educated and able individuals, capable of speaking French and English, and representing a different breed altogether from the usual run of island traders. Fast steamers moved directly between Germany and the islands, supplemented by lines to Sydney and Hong Kong and by a network of interisland vessels. German traders were also able to offer special inducements to planter customers, such as low freight rates in return for trade monopoly.

Godeffroy was eventually liquidated as a result of losses sustained from the French blockade during the Franco-Prussian War, but other German firms glorying in such titles as the *Zweigniederlassung der Deutschen Handels- und Plantagengesellschaft für Südseeinseln zu Hamburg* carried on the tradition and in some cases actually became the government's administrative agency. Against such competition the smaller local firms and those based on Australia and New Zealand had stiff going; nevertheless, many of them survived.

French companies, some of them backed by metropolitan capital and possessing valuable properties, remained paramount in New Caledonia against all outside competition. In French Polynesia (Tahiti and adjacent island groups) commerce did not become as integrated as elsewhere; Chinese immigrants did set up small establishments in nearly every line of business and at every populated center, but they were not under unified management control.

Germany's initial commercial successes did not enjoy government backing. When Godeffroy agents were making their first great gains, Germany was divided into a number of states, and the impetus for trade expansion came from financiers in the Hansa cities. Even the unification of Germany did not immediately change this: Bismarck was at first opposed to colonialism. Eventually, however, expansionists had their way, and the German government turned completely about-face toward empire and world-girdling naval power.

The first product of this policy change was strong support for German trading firms in New Guinea, which led to German annexation of northeast New Guinea and the Bismarck Archipelago in 1884. A year later the Reich took possession of the Marshall Islands, thereby consolidating politically what the Jaluit Gesellschaft, a Godeffroy associate, had already accomplished commercially. The center of German commercial imperialism remained at Samoa. The ranking German trader there, who was also consul, had the backing of German naval vessels which were then almost as much in evidence in Oceania as was the Royal Navy. But Samoa was not so easy to annex as the Marshalls had been: both British and American interests were involved, and the latter had in fact already secured naval rights to Pago Pago, the best harbor in the archipelago. A succession controversy among native Samoans finally provided the powers with excuses for intercession, with Germany backing one side and the Anglo-Americans the other. A providential hurricane wrecked the American and German warships— the British escaped by the skin of their teeth—in Apia harbor before they were able to do more than bristle at one another, so that international complications were avoided. Then, somewhat shaken by these explosive potentialities, the gentlemen in London and Berlin and Washington generously agreed to settle their differences by partitioning Samoa, the western part going to Germany and the eastern to the United States; they failed, however, to consult Australia and New Zealand and, of course, the Samoans themselves. Nor did Britain come out empty-handed, having received a free rein in the north Solomons, and, what was vastly more important to Whitehall, having obtained assurances of German acquiescence for deals then in progress with respect to Egypt and certain African territories.

Germany completed her Oceanic acquisitions after the Spanish-American War, when she purchased the Carolines and the Marianas (except Guam) from a vanquished Spain. As in the other cases, this represented an easy transition from commercial to political control, since German traders were already active in this area.

Perhaps one reason for Germany's steady progress in Oceania was the single-mindedness back of her colonial ventures. She sent out no missionaries to pave the way; in fact, although not violently antimissionary, her traders and officials asked no favors from them and showed little disposition to give any to them. Also, Germany had few subjects resident in the islands except those directly associated with government or semigovernment commercial firms, so that she did not have a troublesome public opinion to deal with. Her aim was commercial expansion, and later on political expansion through commerce. The imperial government even left colonial administration in the hands of company officials for a number of years in New Guinea and in the Marshalls, and turned administration over to government officials only after the companies had failed financially in spite of heavy government subsidy.

Meanwhile Britain was muddling along, taking action only when forced to forestall moves by Germany or when moved by popular indignation in Australia and New Zealand. Her reluctance to assume further responsibilities in Oceania was summarized by one minister who said, "Her majesty already has quite enough black subjects."

Also, treasury officials scrupled against spending United Kingdom taxpayers' money on enterprises that would bring profit, if any, only to the colonists; the home government was not very successful in having Australia and New Zealand share any of the expenses. In all fairness, however, it must be recognized that the London gentlemen had to fry other and larger fish than those occupying the South Seas lagoons. Bigger issues such as Kenya and Egypt deserved, and received, first attention, and when swaps were to be made it was not surprising that Samoa and unknown New Guinea should be passed over for better prizes.

Yet, in spite of this disinterest on the part of the home government, British influence continued to dominate Oceania during this era. British missionaries consolidated their spiritual jurisdictions over Tonga, Fiji, the Cooks, and Samoa, and pioneered throughout the New Hebrides, the Solomons, and New Guinea. They were supplanted by Catholic missionaries, and later by French Protestants, in French Polynesia and New Caledonia, and the Boston missionaries left little unplowed ground in Hawaii; but elsewhere the British had clear fields until the Catholics again moved north and west toward New Guinea. For the most part, the Protestants undertook no further king-making adventures, having relinquished this role to traders and consuls and commodores in Polynesia and having found native political organization too rudimentary in Melanesia.

More important political roles were played by British planters and merchants. Large numbers of them were attracted to the islands by the booms in cotton and sugar and copra; with their funds thus invested and their interests localized, they needed and demanded stable government—preferably British government—to regularize their land acquisitions and protect their property.

During this era Australia and New Zealand also became more directly and vocally interested in affairs in

Oceania. Individuals, companies, and syndicates invested fortunes in South Seas ventures; and large segments of the population supported missionary endeavors with funds and personnel and moral backing. Again and again the British colonial governments urged the home government to annex whole island groups; and in one instance at least, in Papua, the colonials took the initiative, only to have the "annexation" vetoed by London. Jittery Australians and New Zealanders watched with trepidation Germany's swift progress in Samoa and New Guinea. Although they warned Great Britain of the consequences, London went ahead and "negotiated" these areas to Germany. Such events aroused fierce resentment in the colonies and were instrumental in stimulating the Australian colonies to common action and eventually to federation.

Once only did Great Britain move swiftly and purposefully to obtain island possessions. Urged by an intercolonial conference, the home government acquired a number of central Pacific pin-point islands in preparation for the laying of a transpacific cable.

Nevertheless, in spite of general reluctance and indecision, Great Britain did raise her flag over a number of of other island groups during this period. Fiji was annexed in 1874, partly as a result of efforts to control blackbirding. Rotuma was added a few years later. Papua was taken in 1884 at Australian insistence and was later handed over to the Commonwealth. The Solomons became a protectorate in 1892. The Gilbert and Ellice Islands became a protectorate in 1892 and were designated a crown colony twenty-three years later. The Cook Islands and Niue were taken over in 1888 and 1889 and annexed to New Zealand two years later. Tonga, under British influence since the beginning, was brought closer under control. Ocean Island was annexed for its phosphates in 1900. By agreement with France, a joint naval commission was established in the New Hebrides in 1887, and this later changed into an Anglo-French condominium.

All together, between 1874 and 1906, over 112,000 square miles and several hundred thousand unwitting islanders were acquired outright by Britain—"in a state of absent-mindedness."

The Tricolor was raised over several islands in Oceania during these years, representing a consolidation of gains made during the first half of the century rather than a demonstration of continued French colonial vitality. The political climate in metropolitan France, complicated by troubles with North Africa and by the conflict with Prussia, was not very conducive to Oceanic adventures. Furthermore, the marriage of Church and State was dissolved, so that Catholic missions no longer received the official support they had enjoyed during the July Monarchy. This state of affairs was, however, not immediately reflected in Oceania, and for several decades islanders and whites alike continued to associate Catholicism with France.

At the beginning of this era, in 1853, as a result of the momentum gained during the preceding years, France annexed New Caledonia, seizing it out from under the very noses of a British mission. Also, in due course, the protectorate over Tahiti was superseded by formal annexation, as were the protectorates over the remaining archipelagoes which now constitute French Polynesia. Wallis Island was added in 1887, culminating French Catholic control that had existed from the beginning of white contact.

New Caledonia was constituted a penal colony in 1864, and within two decades over seventeen thousand convicts had been incarcerated there. Of these, many were elite supporters of the abortive Commune who eventually were amnestied and returned to France. But large numbers of run-of-the-mill criminals remained in New Caledonia for life, or escaped to Australia or to other islands. So long as they did not return to France, the ministers in Paris were not bothered. Australia, on the other hand, became indignant; the convicts among the founding fathers of New South Wales were at least *British*. Even more indignation was aroused by France's proposal to send recidivists to New Caledonia, and the Australian colonies were not satisfied with the reassurances London was able to obtain from Paris on this score. These issues were enlivened by French activities in the still unattached New Hebrides. Planters and traders from New Caledonia acquired large properties there and French military posts were set up. Annoyance and annexation fever ran high in Australia, but the home government would proceed no further than obtaining assurances from France that annexation was not intended. This agreement eventually crystallized into the form of the Anglo-French condominium, which turned out to be a happy solution only for the diplomats involved.

The interests of the United States in the Pacific received a strong stimulus from Commodore Perry's opening up of Japan about the beginning of this era. There was even some talk at that time of taking over such islands as the Bonins, the Luchus (Ryukyus), and Formosa as American outposts accessible to the rich Far Eastern markets, but this fever abated during the Civil War, and Seward's purchase of Alaska did not immediately succeed in reviving the expansionistic spirit.

Meanwhile Americans were actively engaged in consolidating their supremacy in Hawaii, not only in mere numbers but in spiritual, economic, and political affairs as well. American planters united in movements to bring about closer ties with the United States, and succeeded in 1875 in pushing through a treaty of reciprocity which provided stimulus for a spectacular expansion of plantation activity. American missionaries, turned counselors, retained their influence over state affairs of the Hawaiian

Kingdom and steered the Polynesian monarchy through many critical episodes, domestic and international.

One pathetic development of this era was the effort of a Hawaiian monarch to delay the inevitable by drawing together his "royal" cousins throughout Polynesia into a Pacific federation. In 1880 he went so far as to send a half-caste emissary to Samoa to help effect a reconciliation between warring factions there and to confer upon its "kings" the Grand Cross of the Royal Order of the Star of Oceania! Arriving at Apia, the brown-skinned plenipotentiary proceeded to live a life of champagne revelry until the powers, resenting his "unwarranted interference," forced his recall.

Americans continued to gain in number and in power in Hawaii, and in 1893–1894 they deposed the monarch and proclaimed a republic, which they then promptly invited the United States to absorb. In due course in 1898 President McKinley accepted the offer, characterizing it "a consummation."

The United States' political interest in the islands south of the Line was limited to the acquisition of the coaling and naval station at Pago Pago. This arrangement, together with Germany's commercial interest in Western Samoa, was formalized in 1899 when the three powers (Germany, Great Britain, and the United States) set up a joint commission to rule over Samoa; this body was supplanted ten years later by the partition of the islands between Germany and the United States, the latter being awarded the eastern group.

At the end of the war with Spain, the United States took over the Philippines and annexed Guam as a naval station; the other Mariana Islands did not seem worth taking, since their harbor facilities were poor. At that point Germany stepped in and purchased from Spain the remaining Marianas along with the Carolines, thereby ushering out Spain as a colonial power in the Pacific. About the only remnant of Hispanic memory left in Oceania was Easter Island, which had been annexed by Chile in 1888.

From 1900 to the outbreak of World War I the powers refrained from pulling and tugging at one another in the Pacific, and the islands enjoyed a measure of stability, at least on the international political level. But that does not mean that the islanders themselves enjoyed a respite. Planters extended their holdings along the shores and alienated more and more land. Merchants bound islanders closer to the money economy by stimulating desires for new kinds of imports and by credit fetters. Missionaries continued their pioneering into the wilder islands in the west, and the appearance of new mission societies, such as the Seventh Day Adventists, aroused new mission rivalries. Although these rivalries were not so politically significant as they once had been, they did manage to increase the bewilderment of islanders forced into choosing among several conflicting doctrines. Meanwhile government officials pushed further into the mountains and brought more and more islanders under western rule.

With so much expert supervision, the islanders lost nearly the last vestige of control over their own affairs, and except in anachronistic Tonga even the symbols of their heritage were not preserved. In return for these losses they did, of course, acquire such splendid consolations as salvation for their souls, calico for their loins, canned salmon for their bellies, and cricket or baseball for the dull moments when they were not laboring for their white masters.

X

MINERS AND ADMINISTRATORS:
1914-1939

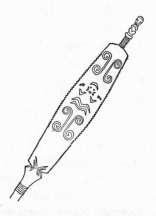

Compared with hurricane-force battles like Pearl Harbor and Saipan, World War I would appear to have struck the islands with the impact of a zephyr. The changes ultimately wrought in parts of Oceania by that First World War were considerable, but the conflict itself was mild.

Soon after the outbreak Australian authorities rounded up a nondescript crew, shoved them into uniform, and shipped them to New Guinea. These rollicking "Coconut Lancers" landed in the vicinity of Rabaul and quickly subdued the handful of German residents there. Thereupon the Australian commander, a better soldier than a linguist, solemnly proclaimed the change of administration to a crowd of bewildered natives with these historic words: "No more 'um Kaiser; God save 'um King." Military rule remained in force in New Guinea throughout the war, but introduced few major changes. German planters were allowed to carry on with their enterprises and German regulations were incorporated in the new laws. The principal effect was a slowing down of economic developments as a result of the disruption of shipping and of uncertainties about the future status of the territory.

On near-by Nauru Island, a German possession, the Australians took over the administration and confirmed the already effective control of British management over phosphate mining there. Meanwhile a New Zealand force seized control of German (Western) Samoa, in exuberant fulfillment of the Dominion's old aspirations.

Throughout the rest of the South Pacific things were placid enough during the war, except for a few gentlemanly raids against Allied shipping carried out by the sporting Count von Luckner in his *Seeadler*. Communications were everywhere somewhat disrupted by the shortage of bottoms, and a few nonessential industries such as pearling were abandoned for the duration. Copra and other strategic commodities continued to fetch very high prices when they did reach markets, and there were several local wartime booms. In Hawaii the war was remembered chiefly for its elevating effect on sugar prices and, consequently, upon the entire economy.

Some islanders actually served on European battlefields; and a Maori battalion distinguished itself fighting alongside the Britons whose fathers their own fathers had clubbed to a standstill a few decades previously.

Far more serious than any of these events was Japan's elimination of Germany in the Marianas, the Carolines, and the Marshalls. A Nipponese naval force seized control at these outposts with a speed and purposefulness that only the myopic western statesmen, preoccupied with Europe, failed to comprehend.

The victorious Allied powers lost no time in expropriating German properties in the conquered island territories, and most of the German colonials eventually returned home penniless. The Peace Conference merely confirmed the conquests and made them a little more palatable to the United States by assigning the islands to the powers—German New Guinea to Australia, German Samoa to New Zealand, Nauru to Britain, Australia, and New Zealand, and German Micronesia to Japan —as trusts or Class C mandates rather than as outright possessions, a distinction that was to prove quite meaningless until after World War II.

Thus, with little fanfare, World War I ushered in a new era in Oceania. By eliminating Germany and introducing Japan, it carried along one step further the process of regional subdividing in Oceania. Before the war Hawaii stood apart from the other islands by reason of its close ties with the United States; and now, with Japan in possession, the Marianas, the Carolines, and the Marshalls were separated from the rest of Oceania and integrated into the Japanese Empire. None of this seemed ominous at first, because in 1921 Japan joined Britain, France, and the United States in concluding a treaty for reciprocal guaranty of their possessions in the Pacific, and during the following year this was substantiated by agreements to maintain the *status quo* with regard to fortifications and naval bases in the Pacific. But with the expiration of the naval limitation treaties in 1936 these assurances lost even official recognition, and long before that Japan had effectively sealed off her islands. Thus, during the period between the wars, Oceania was for most practical purposes divided into four parts: Japanese Micronesia, American Hawaii, Dutch New Guinea, and the Franco-British South Pacific.

The South Pacific, comprising those islands lying south of the Line, moved deeper and deeper into the economic and cultural spheres of Australia and New Zealand. Nearly all shipping lines ended at Sydney or

Auckland, and wherever white men gathered on island
verandas they usually drank Sydney lager and reraced
the Melbourne Cup.

Copra retained its hold over South Pacific economy
in spite of price fluctuations that would have wiped out
most businesses. Many independent planters were forced
out during the hard times and their properties absorbed
by the big mercantile firms; this was especially true of
the "returned soldier" small holders who had flocked to
the islands after the war.

Sugar and shell, along with most other South Pacific
industries, were also affected by the world-wide depression of the thirties. The small holders were of course
hardest hit; the big companies, with their varied interests
and greater resources, managed to weather the storm
and even acquire more holdings.

During the depression the islanders themselves
learned the hard way what it means to be civilized.
Since most of them had become more or less dependent
upon the white man's world for their money income—
earned by selling their services or their products—they
lost the wherewithal to buy the white man's goods they
had learned to want and need. The result was a general
back-to-nature movement: an altogether desirable re-
gression from the point of view of the South Seas addict,
but an unhappy dilemma for the many islanders who
had nearly forgotten how to beat their cloth out of bark
or to illuminate their dwellings with coconut-oil lamps.

The depression might have turned back the clock even
further had it not been for the discovery of immense
deposits of gold in Melanesia. The biggest find, culminating the lifelong searches of a few hardy pioneer prospectors, took place in the wild unexplored mountain
country of New Guinea inland from the Huon Gulf. It
precipitated a gold rush which is quite without parallel
in modern times and led to the establishment of an industry which did more in ten years to open up the hinter-

land than agriculture could have accomplished in fifty. Air transport made it possible to build modern towns in country still inhabited by head-hunters; and revenues from gold provided the New Guinea administration with enough funds to expand its activities in spite of the copra depression. In fact, gold replaced copra as New Guinea's richest business. Smaller gold deposits were discovered on Fiji and Bougainville and Guadalcanal, and all these served to increase the white man's stake in the islanders' world.

Meanwhile the rich phosphate deposits on Nauru, Ocean Island, and Makatéa were turning out to be treasure mines of a different sort. The demand for fertilizer increased in the world despite depression, and these islands were transformed into huge factories for mining and crushing the phosphate rock. Since Australia and New Zealand were especially anxious to obtain their total requirements from these near-by sources and thus reduce dependence upon long overseas hauling, their governments energetically supported the phosphate projects.

The Dominions, lacking petroleum, were even more urgently concerned with locating oil supplies nearer home and encouraged exploration into every promising part of New Guinea. This costly search had not produced tangible results before Pearl Harbor, but it did lead to systematic mapping of some New Guinea hinterland which even the gold prospectors had not covered.

The airplane was instrumental in completing the partitioning of Oceania by the great powers, nearly three centuries after Spain had begun the process. In 1928 Kingsford-Smith completed his epochal flight from California to Australia and set governments to planning transpacific air routes. The United States already possessed a convenient chain of potential runways across the North Pacific—Hawaii, Midway, Wake, Guam, and Manila—and these eventually became bases for Pan

American Airways' flights to the Far East. Also, Japan's chain of islands, the Bonins, Marianas, and Palau, afforded easy stages for regular flights to the Indies. Comparable one-flag chains did not exist in the South Pacific, so the United States and Britain raced to establish sovereignty over several tiny uninhabited coral points that had been earlier cleared of guano fertilizer and then abandoned as useless. In 1936 the United States occupied Baker, Jarvis, and Howland Islands, while Britain occupied Canton Island and Enderbury. The United States also wanted Canton and Enderbury for links with Samoa, but the American occupation force which "invaded" Canton in 1938 shared their British rivals' beer and left it to Washington and London to resolve the problem. The two nations in 1939 agreed upon the establishment of a fifty-year Anglo-American joint administration. In 1940 Pan American began its regular flights to Auckland, via Honolulu, Canton, Suva, and Nouméa. Other air routes connecting Australia with New Zealand, New Guinea, and Singapore shortened Pacific distances to a degree not seen since the outrigger replaced the raft.

While these events were consolidating white man's economic control over the South Pacific, other influences were at work affecting directly the lives of the islanders. The world at large, with some notable exceptions, was tending toward an increasing concern for the welfare of dependent peoples, and these sentiments produced some concrete results in the islands. Missions and administrations gave more consideration to the islanders' health, and the Rockefeller Institute supported a campaign against endemic diseases and against general ignorance of the principles of good health. The attack on other kinds of ignorance was much less energetic, and for the most part what little schooling there was remained in mission hands.

The greatest progress came in connection with administration itself and was inspired by anthropology's better understanding of the cultures of "primitive" peoples. Some administrations even added anthropologists to their staffs. All this had the effect of regulating and moderating white man's impact upon the institutions of the islanders. It was a timely development, too, because some islanders were beginning to reassert their objections to white rule. The ensuing strikes and nativistic movements were much less violent manifestations than earlier uprisings had been, but they nonetheless were most embarrassing to governments which prided themselves on their enlightenment and humanity. Adding to the dilemma of the officials were the loud protests from white communities against the governmental "coddling" of their brown and black wards at the expense of the profits and caste privileges of the whites. The whole labor indenture system became a subject of heated controversy between white entrepreneurs, missionaries, and officials, with the wretched officials trying to maintain a central position. Other complications were introduced by the independence movement in India, which stimulated the Indian community in Fiji to agitate for more political and economic rights; and Nazi Germany's clamor for the return of her colonies also had an unsettling effect. But more foreboding than any of these was the inference drawn from the Sino-Japanese conflict and the shadow cast over the South Pacific by Japan's mysterious activities in her Micronesian outposts.

Most of the world will remember the Hawaii of the twenties and thirties as a tourists' paradise, sullied only slightly by the Massey Case. To the inhabitants, though, it was a somewhat different story. The economy continued to be based upon sugar and pineapples and remained under the control of a small group of interrelated owners and managers, but the structure began to show signs of weakness. In the first place, a few powerful mainland firms successfully invaded the Territory's commercial citadel. Also, mainland labor-union leaders went to the fields and docks and organized membership drives; they were flexing their muscles for a showdown fight against the traditional local paternalism when Japanese bombs brought on a larger conflict. Another disturbance to the *status quo* came by way of the military, who were strengthening Pearl Harbor and laying out airfields and encampments on a scale large enough to challenge the command of the sugar admirals and pineapple generals over territorial enterprises. Finally, as if these indignities were not enough, along came the Federal government and imposed quota restrictions upon sugar exports, to tie in with the international stabilization agreements.

It was no surprise, then, when territorial big business about-faced and joined in the popular agitation for statehood, apparently regarding their previous *bête noire*, the threat from an Oriental majority in the local electorate, as less dangerous than a Federal Congress in which they had no votes to counter the representatives of rival sugar interests on the mainland.

Congress, which opposed Hawaii's request for statehood, ostensibly because of the Japanese element there, also expressed uncertainties about Japan's intentions by holding back in its appropriations for fortifying Guam, which it considered too deep inside the Japanese zone for effective defense. And there was some cause for these uncertainties.

Japan's occupation of German Micronesia seemed anything but accidental. Japanese businessmen were capturing the commerce of these islands long before October 1914, when their "victorious" naval squadron seized military and political control from the handful of German officials. Even during Spanish times Japanese traders had been active in the Marianas and the Carolines; throughout the German years they dominated foreign commerce there, and actually outnumbered all other nonnative residents in the German Marianas. Their infiltration into the eastern Carolines was halted when the German officials expelled them for illegally selling arms and alcohol to the Carolinians.

After ousting the Germans during World War I, the Japanese moved into Micronesia to stay, and the Peace Conference was confronted with the fact that Britain had, during the war, secretly agreed with Japan to confirm the latter's possession. The objections of the United States were overridden, but to sugar-coat the deal the islands were awarded to Japan as a mandate rather than as an outright possession. The United States at first refused to accept this pretty legal fiction, but later did recognize Japan's position.

The terms of the mandate pledged Japan to "promote to the utmost the material and moral well-being and social progress of the inhabitants of the territory." Specifically the terms prohibited slave trade and forced labor, arms trade, the sale to natives of intoxicating beverages, and the establishment of military and naval bases. Further, Japan was required to allow missionaries freedom to exercise their calling, and was asked to present annual progress reports to the League of Nations.

Prior to 1914 the United States depended upon the Guam–Yap–Shanghai cable system as an alternate line of communication to the Philippines and China in case of interruptions in the Guam–Manila–Shanghai line. Before recognizing Japan's authority in Micronesia, the United States insisted upon free access to Yap. This was agreed upon in 1922, but not subsequently honored in practice by Japan.

As the world now knows, few if any of Japan's promises were honored. Within a few years the Territory was fenced off from westerners by a wall of official obstructionism. Only a few white missionaries were allowed to remain, and foreign commerce was completely excluded.

To the rest of the world the Territory became "Islands of Mystery," with the sinister effect increased by rumors about construction of military and naval bases. Up to the end, however, Japan continued to forward to Geneva annual reports filled with pious accounts of native welfare and social progress.

When, as a result of the Sino-Japanese conflict, Japan withdrew from the League, she dropped the "mandate" pretense and held on to the islands as integral parts of her empire. After that the wall closed completely until penetrated by American warships and bombers in 1943.

Meanwhile, behind the wall, Japan moved swiftly to convert the islands into a source of vitally needed sugar, phosphate, fish, and copra. Tens of thousands of Japanese, Korean, and Okinawan colonists were brought in to transform the islands into productive units of the Co-Prosperity Sphere. And, as we now know, in due time plans were perfected and bases laid out to serve as jumping-off places for aggression.

Japanese expansion into Oceania was not limited to Micronesia. From Palau her fishing vessels moved into waters of the Indies and New Guinea. Sampans—some of them officered by naval personnel—turned up everywhere, poaching on others' shell reserves and poking suspiciously into strategic harbors and channels. While this was going on, Japanese-owned and manned plantations were being developed along the northern coast of Dutch New Guinea, and Japanese trading firms were setting up branch stores and extending the markets for their cheap goods into the sacrosanct reserves of British and French companies. Most significantly of all, Japanese merchants secured proprietary interests in some New Caledonian nickel mines and took much of their output. Also, an iron mine owned and manned by Japanese was operated in New Caledonia and the ore sent to Japan. How much of all these enterprises were straight business and how much calculated preparation for aggression remains a problem for the historians. For the student of Oceania, who must project these events on a time-scale of twenty millennia, the early part of this twentieth century of the modern era marks merely a resumption of the movement of men out of Asia, which began during the Old Stone Age and continued unchecked until four hundred years ago. How this latest wave from Asia was checked will be related in a later chapter.

Though geographically and ethnically connected with Australian (eastern) New Guinea, the Dutch (western) half of that vast island had few links with the rest of the Pacific Islands. Politically it was part of the Dutch East Indies, administered out of Java. Along the coasts were a few administrative and mission outposts, and occasional parties went inland prospecting for oil, but the rate of westernization proceeded much more slowly than in the neighboring Australian territories. So remote was this region, it served as a place of exile for Indonesian nationalist revolutionaries. A few Malays penetrated the forested mountains and grassland plateaus hunting for birds of paradise, but most of the interior continued to rusticate in the Stone Age.

METAMORPHOSIS

XI

THE SCOPE OF CHANGE

The four hundred years between Magellan and Tojo
represent only a brief period in Oceania's enormous span
of human history, but during these four fateful centuries
white and yellow men wrought more changes in the
island world than did the hundreds of generations of
black and brown men before them.

These changes cannot be summarized by terse generalizations or neat statistics: each island group suffered
a different fate. In some, like Tasmania, the inhabitants
were annihilated to make room for white men. In others,
like Hawaii and Palau, they were charitably permitted
to acculturate or die out gradually, so long as they did
not interfere with more important affairs. In still others,
like New Guinea, they were encouraged to survive to
provide manpower for white man's enterprises. And in a
few happy places, like Tikopia, they were "discovered"

and then almost ignored, because nothing they possessed seemed worth taking.

During these four centuries a few rare human beings, white and yellow, traveled to Oceania with the object of enjoying without taking, of giving without changing; but the greater number went to exploit, to extract, or to transform. Some took territory for empire outposts and new homes; others used the soil and the climate for producing things wanted in the world's markets; others ripped up ground for minerals or harvested the reefs for marine wealth; still others converted islanders' bodies into profitable labor or their minds into evangelized soul-stuff. With characteristic zeal and energy, white and yellow men applied themselves so vigorously that their various enterprises quickly became the outstanding forces in island affairs. In some places the avarice for productive land or protective bases set the pattern. Elsewhere the preoccupation with copra—or sugar, or shell, or minerals, or souls—dominated island life, with each enterprise exercising a peculiar influence according to its objectives, its technology, and its organization. The following chapters will describe these alien enterprises and will relate the effects they had upon the individual groups of islanders up to September 3, 1939, which ushered in the most violent change of all.

XII

THE DISPOSSESSED

Throughout the more sordid chapters of modern Oceanic history events have shown all too clearly that, next to introducing epidemics or firing bullets into their bodies, the most effective way to destroy natives is to take away their lands. Land is far more than a source of subsistence to the Pacific Islanders. It is a fundament of their social groupings, a measure of their status and self-esteem, and an ingredient of their spiritual lives. If a single criterion were to be used to test the survival value of any native community it would be: To what extent have they retained their lands?

No Oceanic areas have altogether escaped the aliens' quest for land, and in two cases, Australia and New Zealand, the colonists' greed for real estate was the most characteristic and the most devastating feature of culture contact.

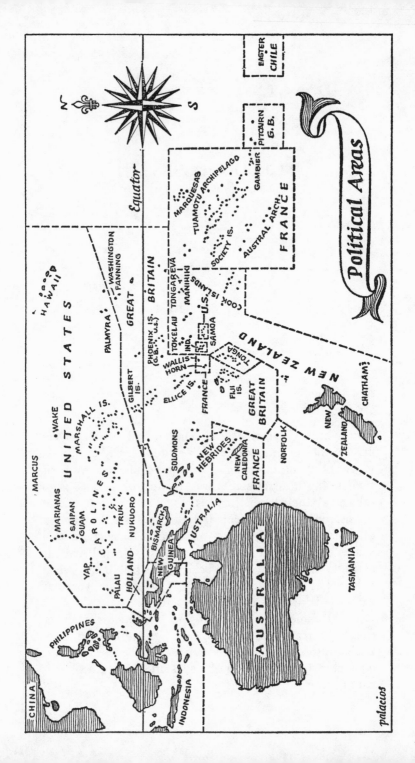

Political Areas

palacios

AUSTRALIA

It is particularly fitting to begin this analysis of
change with a consideration of the fate of the Australian
aborigines, for in this case white man has carried the
process almost to its logical conclusion. The price paid
to the Indians for Manhattan was extravagantly high
compared to that paid by whites for land in aboriginal
Australia. To Captain Cook's fellow countrymen there
was no serious "native problem": the land was there for
the taking, and too bad for any wretched black fellow
who got in the way.

The first permanent white settlement was at Port
Jackson in 1788. Dutchmen discovered Australia as
early as 1605, and in due course sailed near most of the
shores; but with almost incredible consistency they
missed the entire eastern and southeastern coasts, practically the only parts of the continent suitable for extensive white settlement. It was left to Cook to survey
these coasts, and his favorable reports led to the establishment of the penal colony at Port Jackson.

The rest of the story is well known. For a number of
years convicts and their warders were the only settlers;
then came true colonists, nearly all British. Farming and
herding spread up and down the coasts and then pushed
inland. Australian wheat, wool, beef, and hides became
large factors in world trade; and Sydney became an unofficial capital for most of Oceania. The gold rushes of
1850 brought more thousands streaming into the country and pushed the frontiers farther inland. Cotton had
only a short day, but sugar developed into a great industry in Queensland.

By 1939 the white population had expanded to seven
million, 95 per cent of British extraction, with sprin-
klings of Italians, Germans, and Swiss, and with the few
thousand Chinese who were admitted before the "White

Australia" policy barred immigration of all colored races.

Most of Australia's population dwell in large cities and towns along the eastern and southeastern coasts, with a smaller concentration at the southwestern corner. Reaching inland from these coastal centers of trade and industry are belts of farmland—wheat, hay, barley, sugar, and garden crops, dairy pastures, and sheep and beef-cattle ranges. The more fertile pastures nearer the coast will support high concentrations of animals, but moving inland the plant cover becomes so sparse that a square mile is needed to graze one animal, and covering a half million square miles of the center is a true desert which will support neither sheep nor cattle.

It is a far cry from urbane Sydney with its two million population and its skyscraper life to the "outback" sheep or cattle station, but far beyond the farthest stations and on land that even cattle avoid dwell most of the native Australians who have thus far survived the conquest of their continent. They are the lucky ones; their fellow aborigines unfortunate enough to have dwelt in more coveted areas did not fare so well.

By 1939 there remained fewer than 60,000 fullblood aborigines out of some 300,000 living at the time of the first white settlement at Port Jackson. Of these 60,000 survivors, 35,000 to 40,000 carried on their Old Stone Age lives in the comparative security of the central desert or the tropical north. About 10,000 worked at sheep and cattle stations and labor camps along the fringes of civilization, a detribalized people trying to adapt to the white man's ways of life. Another 10,000 were congregated in permanent displaced-persons camps, small enclaves—native reserves and mission stations—surrounded by a civilization they were unable to adapt to and lacking the resources to maintain their aboriginal way of life. As a further complication, there were an estimated 20,000 half-castes, employed at stations or living with their pureblood kinsmen in the reserves, unrecognized by their white fathers and socially unacceptable to color-conscious white Australia.

Meanwhile what happened to the other quarter million aborigines, the number by which their population had been reduced during the previous century and a half? Many of them were the victims of playfulness: the sport-loving British pioneers occasionally relieved the boredom of isolation by hunting "abos" in lieu of other game. More frequently, however, these hunts were serious undertakings: now and then aborigines would be brash enough to kill or steal livestock pastured on their horde territories, and that called for systematic drives of extermination by the white owners. Aboriginal men, women, and children would be rounded up and shot; to slay a pregnant woman was, logically, doubly commendable. Sometimes the same objective was accomplished by leaving poisoned food within reach of the forever hungry blacks. Introduced diseases also were useful in thinning out the unwanted aborigines, whose lack of what we term hygiene made them extremely susceptible.

The tragedy was played to its finish in Tasmania, where all but forty-four of the original two thousand or more aborigines had been wiped out by 1847, and all of these survivors were gone by 1876, victims of disease and drink. One efficient colonial administrator even declared an open season against the Tasmanians, culminating in the infamous "Black Drive" of 1830.

By 1939 disease was as rife as ever, but the cruder forms of extermination were things of the past—the recent past, to be sure. Meanwhile other factors in depopulation remained as effective as ever, perhaps more effective since the white culture had spread out so far. These factors have to do with the breakdown of aboriginal tribal life rather than the liquidation of individual aborigines, but there is evidence aplenty that such indirect attacks have led to a catastrophic fall in birth rate and a rise in death rate among many native groups touched by white civilization.

An earlier chapter described the total reliance of an aborigine on his horde territory for the food he eats, the kinship ties he requires, and the religious beliefs he holds. To take him from his familiar hunting and plant-gathering land reduces his food-getting skill, which is based largely on local knowledge. To force him to move to a strange neighborhood deprives him of his spirit-guardians and confuses his efforts to find food. To disturb his complex and balanced relationships with kinsmen and neighbors upsets the fine balance between man and man and man and environment upon which an aborigine's physical survival is based by such a very narrow margin.

Expanding white civilization shook this balance from all sides. Sometimes hordes and tribes were expelled altogether from their territories and forced to make half-hearted attempts to survive in strange neighborhoods surrounded by unfriendly aborigines. Sometimes they were allowed to remain in their territories, but with their food supply destroyed or their totem sanctuaries desecrated. Such unfortunates usually ended up as paupers, hangers-on around stations and towns, or were collected together into camps and reserves; in either case they constituted excellent factories for disease and half-caste bastards.

On the other hand, some aborigines made fine station hands and domestic servants. Even in White Australia old-timers will admit that much of the outback could not have been pioneered without the labor of blacks, not to mention the more intangible services provided by young aboriginal women at those empire outposts where white women did not go. It might appear that no solution could be better than that aborigines be employed by whites, be given a chance to learn white ways, earn money to acquire white goods, and generally become useful participants in the Great Scheme. But, for the

aborigine, that solution wasn't so splendid. Many did, it
is true, adapt with apparent success to the new life, but
such people only rarely produced families. And even
for those who worked part time for whites, the results
were often unhappy: by remaining away from their
hordes, they could not acquire the training and status
needed to make them productive members of their native community, and their experience at the stations was
of little use at home. Their alternatives were either to
remain and lead an unsatisfactory native life or to drift
back to the fringes of white man's life.

All this provided a heaven-sent opportunity for mission work; and devout folk from many Christian denominations and sects have turned-to with gusto and
good will. Missionaries have penetrated all but the heart
of the nomad country, and these good people have
fought almost alone to protect aborigines from cruder
forms of exploitation and to help them adapt to the intrusive western culture. But despite their altruistic efforts, even their friendly critics credit the missionaries
with little success. In their attempt to school their
charges in western techniques, they taught things utterly
useless for native survival. And in their religious instructions they broke down essential aboriginal values and
left nothing meaningful in their place. Happily, most
aborigines who returned to their hordes after mission
schooling quickly reverted to native ways, and no permanent injury was done. But, unhappily, increasing
numbers remained at or near the missions and towns
and so drifted into pauperism. The men could usually
pick up enough cash to buy food and bootlegged liquor,
and the younger women could turn to prostitution; and
of course there was always the benevolent government
to dole out relief food and blankets to the absolutely in-
digent.

No expert predicted how soon the remaining aborigines would die out or, as mixbloods, lose their racial

identity, but at the 1939 rate it appeared to be imminent. In recent years sympathetic whites attempted to overcome government inertia and undertake protective measures, but nothing substantial was accomplished beyond setting aside a huge "reserve"—on paper; and even this was invalidated shortly afterward to permit miners to prospect. Back of some of this disinterest was the popular opinion that aborigines are biologically inferior and hence congenitally unable to adapt to civilization; and a more vicious corollary to this view was the opinion that aborigines, being inferior, deserve no better fate than painless extinction. But even had the colonizing, conquering whites regarded their black predecessors with tolerance and sympathy, they could hardly have built their towns and expanded their farms and stations without destroying the fundamentals of aboriginal culture and, as a likely consequence, the basis of aboriginal survival.

NEW ZEALAND

In 1939 New Zealand made plans to celebrate the centennial of the Treaty of Waitangi, commemorating the annexation of the islands by the British crown. One and one-half million New Zealanders suitably congratulated themselves on their century of progress: fine cities; keen and athletic people; excellent wool, butter, cheese, and lamb; a brave new social revolution designed to wipe out depression and poverty and privilege; and a surge of gratifying loyalty to empire at the beginning of a great brother-binding war.

Ninety-five thousand Maoris[1] were not so certain they had cause to celebrate. It is true that in 1939 the Maoris were beginning to regain something of their former vitality and numbers, but only after a century of decline during which the count dropped so low (forty thousand

[1] Including about twenty-eight thousand mixbloods.

in 1900) that one contemporary observed: "The Maoris are dying out, and nothing can save them. Our plain duty, as good compassionate colonists, is to smooth down their dying pillow. Then history will have nothing to reproach us with."[2]

Looking about them in 1939, the Maoris saw their lands reduced to a sixteenth of the original area, their share in the Dominion's wealth exceedingly limited, and their once-proud status subordinate in the intrusive white caste system. There were, however, a few bright rays on their horizon: they still retained enough of their tribal organization, their able leaders, and their robust physiques to effect something of a comeback, provided, of course, the whites permitted, and encouraged it.

Two wholly different courses have been followed by scholars in reconstructing the prehistory of New Zealand; one relies heavily upon native oral tradition, the other on archaeology. According to the *traditional* reconstruction, six centuries ago fleets of canoes left central Polynesia and sailed southwest, filled to the gunwales with men, women, and children and all their possessions, escaping from crowded islands and continual conflict. For many weeks these Polynesian *Mayflowers* voyaged farther and farther out of the zone of warmth and calm seas. Finally, gaunt with starvation and nearly dead from exposure, those who survived beached their canoes on the shores of New Zealand's North Island and set about to colonize the land. At a few places they discovered people like themselves already established, descendants of chance immigrants whose canoes had been driven there in the past. Differences between the two groups may have been wide at first, but gradually the better organized, technically superior newcomers absorbed the

[2] Quoted in I. L. G. Sullivan, *The Maori People Today* (Oxford, 1940), p. 28.

original settlers and laid claim to all the lands on both islands.

During recent years archaeologists have begun to cast doubt on the historicity of the Great Fleet tradition. A number of excavated sites, some eight or nine hundred years old, have revealed the existence of a culture much like those of tropical Polynesia but concerned with hunting the famous *moa,* a giant ostrichlike bird, which eventually became exterminated. In *traditional* terms these *moa*-hunters were mainly eastern Polynesians (with perhaps some elements from west Polynesia and Melanesia) who arrived there, more or less accidentally, long before the Fleet voyagers. On archaeological grounds, however, the evidence seems to be accumulating to support the belief that the way of life found by Europeans, the so-called Classic Maori form of culture, was merely an evolutionary development out of the earlier *moa*-hunter or Archaic phase. According to this view, stray canoeloads of Polynesians may have continued to drift to New Zealand, mainly from the northeast, throughout man's occupation there, but there is no need to evoke a hypothetical Great Fleet to account for the Maori way of life.

Tradition does not however need to be historically true to exercise a powerful influence over men's thoughts and actions, and the Fleet tradition will probably continue to enrich Maori lives even if it is proved to be overstated or untrue.

In any event, there is no question about the ultimate source of Maori language and culture, from tropical and probably eastern Polynesia. The principal task of the first immigrants was to adapt their tropical-island culture to the more severe temperate environment of their new home.

The fowl and pigs which the immigrants may have had in their canoes either did not endure the voyage or the new conditions; only the dog survived, to become in time a valued food. Bananas, breadfruit, and coconut would not thrive in the colder climate, so that the immigrants had to depend upon the taro and sweet potatoes brought with them, supplemented with ferns and berries they found in their new home. Cloth beaten out of tropical paper mulberry bark had to be supplanted by cloaks woven out of native flax; huge dugout canoes carved from native timber replaced the graceful sewn-plank and outrigger canoes which had transported them from their homelands. Well-ventilated dwellings had to give way to closed and darkened huts to keep out the unaccustomed cold.

On the other hand, in the new homes Maori social organization retained most of the essential features of central Polynesian life and developed some new features of its own, but it did not evolve the highly complex political or religious institutions which characterized its evolution in Hawaii or Tahiti or Tonga. Kinship remained the fundamental tie among people, and between groups of people and the land. Each household was occupied by a family, and each village by a clan, a group of interrelated families. Related clans occupied adjoining territories and were grouped together into tribes; according to their genealogies, which were carefully and proudly committed to memory, all tribal mates traced descent from some occupant of one of the Great Fleet canoes; and since marriage usually took place within the tribe or even the clan, these larger kinship groups were exceptionally cohesive and enduring.

Chiefly rank followed the Polynesian principle down the senior, and usually the male, line; but here chieftains were not the strong central authorities they were in Tahiti or Hawaii or Tonga. A Maori chief was looked up to as the most respected of kinsmen, but he gave advice rather than orders, and there was a large measure of democracy by council. Since he was the ranking kinsman, the ownership of tribal land was symbolically vested in him, but not to dispose of at will. Chiefs had their greater *mana*, like all Polynesians of status and exceptional capacities, but there were no complex, Shintolike rites over which they could preside. There were priests, also, but they were in general merely experts in the craft of securing supernatural assistance for individual or group undertakings.

Mutual assistance within and among neighboring related households was the basis of economic security, and goods were shared. Thus there was no real poverty, nor was there any need or opportunity for individuals to accumulate property; even high chiefs subsisted much as did their lower-ranking kinsmen, except when they were able to capture slaves in war.

Europeans have had ample proof of the Maoris' skill in warfare. Intertribal feuding was a traditional pastime, and it was carried out almost like a rivalry in sports, with a season of fighting and a season for recouping, and punctilios were observed even toward the bitterest enemies. So prevalent was fighting that most villages were located with a view to defense and were skillfully fortified. Quarrels over land and women along with revenge for real or imagined wrongs kept the tribes continually alerted and their people fierce and fit.

Such were the Maoris when Captain Cook rediscovered New Zealand in 1769: a strong, vigorous, independent people who respected no one but kinsmen, who owed no loyalty to aggregations larger than the tribe.

Being forthright people, most Maoris struck back when the first white visitors massacred a few of their fellows, and they thus acquired reputations for savagery. Others, however, trafficked with the whites who flocked to their shores for flax and lumber and for recuperation from the hardships of voyaging and whaling. It did not take the Maoris long to observe that white man's blankets were warmer than native flax cloaks, metal knives and axes sharper than stone adzes, and—more important —muskets more deadly than clubs and spears. The immediate result of this enlightenment was to transform

intertribal feuding from a serious game into a brutal
scourge. At about that time a Maori chief traveled to
England and returned intent on becoming a super-chief
over a super-tribe, like the English monarch he admired.
This decision added yeast to the ferment, ending up in
an intensification of native warfare which devastated
Maoriland for two decades, shifting many tribes, wiping
out some, and killing altogether nearly sixty thousand
Maoris.

White traders encouraged this slaughter by bartering
firearms for flax and food. Deserters from ships and es-
capees from the New South Wales penal colony even
aligned themselves with tribes, and it was a poor chief
indeed who could not count at least one white aide.
Whalers also added their particular brand of rascality,
so that from all these fine contacts the Maoris were able
to acquire a fair sample of western civilization, including
grog and syphilis. They also began to lose their land,
but that did not seem too serious at first.

New Zealand's North and South Islands together contain over sixty-six million acres, and all of it, from fishing
grounds to mountain peaks, was identified with some
tribe or other. It is true that only a portion of this vast
area was in actual economic use by the Maoris, but that
did not lessen the value of the whole for purposes as
culturally valid for the Maoris as are our tribal lands—
our national parks and reserves—for us. For the Maoris
all the land was tribal, and inalienable save by tribal
consent. The earliest white settlers learned how stubborn
the tribes were in parting with land, so they worked
directly on the cupidity of individual chiefs and succeeded in bribing some of them to "sell" tribal territory.
Also, during the native wars it became a simple matter
for whites to "purchase" land from a tribe which had
just conquered the true owners.

During this period of upheaval, missionaries appeared
on the scene; first the Church Missionary Society, then

the Catholics, then the Wesleyans. The earliest missionaries were good and energetic men; that in itself, and
the contrast they presented with their lay countrymen,
won Maori respect and converts for them. Contributing,
too, was the fact that the Maori pantheon was flexible
enough to admit new deities, and the Jehovah of the
musket-wielding whites obviously deserved an important
niche. Between 1830 and 1840 Christianity spread with
quite amazing vigor; it is estimated that half the Maori
population was converted to at least the theogony and
ritual. Christianity may eventually have weakened Maori
life by nullifying the supernatural sanctions of tribal
authority and economic routine, but its effects were not
so immediate or destructive as the other western influences which ultimately forced the British government
to step in.

There was a very evident need for the establishment
of some kind of authority, and this was plainly recognized by officials in the near-by colony of New South
Wales, who became greatly disturbed by the lawlessness
fomented in New Zealand by white traders. Missionaries, honest settlers, and the Maoris themselves suffered
alike from the acts of those rogues, who went to any
extreme to load their ships with flax and spars. At this
time also an influential group of British capitalists organized the New Zealand Association to undertake an
ambitious colonizing venture, and these men lobbied in
Parliament for the establishment of responsible government in the land, for without that their ambitious
schemes could hardly materialize. But despite these
pressures the evangelical-minded Colonial Ministry
would compromise its policy against annexation only to
the extent of sending out a Resident, with no authority
beyond his moral suasion. About all that miserable fellow accomplished was to solidify the European colony
against him and his works, to move the Maori leaders to
assert a pathetic "Declaration of Independence," and to
draw more attention to the need for stable government.

In the meantime more white settlers moved in and the strife increased.

The precipitant came from an entirely different source. A plausible French adventurer, the Baron de Thierry, self-proclaimed "King of Nukahiva, and Sovereign Prince of New Zealand," succeeded in securing official French backing for a colonial enterprise in New Zealand. This action so greatly alarmed the British New Zealand Association that these gentlemen took matters into their own hands and proceeded to dispatch their own expedition while the French party was still imbibing farewell toasts. With its hand thus forced the British government sent out an agent to negotiate with the Maoris for annexation of New Zealand to the crown, despite the howls of protest from France and the United States. (Washington's ruffled feelings were hardly smoothed down by the realization that the American consul, who happened to be a British subject, exerted all his influence to secure New Zealand for his native rather than for his official fatherland.)

The annexation Treaty of Waitangi turned out to be a document of noble intent but of impossible application. It confirmed the Maoris in possession of their lands and granted them "all the rights and privileges of British subjects"; but it did not take long for the lawyers, acting on behalf of the British colonists, to interpret these treaty guarantees out of existence. For a few years, however, the unsuspecting Maoris were too busy acquiring the new civilization to realize their true predicament.

Instead of tribe fighting tribe, they now all set about with zest to produce and sell and buy. Soon they were supplying all the food consumed in the European settlements and even exporting large quantities of wheat and flax. The old subsistence economy gave way to dependence upon money and outside markets, going even further than Christianity in weakening stability and tribal cohesion. But everything went well when prices were high and demand strong; and it took an economic depression to convince Maori leaders of their people's vulnerability.

The treaty guaranteed political equity to the Maoris, but they were not allowed to vote in spite of the fact that most of the colony's revenue derived from direct and indirect taxes on Maori property and enterprises. No laws were promulgated for them, as their special circumstances required; instead, they were penalized in terms of English municipal law when colonials objected to their practices. It was not Maori ignorance and indifference that led to their shabby treatment. There was in due course a higher percentage of literacy among them than among the colonials, and many of the Maori leaders became sophisticated and articulate statesmen.

Land was the factor that finally moved them to self-defense. Whites flocked to New Zealand by the tens of thousands, and nearly all of them wanted land for farming and grazing, and their elected representatives saw to it that Maori interests did not interfere. The colonial legislature piously continued to express support for the Maori principle that regarded native land inalienable save by full tribal consent, but at the same time the lawmakers adopted sophistries that made it possible for individual Maoris to sell native land to the crown.

These measures led many disillusioned and angry Maori tribes to confederate into a "kingdom"—an entirely novel institution in native New Zealand—for better defense of their persons and property. As a result, in 1860, when the government used troops to enforce an unpopular land sale, there was an organized reaction. The bloody Maori wars which these events precipitated lasted for ten years. The fighting set tribe against tribe, caused enormous casualties on both sides, nearly bankrupted the young colony, and reduced the Maoris to a condition of abject misery. Three million acres of their best lands were confiscated, and their survivors were pushed back into unwanted corners, or allowed to drift along in the town slums.

With the Maoris out of the way, the colonials moved ahead vigorously to build the hardy little Dominion the world now admires. Now and then officials paused long enough to call attention to the picturesque qualities of the Maori life that survived, or to commiserate with the rapidly vanishing minority; but nothing substantial was done by whites to stay the decline.

The Maori revival which New Zealanders now talk about with such pride came about as the result of Maori effort. For decades now, Maori leaders have been working successfully to revive their people's pride in their heritage and to raise their status economically and politically. This has been no mean job.

The war of 1860, which so reduced their numbers and their land holdings, also drove them to town pauperism or to marginal subsistence devoid of the old tribal *esprit* of pre-European days. The task of modern Maori leaders has been to resettle their people on the land and have them work into the dominant pastoral and agricultural economy as independent producers rather than as dependent laborers. At the same time, Maori interests in their old crafts were revived to check a loss of Maori identity in the stronger Europeanization process continually going on.

New Zealand leaders disagreed over goals in this movement for Maori revival. Some of them wished to shape a strong and self-conscious minority of loyal Dominion citizens, equal in cultural, economic, and political status to their white compatriots, but retentive of the tribal *esprit*. Other officials and students wished to see Maori and white blended into a single cultural unit, and pointed to the growing half-caste population to support their predictions. But the real decision would depend upon the ability of future Maoris to hold onto their remaining lands, for without those they would be *Maori* only in shape of head and color of skin.

XIII

SALVATION

Converting islanders' souls from heathen to Christian has in places produced as much economic or political profit for the white agents as converting Hawaiian climate into sugar or Nauru phosphate into fertilizer. Not a few missionaries even turned in their prayer books for the more solid comforts of the life of a planter, a trader, or an "adviser"; and along with the souls they won for Catholicism or Protestantism, many patriotic missionaries acquired loyal subjects for their respective fatherlands.

By 1939 the harvest in souls had been most gratifying to the mission societies back home: out of about two million islanders, 750,000 had been "evangelized"—two fifths Catholic and the remainder Protestant.

But profit seeking, even including the storing up of riches in heaven, has not been the only nor the most important motive behind missionary labors in Oceania.

Hundreds of zealous white men and women have devoted their lives in sincere, though sometimes misguided,
efforts to transform native consciences into something re-
sembling those attributed to western man.

That islanders *had* souls has been fairly generally assumed, although many who went in search of them considered them either brands to be snatched from burning
heathenism or misguided objects to be rescued from the
only slightly cooler purgatory of a rival denomination.

Spanish priests initiated this enterprise in the sixteenth
century, but their field was restricted to the Marianas.
Two centuries passed before missionaries became active
elsewhere in Oceania, beginning with an abortive Catholic mission to Tahiti in 1774 and the more successful
enterprise of the London Missionary Society agents there
in 1797. Since that time dozens of organizations—ranging from the Roman Catholic Society of the Divine Word
to the Pentecostal Assemblies of the World, and including Anglican, Methodist, Presbyterian, Seventh Day Adventist, Salvation Army, Mormon, *Utrechtse Zendings-
Vereeniging*, and the Japanese South Seas Evangelistic
Band—have sent ministers into the islands to transform
the savage raw material into the particular spiritual con-
figurations required by denominational doctrines. Some
of the events have already been noted; the full account
would require hundreds of case histories of sacrifices and
martyrdoms and victories. This short account will relate
only how the many organizations with their different
techniques have affected island cultures in different ways.

To begin with, no two of the mission societies were or
are alike. Added to the differences in theology and ritualism and objectives, which have been considerable,
there have been wide variations in organization and financing. The Protestant societies maintain few white
ministers, their technique being to train native pastors
and catechists to conduct services. Catholics, on the
other hand, depend on direct contact between white

priest and islander. Implicit in the Protestant policy is the long-range objective of a fairly independent Native Church; such a goal would probably be an anathema to the more centralized Roman Church.

Today as in the past Protestant missions generally depend for a large measure of their financing on collections from their native congregations, even to the extent of salaries for white missionaries. Catholics secure their funds from home, supplemented by plantations which they run at their mission stations. Both policies have been vigorously denounced by mission critics. To the planter up against labor shortage and high costs, it is particularly infuriating to see a neighboring mission plantation kept running along prosperously by use of native youths undergoing "schooling."

Protestant missionaries have tended to place great emphasis on a revivalistic kind of conversion, a frontal attack on the heathen's beliefs. Catholic missionaries have in general adopted a longer-range view, concentrating initially upon practices and upon the training of children. The suitability of these techniques differs with the cultures they seek to change.

Many other differences in technique stand out. The Melanesian Mission (Anglican) periodically sends a schooner, a traveling chapel, to its far-flung adherents, instead of maintaining a large white staff at the outposts. Mormon missionaries are usually youths doing their two-year stint in the foreign field before returning to Utah. Congregationalists encourage their adherents to form fairly independent bodies. Methodists insist upon continued supervision from the central Conference. And, of course, Catholics permit no relaxation of strong, disciplined organization.

Complicating this array of denominational differences has been the factional rivalry encouraged in some areas. The earlier Protestant missions, particularly the London Missionary Society and Wesleyans, consented to separate areas of activity, or even worked co-operatively in some places. Catholic missions felt otherwise: to convert a native from Protestantism was almost as worthy as winning the soul of a poor heathen, who, after all, knew no better. And later there entered the arena certain Protestant sects that did not scruple at poaching on the territory of others. Mention was made earlier of the fierceness of the denominational rivalry in Tahiti and Hawaii, when governments even sent warships to back up their chosen instruments. Governments take sides less vigorously today, but mission rivalry persists.

Even with all these differences, the missions appear monotonously alike when compared with the native cultures they sought to transform. The language problem alone was almost insuperable. Even in an island group in fairly uniform Polynesia, the missionary had to operate through a language with no words to approximate the concepts he had to express. If his field was Melanesia, he usually was faced with the problem of working through many languages, all unrecorded and as totally foreign as Chinese or Zulu. Picture his chagrin had an anthropologically naïve missionary realized that many natives in matrilineal communities regarded his "Christ-the-Son" as half-demon, because they interpreted his teaching to mean that Christ was conceived by a ghost in the form of a wild pigeon. Nor were many missionaries prepared to cope with a matrilineally oriented ethos in which a "God-the-Father" was less meaningful than a "God-the-Mother's-Brother."

Yet what most missionaries lacked in linquistic ability and anthropological insight they made up for in energy and zeal, with the result that many forms of native "Christianity" are bizarre to say the least and would be highly entertaining if they were not also so pathetic.

Great things have undoubtedly been done: cannibalism suppressed and areas made safe for trader and official; infanticide discouraged; islanders shielded for a

while from the totally selfish exploitation of nonmissionary whites; and a smattering of education dispersed to
help islanders compete in the white man's world. But
there is a debit side, too.

With few exceptions, every pre-European native culture was a well-integrated set of institutions and beliefs,
peculiarly but satisfactorily adapted to its environment
and to surrounding peoples. Every group had worked
out satisfying explanations of Providence and the
means to establish *rapport* with it. Few of these religious
systems were static, and even before the coming of missionaries many of them were changing radically; but
such changes were usually internally inspired and suited
to the local environment and culture.

Evangelism came along and sought to revolutionize
native religions, putting in their place western systems
of belief and practice radically unsuited to Oceania.
Some native cultures went to pieces under the impact;
few of them survived as integrated systems, and in those
that did, Christianity would hardly be recognized as
such.

One widespread consequence of ruthless evangelism
has been the outbreak of nativistic movements—fighting
it, aping it, or adapting it. Actual heathen uprisings have
occurred frequently, but by 1939 they seemed to be
mainly a thing of the past. More pathetic were the iconoclastic movements like the *Vailala* madness of Papua,
in which natives, made skeptical of their own cultural
values yet lacking faith in the new beliefs, indulged in
mass manifestations of hysteria, destroying all symbols
of the old order and demoralizing everyday life. Another
reaction was the development of the native Messiah or
"Cargo" cults, inspired by opportunists and based on
prophecies of an end of white man's rule. A feature of
some of these millenarian movements was the cessation
of all productive work on the premise that a mystery
ship would soon appear over the horizon bringing

enough food and goods to render all further work un-
necessary.

The early hope of Protestant missionaries and of many
of their supporters at home was that they would be able
to help shape native cultures into strong native states,
capable of maintaining independence and stability in
a civilized world. Home-government statesmen supported
this objective because it meant no perplexing new colonial responsibilities; treasurers backed it because it
meant no new expenditures. But out of all Oceania only
one group escaped total annexation and realized partly
this pious hope. Tonga, according to its mission friends,
exemplifies how Grace and selfless devotion to the task
can transform a savage heathen horde into a progressive,
righteous state.

TONGA

From the decks of a copra steamer pulling in to
Nukualofa, this capital of the Kingdom of Tonga looks
more like Cape Cod than South Seas. The illusion remains even after stepping ashore, because Tongans
learned long ago that the easiest way to remain Tongan
is to appear western; and in the very center of the town
are its western-style churches, conveniently near the
royal residence.

Her Majesty Queen Salote (Charlotte) Tubou,
Honorary Dame Commander of the Order of the British
Empire, Chief Member of the Free Wesleyan Church of
Tonga, is no upstart; she can trace her descent, lineally
or collaterally, back one thousand years through two-
score ruling monarchs of Tonga to the person of Ahoeitu,
sacred king of Tonga, son of a Tongan woman and the
sky-god Tangaroa.

The Tongans are Polynesians, closely related in
language and culture to their cousins in neighboring
Samoa; but during their twenty or more centuries in

Tonga they have adopted many traits from their Fijian neighbors and have developed a degree of political centralization unequaled by any of their neighbors and essentially unchanged even today, after a century of westernization. Their family system was basic to their political and religious life. Authority was vested in the patriarch, and after him in his eldest son, but in family etiquette and ceremonialism women outranked their brothers.

In ancient Tonga, family households were scattered through the land in the midst of cultivations of yam and taro. Families related by close patrilineal blood ties formed lineages and tribes, all tracing their descent from a common ancestor chief. Since chiefly or supervisory status descended through the oldest males, lineages consisted of a nucleus of high-status chiefly families and a large number of commoner families ranked according to their distance from the main line of descent. The importance of a lineage depended upon its numbers and the power and influence of its chiefs. Men sometimes transferred their allegiance from one lineage to another, and many lineages split up or died out altogether.

A thousand years ago the lineage of the Tui Tonga became paramount, its chief—so the myth relates—having been the semidivine son of the sky-god Tangaroa, a hard-working deity who sired many Polynesian heroes. For five hundred years the Tui Tonga line of kings reigned supreme in Tonga, and at times extended their sway by conquest over all western Polynesia. At home their rule was semifeudal; all land ownership was vested in them, and as semidivine representatives of the gods they were hedged about with awesome *tabus*. In addition to the tribute regularly received from chiefs and commoners, the kings were recipients of great annual first-fruits offerings to the gods; and they caused their subjects to construct huge burial monuments for them in the form of truncated pyramids. Over their twenty to twenty-five thousand Tongan subjects their power was absolute and backed by divine sanction.

Within the closely knit royal family the Tui Tonga himself was the actual leader and the high priest of the Shintolike "state" religion, but the characteristic Tongan recognition of women's superiority in ceremonial rank was also maintained. Above the Tui Tonga himself in rank was his oldest sister, and higher still—the highest-ranking living person—was his sororal niece; to both of them he owed ceremonial obeisance.

In the fifteenth century A.D. a Tui Tonga delegated to the head of a collateral branch the administrative duties of kingship, while he continued to function as spiritual head of the kingdom. Then, after a few more generations, the secular authority was redelegated to a third branch which founded a dynasty that in time eclipsed both its elder branches in temporal power. But the Tui Tonga, carrying office from father to son, remained spiritual leader of Tonga until the thirty-ninth and last one died in 1865. At that time the principal chiefs handed the title to the reigning secular king, George I Tubou.

A millennium of feudal rule by autocratic demigods does not particularly well fit a native people to receive the doctrines of John Wesley, and the first earnest but unsuitable Methodists to tackle Tonga would have had rough going indeed had they arrived at a less opportune moment. Previous white visitors, Schouten and Le Maire, Tasman, Wallis, and Cook, had tarried long enough among the Tongans to plant seeds of doubt about the indestructibility of their Tongan universe and the infallibility of their gods. Also, during the early part of the nineteenth century it was customary for Tongans to make the "grand tour" in Fiji—trading, serving as mercenaries in the endless Fiji wars, and returning to peaceful and conservative Tonga with zest for feuding and cannibalism and all the other fashionable things learned during their travels. Contempt for authority and divinity flared into civil war and feuds, converting Tonga into a series of fortress settlements and wiping out large sections of the population. Early in this period several Church Missionary Society representatives tried in vain to preach the gospel of peace, but war was too modish, and they earned only martyrdoms for their efforts.

In 1830 a young chief of Haabai, collaterally related to the secular Tongan monarchs, emerged as a dominant leader and decided to sample Christianity. After a Wesleyan-trained Tongan teacher had converted him, he went about the country pulling down idols, manhandling heathen priests and priestesses, and "converting" all his subjects—before ever a white missionary appeared among them.

This young Christian chief, renamed George I, then set about to spread the tidings among the still heathen chiefs of Tonga. Twenty years of intermittent feuding were required for this, and at the end of that time he was in fact and in title King of all Tonga. His methods were somewhat drastic at times; in the words of a Methodist historian: "He did not consistently exhibit . . . Christian clemency." But he finally won and opened up another market for Bibles, Mother Hubbards, and frock coats. His victory, however, had its bitter fruits for his Wesleyan advisers and strategists: French Marist priests, having been refused permission to operate in George's Methodist districts, were eagerly welcomed by George's enemies and thereby established a large Catholic minority which has endured to this day.

With his own kingdom restored to peace, the restless George traveled to Fiji and aided the hard-pressed Fijian chieftain Thakombau to consolidate his rule over Fiji. In return Thakombau accepted George's practical advice and became a Christian.

Meanwhile the Kingdom of Tonga was enjoying the fruits of *Pax missionis*. Wesleyan missionaries were the king's only advisers, his only link with the great world. Having won the battle against heathenism, these worthies plunged into the fight for Freedom, Anglo-Saxon style, and persuaded the trusting king to establish a constitution, wiping out in one move the thousand-year-old polity and substituting for it executive government on the English plan. "The *Conisitutone*," wrote one observer, "became thereafter the fetish of the Tongan people. Most of them did not know what it was, but it had been introduced by the missionaries, and was intimately connected, they believed, with its outlandish fellow, *Konisienisi* (Conscience), and in some mysterious way it elevated their country to the level of one of the Great Powers."[1] The principal effect of the new order was to place the missionaries in the positions of power from which they had ousted the chiefs.

Critics of these missionaries have had harsh things to say about their motives and statesmanship, but no observer has denied them a certain genius for raising funds. Their appeals were timed to coincide with the sale of copra, and "plate day" became a dramatic substitute for the old first-fruits offerings to the gods. The scene has been described: "A band of men and women would come up together and walk round and round the basin, each throwing in a threepenny piece as he passed. After a few rounds a man whose stock of coins was exhausted would fall out, and the procession continued without him. . . . Then only two were left to circle round each other in a sort of dance, amid deafening applause. At last one of the survivors gave out, and the victor was left alone to stand before the basin and chuck in his coins from a distance. He was the hero of the day."[2]

[1] Basil Thomson, *The Diversions of a Prime Minister* (London: William Blackwood and Sons, 1894), p. 365.
[2] Thomson, *The Diversions of a Prime Minister*, p. 189.

Enterprising European traders would stand at the church door with a bagful of coins, which they doled out against promissory notes on the next copra crop. One evangelist, Mr. Shirley Baker, a man of many parts, solved the traders' coin shortage by handing coin back to them as soon as one collection plate was filled, in exchange for bills on Sydney.

With most of the Tongans' resources thus rendered to God there remained little for Caesar, and tax collections fell in arrears. This, and the fact that a large proportion of the mission collections was sent out of Tonga to evangelize distant heathen lands, caused the Tongan leaders to secede from the Wesleyan Conference in Australia and set up their own Free Church. A moving spirit in this schism was the same Mr. Baker, whose evangelical zeal and financial wizardry were equaled only by his political acumen.

In Mr. Baker we have the prime example of the worldly missionary turned loose among an easygoing South Seas people.

Mr. Baker became Prime Minister, Minister of Foreign Affairs, President of the Court of Appeal, Judge of the Land Court, Minister of Education, Agent-General, and Medical Attendant to the King. As spiritual font of the Free Church, he moved the king to carry out a war of persecution against Tongans who refused to leave the old Wesleyan Church. He lived high, wide, and handsome for several years, until he was deported by the British High Commissioner, who, from his post in Fiji, had jurisdiction over all British subjects in the islands. One Wesleyan chronicle said unhappily, "We would fain draw a veil over the history of this regrettable period."[3]

The King of Tonga continued to reign as an "independent monarch," but the affairs of his kingdom became

[3] James Colwell (ed.), *A Century in the Pacific* (London: C. H. Kelly, 1914), p. 431.

pathetically confused, complicated by the presence of ambitious Europeans and by attempts to administrate the constitutional democratic reforms which conferred political equality upon commoners who, a few years previously, the native religious system did not even credit with souls. Ultimately Great Britain agreed to "protect" the Independent Kingdom and placed a consular agent there to advise on foreign relations.

Relieved of these tiresome administrative worries, Tongans returned to the charming diversion of playing government and attending church. Family relationships had not changed much, nor had subsistence economy, the basis of their everyday lives. Enough copra and bananas were sold to the few white traders to finance the import of the usual European goods. Town life was so pleasant that the authorities had trouble in inducing the Tongans to return to their ancestral acres; and too much cricket playing interfered with practical pursuits until it was *tabued* on certain days of the week.

Meanwhile the Tongans retained their land, safe from alienation by outsiders, and there was enough of it to fill the predictable needs of their growing population, already thirty-four thousand by 1939 and probably larger than it ever had been. Everyone now had a soul, and a good Catholic or Methodist soul; everybody was well covered; and the use of English was improving steadily. Moreover, their old Polynesian gods had been conveniently transformed into *tevalo* (devils), and continued to haunt the bush as a reminder to little Tongans that they must obey their father, respect their sister, harken to the minister, and honor their queen, who still remained the legitimate successor of their sacred Tui Tonga.

XIV

COCONUT CIVILIZATION

By 1939 there were about fifty million coconut palms in Oceania, enough to cover completely three islands the size of Oahu, where, incidentally, the few that actually survived made up for their small numbers by their very active service to amateur photographers and the local tourist bureau.

South Seas sugar statistics were far more impressive in tonnage and in value than those of the South Seas coconut, but sugar's influence was limited to Hawaii, Fiji, and prewar Saipan-Tinian, and only whites and immigrant Asiatics benefited directly from it. The influence of the coconut, however, stretched from Truk to Tonga and from Hiva Oa to Hollandia, and directly or indirectly affected the life of nearly every islander in this vast area, even including those primitives dwelling in the remote mountain regions of Melanesia, who never saw a coconut palm until they went to work on white man's plantations.

Coconuts require year-round warm temperature, a well-drained soil, and plenty of moisture and sunlight; they grow best of all in low altitudes near the coast. The palm grows out of the mature, fallen nut, and requires from eight to ten years to reach the bearing stage. After that it lives for nearly eighty years and bears nuts at the rate of about fifty a year for sixty or seventy years.

The mature nut consists of a hollow kernel of oily white meat, one half inch thick, encased in a hard woody shell. Around this is a fibrous husk one half to two inches thick. The cavity of the unripe nut is filled with a thin "milk," a nutritious and refreshing beverage with a tangy taste. As the nut matures, this "milk" is absorbed into the coconut meat, which when dried and removed from the shell becomes the copra of commerce.

Throughout Oceania the coconut leads a double life. In one way it is a source of food, shelter, and income which helps support native life nearly everywhere. In another way, however, it has been the instrument by which white men have done most to change native life.

To islanders the milk of the unripe coconut is a prized beverage, the only one, in fact, on many islands lacking potable water or rain catchments. The meat is scraped from the shell and eaten either by itself or mixed into puddings of taro and yams and sago. Or the oil is squeezed from the meat and used as a food, an unguent, or a cosmetic. The hollowed shell becomes a flask, the clean-scraped shell a cup or a spoon or a material for carved ornaments. Cord is manufactured from the fibrous husk; furniture, utensils, and building timbers from the tough trunk. Leaves are used to thatch huts or weave baskets; and even the pith of the palm is eaten when for some drastic reason the palm is felled. On islands nearer to Asia's influence, the sugar-rich sap is drawn off by tapping the flower bud and is allowed to ferment into inebriating toddy. To deprive an islander of his coconut palms is to take away much of the basis of his living. Even the white man's world would be a much poorer place without them.

From the copra of commerce, oil is expressed to produce margarine, cooking and salad oils, fine soap, and cosmetics. Copra cake, the residue after most oil has been expressed, is an important stock food rich in protein. Coir mats and rugs are manufactured from the fibrous husks, and coconut-shell charcoal was one of the best vapor absorbents known, especially valuable for absorbing industrial odors, for recovering gasoline and benzol from the air, and for use in gas masks. In the manufacture of soap, coconut oil plays a unique role; it hardens well, and its highly soluble acids possess exceptional lathering qualities, even in salt water. It has consequently become a favorite for toilet and salt-water soaps and for soap chips. And, in addition to all these, consider how empty life would be without coconut pie!

But most of these good things are end products, processed in factories thousands of miles from the islands. With the exception of a few tons of coconuts used in the local manufacture of desiccated coconut and some locally used cooking oils, most palm products leaving the islands do so in the form of copra.

Copra is merely coconut meat removed from the shell and dried sufficiently for shipping. To obtain it, mature nuts may be picked from the palm or they may be collected after they have fallen. Then the whole coconut is split in half and the meat either immediately cut out of the shell or allowed to dry a bit before removal. Excess moisture must then be removed from the meat by some method of drying, and the resulting copra bagged in hundred-pound sacks for overseas shipment.

South Seas copra is dried by sun, or over smoke and heat, or in hot-air ovens. In the drier, less cloudy eastern islands, native-made copra is mostly sun dried, re-

sulting in a clean and fairly high-grade product. Elsewhere natives and some of the less progressive white
planters dry their copra on racks over smoldering husk-
burning fires; this produces a dirty and smelly product
which is not very suitable for the manufacture of food or
toilet soaps. High-grade plantation copra is dried on
wire-screen racks built in house-size hot-air ovens. This
method dries the copra in about twenty-four hours, several times as fast and much more thoroughly than the
sun and smoke methods, with the result that the copra
becomes less rancid. South Seas hot-air dried copra com-
pares favorably with copra produced anywhere else in
the world, but South Seas smoke-dried is an inferior
product.

Just prior to 1939 Oceania had produced about one
eighth of the world's one and one half to two million tons
of commercial copra, coming after the Netherlands East
Indies, the Philippines, Ceylon, and Malaya. From the
producing island groups in Oceania the following ton-
nages were exported in 1938:

Mandated Territory of New Guinea	73,720 tons
Fiji	33,480
Solomons	22,940
French Polynesia	20,680
Japanese Mandated Islands	13,100
Tonga	12,430
New Hebrides	11,450
Papua	11,250
Western Samoa	11,240
Gilbert and Ellice Colony	4,850
New Caledonia	2,950
Guam	1,660
Cook Islands and Niue	1,300
Eastern Samoa	800
Total	221,850 tons

In nearly all these island groups, copra has been the

chief industry, employing more people and touching more lives than any other enterprise. On most all island wharves rancid coconut oil is the pervasive odor and tiny copra bugs a chief annoyance; but there the exact similarities end. In every island group the copra industry has had a different effect on human life, according to the extent of the plantations and the organization of production. From this point of view there were three main types of producer: native, small planter, and big company.

Native production supplied part of the copra exported from all Oceanic island groups, but it accounted for all copra exported from the Gilbert and Ellice Islands, Guam, American Samoa, the Cook Islands, and Niue, and for over 60 per cent of that exported from Tonga, French Polynesia, Western Samoa, New Caledonia, Fiji, and the Marshall Islands. Under this system, islanders harvested nuts from their own groves, extracted and dried the copra—by sun or smoke—and sold it to traders for marketing. The small trader, either a Chinese or a white, then sold to a larger central firm for overseas shipment or shipped the copra on consignment. The picture was a familiar one: a small, tin-roofed trade store, stocked with hurricane lamps, kerosene, matches, calico, rice, stick tobacco, canned beef and salmon, mirrors, hair oil—"civilization" itself set out on rough board shelves. Sometimes copra was paid for in trade or in coin that never left the store. Just as frequently, the copra maker received nothing but a credit against his perennial debt, for no trader could survive long without offering credit whether local statutes permitted it or not: "native exploitation" this was termed, but the wretched trader was just as likely to be exploited by his dark-skinned customers. Native boycotts had back of them all the solidarity of kinship groups, and an unscrupulous trader or an unco-operative one would not have lasted very long in a South Seas community.

A variation on this theme occurred in the Gilbert and Ellice Islands, where the government stepped in and helped the islanders to set up co-operatives for marketing their copra and procuring trade goods directly from overseas firms, thereby cutting out the small trader. This "bloody communism" was, of course, something less than popular in white commercial circles.

The "Chinee" and the pajama-clad white storekeeper were familiar types on the coconut islands, but one looked almost in vain for the native trader, and for a reason. Not that islanders did not learn to write and read and calculate; they did, and frequently with more skill than many white traders. Nor were islanders inferior in the fine art of abstracting profit from exchange. But until commercialism and individualism altogether supplanted Oceanic communalism, few native storekeepers could keep shelves filled and relatives satisfied at the same time.

There was one factor in the economics of native production which reduced the conventional western-minded economist to despair. The amount of native copra sold for export fluctuated greatly from year to year, and usually islanders produced less when prices were high. Not so devoted as westerners to acquisition for its own sacred sake, they made and sold only enough copra to fill the lamp with kerosene or the pipe with tobacco, and worked for the morrow on the morrow.

Coconut economy, native style, was the South Seas of memory and romance. It began in the early nineteenth century, and it persists more than is generally supposed.

By 1939 the small planter was fast becoming an anachronism in Oceania. He was independent in name only, for his business was usually mortgaged beyond hope of redemption, and he was utterly dependent on the highly variable world price of copra, with little or no savings to tide him over the lean years. Despite this predictable outcome, for decades adventurous men flocked to the islands, from Hamburg, Marseille, London, and Sydney, cherishing the dream of a South Seas homestead and excited by the prospects of the huge profits which occasionally materialized in years of high prices. It seemed such a simple matter: plant the palms, let them grow for a few years, then settle back and count the nuts as they drop. But the hard fact was that it cost nearly one dollar to bring each palm into bearing, and thereafter from twenty to forty to produce each ton of copra. And while the costs were usually fixed—or rising, if anything—the world market price for copra has been subject to great variation: London market quotations on South Seas copra dropped from £ 39. 14s. a ton in 1920 to £ 8.0 in 1934, back to £ 22. 12s. 6d. in 1937, and down again to £ 9. 5s. at the outbreak of World War II. (These prices included overseas freight charges; the price at out-district island ports averages about one half the London quotation.) These figures, probably better than any other index, provided a barometer of economic climate in the coconut islands, and hence for nearly all of Oceania.

For the small planter without large reserves, a sustained rise in copra price meant a partial liquidation of indebtedness to the mercantile firm which lent him cash and extended credit for supplies, and it sometimes meant a glorious holiday in Australia or New Zealand (the traffic in Usher's Hotel Bar in Sydney was nearly as reliable a guide to island booms as the market quotations themselves). A sustained price drop, on the other hand, often meant foreclosure and operation of the plantation by the creditor company.

Aside from the infrequent trips back home, most small planters led lives of hard work and monotony and loneliness. The corrugated iron roofs of their houses usually covered two or three sleeping rooms surrounded by a wide veranda, with a cookhouse off to the rear. Palms covered all of the five hundred or so acres, the average extent of the small plantation, and extended even up to the veranda. A few hundred feet away were the rough barracks of the planter's native laborers, and close to the water's edge stood the drying and storage sheds. Just offshore was sheltered the small launch which linked the plantation with the comparative civilization of the government outpost or trading village.

Day in and day out, year after year, the planter arose at dawn and lined up his fifty or so laborers for the day's work. After doctoring the sores and coughs, he inspected ovens and sheds, or struggled with the launch's eternal ailments. He was his own commissary officer, store-keeper, engineer, bookkeeper, and, unless he was lucky enough to acquire a wife and persuade her to share his island existence, he had to be his own housekeeper and doctor himself when fever or dysentery brought him low. Usually his nearest white neighbor was hours or days away by launch or trail; during the one event he could look forward to, the periodic visit of the copra ship, he was usually too busy supervising the loading of copra or unloading of stores to do more than enjoy a hurried meal on board. In recent years, with the arrival of home refrigeration and power, he could at least drink his beer cool and tune in on the BBC.

For all his white supremacy, he did not possess the power to enforce authority over his native employees; only the distant government official could do that. But even controlling his labor force and making efficient use out of it was not so serious a difficulty as acquiring it in the first place. There was probably never a time when native labor was adequate for white man's require-ments. The early planters in eastern Oceania quickly realized that Polynesians were not suited to the monot-ony of commercial agriculture, so they turned to Melanesia for labor, with results that have already been described. In time even Melanesians came to be re-garded as unsatisfactory: too few of them rushed to labor in white man's groves at a shilling or less a day, and those who did sign on were not up to European standards of efficiency. Added to that was the increasing tendency of governments to formulate tiresome regulations which limited indentures, controlled recruiting, specified diets, defined housing standards, set wage minimums, outlawed punishments, and generally restricted the planter's freedom of action. French planters were permitted by their government to import Asiatics, but British planters had to rely on local islanders.

Not the least of the difficulties of the planters—large and small—were the diseases and insect pests which frequently infest the groves and play havoc with production. The small planter could make little headway against these natural enemies, and even the huge resources of Lever Brothers did not prevail against an infestation which devastated many of their Guadalcanal acres long before our naval gunfire supplied the finishing touches.

Clearly the small planter had no sinecure. Not all of them, however, lived as colorless and unrewarding lives as that depicted above. Near the larger white settlements—Rabaul, Apia, Samarai, and so forth—there were many compensations; and some exceptional planter families, even in far-isolated places, surrounded themselves with gardens and books and had pleasant, leisurely lives. On the other hand, some small planters led still poorer lives than that described: even without *cool* beer!

Regardless of their difficulties in material well-being, however, nearly all small planters shared some things in common: their fierce individualism in the face of encroaching government controls and big-company absorption; their unsentimental attitude toward native welfare; and their increasing insecurity in a world moving toward larger production units and copra substitutes.

Almost a different world was the big-company plantation enterprise, comprising thousands of acres of palms and many separate properties, and employing a small colony of whites plus hundreds of islanders. Salaried managers directed the day-to-day plantation operation, but gentlemen in Sydney, Auckland, and London board rooms really ran the businesses.

Big-company plantations were not recent developments in Oceania. Most of the German enterprises in Samoa and New Guinea were conducted along these lines, and big companies have always dominated the Solomons and parts of New Guinea. Some of these big companies, such as Lever Brothers and the Samoan Reparations Estates, were concerned only with production; but to others, such as Burns Philp and W. R. Carpenter, production was only one phase of an all-embracing mercantilism.

One suspects that most small planters instilled in their children the fear of God *and* Lever Brothers, as forces of good and evil, respectively. Lever's Pacific Plantations, Ltd., the Oceanic branch of world-encircling Unilever Trust, operated large plantations in the Solomons and Fiji and survived and apparently prospered despite pests and prices. Less durable planters muttered darkly of price-fixing, complaining that the Unilever plutocrats in London kept prices low to buy more cheaply the copra they needed to supplement their own in the manufacture of Lever's shortening and soap.

Whether one was squatting in a native hut or lounging on a club veranda in the British Islands, the conversation sooner or later got around to "B. P." Notwithstanding many of its critics, B. P. does not stand for "Bloody Pirate" but rather for Burns Philp (South Seas) Company, Ltd. If you traveled by steam from Australia to an island port or from one island port to another, in all statistical likelihood you traveled in a B. P. vessel. Almost as likely, the largest building in each island port of

call was the B. P. store, and much of the copra you
smelled would eventually be carried to market in B. P.
bottoms. In the beginning, B. P. was mainly a trading
firm with a network of stores and shipping covering
nearly all Oceania. Canny British management put the
firm even with the heavily subsidized German companies, and, after the liquidation of Germany in Oceania,
raced far ahead of all rivals. In due course B. P. set up
its own plantations and, with loans and extended credit,
supported the efforts of small planters as well: obviously
more copra and more settlers made more freight and
merchandising. Thus, eventually, B. P. acquired the
properties of many of its debtors and consequently became a major producer in its own right.

Though younger and more concentrated, the British
firm of W. R. Carpenter has had a somewhat parallel
evolution. Trailing behind these, but still quite large,
were several other English, Australian, and New Zealand
companies producing or trading throughout Oceania.
Similarly, but on smaller scales, French mercantile concerns have expanded their activities throughout New
Caledonia and the New Hebrides.

However violently small planters or big companies
complained about one another's inefficiency or monopoly,
they joined as allies in their criticism of mission plantation enterprise. The Catholic missions in particular have
gone in for copra production to support mission work.
It provoked unprintable comments from the lay planter,
struggling to obtain copra and native labor, when he
pondered the fact that natives were paying their tithes
in coconuts or working in mission plantations while training in mission schools.

For better or for worse, the simple process of obtaining the meat and the oil of the coconut to spread on
western bread and bathe western bodies has had greater
influence on recent Oceanic history than any other

factor. Copra has to some degree affected all Oceanic island groups, but it has been so dominant an economic force in the affairs of some groups that one is justified in speaking of "copra areas." In the next few sections will be told the stories of the principal copra areas: of the Gilbert and Ellice Islands, where native production predominates; of Tahiti and other islands comprising French Polynesia, where native production exists side by side with the enterprise of foreigners; of Samoa and its neighbors, constituted like French Polynesia but with a larger proportion of foreign plantations; of the Cook Islands—small-scale Samoas; of the Solomons, coastal New Guinea, and the New Hebrides, where copra production is mainly in the hands of whites. These are not the only copra areas of Oceania, but they are the principal political or geographic areas where most of the inhabitants are affected in their daily lives by world price fluctuations in this commodity. Other copra areas, such as the Lau Islands and Rotuma, the Marshall and eastern Caroline Islands, and even Tonga, could with much justification be added to the list; but other considerations have led to their stories being told under different headings. Lau and Rotuma are coconut-covered, but, as political subdivisions of the crown colony of Fiji, they are indirectly but significantly affected by the colony's dominating sugar industry. Islanders of the Marshalls and most of the Carolines have for generations depended upon copra to secure the gadgets which foreigners taught them to want, but between World War I and II an influence over their lives far more important than any single commodity was the colonizing activities of their Japanese masters. Tonga, also, is a copra area, but even more important to Tongans than copra commerce have been the activities of proselyting missionaries.

The travelogue through the copra area begins logically with the Gilbert and Ellice Islands, where production has remained in islanders' hands and where consequently the effects of foreign technology have been least disturbing.

GILBERT AND ELLICE ISLANDS

The Gilbert and Ellice Islands[1] offer the typical example of coconut economy—*native* style. Owing to the happy circumstance that these islands produce nothing of interest to civilization except coconuts, and not many of those, the inhabitants managed to survive the first century of contact by a safe margin despite the early depredations of whalers and blackbirders. Many of their beliefs changed, as did their rules governing kinship and inheritance; but the fundamentals of getting a living remained the same, for iron hoes cannot help grow new foods where there is little or no soil, axes are of scant value without trees, and no western gadgets or tricks can improve on the consummate skill of these islanders in sustaining life on these physically unfavored atolls.

The twenty-five atolls comprising the Gilbert and Ellice Islands are scattered over thousands of square miles of the mid-Pacific, but their total land area is only 180 square miles. They extend above and below the equator; those in the extreme latitudes enjoy year-round breezes and rains, but a few nearer the Line suffer periodic droughts which make native life even more precarious. Soil is thin or almost lacking, and on most islands only coconuts and pandanus will grow naturally. By prodigious effort an inferior kind of root crop has been induced to grow in pits excavated by hand and filled with humus.

[1] The Gilbert and Ellice Islands Colony, coming within the jurisdiction of the British High Commissioner for the Western Pacific, headquartered at Guadalcanal, contains, in addition to the Gilbert and Ellice Islands, the Phoenix group, Christmas Island, Fanning Island, Washington Island, and Ocean Island. Ocean Island is described in some detail in Chapter XVII; its phosphate industry removes it from the coconut area and puts it in a separate category.

Notwithstanding all this, there once lived 44,000 robust people on these infertile specks: 40,000 Micronesians in the Gilberts and 4000 Polynesians in the Ellice group. This large population was made possible by the circumstance on most islands that for every acre of dry land there were on an average three miles of fish-filled lagoon.

These islanders, Micronesian and Polynesian, were much alike in their skills of extracting a living from land and sea. By mixing the few staples in various proportions and by preparing them in various manners, they were able to escape what could have been a diet of deadly monotony. Every part of every kind of growing thing was made to serve a practical purpose, and the natives' artistry in fashioning fibers into beautiful pliable mats has rarely been excelled. Both peoples were skilled in the handling of their canoes, and they were truly as much at home in water as on the land.

In many respects, however, Micronesians and Polynesians differed from one another. The language common to all the Gilbertese was Micronesian; that of the Ellice Islanders was Polynesian, their dialect being closely related to the language of Samoa, whence they emigrated in the sixteenth century according to their traditions. In fact, the Ellice Islanders are like Samoans in many details of culture, and that is also true of their physical appearance. The Gilbertese are shorter, darker skinned, and, according to early white visitors, they were more warlike than their southern neighbors. With so many Gilbertese crowded together on their few small atolls, it is no wonder that they feuded continually and developed ingenious weapons of offense and defense, including swords studded with shark teeth, spears embedded with sting ray, and coconut-fiber armor.

The Ellice Islanders belonged to descent units structured according to the Polynesian pattern. The Gilbertese had lineages, which were patrilineal and exogamous. Throughout most of these islands authority rested in the hands of kin elders, and ranking according to class did not develop to any extent; but on two atolls of the Gilberts chieftianship evolved into highly autocratic institutions.

Mendaña sighted some of these islands in 1567; other ships contacted the rest of them between 1764 and 1824, and therewith ushered in the dreary procession of whalers, traders, and blackbirders. Although food and fresh water were scarce on these islands, whalers discovered ample compensation in the favors of the comely women; the islanders can probably thank their whaler guests for most of the new diseases which decimated several of the atolls. Then came the blackbirders, who removed hundreds of natives to work in the mines and plantations of Latin America; but to give these gentlemen their due, one cannot hold them overmuch responsible for the foreign ideas which were introduced into the islands, since so few of their victims survived to return home.

More revolutionary than either whalers or blackbirders was the influence of missionaries, who began their direct assault on native institutions very early. The first to enter were Samoan teachers sent by the London Missionary Society, and they must be credited with almost miraculous success. In no time at all they were installed throughout the Ellice Islands as persons of paramount authority, usurping leadership from the clan elders and in fact banishing traditional beliefs and practices to such an extent that the whole clan system became obsolete. The new beliefs and relationships were based on their versions of the Old and New Testaments, and most communities became theocratically reorganized.

In 1856 the Reverend Hiram Bingham of the Boston Mission began his labors in the Gilberts, but this field was subsequently turned over to the London Missionary Society. A Catholic mission also became established in the Gilberts, but did not find foothold in the Protestant Ellices.

Traders invaded these islands for copra and established shore stations on the larger atolls, but the shortage of arable land kept planters away.

In 1892 Britain's long arm reached out and placed the islands under a protectorate; later they were transformed into a crown colony. Even the sharpest critic of imperialism must concede the need for such action. Until then the islands were completely vulnerable to any white rascal who happened along. Some islands were run by traders, others by beachcombers, others by strong-willed chiefs whose rum-inspired ambitions made community life something less than idyllic. With little apparent effort and with a very small staff, the British administration quickly imposed order and set about to restore the islands to the islanders. Perhaps it was the islands' slight economic value which kept away most white men and thereby made the task of governing easier. Or perhaps it was the very small size of the administrative staff which compelled officials to allow islanders to run their own affairs. At any rate, the product was almost unique in Oceania. Ultimate authority rested with British officials, but there were only a handful of these administrators, and native customary laws together with large segments of white man's law were administered by native headmen and magistrates. There were few white settlers to influence native affairs, and many islands remained unvisited by whites for months at a time. It should not be thought, however, that isolation and self-government encouraged the islanders to revert to their older ways—far from it. The new needs and desires for white man's goods were just as real here as elsewhere in Oceania; the difference lay in the way they were satisfied.

These islanders could earn the money to buy trade goods by marketing their labor or their copra. Every year scores of them went away to work in the phosphate mines on Ocean Island or on the plantations at Washington and Fanning. But, because of a government ruling, they could remain away from home only a year or two at a time, and they were encouraged to take their wives along with them. Thus the break in village life was neither long nor abrupt. Copra, the other marketable resource, was produced on every island. The colony exported from five to six thousand tons annually, all produced by islanders and with every family sharing in the proceeds. Prior to World War II, one Japanese and two British mercantile firms had agents stationed on many of the larger atolls, but since they were not natives they were not allowed to purchase land or even to lease it in parcels larger than five acres. And even retailing and buying of copra remained in islanders' hands on the many islands possessing native trade co-operatives.

Under conditions like these, it is little wonder that before the war these islands were fast regaining the numbers they once possessed. In 1939, Ellice Islanders numbered only 4000, but they were increasing; and Gilbertese numbered 27,000. So numerous, in fact, were the latter becoming that the administration resettled several hundred of them upon the neighboring uninhabited Phoenix Islands.

However admirable one might consider the old life of Oceania, untampered and unspoiled, it would require a blindly unrealistic sentimentalist to suppose the islanders could or should retain intact their old ways when surrounded by an expanding westernism. The most that the sentimentalist can sensibly hope for is that islanders be left in sufficient isolation to permit them to swallow westernism in homeopathic doses. To the extent that the native patient was not already infected by the earliest white contacts, this regimen was being successfully followed in the Gilbert and Ellice Islands before Pearl Harbor changed it all. By comparison, however, the therapy was differently conceived and only casually administered in French Polynesia.

FRENCH POLYNESIA

Scattered over two million square miles of the southeast Pacific is French Polynesia, containing the fairest islands and some of the handsomest people on earth. So much beauty and so much grace have been sources of wonder to white visitors from Bougainville to Pierre Loti. But the greater wonder is that any of it has survived nearly two centuries of western savagery.

There are both ancient and modern reasons for considering all these thirty-nine atolls and extinct volcanic masses together: the Polynesians who inhabit them were once linked by common blood and many similarities of culture; coconut economy and Christian worship brought them even closer together; and now one French governor administers them as a single unit.

Tahiti itself is queen of these islands, largest of any of them and central to all. Its jagged volcanic center rises steeply seven thousand feet above sea level and is covered with luxuriant tropical grasses and trees. An island-circling reef shelters most of its shores from the Pacific swell. Between its lagoon and mountains is a narrow belt of shore land, and here the people dwell.

Northwest, south, and southeast of Tahiti are the Leeward, Austral, and Gambier archipelagoes: little Tahitis in conformation. Far to the northeast lie the Marquesas: rough mountains plunging precipitously into the ocean, their nearly unscalable walls separating shallow valleys. And finally, stretched out over an enormous arc, are the Tuamotus: low, flat atolls and reefs aptly called the "Dangerous Islands."

"High island" and "low island" have important meaning to Polynesians. Valleys of the high islands support luxuriant vegetation, including taro, yam, sweet potato,

banana, and breadfruit, together with materials for
building canoes and shelter. Low islands contain only
poor shallow soil and support few edibles beyond coconuts and pandanus; hence low islanders have to depend
upon the sea for most of their nurture. And, when hurricanes drive walls of water over the low islands, survivors have to seek refuge on high islands and wait for
vegetation to re-establish on their atolls. Despite these
hazards and the narrow margin of survival on low islands, those atolls favored with frequent rainfall and
covered with palm and pandanus have produced admirable cultures and vigorous people. The drier, treeless
atolls do not possess permanent settlements, but make
fine fishing camps and resting places for canoe voyagers.[2]

A previous chapter described the peopling of this
southeastern Pacific area. When white men first arrived,
nearly every habitable island in the area was populated,
and communication among some of the islands was
maintained by much voyaging back and forth, trading,
visiting, and feuding. Raïatéa was spiritual center for
some of the islands, and Tahiti possibly a cultural center.
But there was no area-wide political subordination to
these centers. The Marquesas, the scattered Australs,
and most of the Tuamotus were, in fact, isolated and independent.

Mendaña, Quirós, and Schouten visited some of these
islands during the first decades of Pacific exploration, but
continuous contact began much later, after the visits of
Wallis, Bougainville, Cook, Bligh, and Vancouver, and
after an unsuccessful attempt by Spanish priests to set
up a colony on Tahiti. It has already been related how
the band of pioneers from the London Missionary

[2] North of Tahiti about two hundred miles lies the raised-
coral island of Makatéa. As a source of valuable phosphates
and site of a large mining operation, its recent history has
differed from that of coconut-economy French Polynesia, and
it will be described in a later chapter.

Society arrived in 1797 aboard the *Duff* and laid the foundation of the missionary kingdom, which transformed Tahiti outwardly into a Protestant culture and endured until supplanted by French sovereignty and, throughout most of the area, by the Roman Church. By British default, France was ultimately able to extend her hold over all the surrounding archipelagoes. Catholicism was usually the partner, and sometimes the senior one, in this empire building.

Like much of Oceania, these islands suffered the visits of traders, whalers, sandalwooders, and blackbirders. They also went through an era of planter imperialism in sugar, cotton, and coconuts. During this era Chinese and Annamese were imported for labor, but the foreign planters did not wholly succeed in establishing their enterprises. Instead, the indigenes continued to supply raw materials from their small groves and marketed their coconuts, coffee, and vanilla through the Chinese, who eventually set up their small trade stores on nearly every island. Pearl diving became a major industry, especially in the Tuamotuan lagoons. In many communities pearls and nacre took the place of copra as the major source of income, until the shell beds were exhausted by overexploitation.

The entire area eventually became united under an appointed French governor, assisted by appointed counselors and an administrative bureaucracy, including an administrator for each archipelago and a gendarme on each large island. The colony was financially self-supporting, and most of its revenues came from import duties. The codes of France constituted the laws of the colony, but a distinction was drawn between Polynesians of the Leeward, Gambier, Marquesas, and some of the Austral Islands, who were "subjects," and those of Tahiti and the other islands, who were given French citizenship.

Beyond these generalizations, which apply to all of

French Polynesia, each archipelago had by 1939 undergone a different development as a result of western influence.

It was quite natural that eighteenth-century Europeans should gratuitously single out the first chief they met and dub him "king" of Tahiti. At that time, however, there were several tribal chiefs and no one paramount leader on Tahiti. Europeans, however, picked out the Pomare dynasty of one tribe and favored its head with special honors and responsibilities; it suited the purposes of the early *Duff* missionaries that their first chiefly convert, Pomare, should be sovereign of the Protestant kingdom that was their objective. For they felt that a native "kingdom," shaped by a theocratic missionary council, could obviate the need for annexation by a European power and eventually evolve into a modern Christian (*i.e.*, Protestant) state. Perhaps it might have, but Catholic intervention and French annexation spoiled that plan.

The Protestant British missionaries at first succeeded in containing the natural Tahitian exuberance with Mother Hubbards and scriptural commandments even after the onslaught of whalers and traders; but under the easier French regime Tahiti again became the refuge of adventurers and escapists, and some of the old freedoms revived.

Western capitalists have never been happy about Tahiti. Attempts to set up large plantations have not succeeded: local Polynesians could not be induced to work them, while imported Chinese promptly graduated from wage labor to commerce and eventually came to dominate vegetable growing, merchandising, and service occupations. Most of the copra and vanilla which constituted the colony's major exports were produced by Polynesian householders and sold to Chinese middlemen for overseas marketing, the income being used to buy trade-store calico, kerosene, tobacco, and such things, to supplement the subsistence economy which continued to be the basis for Tahitian native life.

Numbers of Frenchmen settled in Tahiti, as civil servants, shop owners, and artists, and were followed by westerners from many other nations; but to a degree almost unique for Oceania, caste lines between Europeans and islanders failed to materialize. More than any other group, the Chinese kept socially to themselves, maintaining their own schools and clubs. But like westerners, many Chinese intermarried with Tahitians, and their numerous side issue include some of the handsomest people in a population generally noted for its beauty.

Papeete, Tahiti's largest town, is political and commercial capital of French Polynesia and port of entry for the entire group. There overseas vessels bring goods from Marseille, San Francisco, Auckland, and Sydney, and carry away copra, shell, and vanilla for world markets. Schooners, many of them built, owned, and manned by natives, transport store goods from Papeete to the outlying ports and bring back island produce for overseas shipment.

Far from Papeete, the Leeward, Austral, and Gambier Islands retained much of the old Polynesia that westerners effaced in Tahiti. A French gendarme, a Marist priest, and some Chinese traders were usually the only outsiders on most of these islands. Schooners carried their copra, vanilla, coffee, arrowroot, and craftwork to Papeete, and occasionally the more adventurous islanders visited the metropolis, where some of them were caught up in the faster life. For this commerce nearly every out-island had its specialty: Rapa and Rurutu men were the best sailors in the colony; the fiber weaving of the Gambiers was unexcelled in southeast Polynesia; and Tubuaï's chief export to Papeete was turkeys!

Mangareva's Catholic church was capable of seating

the whole local population, and regularly did. Throughout these out-islands the influence of the missions continued to be all powerful. For many decades after
French annexation of Tahiti itself, these out-islands were
left open to the inroads of aliens and their diseases, and
their populations were literally decimated in some cases.
Only the missions served native welfare until the French
government tardily stepped in and barred the more
vulnerable islands to outsiders.

Geography has been the decisive factor in the lives of
the Tuamotuan atoll dwellers. Their lands are low and
narrow, shallow in soil, and usually lacking in permanent
fresh water, but their broad lagoons are reservoirs of
fish, so that the Tuamotuans must lead practically amphibious lives. In former days the shell and pearls in
their lagoons provided them with income, until insatiable traders caused them to exhaust the beds. In recent
years it was not usually permitted to work with diving
gear and the diving season was officially limited, so that
the beds began to recuperate.

A different world altogether was that of the Marquesans. Even in pre-European times they remained isolated
from the refining influence of Tahiti and Raïatéa.
Reasonable estimates of the pre-European population go
up to 80,000; in 1939 there were less than 3000 left to
wander around among the ruins. Extensive archaeological remains and deserted cultivations bear out early accounts concerning the size and complexity of the earlier
culture; even as late as Melville's day the remnants were
impressive.

Pre-European Marquesans lived separate tribal lives
in their fertile and inaccessible valleys. Although feuding
was commonplace and cannibalism traditional, such customs apparently did not impair the growth and vigor of
the population. In 1595, however, Mendaña started the
familiar procession of horrors; during a week's stay at

Fatu Hiva, his crew raised three crucifixes and massacred two hundred natives. Later, Americans shared in the butchery. In 1813 the frigate *Essex* was based on Nuku Hiva to attack British shipping; its officers went further and, after assisting one tribe to conquer its neighbors, proclaimed United States sovereignty over the whole group. But the *Essex* was subsequently captured by the British and the annexation never ratified.

For many years whalers and blackbirders flocked to the islands to refresh themselves, enjoy the favors of the handsome native women, and recruit fresh crews for their vessels. Some ports became notorious for their lawlessness and debauchery, and Marquesans acquired western diseases and the taste for rum with equally disastrous results. Some chiefs, alarmed at their inability to control the lawless whites, petitioned France to move in, and French sovereignty was proclaimed in 1842. After that the decline was better regulated.

It required many years and many bloody campaigns for the French to subdue all the tribes, and official metropolitan interest was never very strong. Once, in 1859, they administratively abandoned the islands altogether; and when they subsequently set up a new headquarters at Hiva Oa, it was a mere gesture of sovereignty.

A planting boom inspired by the American Civil War brought other adventurers to the islands; and Chinese, Annamese, and Martinique Negroes were imported as laborers. As in Fiji, the boom quickly passed and the plantations were abandoned, but the diseases and drugs introduced by the immigrants remained. Natives proved especially susceptible to opium, and little effort was made to halt the trade.

Eventually the whalers and blackbirders and planters moved on. Throughout that dismal epoch the Catholic mission was the only benign influence in the Marquesas, but it proved quite incapable of staying the decline.

By tourist steamer the distance between French Polynesia and Samoa was a matter of days only, but in colonial terms the cultural distances were as far apart as Papeete's waterfront saloons and Apia's milk bars.

WESTERN SAMOA

Rotting on the reef just off the beach of Apia, largest town of Samoa, lies the broken hull of the German warship *Adler,* which was wrecked there in the hurricane of 1889, a stark reminder that more of white man's hopes and intentions—good and bad—have been wrecked in this Polynesian archipelago than on any other island group in the Pacific. The Samoans, sitting cross-legged on their fine mats and whisking flies off their brown torsos, may well chuckle at the hundred-year impasse that they constructed against the pale and puny outsiders. These inhabitants of the islands of Savaii, Upolu, Tutuila, and Manua have driven foreign governments almost to war with one another; they have ruined official reputations, forced planters and traders into bankruptcy, and divided white settlers into hostile camps—all this just by remaining *Samoan.* And in the process they have taken what they wanted from the white civilization and have gained steadily in numbers and in vitality.

Samoa presents a radically different picture from the usual South Seas spectacle of native peoples cheerfully and unknowingly losing their identity and their heritage in a setting of successful and expanding economy established and controlled by white men. For that reason, Samoa was until recently pronounced a "failure," and the white man's money lost in commercial ventures and well-intentioned administrative reforms was exceeded only by the sums spent in official inquiries into the causes of "failure." The causes actually go back many centuries.

The massive islands of Sávaii, Upolu, Tutuila, and

Manua must have been a welcome sight to the first Polynesians arriving there; their descendants came to regard Samoa as the best place in the world and *fa'a Samoa* (Samoan custom) the only correct way to live. These sentiments were furthered by the ideal environment they dwelt in and by the degree of isolation they enjoyed. This isolation was, however, not complete: their traditions contain many allusions to contacts with Tonga and Fiji, including marriages with chiefly individuals from those places. Wars with Fiji and Tonga also took place, and raiding parties from both groups conquered regions of Samoa on occasion. In addition, canoeloads of settlers from Samoa colonized the Ellice and many other islands near and far.

Samoan economy was not greatly different from that of other high-island Polynesian communities—growing taro and yams, collecting breadfruit and coconuts, fishing, hunting wild pigs and fowl, and tending domesticated ones—but it must have been easier, permitting more time for the more refined arts of ceremonial, politics, and fighting. Samoans were, and continue to be, accomplished politicians: "Irishmen of the Pacific," they have been called.

The basis of their dwelling, working, eating, and sharing was the large descent unit, each possessing traditional duties and privileges and honorific titles accumulated through the centuries and deriving in many instances from divine ancestors. Each unit designated one or more of its influential members to bear the family titles and perform the family ceremonials.

Several units dwelling in the same locality and usually linked by kinship ties formed a village unit, which was the political basis of Samoa. The whole population, about 56,000 a century ago, was divided into 122 of these villages. The village was largely autonomous, having its own council of family leaders (*matai*), but villages were grouped into larger district or subdistrict combinations, generally with kinship interrelationships and held together by the need for common defense. Each village within the district had its traditional role in ceremonial and warfare; for example, one served as the place of assembly for district councils, another as the center of oracles, and a third furnished leadership in war.

In time there developed larger combinations of districts into two great factions, Tumua and Pule, in addition to the easternmost district of Manua, which remained independent. Either the Tumua or Pule faction was alternately ascendant as a result of warfare or intrigue, and the struggle for gaining or maintaining supremacy went on continually. Supremacy did not mean domination as much as prestige and precedence in social-ceremonial affairs, but these latter were the valued factors in Samoan life and the great families were forever intriguing and fighting to push their own leaders ahead.

In tradition-minded Samoa high position meant title, precedence in ceremonial, and freedom from the activities and responsibilities of workaday life. For the practical side of politics the revered titleholders (*alii*) depended upon their own cunning and that of aggressive orators (*tulafale*), who not infrequently possessed more ability than they. Throughout this polity communalism was the rule. The individual mattered less as individual than as titleholder. Innovation gave way to imitation. High value was placed on correct conformance to glorified past behavior. Yet there was extreme rivalry to obtain the privilege of performing the great social ceremonials. Under these circumstances neither faction maintained its ascendancy for very long, and a unified, stable Samoa was quite impossible so long as autonomy in practical matters remained with the village and district.

Such was the situation when the first significant European settlement took place in 1830. In that year the

London Missionary Society pioneer, John Williams, arrived from Tahiti and began his work. A few beachcombers had preceded him, but their influence was slight. Williams' reception was far from hostile: he was immediately adopted by the faction then in power, accorded the high honors due a great teacher, and assisted in his mission. The rituals and cosmogony of the new religion were promptly incorporated into the native system, the Christian God occupying a high position in the supernatural hierarchy; and before many years Samoan converts were spreading the gospel elsewhere in Oceania. Later on, Wesleyan, Catholic, and Mormon missions secured followers, thereby increasing the factionalism inherent in Samoa.

The missions were able to outlaw a few pagan customs, such as the ceremonial defloration of brides, and to add new customs, such as observance of the Sabbath, but they did not bring about a reformation in native philosophy or morality. In Samoa, where religion was never so highly institutionalized as elsewhere in Polynesia, the mission teachers simply replaced native priests in the new system, and the *matais*, formerly the families' intercessors with supernatural forces, simply became deacons in village churches. Ultimately the Protestant congregations developed into peculiarly Samoan native-church organizations, possessing many local twists in doctrine and practice.

Samoans took over white trade much as they had taken white religion, choosing those aspects and items that fitted comfortably into the *fa'a Samoa* and rejecting the rest. From the very beginning traders remarked at the lack of awe with which Samoans greeted the appearance of the iron and cloth that had sent other islanders into transports of wonder and excesses of acquisitiveness. Samoans made enough copra to buy a few trade goods and to place offerings in the church boxes, and then relaxed to the enjoyment of their politics and

subsistence economy. There was little incentive to acquire many European goods: to do so would merely
have invited relatives and friends to divide them according to traditional practices of communalism and gen-
erosity.

In 1856 the powerful Hamburg firm of Godeffroy and
Son established a trading station at Apia, developing it
ultimately into headquarters for Germany's commercial
and political expansion throughout Oceania. Other companies, British and American, followed suit, and soon
Samoa was a center of plantation and commercial life.
But the Samoans did not succumb to the new philosophy
of work and gain. To assure plentiful supplies of copra
for the expanding world markets, planters had to acquire land and start their own plantations. And when
they learned they could not induce Samoans to work for
them, they had to import Melanesians and Chinese
coolies.

By 1870, Samoans had accepted as much of the white
man's religion and economy as they could comfortably
swallow and were well on the way to assimilating it. At
that point, however, rivalries among the whites living
on their beaches disturbed the process.

Throughout the early period of white contact, native
Samoan factional strife went along merrily and naturally. On one occasion a truce succeeded in uniting in
the person of one individual most of the important titles,
so that there was the appearance at least of a unified
native Samoa. Naïve foreigners took this at face value
and assumed that it represented a fundamental political
evolution; its inevitable breakup led to side-choosing,
the Germans backing one aspirant and the Anglo-Americans the other. There were the usual angry conferences,
the pleas for protectorates, the suspicions of annexation,
and the visits of warships, all gleefully observed by the
Samoans, who enjoyed the novelty of harassing their
traditional enemies with modern weapons and trained

Europeans as fellows-in-arms. The German side had the advantage of having more intelligent conspirators, more able personnel in their trading firms, and stronger naval support. To complicate the issue, a clever rogue of an American, Colonel A. B. Steinberger, arrived on a semi-official mission, sold out to the Germans, and was established as "Premier" until the British and American consuls had him deported. Serious fighting involving nationals of the three powers broke out and might have led to an international conflict but for a most timely hurricane in 1889, which wrecked the warships preparing for hostilities and thus drew the attention of London, Washington, and Berlin to the seriousness of the situation.

Jealous of one another's advantage, the three powers in 1889 declared a joint protectorate over the "Independent Kingdom of Samoa," solving nothing but the temporary dilemma of the diplomats. Ten years later, after the admitted failure of this arrangement, Britain withdrew from the Samoan scene in consideration of other international arrangements. Germany and the United States thereupon divided the group, the former taking Savaii and Upolu and the latter Tutuila and Manua in the east, thus recognizing Germany's paramount commercial stake in more highly developed Upolu, and America's naval establishment in Tutuila's fine harbor of Pago Pago. From this time onward Western and Eastern Samoa went different ways. Copra continued to play important roles in both divisions, but in the American area it was subordinated to the dominant preoccupation of maintaining a naval base and coaling station there—a development described in a later chapter.

German administrators had very definite ideas about the role to be played by Western Samoa in the grand strategy of expanding German colonialism. First of all, Samoa must be a rich tropical garden, producing coconuts, fruits, spices, and other things needed in the western world. Secondly, the government must demonstrate to the world how Germany, late arrival though she was among the colonial powers, could govern skillfully and justly the native inhabitants of its new dependency.

A vigorous program of agricultural experimentation was undertaken and almost every tropical crop tried out, with copra maintaining its first place and cocoa and rubber emerging as important supplements. The *Deutsche Handels- und Plantagengesellschaft,* successor to Godeffroy and by far the largest operator in the colony, retained its semiofficial status, but the government dealt tactfully and sympathetically with the large community of non-German planters and traders already established at Upolu. Times were prosperous, although not all the foreigners profited equally. The colonists who flocked to Samoa from Germany with more enthusiasm than knowledge and capital soon learned that tropical agriculture was a big-scale enterprise, unsuited to the small holder. These new settlers joined with other dissidents in the European colony and expressed their frustrations by criticizing the government's "big business" and "pronative" policies.

The Germans approached the task of governing Samoa with firmness. They informed themselves thoroughly concerning Samoan matters and shaped their practices accordingly. They soon did away with the artificial "kingship"; and though respecting ceremonialism and village autonomy, they firmly suppressed all show of factionalism. Perhaps after a century or two they might have succeeded in wiping out politics and intrigue, but in the few years of their administration they only drove it underground.

In opposition to the government's absolute rule and quick reprisals, there developed a native *Mau* ("Opinion") movement, led by thwarted leaders and probably encouraged by dissidents in the European colony. But the solution to this new problem was left to the next masters.

In August 1914 a New Zealand expeditionary force occupied Western Samoa without opposition and set up a military administration. The Versailles Treaty ultimately awarded Western Samoa to New Zealand as a Class C mandate, to be governed as an integral part of the Dominion in the interest of promoting "to the utmost the material and moral well being and the social progress of the inhabitants of the Territory." The League of Nations Covenant of the treaty prohibited slavery and forced labor, liquor and military training, and outlawed interference with mission work and with freedom of conscience and worship. Brave new world!

New Zealand officials approached the task with the best of intentions to carry out the letter and the spirit of the mandate, but their failure became so apparent at one point that New Zealand might have been relieved of her responsibilities had the League been stronger. It is improbable that any nation could have brought about a solution in Samoa without using force, which however was foreign to the spirit of the League Covenant and to the humanitarianism of the New Zealand government and public.

First of all, the prosperity promised and to some extent realized during the German days did not materialize under the new regime. During the next two decades copra prices fell off sharply and this slump affected Samoans as well as Europeans. The Samoans, who normally produced about 60 to 70 per cent of the copra exports, dried and sold only enough to obtain basic necessities and left most of their groves unworked.

White planters suffered even greater reverses. The New Zealand administration deported all Germans and took over their holdings for reparations; a government-owned and managed Reparations Estates Company was organized for the purpose of operating the plantations, and some portions were leased to New Zealand settlers. The substitution of untrained New Zealand personnel for the experienced German planters would have had unfortunate consequences in any case, and that was particularly so during the postwar depression. Only the large and efficiently managed estates survived; and, as inevitably happens, the less successful among the Europeans blamed their misfortunes on the administration. As a matter of fact, they had some cause: the New Zealand administration was far less concerned with the welfare of the nonnative population than the German officials had been. But ironically enough, the white dissidents spread their poison among their native Samoan friends and helped to arouse native opposition to the very regime that was acting on behalf of native welfare.

In this crisis the noble intentions of the administration did not suffice. In general, the New Zealand officials had less understanding of Samoan problems than their German predecessors had had, nor did they have the will or the authority to impose drastic measures, since most decisions had to be cleared with Wellington.

In a sincere effort to give natives more voice in managing their own affairs, one administrator set up a Samoan council with representatives from each community —a "democratic" reform, fundamentally different from traditional Samoan intrigue, factionalism, and abhorrence of responsibility in practical affairs. This council met in continuous sessions, indulged in long-winded oratory, and rubber-stamped proposals of the administration. Their "constituents" ignored them and set about to oppose on principle all regulations of reform. Before very long the extreme conservatism of *fa'a Samoa* reasserted itself in a revival of the *Mau* opposition movement. The slogan "Samoa for the Samoans" was adopted, uniforms and symbols devised, and an entirely separate native government organized.

Strong support came from antiadministrationists among the European colony and from "native sympathizers" in New Zealand who wrote countless letters to editors and kept Samoan hopes high by promising material aid. The government sought to dissolve opposition by deporting the leaders, especially its part-Samoan organizer; this action merely provided the movement with a very useful martyr. Finally, open hostilities broke out and brought about vigorous administrative action.

Underlying the *Mau* was the conservatism inherent in Samoan life. It manifested itself in a native boycott of things European: Samoans made little copra and traded only with friends; they disobeyed regulations; and they refused to pay taxes. In addition, their more sophisticated leaders and backers made up fine-sounding platforms, demanding autonomy and the end of European controls and exploitation. For the average Samoan native, however, *Mau* was simply an inarticulate expression of opposition to everything he couldn't assimilate and didn't want from the white culture. Later, upon its accession to power in New Zealand, the Labour Government reversed official policy, interpreted the *Mau* as being a "legitimate" expression of native aspiration, and set about trying to govern accordingly.

Meanwhile European enterprise declined, and it looked as if "Samoa for the Samoans" would become a reality. The government undertook to market copra and bananas for native producers, and did in fact assure some income for Samoans; but this represented a loss for the trader, who no longer secured the profits due the middleman. Planters found it more and more difficult to secure labor and to survive in the face of world depression. All but a few of the indentured Melanesians had been repatriated when Germany lost control, and the importing of coolies became increasingly hedged about with regulations, so that their numbers dwindled.

The half-caste population—Samoan mixed with whites or Melanesian or Chinese—increased and created even more problems for the harassed administration. Some of the mixbloods were absorbed into the native community, but others attempted to retain the European status of their fathers and lived the almost inevitably unhappy half-life of half-castes, unwanted by whites and natives and unprovided for by government.

Under all these conditions most fullblood Samoans continued to increase in numbers and to follow their accustomed routines: garden and grove work on Friday; Sabbath preparation on Saturday; church attendance, hymn singing, and feasting on Sunday; recuperation on Monday; fishing, visiting, politics, and cricket playing on Tuesday, Wednesday, and Thursday; and then begin again. To the missionary they appeared devoted adherents and generous supporters of the church, little understanding the doctrines they enthusiastically sang about and ill prepared to manage their own spiritual affairs. To the planter they seemed lazy and undependable, unsuited and unwilling to work, the spoiled darlings of an "unrealistic bureaucracy." To the administration they were a profound enigma, stubbornly resistant to all government efforts on their behalf. To the tourist they appeared a beautifully formed, generous, and jolly people, living idyllic lives in beautiful surroundings. To the scientist they provided a fascinating and almost unique example of Polynesians surviving the strong impact of western civilization without changing their everyday lives and without losing their numbers, their strength, their dignity, or their zest for a good controversy.

COOK ISLANDS

To say that the Cook Islands are located between Tahiti, Samoa, and Tonga is to characterize them in nearly every respect. Their consolidation into one political unit, a New Zealand dependency, came about as a by-product of the powers' struggle for control over the more strategic Papeete, Apia, and Tongatabu; the Cook Islands were literally the crumbs that were left after the

choicer morsels had been swallowed up. Otherwise, aside
from the common Polynesian origins of all Cook Islanders, there was little logic in unifying them under a single
administration. The northern Cooks, typical low-lying
coral atolls, crowded with coconut palms, had more geographic affinity with Samoa's coral outlyers; and the
larger, volcanic southern Cooks had the same relationship with their neighboring French islands to the east.
However, with Germany and the United States occupying Samoa, and the French on the islands to the east,
Great Britain wasted no time in academic geographic
argument but took everything that was left and handed
it to New Zealand for safekeeping. That was in 1901.

Long before then, British missionaries were at work
in both the northern and southern Cook Islands transforming the lusty islanders into pious parishioners,
thereby adding a *soupçon* to the Samoan and Tahitian
ingredients which help to make up the Cook mixture.

In their traditional histories many Cook Islanders
trace their lines back to legendary expeditions from the
same Polynesian homeland, but after century-long residence on their separate islands their ways of life took on
local forms. The northern islanders had to adapt aus-
terely to the limiting environment of atolls with very
sparse soil. But even in the larger and more fertile
southern islands, no one island achieved the kind of cultural hegemony which permitted Tahiti and Upolu to
maintain homogeneity among their neighbors. Of course,
like all Polynesians, the Cook Islanders voyaged in their
canoes beyond their own reefs, but these voyages were
not frequent or long enough to draw northern and
southern Cook Islanders into any kind of institutional
relationships.

The unsavory trio—whaler, trader, and blackbirder—
left their marks on these islands, and slavers recruiting
for Peru nearly solved the native problems on one northern atoll by the simple expedient of carrying off the na-

tives. Missionaries then stepped in. The indefatigable
John Williams of the London Missionary Society pushed
on from Tahiti to the Cook Islands in 1823 and laid the
foundations for a really remarkable evangelization.
Within a very few years most Cook Islanders were zealous converts and in fact some of them were actually
spearheading mission work in neighboring heathen
areas. Theocratic control was complete; strict Blue Laws
were enacted. It became unlawful to remain abroad
nights after the eight o'clock curfew. "Cohabitation out
of wedlock" became a punishable crime. Mother Hub-
bard had all the authority—and considerably more legal
force—than a modern Dior.

Meanwhile copra trading developed, supplemented
by pearl diving in the northern atolls; and when the
New Zealand market opened up, some enterprising New
Zealanders encouraged the production of tropical fruits
in the southern Cooks.

Annexation of the two groups to New Zealand in 1901
further stimulated fruit production, and the main island
of Rarotonga along with its close neighbors went over
almost entirely to the growing of citrus fruits and bananas. Many white planters and traders settled on Rarotonga and transformed it into a small facsimile of Apia;
but few of them settled outside Rarotonga, and the
other islands carried on their subsistence living, producing just enough copra and trade handicraft to purchase
western-made luxuries and to support their churches.

Lacking strongly centralized native political systems,
the Cook Islands afforded less opportunity for western
adventurers to move in and become king-makers, as they
had done with such profit in Fiji and Tahiti. Nor was
New Zealand far enough along in the development of
its own resources to stimulate many of its white residents
to leave and seek their fortunes in the South Seas. Such
factors as these, coupled with the Cook Islands' relatively uninviting resources, may have helped preserve

these islands for the islanders. In addition, the New Zealand administration enacted protective land laws which made it impossible, anyway, for nonnatives to acquire more than limited lease rights in island real estate. And although the New Zealand government retained final controls, large areas of authority were left in the hands of the islanders themselves.

After World War I economic ties with New Zealand were further strengthened and political fusion made rapid headway. Elsewhere in Oceania white settlers, subjects of the metropolitan governing powers, were usually the instruments for this kind of fusion; in the Cooks the islanders themselves played that role. Associations of islanders were formed to produce and market income crops, and more and more administrative responsibilities were returned to islanders' hands, but always with the apparent objective of encouraging their greater participation in New Zealand affairs. Unlike the case in Western Samoa, New Zealand's mandated dependency, the colonial alternative of evolution toward independence seems not to have been considered for the Cook Islands.

SOLOMON ISLANDS

Tens of thousands of GI's will remember the Solomon Islands for their climate and coconuts. There alone could you wade in mud one moment and be blinded with dust the next. And there alone were the palms so thick that they seemed to live and move, crowding in after six months' staring at them, but receding after a year: South Pacific veterans will know what is meant!

For sheer cussedness of climate the Solomons are hard to beat; and when malaria, dysentery, and blackwater fever are added to oppressive humidity and torrential rainfall, it is not strange that these islands have remained, by Colonial Office standards, the most backward of Brit-

ain's Pacific dependencies. And as for the animated coconuts, they are in fact almost the only living productive
items in the few narrow coastal zones where white man's
influence extends.

Three hundred and eighty years had passed since Europeans first discovered the fabulous Islands of Solomon,
but by 1939 only a few hundred aliens—whites and Chinese—eked out existences there, and most of these settlers
were in one way or another concerned with copra, with
producing it or buying it or transporting it.

Geographically the Solomons comprise one sector of
the double chain of islands extending from New Guinea
to New Zealand. Some of these islands have fundaments
of old continental rocks upthrust as massive mountain
ranges, through which lava has burst to form volcanoes.
Rich soil and heavy rainfall have helped to clothe the
larger islands with rain forests and swamps. Cluttering
up the sea between the large islands are numerous
smaller and flatter islands covered with jungle and scrub.
A few active volcanoes and frequent earthquakes serve
to remind visitors that geologically these islands are
still young and subject to violent change.

By 1939, cultural changes had been quite gradual.
Back in the hills were to be found natives who had only
recently replaced stone with steel, and even those more
accessible to trader, missionary, and administrative officer had adopted steel tools, calico, and nominal Christianity without changing radically their millennia-old
economics and rituals.

Not that all the native cultures were alike; far from
it. It is true that most of their economies were and are
based on the growing of taro, yams, plantains, and coconuts; on the collection of sago and wild plants; on the
raising and hunting of pigs; and on some fishing. On the
other hand, social organization and languages varied
from island to island and even in some cases from village

to village. Most Solomonese speak Austronesian languages, although these differ so much among themselves as to be as mutually incomprehensible as, say, English and Italian. There are also isolated pockets of people speaking Papuan tongues, and a few islands—Ontong Java, Sikiana, Rennell, Bellona, Tikopia, Anuda—were and are inhabited by colonies of Polynesians. Polynesian influences are also noticeable along the eastern shores of some of the larger islands such as Isabel and Vanikoro.

The official limits of the British Solomon Islands Protectorate extend only up to Bougainville, but ethnically and racially Bougainville and its northern appendage, Buka, should probably be grouped with the western Solomons—Shortland, Mono, Choiseul, Vella Lavella, and the New Georgia group—constituting the so-called "Black Spot," because the skin color of their natives is darker than that of any other peoples in Oceania. The culture of one of the Black Spot tribes was described earlier, but nothing short of an encyclopedia could fully describe the great variety of social forms and religious practices of all the Solomons. There are the usual characteristic differences between coast and inland tribes, and the basic institution of family and extended family exists throughout; but marked tribal differences in matters such as kin alignment (matrilineal, patrilineal, bilateral), rank (inherited versus acquired), totemism, age grading, and cultism, spell despair for anyone seeking a simple formula for understanding the Solomonese as an entity.

Even their world-wide reputation for "natural" ferocity requires qualification. From the time of Mendaña's first visit in 1567, most native attacks against Europeans have been the result of provocation. Mendaña's crew left a trail of blood, and this event was probably remembered even during the centuries when the Solomonese were "lost" to Europeans. Whalers used to call in for fresh water and food, and they were not noted for their diplomatic treatment of native peoples. Then, about 1840, traders began to visit the islands in search of sandalwood, trepang, and turtle shell; and to the usual tactics of their kind they added such refinements as the aiding and abetting of head-hunting to curry favor with chiefs who could provide good trade. But none of these harbingers of civilization made such impressions on the natives as did the blackbirders.

Beginning about 1865 Solomonese were induced to go to Fiji to work on cotton and coconut plantations. Ten years later they began to be sent in shipload lots to the sugar fields of Queensland. In addition to outright shanghaiing, cargoes of black and brown humanity were obtained by offering such incentives as rum and firearms. No official notice was taken so long as the muskets were used only in intervillage feuding, but when they were turned against traders and blackbirders British warships were compelled to shell villages and establish the usual law and order. Recruiting for work in Queensland ceased in 1903, after sixty thousand natives had been sent there, and Fiji traffic ended in 1910. Meanwhile recruiting for labor for use within the archipelago has continued down to the present.

As an inevitable consequence of the annexation of Fiji in 1874 and the campaign against blackbirding, Britain consolidated its rule over the central and eastern Solomons between 1893 and 1899, and a Resident Commissioner was placed in charge in 1896. At that time there were only fifty Europeans residing in the group— four missionaries and forty-six traders, with not one white woman among them. Fifty years later there were still only five hundred Europeans, including officials, planters, merchants, and missionaries, along with about two hundred Chinese traders. Altogether these outsiders numbered ninety-four thousand fewer than the natives they were there to employ, civilize, or succor.

In the decades before 1939 three kinds of white man's culture impinged on the Solomonese. Foremost was the coconut economy: labor-recruiting schooners, plantations, and trade stores. Next was the mission, at least for the Christian half of the population. Third was the government, that awesome institution whose agents collected taxes and put you in the calaboose if you acted like a Solomonese when you should have acted like a European.

The planters were the last to arrive. Traders had begun buying native copra long before, but organized plantation enterprises were not started until 1905, when the British firm of Lever Brothers acquired land in the central Solomons and laid out cultivations ultimately covering twenty thousand acres. Shortly thereafter the Australian firms of Burns Philp and the Malaita Company started plantations. Later on they were joined by the Carpenter Company and a few independent planters, until eventually there were over sixty thousand acres in coconut cultivation, not including the thousands of smaller plots owned by Solomonese. There were marked differences between the large integrated organizations (Lever's, Burns Philp, Carpenter's, and so forth) and the smaller "independents." Missions also owned and operated plantations, and these were comparable in size to the small planter enterprises.

From the native point of view, the main difference between plantations was the distance of the plantation from home. Some natives preferred to work near home, but others liked the adventure and glamour of traveling to another island and the identification with a big-company enterprise.

"Government" meant the central administrative headquarters, the jail, and the native hospital, all at Tulagi; the district administrative outposts, eight in all; and the annual census and tax-collecting patrols of district officers. The chief official was the Resident Commissioner, a British career colonial officer, directly responsible to the British High Commissioner of the Western Pacific, then with headquarters at Fiji.

The Solomons are not white man's country, and no encouragement was given to white colonization. Certainly, in theory at least, the administration was pro-native. As a group, the officials appeared to have the best of intentions toward native welfare; but from the standpoint of numbers and facilities, they were ill equipped to carry out these intentions. And, in one respect, the administrative regulations involved a major paradox: a complex set of regulations protected the native from exploitation and mistreatment by planters, recruiters, and traders, but the head tax imposed on native adult males indirectly compelled nearly all of them to work at least for a few years on plantations, there being practically no other way to earn tax money.

The pioneer attempt to missionize the Solomons began in 1845, but native hostility forced the Marist fathers to postpone their endeavors for fifty years. Next in the field was the Anglican Melanesian Mission, whose work was first directed from New Zealand, then from Norfolk Island, and later from headquarters in the Solomons. This enterprising organization depended greatly upon native pastors, and dispensed salvation and welfare from the deck of its circuit-traveling schooner, the *Southern Cross*. In due course Methodist, South Seas Evangelical, and Seventh Day Adventist missions were established; but by 1939 all the missions together had won adherence from only half the native population.

These white cultures, commercial, official, and missionary, influenced the native Solomonese as three distinct forces and not as a unified "European civilization." The planter hired the Solomonese's labor; the missionary invited his adherence to a set of bizarre rules about bishops and human conduct; and the official demanded his tax money and his obedience to a set of equally bizarre foreign laws. Sometimes the three sets of demands clashed. The native's dilemma was pathetically sharpened when, too frequently, he heard the white masters commit that worst of all caste crimes: criticizing one another within native hearing. The ideological differences between official and missionary were particularly unfortunate; occasionally the wretched Solomonese had to choose between a mild but immediate calaboose and a drastic but distant Hell.

The planter, on the other hand, was singularly unconcerned with native polity and native souls, although he had ample opportunity to transform both. At some point in their lives nearly all native youths signed on for a two-year contract to work on plantations, and many of them renewed their indentures. Prior to World War II, there were about five thousand—5 per cent of the whole population—so engaged at all times. The starting age was about seventeen or eighteen years old; men with families seldom risked leaving their wives for such long periods.

Curiosity about the great outside world was certainly one incentive for signing on; the need for tax money was another. White recruiters periodically visited the outlying islands to pick up the new workers, and plantations were obliged to repatriate them upon completion of indenture. Plantation natives dwelt in barracks and for about fifty hours a week carried out all the unskilled jobs and many of the semiskilled ones. At the bottom of the scale was the raw youngster, probably for the first time wearing a calico *lava-lava* around his loins, whose job it was to scurry up palms monkey-fashion to catch harmful insects. At the top of the scale was the seasoned "bossboy," the veteran of ten to twenty years of plantation work, completely expatriated from his native village. Between these two extremes were the coconut collectors and cutters. Each cutter was expected to cut five to six hundred pounds of copra a day, with a small bonus for larger amounts. Wages ranged from ten shillings to several pounds a month, supplemented by an officially approved ration scale of food, a calico loincloth each month, blankets, a mosquito net, soap, and tobacco.

Life at the plantation was completely foreign to the native way of living. Work was regimented and steady, and the government-backed contract, once entered upon, could not be broken without exceptional cause. Any one plantation would generally employ laborers from a number of different villages and islands, so that the native workers usually had to converse in pidgin. Since there were usually no native villages within visiting range and no unmarried native women on the plantation, sex aberrations not infrequently developed among the male workers.

The only natives who saw much of the white planters' civilization they helped support were the few who worked as domestics. The common plantation hands had to learn at secondhand about these wonders and rituals, notwithstanding the airs of sophistication they assumed when they returned to their villages. This situation raised the question: What effect then did plantation life have on native culture?

The "finish-time" boy usually returned home with a handful of shillings and a small wooden chest—with the all-important padlock—filled with trade-store knives, tobacco, pipes, calico, curios, blankets, and a multicelled flashlight (with no extra batteries!); the use he made of these items provided one answer to the question.

Anyone dealing with Solomonese after having sojourned in the eastern Pacific was struck by the strong individualistic sense of property of these Negroids. It had not developed as far as our sacred principle of dog-eat-dog, but, unlike most of Polynesia, it was possible for a Solomonese to rise to fame and power in his own community through accumulating and distributing material things. Most of the native cultures distributed between New Caledonia and New Guinea possessed some kind of rudimentary "money": durable items such as necklaces of shell beads or dog teeth, or boar tusks curved into arm bands. These items may on special occasions have been worn as ornaments, but they functioned chiefly as repositories of value, used in ceremonial exchanges to cement pacts, to acquire wives, to reciprocate hospitality. Some of the commoner types of money were used as we use currency, to buy weapons, pottery clay, and so on, but the high "denominations" were reserved for more ritual occasions.

Solomonese did not customarily collect native money for the mere sake of accumulation; they generally used it to give social-climbing feasts or to assist young kinsmen pay their ceremonial obligations and thereby secure wives and status. The older men, who generally possessed more of the native money, were thus by that fact more influential than their juniors, who were usually poorer. And no small part of their tribal authority derived from this balance. This was the indigenous system; by 1939 it still prevailed in many communities, although the influences of plantation and mission served to undermine it. For one thing, the importance of young men was materially enhanced by plantation work, since the elders had to depend upon them for the shillings to pay head tax and buy trade goods. And although youthful finish-timers continued the practice of distributing their earnings among the elders to ensure obtaining native money for marriage and rituals, they returned to their villages feeling less respect for status based on old age alone.

In yet another way the plantations affected native life. The absence of numbers of young males from their native villages inevitably put more burden on females and the very young and old in producing food and maintaining other standards of living. This also tended to warp the conventional patterns of courtship and betrothal; few betrothed or married men could have expected young fiancées or wives to remain faithful during their yearlong absences.

Thus, although white plantation "culture" was not in itself carried to native villages, the indentured-labor system did induce changes in native institutions.

The effects of missions were considerably more direct. Missionaries, unlike most planters, did attempt to change native life, and among half the population they had succeeded in some respects. The first conversions may have come about through natives' desire to emulate whites, but that motive came to have considerably less force for the disenchanted Solomonese of this century. Education was a more potent factor in recent years, for the missionaries alone conducted schools. In this connection, many Solomonese attributed their caste subordination less to skin color than to whites' superiority in economics and education, and expected someday to level these differences by schooling. (Remarkably, the inevitable disillusionment of the "educated" ones did not seem to dampen the hopes of others.) Other religious conversions were brought about by the desire of young men to break away from the authority of their elders. The missions frowned on the heathen institutions and practices by which men rose to affluence and power over their communities; and they attacked these, directly, by inveighing against them, and, indirectly, by encouraging young converts to ignore them, to disbelieve the supernatural sanctions which helped maintain the native institutions.

This discrediting of native practices and undermining of local authority was a principal effect of mission activity. It is doubtful that the missions brought about many fundamental changes in native morals or in the forms of native religious beliefs. In fact, Christianity became fairly well assimilated to Solomonese religions and filled many of the same functions, except, perhaps, the important one of stimulating natives in their economic activities. Jehovah appears not to have had the same connection with good crops and fine canoes that the old pagan deities had, with the result that natives became more apathetic about careful cultivation and workmanship.

Government, the third outside influence upon native life, operated principally as a restraint. Natives learned by experience what they should *not* do, but the administration, unlike the missions, did not see fit to advise them what they *should* do and become. Before World War II, the natives did not seem to object too strenuously to government; even incarceration in the Tulagi jail may have been inconvenient, but it left no great stigma. In one respect only was there a grievance: natives did not understand why the relatively richer white men, with shillings to throw away, persisted in taxing them for their few hard-won pence.

All in all, the Solomonese did not fare too badly under white rule after blackbirding was supplanted by comparatively innocuous plantation indenture. Numerically the population had begun to reverse the decline which accompanied the first introduction of white diseases. The missions and the government did, it is true, remove some of the *esprit* formerly associated with feuding and ceremony, but other enthusiasms were taking their place. And although the old systems of group cohesion and authority were breaking down, new institutions were forming. Prior to Pearl Harbor, their land was nearly intact and likely to remain so, and their self-respect was inviolate. For this they could thank, among other things, a well-meaning administration and a wretched climate.

COASTAL NEW GUINEA

The continental island of New Guinea sprawls across the top of Australia like a great flapping bird, with its head pointed toward Borneo and its tail toward Fiji. Through the center of its 1500-mile-long mass are ranges of rugged mountains reaching to heights of 17,000 feet. In places the mountains fall away abruptly into the sea; elsewhere they slope gently and provide wide alluvial plains covered with rain forest. In the interior there are also rolling, grass-covered plateaus, but these are isolated by mountains, by belts of rough limestone or by wide swamps. A few great river systems, including the Fly, the Sepik, and the Purari, provide some access to the interior, but these same rivers also create thousands of square miles of treacherous fen country.

To discouraging topography and disconcerting vegetation have been added deadly anopheles by the billions, centipedes, scorpions, crocodiles, and human savages, so that it is not surprising that by 1939 there remained large areas of New Guinea unvisited by white man and unchanged by the outside world since polished stone began to replace chipped flint as mankind's basic artifact.

In 1939 New Guinea's million and a quarter known native inhabitants continued to dwell in small settlements, separated from each other so distinctly by mountains or forests or swamps that no groupings had developed larger than kin or village communities, although the anthropologist classifies New Guinea hamlets and villages into larger units on the basis of language or other cultural similarities. A universal suspicion toward outsiders, along with intervillage feuding, head-hunting, and cannibalism, reinforced the environment's own discouraging features to keep New Guinea savage and inaccessible.

Except for some enclaves of Austronesian-speaking

peoples along the eastern fringes of the island, most of
New Guinea's natives speak Papuan languages. Physical types range from pygmy-statured Negroids dwelling in inland refuge areas to tall coastal types. Many of
them bear the unmistakable imprint of Australoid inter-
mixture; others are lighter skinned and have straighter
features, suggesting Mongoloid genes. Almost the only
features common to all are their relatively dark skins and
their frizzly hair.

Culturally they also differ among themselves in such
fundamental features as the manner in which they reckon
descent and the relative importance they attach to initiation rites, totemic affiliation, cultism, and so forth.
And they also exhibit differences in the shapes and arrangements of their dwellings, the size of their communities, their forms of clothing or lack of it, and the accent
they put upon art work. But underlying these differences
there are certain fundamental similarities throughout:
the natives are all horticulturists, paced by the slowness
of their tools of polished stone, ground shell, or split
bamboo and, more recently, steel; and they all carry on
fishing, hunting, and gathering of wild plants to supplement their monotonous diets of taro, yam, sago, or sweet
potato.

North and east of New Guinea lie scores of smaller
islands that have come to be identified with it for white
man's administrative convenience. The Bismarck Archipelago, comprising New Britain, New Ireland, New Han-
over, the Admiralties, and numerous smaller islands,
have had a special recent history owing to their easier
accessibility and their suitability for coconut growing.
The Admiralties, including Manus, are the homes of
skilled Austronesian-speaking sailors. New Britain is a
kind of miniature New Guinea and is especially notorious
for its active volcanoes. Clustered around the tail of the
New Guinea "bird" are the Woodlarks, Trobriands, and
Louisiades, inhabited by artistic sea rovers.

Given a few more millennia, these and other Austro-nesian-speaking islanders, with their far-traveling canoes and less circumscribed ideas, might have spread their influence beyond the eastern coastal fringes into the very heart of Papuan New Guinea, but the trend was halted by another development.

Portuguese and Spanish navigators sighted New Guinea in the early sixteenth century, but gave it wide berth. During the following century Dutch explorers skirted its shores, but passed it up for their more profitable colonies to the west. English and French navigators, Dampier, Carteret, and Bougainville, defined its outlines more precisely, but no one seems to have considered it worth colonizing.

The first proprietory move toward New Guinea was made by Holland in 1828, when Dutch suzerainty was established over the western half of the island. But that was only a gesture, for although the claim was internationally recognized, for a hundred years the Dutch did little to consolidate their gain beyond establishing small administrative outposts and planting a few coconuts along the more accessible coasts. Natives in the interior went about their neolithic ways and saw nothing of the outside world except occasional bands of Malayan hunters searching for birds of paradise.

Coastal natives along the western fringes kept up their age-old trade with the Moluccas, and through them such exotic commodities as dammar, ebony, ironwood, and trepang reached world markets. Also, the Japanese South Seas Development Company, reaching out from its Palau Colony, established a station on the head of the New Guinea "bird." Missions, Catholic and Protestant, made some headway along the coasts; and a few converts were won over for Islam through the efforts of Ceram traders. But the first real stimulus to exploration and development came in 1932, when several Dutch interests organized mineral and oil surveys.

Meanwhile the unclaimed eastern half of New Guinea began to feel the first tentative effects of white contact. Fortunately for native lives and property, the whalers and sandalwooders avoided New Guinea: whaling grounds were too far away, and suitable trees were not easily available. Consequently, until about 1870, almost the only white visitors to New Guinea were explorers and a few Australian traders who were intent on exchanging their calicos and "Nigger head" tobacco for coconuts, shell, and curios. The first recorded shore trade station was set up in 1872 by an Englishman in the Duke of York Islands between New Britain and New Ireland. This pioneering enterprise was quickly followed by agents of the aggressive German merchants, Godeffroy and Son, operating out of Samoa. At about the same time a Wesleyan missionary began his labors here; and within ten years the white population of eastern New Guinea had swelled to the impressive total of thirty souls, mostly concentrated around the northeastern end of New Britain. Most of them were traders, dangerously engaged in bartering their calico and tobacco and iron tools for the coconuts and shell of semihostile natives.

Around 1880, some traders began to lay out coconut plantations. Throughout the decades that followed, only a small fraction of eastern New Guinea land was alienated to white man's plantations, mines, and settlements; but through the large native labor forces employed on these enterprises, eastern New Guinea was transformed into a more homogeneous native civilization upon which was superimposed a numerically small caste of white masters.

On the whole, the natives of eastern New Guinea had up to 1939 fared better under civilization than other Oceanic Negroids. In addition to escaping the attentions of whalers and sandalwooders, they experienced only a few years of blackbirding, and that of a much milder variety than the scourge which nearly depopulated the

New Hebrides. During the early eighties boatloads of eastern New Guinea natives were transported to plantations in Queensland and Samoa but the commerce was better regulated and less scandalous than elsewhere.

During those early days eastern New Guinea was a lawless place, or rather a place of many codes. The few white planters and traders individually policed their own neighborhoods; even the missionaries were not above fighting—and killing—hostile natives, to make the way safe for the Word. This state of affairs persisted until 1884. Traders felt out some of the main island coasts, but missionaries and planters, along with a handful of prospectors, limited their activities to the islands around the eastern end of the main island.

Meanwhile German merchants conceived more ambitious plans. Although Germany entered the colonial picture late, she made up for this in zeal. The prospect of a South Seas empire to rival Britain's was hugely appealing, and there developed in the fatherland a popular agitation to take on new territories. At first Bismarck's government was cool to overseas expansion, but the merchants soon changed that.

As more and more Germans appeared in New Guinea, the realistically suspicious and blunt-speaking Australians warned London of German ambitions and urged annexation of New Guinea in the interest of Australian security. A Queensland official actually raised the British flag near Port Moresby in 1883, but London repudiated the action. Shortly after, while London and Berlin were exchanging polite disclaimers, the government-backed Neu Guinea Kompagnie raised the German flag over northeastern New Guinea and the Bismarck Archipelago. Howls of anger and disgust from Australia finally moved London to assert British sovereignty over southeastern New Guinea and adjacent islands, thereby completing the partitioning begun by the Dutch. From this time on the three parts of New Guinea, Dutch, German, and British, evolved along separate courses; but in one respect these courses led in the same direction, toward coconut economy, until after World War I, when the discovery of rich gold fields and the quest for oil opened new horizons.

Northeastern New Guinea

Included in the German territory were Kaiser-Wilhelmsland (northeastern New Guinea), Neu-Pommern (now New Britain), Neu-Mecklenburg (New Ireland), Neu-Hannover (Lavongai), and the Admiralty Islands. Later, by agreement with Britain, the northern Solomon Islands of Buka and Bougainville were added. Until 1899 administration was left in the hands of the chartered Neu Guinea Kompagnie; but the expense of exploration and governing, added to the usual costs of developing plantations, setting up trade stations, and maintaining interisland and overseas shipping, forced the company to hand over administration to the German Colonial Office. Earlier, an attempt was made to establish administrative headquarters for the whole territory on the main island, at Finschhaven and Madang, but malaria and isolation eventually induced the officials to locate at Rabaul, in the heart of the settled plantation area. From Rabaul the administrator also governed the German-owned Marshalls, Carolines, Marianas, and Nauru.

German explorers penetrated far into the interior of the main island, and missionaries fanned out along all the coasts, but planters and traders concentrated their efforts upon New Ireland and northern New Britain, and there they prospered. Enterprises controlled by large chartered companies predominated, but smaller independent planters and traders also shared in the increasing profits from copra and shell. When the supply of native labor thinned out, Javanese, Malayan, and Chinese coolies were imported. The firm-handed government protected natives from excessive abuses, but otherwise made it clear that New Guinea was a *colony*, to be utilized for economic and political profit, rather than a *trust*, to be administrated solely for native welfare.

Upon the outbreak of World War I, an Australian expeditionary force landed on New Britain and forced the Germans to capitulate after two days of skirmishes. Then, for seven years, the territory remained under military rule. The Australians were unprepared for the job and wisely maintained, with few changes, the laws and procedures of the Germans. They even permitted German planters and traders to carry on their enterprises under oaths of neutrality, so that commercial life went on as before. During this interim no real efforts were made to open up new areas or start new enterprises, since the legal status of New Guinea was too uncertain. In 1920 New Guinea was awarded to Australia as a Class C mandate, and a year later civil administration was inaugurated.

Some changes were made in the laws regulating acquisition of land and use of native labor, but the coconut economy continued to develop along lines that had been established in German days. Malays and Javanese were sent home, but most of the Chinese, who had meanwhile become artisans and small traders, remained. The German planters returned home and their estates were expropriated and sold; although an effort was made to distribute these estates among small holders, and particularly returned soldiers, the big companies (including Burns Philp and Carpenter's) eventually gained control of the largest share.

New Britain's coconut economy spread to the New Guinea mainland, and clusters of plantations grew up around Finschhaven, Madang, and Wewak. In time the area under coconut cultivation reached 265,000 acres, with annual exports averaging 70,000 tons, over half of which came from New Britain and New Ireland. World depression did not spare New Guinea's coconut industry and would have seriously crippled its administration (under Australian rule the Territory was forced to be financially self-sustaining) if the discovery of gold had not in the meantime uncovered another source of revenue. But that is another story,[3] a specialized chapter in the history of New Guinea; coconut economy continued to dominate the lives of most natives and whites. Within this setting there were three main forces active in transforming first-rate savages into third-rate subjects. These forces were plantation, missionary, and government, and the results were much the same as in the Solomons. The differences that did exist between the Solomons and New Guinea were mainly due to the latter's greater size and larger population. The more accessible populations of the Solomons were nearly all partially westernized, whereas the mountains and swamps of New Guinea still harbored tens of thousands of untaxed heathens.

Until World War II half of the total number of the Mandated Territory's 40,000 indentured native laborers worked on plantations, and the turnover was great, especially at the end of the standard three-year term of contract. It can be estimated, therefore, that a large proportion of the total population worked for white planters at some period of their lives, and the effects of this contact were like those in the Solomons: village life became disrupted by long absences of the young males; money began to supersede native systems of exchange; and the tribal authority underwent reorientation.

The eleven missionary societies active in the Territory claimed over 300,000 converts, with annual additions averaging 20,000. Here, as in the Solomons, missionaries launched direct attacks upon the "heathen" aspects of native life, and frequently upon the doctrines preached

[3] See Chapter XVII.

by rival missions. If the extent of their success were to be measured by the numbers of village churches, memorized catechisms, schools, and sanitary reforms, then missionaries should be credited with many tactical victories. But it is most unlikely that they succeeded in changing many basic institutions or attitudes toward the supernatural.

Government, the third factor of change, was a very large enterprise in the Territory. It sought to regulate relations between white and native, to improve native economy, and to bring all of the islanders under "control." It directly employed about 1700 natives in this administrative work and through taxation, patrols, policing, courts of justice, and medical service, affected to some extent most native lives. It was staffed by men specially trained for the work and dedicated to the objectives of the mandate. It did, of course, wipe out such customs as feuding and head-hunting and, through its procedure of appointing native village officials, institutionalized and concentrated chieftainship far more than the native cultures did.

These three agencies of change did not constitute the whole story. Many thousands of natives were employed as stevedores, truck drivers, boat crews, domestics, and so forth, and these workers probably more than plantation laborers received close views of white civilization. Most finish-time laborers carried their impressions back to their villages, but more and more of them tended to remain at the white settlements, to become "detribalized," and to work as casual day laborers, thereby earning higher wages and retaining their full freedom. Some New Guinea laborers even indulged in a strike, which had rather paralyzing effects upon the white community. (So far had they become civilized within a few decades!) But in this case the white planters and businessmen quickly made it clear that, mandate or no mandate, white men were masters and commerce supreme. And, in this rich Territory, the commercial future seemed so promising and white masters so numerous that, regardless of published policy, events were moving toward a white man's empire in a brown man's setting. Meanwhile Papua, with its fewer resources, followed a slightly different course.

Southeastern New Guinea

The prewar history of the Territory of Papua, comprising the southeastern corner of New Guinea, falls properly into two periods: from 1884 until 1906 it was administered by agents of the British Colonial Office; since 1907 its administration has been carried out by Australia.

During the first period Papua (or, as it was then called, British New Guinea) did not keep pace with the agricultural and commercial developments pushed by the Germans in the neighboring territory. In fact, European plantations were almost nonexistent; and except for some trading, European economic activity was limited to prospecting for gold. Scores of adventurers underwent epic hardships to find gold, and some of them succeeded; but a permanent industry failed to materialize because, as one prospector said: "There's plenty of gold in Papua; but there's too much of Papua mixed in with it."

The main preoccupation of the administration was exploration and pacification of "wild tribes"—quite the reverse of the German policy, which was to develop a prosperous and comfortable coastal colony before opening up inland areas.

The second period was characterized by the encouragement of white settlement and the evolution of a definite native policy. Throughout this period Papua had the extreme good fortune of having an administrator of exceptional enlightenment; Sir Hubert Murray and his staff conceived of their task as a balanced course of action between the development of natural resources and the trusteeship of native welfare. Toward the first objective they inaugurated a liberal land policy to encourage "persons of means" to settle in Papua and start plantations. Individual adventurers and large speculator syndicates were not admitted, but substantial individuals and companies were welcomed. There was a minor real-estate rush for a while, but it petered out when it was learned how infertile most of Papua actually is. By World War I over thirty thousand acres had been planted in coconuts, but the trees did not mature in time to enjoy the wartime boom in copra prices, as was the case with the older plantations in the neighboring territory. By the time Papuan copra was ready to begin exporting, the prices were low again. Also, the Australian Navigation Act abolished competitive marketing by restricting Papua's trade outlet to Australian ports alone, which in fact meant only one vessel a month, to Sydney. Later the shipping situation improved, but world depression moved in to keep Papua poor.

Meanwhile thousands of acres of Pará rubber trees were planted and proved well suited to Papua's soil, climate, and type of labor; but the industry suffered from the same economic pains as copra, and not until the late thirties did prospects begin to improve.

Discouraging as this was to the planters, it may have been a blessing in disguise for the native population. Freed from pressures to secure land and laborers for white enterprise, the government was able to follow an evolutionary program of native acculturation. Exploration went on apace, and new areas were placed under control. Natives were taxed, according to their ability to pay, and all tax revenue was set aside for native education and medical welfare. And, although the administration favored having natives work for short periods in white enterprises, no pressure was exerted to make them do so, either by official encouragement or by preferential tax treatment. The administration even advanced to the near-heretical position (according to colonial standards) of assisting natives to set up their own income enterprises in order to guard against their becoming detribalized and disinherited wage-laborers.

Government revenue in Papua was limited by the poverty of the territory and the ridiculously small Australian subsidy (£30,000 to £50,000 annually), so that missions were encouraged to maintain native schools. And in this connection, to anyone coming from northeastern New Guinea and its inter-mission rivalries or mission-planter-government squabbles, the equivalent Papuan relationships seemed harmony itself. For one thing, mission areas did not seriously overlap. Also, the administration regarded evangelization as an essential substitute for the native religions which were said to be disappearing.

The effect of all these circumstances was that the natives of Papua were transformed just as surely as those of the Mandated Territory of New Guinea, but the changes were administered in small doses and the patients' survival seemed better assured.

NEW HEBRIDES

Between the Solomons, New Caledonia, and Fiji lies the cluster of islands, reefs, shoals, and live volcanoes which Captain Cook, with singular inappropriateness, named the New Hebrides. To a confusion of topography, vegetation, and native peoples, white man has added his destructive genius, so that the archipelago now stands unchallenged as one of the unhealthiest, wildest, most mistreated, and most mismanaged spots on earth. According to his tastes, today's visitor may squat down in a jungle hut, eat grubs, and watch cannibals plan man hunts, or, a few miles away, he may dine elegantly and swap international gossip with urbane officials. And whatever else it proves, the New Hebrides story beautifully demonstrates how successfully white men can exterminate native peoples.

Central in the archipelago are Espíritu Santo and Malekula, large, mountainous, heavily forested, and inaccessible. Near-by is tame Efate, with grassland plateaus and charming garden areas. Lopevi Island is an active volcano, Aore a vast coconut grove, Aneityum a valuable timberland. Dangerous reefs and mangrove swamps, insects and parasites, all combine to give these islands an unhealthy reputation. Malaria and blackwater fever have proved particularly vicious for whites, and natives suffer more than the usual quota of yaws, leprosy, and tuberculosis.

New Hebrides natives are like those of the Solomons: dark skinned, prognathous, and woolly haired, except in the eastern islands, where the Polynesian element is noticeable. As elsewhere in Melanesia, linguistic and cultural differences are exceedingly great from island to island and even from community to community.

An outstanding feature of many New Hebrides cultures is the elaboration of secret cultism. Throughout most of Melanesia men are preoccupied with pigs—with breeding, trading, accumulating, and distributing them for profit or prestige; but this has become even more intensified and formalized in the central New Hebrides. Size of tusks rather than size of pigs is what counts, the object being to train the boars' lower incisors around until they form circles which eventually become prized ornamental bracelets. Social status depends upon a man's progress through a series of masoniclike grades, with promotion based on accumulation and distribution of pigs. But before youths are allowed even to embark on this social climb, they are subjected to arduous and bloody initiation rites. Nor is the status merely honorific; each grade marks a further release from taboos and food restrictions which burden the lives of the uninitiated.

Some ethnologists have drawn attention to Polynesian religious elements in these Melanesian cultures, particularly to myths and rituals associated with the New Hebridean equivalent of the Polynesian god, Tangaroa. It would have been rather surprising if some stray canoeloads of Polynesians, sailing with the southeast trades, had not reached these shores. But nothing that the Polynesians brought or did could have prepared natives for the visitation of still lighter-skinned travelers from the east and south.

Quirós started the procession in 1606; but then Providence and poor navigation spared the islands further visits for 160 years, after which Bougainville, Cook, Bligh, La Pérouse, and D'Entrecasteaux came in quick succession. All met trouble, even the usually mild Cook. La Pérouse's entire party was lost and probably eaten; not until later did the natives learn to dislike the saltiness of white flesh.

After these visitations there were three decades of peace, until 1828, when traders and whalers came ashore seeking refreshment and sandalwood. The southern islands were hardest hit, but none was completely spared. For a period, cheap trade goods—red calico, axes, knives, beads, tobacco—brought in the sandalwood; and some vessels took along their own logging crews of Polynesians, who succumbed to fevers in droves. Then there followed the inevitable clashes between traders and natives, with the usual results: the traders had the guns. When the sandalwood became scarce and natives reluctant, persuasion was used—kidnapping, village destruction, and murder. White-introduced diseases were even more devastating than guns and alcohol, and many communities were literally wiped out. Here are a few samples:[4]

—In 1842 a British vessel landed Tongans on Erro-

[4] From Harrison, *Savage Civilization*.

mango to cut sandalwood. The arrogant Polynesians soon picked a fight with natives, killed sixty of them by gunfire, drove the survivors, including women and children, into caves, built bonfires in the entrances, and roasted the lot. Then the vessel was loaded with sandalwood—no troublesome owners to barter with!—and sailed to another unsuspecting island.

—In 1861 one schooner deliberately landed some measles-infected Tanna Islanders on Erromango, promptly causing the death of one third of the population.

—A favorite trick was to capture a chief and hold him as hostage until his people ransomed him with sandalwood. Then, instead of releasing the man, he would be traded as cannibal fare to another island for more sandalwood.

Sometimes, after natives had supplied wood to a trader, he would shoot a few of them and burn their houses, to discourage competitors from calling there in the future. This stratagem, together with others applied less deliberately, soon caused the natives to suspect that traders and whalers were not the reincarnated Sailing Gods they had originally thought, and following this disillusionment the murdering became a two-sided affair.

Into this turmoil moved the missionaries. The London Missionary Society was the first to arrive. Ubiquitous John Williams, the pioneer missionary in Polynesia, turned to the New Hebrides in 1839 and quickly secured martyrdom by walking about unarmed on Tanna Island, where natives had become justifiably dubious about white men's motives. Williams' murder did not, however, weaken the courage of his colleagues, who continued their good work by depositing ashore several mission teachers—native Samoan mission teachers, that is! Other martyrdoms followed, Polynesian ones this time, but a little evangelical progress was made.

A case on Efate was typical. A Reverend Murray landed several Polynesian teachers there in 1853 and rejoiced: "When we took the teachers on shore to introduce them to this most inviting sphere, the joy of the people seemed to know no bounds."[5] Nineteen days after Murray left, the teachers were all murdered. But, nothing daunted, the missionaries tried Efate again in 1854; result: four teachers and their families eaten, one dead of fever, another of dysentery.

The Presbyterians, who next entered the field, were sufficiently tough in body and determined in will to survive the black savagery they ministered to as well as the white savagery they fought. For, not the least of their troubles stemmed from traders who were shrewd enough to foresee the curtailment of "free trade" in a missionized area.

With diminishing sandalwood supplies and fewer traders, the missionaries might have prevailed and brought some order into this chaos, had it not been for the blackbirders, who beat the traders at their own game. That sordid history has already been told: how Melanesians were recruited to man the plantations of Fiji and Queensland; how the commerce became so appallingly ruthless that British warships had to patrol the islands to capture the blackbirders and pacify their victims. No area suffered this evil so intensely or so long as the New Hebrides. Thousands and thousands of men were abducted, forcibly or by false promises, and held for years on foreign plantations without redress. Those who managed to return brought back with them diseases, muskets, a taste for liquor, and a cold hatred of whites. The diseases did their trick, and the muskets added efficiency to tribal warfare; furthermore, obliging traders saw to it that ammunition supplies were replenished.

This state of affairs—blackbirding and, before that, sandalwooding—prevailed in the New Hebrides for two thirds of a century, and throughout most of this frightful

[5] Harrison, *Savage Civilization*, p. 151.

era the only good whites the natives knew were a handful of missionaries.

Toward the end of the era French and British planters arrived on the scene. Large areas were cleared, and coconuts, coffee, and cocoa were planted. New Caledonia capitalists invested in enterprises and encouraged French settlement. For a time it appeared that France might annex the islands, but Britain intervened and, anxious to keep other powers out but unwilling to assume responsibility herself, compromised to the extent of joining France in setting up a joint naval commission to safeguard the interests of their nationals. This farcical measure was undertaken in 1887; it proved so unworkable that twenty years later it was replaced by an Anglo-French condominium administration, a slightly more workable, much more elaborate, and distinctly more entertaining system. It "works" like this:

There is a British Commissioner and his staff charged with safeguarding the interests and curbing the delinquencies of all British subjects, and a corresponding set of officials for the French. Each government maintains its own courts, police force, prisons, currency, weights and measures, and sundry regulations. In addition, there is a joint condominium staff, in control of customs revenue, radio-telegraph, and certain phases of justice. The jurisdiction of the Joint Court is mainly limited to questions of land ownership, to cases referred to it by mutual consent of the parties, and to offenses involving natives. The first Judge President, who presided over French and British national judges, was, according to the terms of the treaty, appointed to his office by the King of Spain. He was truly neutral, having understood little French, less English, and no Melanesian; but this was no additional handicap, because he was also deaf.

Along with such comedy, the condominium also had its tragic side. France looked after Frenchmen and Britain after British, but only the politically impotent missionaries looked after the forty thousand natives who had managed to survive a century of white conquest. There are native regulations aplenty, and pages of legal safeguards protecting black and brown from white, but the machinery to enforce these measures was ridiculously inadequate and the loopholes miles wide.

Out of this mess French nationals and French influence emerged dominant. The British regime imposed the usual restrictions upon its own nationals, regulating carefully their alienation of land and use of native labor. The French regime, on the other hand, consistently supported French colonization by laws favoring expansion of plantations. French, but not British, were permitted to import indentured Asiatic laborers, and many thousands of Tonkinese helped the French to survive and prosper, while their British neighbors failed because of dependence upon reluctant native workers. Also, the French government supported its nationals financially when hurricane devastation or price declines threatened failure. The result was that just prior to World War II there were 750 French and only 200 British in the islands, many British subjects having given up and left or become naturalized Frenchmen.

For the native it was not quite so simple; he could not become a Frenchman. On the other hand, he could have become a Protestant and wear a shirt, or he could have become a Catholic. In fact, the missions appear to have been the only effective champions of native welfare in the New Hebrides. Missionaries have undoubtedly proceeded with their conversions in manners culturally ruthless enough to make pedantic anthropologists shudder, but they at least helped to keep the patients alive. Some students, working through archaeology and early accounts, believe the pre-European population of the New Hebrides to have been near one million. That is probably far too high an estimate; but there were certainly many more New Hebrideans then than the forty thousand of

1939. The missions alone have consistently fought the causes of this decline—murders, kidnapping, muskets, disease, and alcohol—and should therefore be forgiven their internal squabbles and their bigoted iconoclastic attacks on native institutions.

The effects of all these decades of white conquest—economic, political, and spiritual—were to produce a cultural crazy quilt. By 1939, cannibals still held out on Santo and Malekula, while a neighboring island was inhabited entirely by beskirted, pidgin-speaking, hymn-singing native copra producers. Throughout the archipelago there were few natives who had not seen and experienced white man's culture; many of them had mastered it to their own satisfactions and led "civilized" lives. On the other hand, there were many others who had spent years on plantations or wharves or schooners and, not liking what they saw, had returned to their jungle huts to live as they had before.

XV

SUGAR REVOLUTION

The "honey-bearing reed" was merely another souvenir of the fabulous East when Alexander brought some specimens home from India in 325 B.C., but as mankind's sweet tooth developed through the centuries, sugar cane became a factor in international politics and even shaped the course of history in several small nations as well as in three Pacific archipelagoes.

In the period immediately before 1939, world consumption of sugar (raw sugar value) averaged over thirty million short tons annually, and about 60 per cent of this derived from sugar cane. Some sugar is used for manufacturing industrial alcohol, but it is principally a food, and probably the least expensive of all foods in terms of its cost per calorie.

Sugar passes through five processes before it reaches the consumer in white granulated or powdered form.

Initially, juice is extracted by crushing the cane and passing it through rollers pressed together by powerful hy-
draulic rams. The juice is then clarified by heating and
liming; and the clear liquid is subjected to vaporizing to
remove excess water. From the resulting thick syrup, raw
sugar is crystallized and dried in centrifugal machines.
Processing up to this point usually takes place at the
locations where sugar cane is grown; the actual refining
of the raw sugar into the final product nearly always is
done in refineries near the consumers' market.

Sugar is universally such an important item, in peace
and in war, that most nations strive for self-sufficiency in
it by subsidizing domestic production and by raising
tariff barriers. The international sugar picture is further
complicated by the competition between sugar cane,
produced in faraway cheap labor areas, and beet sugar,
costing more to produce but grown in the strategically
safer areas nearer consumption centers.

Australia's sugar, for local consumption and shipment
to the United Kingdom and Canada, is produced in
Queensland. In the early days islanders were imported
for labor in the cane fields, but since 1902 the industry
has had to depend upon white workers and has had no
special direct influence upon the lives of native Oceanic
peoples.

Elsewhere in Oceania, however, in the Hawaiian, Fijian, and Mariana Islands, sugar has been the greatest
single factor for change. In each of these groups the industry has been economically linked to the parent power:
Hawaii with the United States, Fiji with parts of the
British Empire, and the Marianas with Japan. Also, in
each case, sugar has been the dominant factor in island
economy and has brought about radical population
changes.

The effects of sugar on island life have been quite different from those of copra. For one thing, sugar growing
in the islands has developed by means of tightly inte-

grated mass-production methods. Even within each protected national sphere, prices have been highly competitive, and profitable operation has depended upon installation of expensive machinery kept in continuous use to reduce unit costs. All this involves centralized control, large capital resources, and assured access to very extensive cane plantings. Under such conditions it has not been economically practicable to produce cane, like copra, in small scattered plantations. The islander can trade a few coconuts to a Chinese trader, and copra from those coconuts is as marketable as copra from a huge plantation; but cane is another matter. Before it can become a valuable, transportable commodity it requires processing, and it is estimated that a modern sugar mill cannot operate profitably on plantation units of less than ten thousand acres. How different from the Gilbertese coconut grove, or even the isolated 500-acre coconut grove of some white planter, for that matter.

From the outset, then, the island sugar industries have involved resources and management skills beyond the capacities of islanders. Nor have islanders participated even as laborers; they showed little inclination for the monotonous, sustained work of cultivating and cutting cane. Planters had to go outside Oceania altogether for workers. Under these circumstances scores of thousands of Asiatics were imported, and through the tens of thousands who remained as residents many islands lost nearly all semblance to the Oceania of the palm tree and outrigger canoe.

HAWAII

From Captain Cook to Pearl Harbor Day, "progress" in Hawaii consisted mainly in the substitution of one form of autocracy for another. Economically, taro and fish were replaced by sugar, pineapples, and beef; politically, a hereditary ruling caste of sturdy brown-skinned warrior chiefs was supplanted by a semihereditary ruling caste of white-skinned bankers and traders. During this era of transformation some new lands were opened up, and some old lands were abandoned. Although the population altered radically in racial composition, numerically it increased by only one third: an increase which might well have taken place in time under the old native order, quite without benefit of clergy, mass immigration, industrial paternalism, or medical science.

Anthropologists consider that native Hawaiian culture was derived from a series of migrations of Polynesian-speaking peoples from central Polynesia, beginning about eighteen hundred years ago. During the eleventh and twelfth centuries there may have been other migrants from Polynesia, and then this contact ceased and Hawaiian native culture developed in relative isolation until visited by Captain Cook in 1778.

Cook discovered a population of about 300,000 large and well-proportioned people, living in villages at or near the shore, subsisting mainly on taro and fish, and organized into large tribal units under the rule of warrior chieftains.

The basic type of Polynesian culture has already been described, but it might be well to recapitulate. The society was characterized by large extended-family units and strong parental authority, by descent and family membership reckoned bilaterally. Individuals usually found their marriage mates outside the family unit, but were not limited in choice by rules of kinship group exogamy. Leadership in the family and in the larger tribal units was hereditary and based mainly upon primogeniture. Religion was centered around reverence toward deities personifying natural phenomena (including rain, sun, heaven, and volcanoes) and around the concepts of *mana* and *tabu*. Technology remained at the level of stone and shell implements, and economy rarely progressed beyond subsistence needs: dependence upon taro, breadfruit, yams, pandanus, fish, fowl, and pigs.

All these elements were fundamental to most Polynesian cultures, but in Hawaii the leadership system became hypertrophied, and three distinct castes developed. At the top were the *alii*, or nobles, represented by tradition as having immigrated hence from central Polynesia during the eleventh and twelfth centuries, and as having introduced the more advanced elements in the culture. As a group these *alii* were possessed of unusual *kapu* (*tabu*), which served to enforce their superior status. The mass of commoners (*makaainana*, "dwellers on the land") were devoid of *kapu*. Below these commoners was a smaller caste of pariahs and slaves (*kauwa*), possessed not with the *kapu* of sacredness of the nobles but with the *kapu* of defilement, somewhat similar to the untouchables of India.

Among the nobles there were degrees of *kapu*, based upon genealogy and primogeniture and upon function. Each island or part of a large island was ruled by a monarch (*moi*), who was regarded as a god incarnate, and who possessed supreme *kapu*. So refined did this concept become that monarchs would occasionally marry their own sisters in order to maintain purity of descent, and as late as 1840 this practice persisted.

The monarch, assisted by advisers and by priests, was absolute leader in peace and war as well as in religious rites, and he was proprietor of all land in his domain. Hierarchical relationships were sustained by *kapu* and were periodically intensified by levies of tribute in the forms of food and other materials and of warriors for the frequent intertribal wars.

Shortly after Cook's visit one tribal monarch, Kamehameha, succeeded by conquest and threat of conquest in subduing all the Hawaiian Islands and uniting them under his rule. But white-introduced diseases and practices were beginning to make inroads in the native population and institutions, so that the high point in native culture was almost immediately followed by a precipitous decline. For several decades, however, the shell of the monarchy was retained. Prior to its overthrow in 1893 by a faction of Euro-American planters and traders, the Hawaiian monarchy adopted all the manners and regalia of a European court, with a hideous Victorian palace, privy counselors, and royal debts running into hundreds of thousands of dollars.

Before the white man landed, the Hawaiian Islands supported a population of a third of a million people. Early white voyagers remarked at the industry and ingenuity with which the Hawaiians had laid out their extensive cultivations and irrigated them with water led in through large aqueducts and ditches. In hundreds of man-made fishponds mullet were impounded and propagated, and this source of food was supplemented by lagoon and deep-sea fishing.

What a different picture in 1939! Some entire islands and large portions of other islands which were once populated and intensively cultivated had been abandoned or given over to cattle and goats. The few taro patches remaining were being cultivated by Orientals producing for plantations or for Honolulu markets. Forests had been cleaned out of all sandalwood. Fishponds were nearly all gone; those remaining bred more mosquitoes than mullet. Lagoon fishing had become a sport indulged in by Japanese workers on their days off. Deep-sea fishing was carried out by professional Japanese fishermen in their foul-smelling little sampans, but hardly enough fish were caught to provide *hors d'oeuvres* for Honolulu's appetite.

Instead of dwelling comfortably spread out in villages situated at picturesque spots along the coast, Hawaii's 1939 population was cramped together in large urban and plantation settlements; Honolulu alone contained nearly 40 per cent of the population.

There was, to be sure, another side to this picture. Tens of thousands of acres barely used in ancient times were producing sugar and pineapples and cattle; and, through stupendous feats of irrigation engineering, whole plateaus had been transformed from wasteland into some of the most valuable agricultural land in the world.

Even more striking than the transformation of the land was the change in composition of the population and in content of the culture. In place of the estimated one third of a million native Polynesians living there in Cook's time, Hawaii's 1939 population included some 156,000 Japanese, 115,000 "Caucasians," 100,000 Filipinos, 50,000 part-Hawaiians, 28,000 Chinese, 6000 Koreans, and only 14,000 "pure" Hawaiians.[1] And instead of semifeudal native super-tribes, the Hawaii of 1939 was a thoroughly westernized community dominated by a small group of Euro-American businessmen who controlled nearly all the productive enterprises of the islands. The bulk of island industries and business, comprising most of the resources and 75 per cent of all wage earners, were integrated under the control of a handful of local white businessmen. Government was also an important employer, but aside from engaging in public construction works (two thirds of all construction carried out in the Territory) and in national defense, most government employees entered into the islands' economic life only as consumers. In addition, there were many small enterprises which provided livelihood for several hundred inhabitants; and a few mainland firms had succeeded in establishing branches there, but only in the face of tough opposition from local big business.

Almost daily, editorials in the local newspapers commented upon the happy state of interracial relations, and for such a complex racial conglomeration there was in fact a surprisingly small amount of racial antagonism. There was, nevertheless, a distinct class system along ethnic lines in spite of a large number of interracial mar-

[1] These are approximations based on the Federal census figures for 1940.

riages. Whites comprised the upper class, and white-Hawaiian mixtures came next. Then followed Chinese, Japanese, Filipinos, and Puerto Ricans, in about that order. Hawaiians and Portuguese were usually classified according to economic status and were distributed among all but the highest and lowest classes.

Several factors led to this complete transformation of Hawaii from a Polynesian super-tribe.

Hawaii's strategic central position was from the very beginning a factor inviting change. Ships en route to the Far East and the Antipodes, or ships whaling throughout the Pacific, dropped anchor in her safe harbors, restocked with water and provisions, traded for sandalwood, took on fresh crews of Polynesians, and tarried while weary ships' companies caroused ashore and recuperated in the mild climate. In increasing numbers sailors and traders left their ships and settled in the islands. Hawaii also soon attracted the attention of strategy-minded admirals and statesmen, and men-of-war paid frequent visits.

As a result of all these contacts, natives acquired new diseases and appetites for new gadgets and ideas. Iron of any kind was clamorously welcomed; textiles, implements, tobacco, and rum were traded for fruit, vegetables, pork, and fish. Through the maladies of civilization—syphilis, smallpox, and the rest of the awful inventory—the native population was reduced by over one half within fifty years of Cook's visit.

Before a single missionary had set foot on Hawaii, the native institutions and symbols already had been profoundly altered by contact with whites. The *kapu* concept was officially disavowed by a native monarch in 1819; and, to show contempt for their customary beliefs, Hawaiians destroyed their own idols and flaunted many of their strictest conventions. Ironically, it was the native nobility, who lost most in power and prestige by the action, who took the initiative in these iconoclasms.

Sweet-smelling sandalwood, highly valued in China for incense and fine cabinet work, was discovered in Hawaii by whites in 1790, and by 1805 there had developed around it a serious commerce. For the next twenty-five years in Hawaiian history, until the forests were cleaned of sandalwood, the avaricious trade for this commodity brought to the islands a vast quantity of trade goods, from beads to billiard tables and complete sailing vessels.

Yankee merchants were paramount in the trade. They bartered for the wood in goods or dollars and then shipped it to China to exchange for Oriental goods for the American market. (Measure in sandalwood was reckoned in piculs [133⅓ lb.], worth on an average ten dollars per picul.) When the native monarch Kamehameha learned the value of this produce of his forests, he monopolized the trade to provide revenue for his court. To collect wood for bartering with white traders, the monarch simply directed all able-bodied subjects to scour the forests and cut specified quotas of wood for deposit in the royal warehouses. As the wood became scarcer and the ruler's appetite greater, Hawaiians spent more and more time at this labor, remaining away from home for long periods while they searched through the remote mountain forests. Garden work had to be neglected and near-famine resulted; the Hawaiians were further weakened by continual exposure to the cold mountain rains.

Kamehameha's successor relinquished the royal monopoly in the sandalwood trade by permitting his subordinate chiefs to deal directly with white traders; but this move proved even more disastrous than had the previous monopoly control, for the shrewd Yankee traders soon initiated the naïve and greedy chieftains into the mysteries of the promissory note, and the levies of sandalwood upon the commoners increased with the demands of the white creditors. At one point American warships visited the islands to enforce the debt payments and "protect American Commerce." The commitment of the monarch to undertake to pay this debt, which amounted to about $200,000, constituted the first Hawaiian national debt and therewith introduced the kingdom into the company of civilized states. Still further levies were made upon commoners for sandalwood, and the supply was all but wiped out by 1830.

After the peak of sandalwood trade there began the era of whaling-ship visits, which continued for several decades and led to the establishment of a number of large, white-owned mercantile firms supplying vessels with local and imported goods. Commercial centers like Honolulu, Hilo, and Lahaina attracted increasing numbers of Hawaiians, and contact with whaling men further hastened the disintegration of native community life.

The missionaries, who began arriving in 1820, changed somewhat the direction of this decline by introducing modes of life better calculated to produce social, economic, and moral stability as conceived by sober New England standards. Boston missionaries succeeded in Protestantizing most of the Hawaiians and were particularly influential among the nobility. Most of the pioneer missionaries remained at their labors, but a few turned to agriculture and commerce or entered the service of the native monarchs, thus helping in a very large measure to shape the islands' economy and policy; their descendants constituted the most influential group in the 1939 community.

Sugar succeeded the procession of whaling vessels as the most important factor in the transformation of Hawaiian lands and population and culture. When Europeans first visited the Hawaiian Islands, they saw small patches of sugar cane growing near native dwellings, possibly serving as windbreaks for gardens. How long ago sugar cane was introduced into these islands no one knows; the probability is that it was brought by one of the migrant groups of Polynesian ancestors of the Hawaiians, for cane is believed to have originated in southern Asia whence came the ancestors and most of the material possessions of the Pacific Islanders. In Hawaii as elsewhere in Oceania natives chewed cane for its sweetness but did not extract the juice in any other manner.

As early as 1802 a Chinese immigrant set up a simple stone mill in Hawaii and turned out loaf sugar in small quantities, but his enterprise lasted for only a year. Not until 1835 did sugar production become established on a commercial scale; during the intervening years most Hawaiians and foreigners were too preoccupied with gathering and selling sandalwood and supplying the needs of visiting fur traders and whalers. Beginning in 1835, more and more acres were converted to cane growing, owing mainly to the efforts of a few American and British settlers who foresaw the eventual need for placing island economy on a firm agricultural basis. The new industry went ahead very falteringly at first, but eventually became the leading wealth-producing enterprise in all Oceania. Progress in the internal development of the industry was marked by the establishment of land-tenure reforms, by procurement of adequate capital, by technical advances in cane growing and sugar extraction, improvement of cane varieties, introduction of irrigation, control of harmful insects, and importation of labor, and by rationalization of the industry into a large-scale, mass-production organization.

White men, mainly Americans and Britishers, pioneered the industry and have always controlled its operations and owned most of its assets. On a few occasions native rulers made ineffective attempts to participate, but for the most part Hawaiians neither shared in the ownership nor served as workers in the industry.

The native system of land tenure was one major obstacle to the sugar industry, as it was, in fact, to all forms of capitalistic enterprise. As elsewhere in Polynesia, land tenure in Hawaii followed tribal, communal, and patriarchal lines, but possessed distinctive "feudal" features reflecting Hawaii's heavy emphasis upon the authority and prerogatives of chieftainship. These islands were divided into several large tribes, generally two or three to an island, each led by a paramount chief; and "ownership" of all land in a tribal area was vested in the paramount chief. Chiefs apportioned their holdings to subchiefs, who in turn reallotted subdivisions among their dependents, and so on down to the native farmer tenant. Theoretically, upon the death of a subject, or at the pleasure of the tribal chief, the subject's allotment of land was redistributed by the chief; but, in fact, generation-long identification of a family or a subchief with a plot or a district was tantamount to ownership and was usually thus recognized in redistribution. Following upon the death of a tribal chief, his successor usually reallotted residual titles among his subchiefs and managed thereby to secure his authority by rewarding loyalty.

Intertribal warfare was common, and a victorious chief took control of his foe's tribal land, setting aside some of it for his personal use and allotting some of it to his followers, but confirming the tenancy of most of the defeated commoners and subchiefs.

Tenants were not bound to the land; they were free to move from the domain of one chief to that of another, but once established they were obligated to pay fealty in the form of produce and service. Commoners' privileges extended to use of their chief's forests and waters for building materials and fishing.

The semifeudal character of Hawaiian land tenure was accentuated by the campaigns of Kamehameha. After conquering all his rivals, he redistributed their holdings among his subjects, but reclaimed large areas for his direct personal use. The residual ownership of all land by this native king, coupled with the practice of permitting no alienation of it, actually led to some evictions and to oppressive tributes in produce and service; but the system was merely an elaboration of the traditional pattern, and most Hawaiians meekly accepted it. Much more scandalized by the system were the foreigners, who cherished the concept of fee simple ownership. Early missionaries characterized the native system as a monstrous violation of individual rights and spread their dissatisfaction among their native flocks. Foreign businessmen objected to the system for more practical reasons: their hopes for building fortunes for themselves were tempered by the realization that they could not own outright the land in which they invested money and energy. Sugar planters were particularly affected, and they began a co-ordinated campaign to force "reforms."

Missionary, trader, and planter exerted so much pressure upon Kamehameha III that he agreed to revolutionary changes. He forthwith surrendered his feudal rights to all the land and retained only certain portions for his private use, while other portions were allotted to his government. The remainder was divided among chiefs, commoners, and those foreigners who had previously received land grants; and all this land was thereafter held in fee simple. With outright ownership now possible, sugar planters confidently expanded their enterprises, and, as was to be expected, they proceeded to buy from the Hawaiians most of the desirable agricultural land in the islands.

Cane matures slowly in Hawaii, and a plantation requires a very large financial investment. Outside capital was needed to bring about any real expansion, and it was not until the land reforms had been passed that foreign investors, mostly Americans, were attracted. The industry received another financial fillip as a result of the higher prices paid for sugar during the Civil War;

but the most significant increase in capital investment came about after 1876, when a treaty of reciprocity was signed between Hawaii and the United States, admitting the products of each country duty-free into the other and thereby assuring a favorable and expanding market for Hawaiian sugar. Annexation of Hawaii by the United States in 1898 stimulated an even greater movement of American capital into the Hawaiian sugar industry and consummated American domination over the industry. After that the industry itself built up reserves sufficient to finance its own expansion.

Technical improvements in cane growing and sugar extraction placed the Hawaiian industry ahead of all competitors in operational efficiency. The local planters were quick to substitute ox-drawn for steam-driven vehicles to pull the massive plows required, and enormous sums of money were spent on developing mechanical means of harvesting cane. The local mills were also transformed into models of mass-production efficiency.

The cane found growing in Hawaii by the first white settlers was hardy and immune to endemic plant diseases but not very sweet or highly productive, so it was supplanted by a sweeter variety imported from Tahiti in the middle of the last century. This newcomer, named the "Lahaina" variety, remained the mainstay of the industry until early in this century, when it, and the industry along with it, almost succumbed to a root-rot disease. The day was saved by the development of better varieties resistant to the disease and high in sugar content. Meanwhile Hawaiian botanists continued their worldwide explorations and intensive experiments in search of cane varieties that would combine the desirable characteristics of high sugar content, quantity production, quick growth, brittleness (for ease in harvesting), and resistance to weather, insects, and disease.

Cane requires great quantities of sunshine and water. Hawaii has both, but less than half the good cane-growing lands are so located that they receive sufficient rainfall; hence irrigation is required. The amount of irrigation needed is indicated by the fact that about four thousand tons of water are required to grow enough cane for one ton of sugar. Some plantation irrigation systems derive water via ditches, tunnels, and aqueducts from rain-soaked mountain areas; other plantations are supplied from artesian wells. These irrigation projects are quite stupendous. One ditch carries 60,000,000 gallons of water daily, through a tunnel six miles long. The artesian wells and gravity systems on another plantation supply 300,000,000 gallons a day—over four times the amount daily used in prewar San Francisco.

Hawaiian sugar planters have had to maintain a constant vigil to keep out harmful insects. As new and better cane varieties have been introduced into these islands, the pests that retarded their growth were left behind; but at the same time there were left behind the natural enemies of these pests—the "fleas on the fleas" that kept the pests in check—so that when harmful insects did slip past quarantine they multiplied unchecked and ravaged the crops. Early in this century an infestation of leaf hoppers destroyed thousands of acres of cane, and was only finally checked when small egg-killing parasites were brought in from Australia. Another devastating pest was the cane borer, which was finally controlled by the tachina fly, brought from New Guinea by industry entomologists.

Probably the most vexing of all problems which faced the Hawaiian sugar industry was the maintenance of an adequate labor supply. It was just as serious in 1939 as it was in 1839. Cane growing requires large numbers of hand laborers. The industry had progressed far past its primitive beginnings when everything was done by hand, even including native-drawn plows; but some processes like weeding and harvesting had not yet advanced beyond dependence upon hand labor, and in

1939 the plantations still employed about 45,000 workers.

While the industry was in its infancy it was almost wholly dependent upon native Hawaiian workers, but it would never have grown past infancy if other labor had not been found. The native Polynesian population, estimated at about 300,000 at the time of Captain Cook's first visit in 1778, had decreased to about 70,000 by 1853. Only a few thousand of these people were willing to work on plantations; earlier, many of them had been released by their chiefs to work on white men's plantations located on land leased from the chiefs, but even the volunteers were not ideal workers. Their way of life had not prepared them for the steady grind of plantation work, and their physical survival did not depend upon wage earning.

Various projects were undertaken to make up for these deficiencies. First, there were attempts to reverse the population trend and to introduce incentive systems involving a piecework wage scale. Then, attempts were made to bring in other Pacific Islanders as plantation workers, the argument having been that these racial relatives of the Hawaiians would become quickly acclimated and would blend easily with the local islanders; but only some 2500 Gilbertese immigrated, and when they too turned out to be unsuited for plantation work, the plan was given up.

Chinese coolies, mostly from the vicinity of Canton, were the first laborers to be imported in numbers. Beginning in 1852 and continuing until the Exclusion Act was called into effect by annexation in 1898, about 46,-000 Chinese immigrated to Hawaii. Most of them eventually left the plantations and either returned home upon completion of their contracts or remained in the islands and established enterprises of their own, including the production of taro and truck crops and the management of stores and restaurants.

From 1878 to 1913 about 17,500 Portuguese immigrated to Hawaii, mostly from the Azores and Madeira Islands. Some of those who stayed in Hawaii upon completion of their contract terms remained at the plantations and became skilled workers and foremen.

The greatest influx of immigrants came from Japan. From 1894 to 1939 about 180,000 Japanese laborers and their relatives were landed in Hawaii. Some eventually returned home and other thousands moved on to the United States, but enough remained in Hawaii to constitute the largest ethnic group there. After the turn of the century their numbers on the plantations decreased steadily.

In 1939, Filipinos were the largest ethnic group working on sugar plantations; immigration was continuous after 1906, and over 120,000 were brought in. Many of these immigrants came without their families and returned home upon completion of their contracts.

Numbers of Koreans, Puerto Ricans, Spaniards, northern Europeans, and even Russians were attracted to the islands to work as plantation laborers; but in 1939 the only likely source for additional labor was the Philippines.

From its very beginning over a hundred years ago, the Hawaiian sugar industry has moved in the direction of larger and larger mass-production units, and in 1939 it was one of the most completely integrated agricultural enterprises in the world. The reasons for this development were mainly financial. Some degree of integration was present in the beginning. Whereas on the mainland plantations and sugar mills developed as separate enterprises, the individual farmer selling his cane to the mill for sugar extraction, in Hawaii there was no established pattern for this kind of relationship and the white pioneers who established the first plantations had to set up mills in connection with them.

In the early days sugar extraction was slow and simple. Individual stalks of cane were fed into presses which expressed only about 50 per cent of the juice, and from this juice sugar was extracted by a process of liming, condensation, and drying, all of which took weeks. The output of a mill was consequently meager and not much cane was required to keep it busy. Later on, technological improvements in sugar extraction speeded up the process, but the new machines were costly and in the interests of economical operation they had to be kept busy. This called for more cane and larger planted areas to be serviced by each mill.

The need for irrigation water was another factor in the movement toward integration, since small plantation units could not capitalize the costly irrigation projects. Co-ordinated efforts, moreover, were required to bring in labor, finance experimentation, combat plant disease and pests, procure supplies, and ship and market raw sugar. In the past these efforts were applied effectively to force changes which have strengthened the position of Hawaiian sugar: the land reforms, the Treaty of Reciprocity, overthrow of the native monarchy, and annexation. And in 1939 this same co-ordination was apparent in the publicity campaigns—"lobbying" was an impolite word—then being conducted to ensure Hawaiian sugar equitable treatment by Congress. Spokesmen for the industry claimed, with what appeared to be some justification, that only through integration could Hawaiian sugar be produced economically enough to compete with other sugar industries producing for the United States market.

Basic units in the sugar industry are the plantations. In 1939 there were thirty-eight of them, containing a total of 240,000 acres planted in cane and 510,000 acres given over to forests (for water supply), grazing land (for plantation cattle), and for community sites. The 1939 dollar value of all these plantations was estimated at between 155 and 180 millions. Throughout the prewar decade about one million tons of raw sugar were produced annually. During the same decade an average of about 50,000 workers were employed, in the following order of numerical importance: Filipino, Japanese, Portuguese, Hawaiian and part-Hawaiian, "other Caucasians," Puerto Rican, Chinese, and Korean. With their families these employees made up a total of 100,000 persons, one third of whom were aliens.

A Hawaiian sugar plantation was an intricate, factorylike organization, with all operations directed toward keeping the sugar extraction mill working full time. Under the supervision of a manager, who had full authority over all operations and, in fact, over the community lives of plantation employees, were the following main departments: agricultural operations, industrial operations, office, and industrial relations; and several subsidiary departments: store, machine shops, railroads, hospitals, and so forth. Similar patterns of organization and procedure, as well as similar wage rates, worker prerequisites, and most other details of plantation life, obtained throughout all the sugar plantations, affording further evidence of industry-wide integration.

The dominant position in the sugar industry was held by the "factors," the commercial agencies which controlled the assets and activities of thirty-three of the thirty-eight plantations. These factors date from the whaling era, when several trading firms sprang up in Honolulu to cater to the needs of the visiting ships. With the decline of whaling, these companies began servicing the plantations. Planter-owners were kept busy managing the day-to-day activities of growing and milling cane. They did not have the time to visit Honolulu whenever supplies were needed, nor were their knowledge of and contacts with world markets close enough to enable them to sell their product profitably under circumstances of increasing competition. The factors consequently became Honolulu agents for the plantations and went on to extending credit, making loans, procuring labor, arranging shipping, and handling all other business connected with sugar. Ownership of plantations soon passed from planter to factor, and by 1939 five Honolulu factors—the "Big Five"—owned and bossed the industry, as in fact they owned and controlled most other phases of island economy, including importing and wholesaling, retailing, interisland and mainland shipping, banking, utilities, hotels, canneries, and mainland sugar refineries.

Competition did not exist among these five factors, which were linked by interlocking directorates, by inter-family relationships, and, with respect to sugar, by membership in the HSPA (Hawaiian Sugar Planters' Association). The stated functions of the HSPA were the discovery and adoption of new agricultural techniques and laborsaving devices, formulation of a general labor program, and political lobbying or "representation." The most conspicuous phase of HSPA activity was its experiment station, expertly staffed and liberally financed, and responsible for some quite remarkable technical improvements in the industry.

In recent years the Hawaiian sugar industry became the center of heated controversy. It was attacked from one side as a despotic, monopolistic, industrial monster, holding island economy in capture, stifling individual enterprise, and maintaining labor at a peonage level. On the other side it was supported by assertions that it had made Hawaii into a productive and wealthy Territory, that its employees were well paid and amply provided with essentials for happy living, and that no other type of organization could have succeeded under the peculiar physical and human circumstances that prevailed in the islands. The correct evaluation lay somewhere in between: the essential fact was that the social concepts of the United States had been continually changing, but the industrial leaders of isolated Hawaii were unable or unwilling to follow the trend.

The assertion that sugar made Hawaii what it was before 1939 can be amply documented. The face of the land was changed. The total four million acres of the islands were altered only slightly by the early Hawaiians; patches of taro, sweet potatoes, plantains, and sugar cane, small groves of coconut palms, a few fishponds, and scattered village settlements were almost lost against the background of extensive forests and grass and wasteland. Mountainous forest land and wide pastures and wastelands still dominated the Hawaiian landscape of 1939, but over 300,000 acres had been transformed into cultivation, and of this area four fifths was planted in sugar cane. Cane will not grow well on low taro lands and has been planted mainly on forest land, semiarid pasture, and useless arid land rendered productive by irrigation. In other words, the change-over from native subsistence gardening to sugar growing was not directly due to the displacement of one crop by another. It can be fairly claimed that sugar growing, with its careful irrigation and use of fertilizers, has if anything enriched the natural resources of the islands.

Sugar also altered the population of the islands. Native depopulation was proceeding rapidly even before sugar entered the picture, so that any hastening effect on the process which the industry might have had was indirect. This is not true, however, regarding other population changes. Sugar was directly responsible for introducing nearly 300,000 Orientals, about 20,000 Portuguese, and smaller numbers of Puerto Ricans and Spaniards. Many of these workers remained, so that they and their offspring comprised the bulk of the prewar population in the islands.

Sugar also altered the economy of the islands and determined the course of political history. Half the total population was employed, directly or indirectly, in this industry. Sugar planters, acting in sugar's interest, broke the native monarchy, secured annexation by the United States and, publicly at least, were forcefully behind the move for statehood in order to give the industry votes in Congress and thus protect it from discriminatory legislation.

In 1939 the outlook for Hawaiian sugar was this: Practically all suitable land was already under cultivation and future increases in production would have to come from the discovery of better canes. Further large-scale import of labor other than from the Philippines was blocked by immigration laws, and most future plantation laborers would have to be recruited from among locally born, democratically educated, and increasingly union-conscious descendants of immigrants. Under these circumstances the search for laborsaving devices, especially for field operations, would have to be prosecuted vigorously. Because of general overproduction in sugar throughout the world, the dangers of ruinous competition from cheap-labor areas, and the resultant international sugar agreements of 1934 which restricted the movement of free sugar on the world markets and created several closed-market blocs of political and regional lines, the maximum quantity of sugar which Hawaii was allowed to produce depended upon the decision of the Federal government. Manifest Destiny had slowed down.

The pineapple industry began late and fell into the pattern already established by the sugar industry. Whether the fruit was introduced into the islands before or after Cook's visit is not known; at any rate, pineapples were growing in Hawaii early in the nineteenth century, although natives made little use of them for food. Quantities of the fresh fruit were shipped from time to time to the mainland, and late in the last century white homesteaders cultivated it for export on a small commercial scale. However, so much of the fruit spoiled during the long ocean voyage to San Francisco that interest in the project waned. An enterprising homesteader named Dole (a distant relative of Judge Sanford B. Dole, first governor of the Territory of Hawaii), whose name has since become almost a synonym for pineapples, realized that canning was the answer and secured mainland capital for his pioneering venture. From that small beginning at the start of this century, the Hawaiian industry grew to the point where, in 1939, it produced 80 per cent of the world's canned pineapple, turning out in a peak year a pack valued at $60,000,000.

This young industry did not go through the long, slow, and tortuous career experienced by Hawaiian sugar, but its development was anything but smooth and steady. To sugar-bound Hawaiian businessmen, pineapple growing was an unwanted foundling left on the doorstep. The fear was that it would compete with sugar for land and labor. Because its success was uncertain, no local encouragement was offered it in the form of capital or other aid, and pioneering capital had to be obtained on the mainland. This situation changed, of course, when local businessmen observed how the profits rolled in.

The problem of market was also serious at the beginning of the enterprise, and still loomed large in 1939. The American public had to be educated to eating canned pineapple, and that was no mean undertaking in an era not yet advanced to million-dollar huckstering. In some years the overzealous young industry glutted the undeveloped market and suffered financial setbacks, and even after advertising had established a public demand, consumption fell precipitously during the depression. This uncertain market remained subject to further disturbances as a result of competition from other domestic canned fruits and from canned pineapple imported from nations enjoying reciprocal-trade treaties with the United States.

Land for growing pineapples, on the other hand, was not much of a problem. It was learned that pineapples grow best in the high, cool plateau lands unsuited for sugar, and that they will grow in a wide variety of rainfall situations. Thus, pineapples did not displace sugar anywhere, or any other agricultural activity for that matter. A good example is the small island of Lanai: formerly a wasteland supporting only a handful of people and a herd of about four hundred cattle, it was transformed into thirteen thousand acres of pineapples and a modern plantation community.

Throughout Hawaii laborers who had been brought in for the sugar plantations were already on hand to grow and can pineapple. Since nearly all pineapple operations except harvesting are mechanized, the labor force required is relatively small. Notwithstanding this fact, the pineapple industry was confronted with the same problem that sugar faced: the necessity of obtaining its labor force from second- and third-generation citizens educated to expect higher standards of living and better working conditions than their immigrant parents put up with.

Pineapples no less than sugar are vulnerable to pests and diseases; a wilt almost wiped out the industry a few years ago. Another set of problems is posed by the seasonality of growth; sugar is harvested all during the year, but the bulk of the pineapple crop matures in the summer and has to be harvested and canned immediately. This circumstance causes marked seasonal employment: at the peak of the harvest season, field labor has to be doubled and cannery labor quadrupled. Some of this increased labor need is met by employing housewives and school children and by "borrowing" labor from sugar plantations, but the net result is a less stable manpower for pineapples than for sugar. Management attempts to mitigate this by lengthening the harvest season by chemically accelerating and retarding the growth of different portions of the crop; and the search for mechanical aids to harvesting has also been vigorously pushed.

Many of the causes which favored integration in the Hawaiian sugar industry led to consolidation in the pineapple industry, but since an important part of the latter was owned by mainland firms having other interests, integration was not carried as far as it was in the almost completely locally owned sugar industry. But, excepting the plantations and canneries owned by mainland companies, pineapple enterprises came to be controlled by the same five factors that controlled sugar, and the pattern of control was similar. Regardless of ownership, however, all the pineapple companies voluntarily established production quotas among themselves in order to limit production to market needs and thus protect prices.

Whereas sugar plantation and mill are physically integrated into a single community—except for individual "adherent planters," who sell their crops to plantations but do not necessarily dwell on the plantation—pineapple plantations and canneries are usually separated physically, the canneries being principally located near Honolulu, where casual labor is more readily available to meet the seasonal demand. In 1939 plantation labor consisted mainly of Japanese, Filipinos, and Portuguese; and plantation communities contained much the same facilities—company housing, hospitals, recreation—as did sugar plantations.

By 1939 fifty thousand acres of former pasture and wasteland had been converted into productive agricultural land by pineapples, but otherwise the industry has had far less effect than sugar in shaping Hawaii's social and economic life. The dominant patterns were already drawn when pineapples entered the picture. True, this industry did serve to diversify island economy and to stabilize its earnings during years of sugar depression; but the native Hawaiians and their culture had already been relegated to marginal insignificance before ever a pineapple was canned.

In 1939 the industry still had room for expansion, provided labor and market problems could be solved, for suitable land was available to the extent of doubling the annual pack.

Coffee production, in comparison with sugar and pineapples, did not transform the native culture or enter importantly in the economic life of the islands, but it did open up new areas to cultivation and provide livelihood for hundreds of Japanese immigrants who sought escape from what they considered to be the peonage of plantation life.

Coffee was first introduced in 1810 and began to be produced for market fifteen years later. For a while it was a lively industry; native Hawaiians grew it by royal decree and paid taxes with their crops. Indeed, until the middle of the century, coffee shared first honors with sugar, but four obstacles edged it out of the race. For one thing, the climate was not particularly suited to coffeegrowing. Also, labor requirements were greater than those of sugar, and price fluctuations kept the market unstable. On top of all this a fungus blight played havoc with crops, so that when the Civil War stimulated sugar production, coffee was left far behind. A short-lived boom in the nineties induced some whites to undertake large-scale planting again, but another price decline relegated the industry to the marginal position where it has since remained.

The crop before the Second World War averaged about 8,500,000 pounds per annum and was shipped to the mainland for blending with other coffees. The principal growers were Japanese tenant farmers who eked out existences on submarginal land in the Kona region of the Island of Hawaii. These growers sold their crops to small storekeepers, who held the farmers in debt by advancing credits for fertilizer and subsistence; but here as elsewhere in the Territory the big factors played dominant roles through their financial hold over the storekeepers.

In 1939 the picture was changing to the extent that Filipinos were beginning to replace Japanese as coffeegrowers, while the latter were moving into easier or more profitable occupations.

Hawaiian cattle ranches do not provide even enough meat to satisfy all local consumption requirements, but they cover more area than all plantations combined and have provided hundreds of native Hawaiians with employment well suited to their ways of living.

In Hawaii is located one of the largest ranches in the United States. In fact, in 1939 a quarter of the land area of these islands was in pasture, which supported about 120,000 head of cattle. It came as a distinct surprise to visitors who ventured beyond the beaches and the Honolulu bars to see typical western cowboy life reproduced on several islands.

Native Hawaiians possessed only pigs, dogs, and poultry. The handful of cattle brought in by Captain George Vancouver in 1793 and presented to the native monarch were objects of such curiosity and awe that they were freed and for many years protected from killing by royal *kapu;* as a result, they increased to such numbers that they became pests to farms and to the expanding plantations. Three Mexican cowboys were imported a hundred years ago to help herd the cattle, and these men brought in a way of life which caught the imagination of the native Hawaiian as plantation agriculture never could. By 1939 nearly half of the eight hundred families employed as herdsmen were Hawaiian or part-Hawaiian, the remainder being Japanese and Portuguese.

In terms of money value, the prewar income from Hawaii's livestock industry amounted to approximately

$5,000,000 annually, about half in meat and the rest in milk, eggs, wool, hides, and tallow. Even so, meat, dairy, and poultry products had to be imported to satisfy local needs.

Cattle ranching was the one white-introduced agricultural industry which native Hawaiians found to their liking. The cowboy life, exciting and varied, without the sustained daily monotony of field labor, corresponds to the Polynesians' old-time existence. The dangers of galloping across treacherous, hole-ridden ranges were enjoyed with the same zest shown by their forefathers in racing along after fish through heavy seas in their narrow canoes.

Though management's paternalism was even more evident in ranching than in the strongly paternalistic sugar and pineapple industries, the lot of ranch laborers was better in some respects. Seasonal employment was practically nonexistent. Owners and employees, linked by generations of master-man relationships, were usually on the friendliest of terms, and in this setting the non-competitive Hawaiians probably had a better chance of survival than in the urban areas to which most of them had moved. The small island of Niihau stood out in this connection.

Niihau was purchased outright in 1863 by a Scottish family escaping from the stresses of civilization. In 1939 the part-Hawaiian grandsons of the pioneers dwelt on their plantation on neighboring Kauai Island and permitted no outsider to trespass on Niihau itself. Niihauan inhabitants, about two hundred in all, were employed by the owners in herding the cattle and sheep which constituted the island's main resource. The only link with the outside world was the owners' sampan, which carried in supplies each week. Niihauans were nearly self-subsistent, conducted their own school and church (without benefit of outsiders), punished their own misdemeanors, and generally managed their own affairs.

Even in 1939 the Territorial government exercised practically no jurisdiction over them.

In addition to all these primary industries, large-scale commercialized tourism provided business opportunities for an increasing number of individuals with modest incomes, thereby adding recruits to the middle-class ranks, which were previously almost empty.

And finally, the Federal government, though entering the stage quite late, nevertheless played an important role in shaping Hawaii's economy. Large land and water areas were set aside for military and naval reservations, and their prewar personnel annually purchased millions of dollars in services and supplies. In addition, the Federal government was a big employer of local labor for construction projects.

Between 1778 and 1939 the population and culture of the Hawaiian Islands had become so completely transformed that it was practically unrecognizable, but no wise observer believed that the current pattern would endure. The children of Oriental immigrants were being educated in schools which taught democratic ideas, and these new citizens were beginning to demonstrate impatience with the status and earnings of plantation laborers and with the concentration of economic power that limited their economic opportunities. The time was ripe for the development of unionism, and the initial impulse came from the mainland. A battle with local capital loomed unless both sides agreed to compromise, and that word did not appear prominently in the local vocabulary.

The almost absolute authority of big business over island affairs was also being threatened from another direction. Military and naval leaders, and particularly the latter, were beginning to voice their belief that, sugar or no sugar, Hawaii's main function was to serve as a defense outpost. With war against Japan a definite possibility, these same leaders indicated increasing uneasiness about having a large Japanese population near Oahu's depots and harbors and air fields. As a matter of fact, fear of this eventuality was a major factor in the prewar recommendation of Congress against Hawaiian statehood.

Still another threat to big business was the Federal government's sugar-quota legislation, which, in the interests of helping to stabilize the world sugar industries, restricted Hawaii's production to a figure one sixth below its previous capacity.

These and other lesser considerations stimulated most island factions to agitate for statehood, in order that Hawaii might have a vote as well as a voice in the Congress and therewith keep outsiders—especially mainlanders—from interfering with Hawaii's affairs.

FIJI

In 1939 the best vantage point for observing Fijian savagery was from the wide, second-story veranda of Suva's Grand Pacific Hotel. From a comfortable reclining position, a visitor could look inland across the coastal highway onto the green-turfed athletic field and watch Fijians beating their white masters at cricket. If the excitement of watching the match aroused thirst, the observer could call out and be served an excellent whiskey-soda by another dark-skinned fellow, whose smaller stature, sharper face, and straighter hair proclaimed him an Indian.

Altogether, an idyllic scene. South and a few yards away the Pacific lapped at the palm-fringed shore. Inland rose a wall of fantastic mountain shapes—surviving volcanic plugs and crater rims. Extensive sugar cane plantations, kept productive by industrious Asiatics, spread out on either hand. And near-by were picturesque villages of loyal and literate native Fijians. Fiji, unofficial capital of the lovely South Seas, monument to the white man's humanitarianism and administrative genius! Or so it seemed.

Away from hotel verandas, Fiji presented a somewhat different picture. By 1939 part of Fiji was losing its character as a South Seas island and was becoming a "Little India." Natives still claimed most of the land, and white men still drained off the productive wealth; but birth rates and working habits placed the future in the hands of the Indians. This is how it came about.

The Fiji archipelago consists of a western leeward group of massive volcanic islands (including Viti Levu, Vanua Levu, Ovalau) and an eastern windward scattering of smaller islands. Negroids were the original inhabitants of the whole archipelago, but centuries before white men came there was intercourse between Fiji and Samoa and Tonga. Tongans canoed frequently to the Lau (eastern) Islands, trading, warring, and sometimes settling down, and in any case leavening the local culture with Polynesian traits. Later, under the stimulus of western ideas, a Tongan monarch even sent to Lau one of his lieutenants, Maafu, and set up a Tongan hegemony over these islands. Long before these events, however, all Fiji was divided into a large number of social and political units, constantly warring with one another in the usual South Seas fashion.

The family was the social nucleus, and several interrelated families comprised a village. The father was absolute head of each family, and upon his death his formal status was passed on to his eldest son. In the basic form of the social structure, all families in a village traced their relationships through males back to a principal male ancestor, who had perhaps left his own village and set up a new home at the present village site; and that ancestor's direct male descendant, through primogeniture, was the village headman. Among these Austronesian-speakers of shallow memory actual genealogies were not remembered for many generations, and the traditional ancestor was venerated as a demigod.

Each family had its own house site and enjoyed proprietary rights to the land it gardened in; all other land identified with the village, reaching up to the boundaries of other villages, was held in common, with the chief exercising strongest power over its disposal.

Each village had its men's clubhouse where youths slept and learned the arts of warfare. At puberty, boys were circumcised and girls tattooed, as marks of advance up the age-ladder. Opportunities for premarital love-making were guarded against, but many married women had their youthful lovers. The preferred marital link was between cross-cousins, that is, offspring of a brother and sister. Every man took as many wives as he could support, but most men had only one. Upon the death of a great chief his widows were usually strangled, so that they might accompany him to the afterworld.

Three native concepts which significantly affected Fijian history were communal *lala*, *kere kere*, and personal *lala*. The first signified the mutual aid exercised by all members of a community; the second specified the process of sharing goods among members of the community: those who had not might beg and receive from the surplus of those who had. Both of these concepts strengthened the communalism of the native community. Personal *lala* referred to the tribute exacted by a chief from outsiders allowed to settle on the community's unused land, over which he as chief had strongest proprietary rights. This factor contributed to the strengthening of chiefly powers which eventually made possible larger political units.

Warfare—or, better, feuding—was chronic among the small Fijian communities, but large-scale organized aggression developed only after native clubs and spears were supplemented with white man's firearms. During the first half of the nineteenth century there developed several great confederations of coastal tribes which proceeded to demonstrate how effectively primitive men can destroy themselves when aided by civilized weapons. Also, the few white men cast up on the beaches who escaped the baking ovens—white flesh was not so tasty as dark—added to the sport by serving as military advisers to native chiefs. For all these adventures, sandalwooders willingly supplied muskets and powder.

Strongest of all the confederations was that owing an uneasy allegiance to the Mbau tribe of western Viti Levu and to its chief, Thakombau ("destruction to Mbau"). Mbau began as a single village on a small island; through intrigue and warfare its influence was spread to the main island of Viti Levu. Its proximity to ship anchorages of the early white traders increased its influence, so that many white visitors began to refer to Thakombau as "king" of Fiji, despite the existence of rivals who would have eaten him with pleasure.

Chiefs of Thakombau's status had large responsibilities and dread power. In each super-tribe one chieftain held temporal power, planning battles and administering affairs, and a second held spiritual powers, directing the priests in their sacrifices and petitions to the tribal ancestral gods and other supernatural forces. Some chiefs could call forth hundreds of warriors to do battle, and received tribute from scores of villages settled on their land. Their households contained many concubines and personal retainers, and their appetite for human flesh kept the court baking ovens always hot.

Into this island paradise moved the missionaries, first Wesleyan and then Catholic. The Wesleyans came in the wake of Tongans, whose newly found missionary zeal armed them with one more weapon for extending their influence over Fiji. From the Tonganized Lau Island group, Wesleyans moved to the larger islands and began the tedious task of substituting hymn-singing for the cannibal feast. They attacked the native religious beliefs with gusto, one enthusiast courting disaster by destroying temples and idols; the fact that so many survived may have been due not only to the native prejudice against white flesh but to the frequent visits then being made by western warships.

When the practical advantages of Jehovah worship became evident, many ambitious chiefs put aside some of their wives, let their cooking ovens cool off, and became converts, probably not realizing at the time that disavowal of their old gods removed one of the strongest props under their temporal power. For a period there was fierce warfare between converts and holdouts, but the issue was finally decided when, in 1854, Thakombau finally acceded to the request of the King of Tonga and accepted the Wesleyan mission. Shortly afterward Tonga lent to Thakombau a force of two thousand warriors, who routed his last remaining enemies and extended Thakombau's power—and the mission's—over most of Viti Levu.

Meanwhile planters and more traders were moving to Fiji, acquiring land, setting out coconuts, trading for shell and sandalwood, and entering into native politics. Salem traders were predominant, and the United States designated a consul there. On one fine Fourth of July that convivial gentleman carelessly burned down his home with fireworks and lost a few of his possessions to looting natives. On this and other grounds he presented a huge claim to Thakombau on behalf of the United States, demanding that the King of Fiji must be held responsible for the actions of his subjects. The harassed Thakombau may have been flattered at the implications, but he did not have the money. This "national debt" doubled and quadrupled by saltations understood only by the consul, and when American warships were called in to help collect, the anxious Thakombau followed the familiar practice of offering his insolvent kingdom to western powers; but there were no takers.

The world cotton shortage brought on by the American Civil War sent numbers of would-be planters to Fiji and increased the foreign stake in land and political influence. Fijians proved to be unwilling and unproductive workers in the cotton fields and coconut plantations, so that natives were imported from the New Hebrides and the Solomons. The blackbirding evils which accompanied this traffic set off the chain of events which ultimately induced Great Britain to overcome its reluctance and annex Fiji in 1874. By that time the motley assortment of adventurers, traders, missionaries, planters, and consuls, all intriguing with native factions and competing for souls and land and loot, had created such hectic conditions that some power had to step in. Since Britain's interests in the area were larger than those of any other nation, and since her New Zealand and Australian colonies were urging clamorously, she was forced to extend Her Majesty's sovereignty over a few more black subjects. The most noteworthy aspect of the annexation was the promise given to the new subjects that their welfare, including their titles to their lands, would be vigorously protected for all times. Subsequent failures to keep this promise have resulted not from a cynical disregard for native rights but more from lack of foresight in estimating the long-range consequences of certain day-to-day decisions.

The British government made a sincere effort to guard native interests and "improve" native society. At the time of annexation about one tenth of Fiji's four and a half million acres had been alienated by white settlers under conditions confirmed by the government as having been "legal." The remaining nine tenths were constituted inalienable native lands, which could be leased to nonnatives only with the consent of the native proprietors and the government. This regulation protected the Fijians' chief resource, bound them closer to their native communities, and provided them with income from rents. (Sixty-five years later Fijians still retained most of their lands, only an additional one tenth having been leased to nonnatives.)

Indirect rule was established; native leaders were confirmed in their rank and their influence over tribal and community affairs. Warfare, cannibalism, and human sacrifice were of course abolished, but for the most part other native affairs were not at first interfered with. Later on, however, other changes were brought about, either consciously or unconsciously. Personal *lala*, the tribute paid to a chief, was "legalized" to a point of importance beyond its real native scope, and the rights of chiefs were thereby increased. On the other hand, chieftainship began to assume more of a territorial and less of a 'kinship basis, and the prestige of chiefs was weakened by Christianity, which denied their supernatural powers, and by official prohibitions against "wasteful" social-climbing feasts, which lessened intercommunity competitions and tribal *esprit*.

A few native rebels appeared from time to time and made rather pathetic efforts to secure popular backing for reclaiming "Fiji for the Fijians," but the government dealt decisively with these upstarts, and for the most part natives adjusted easily to the new regime. From an estimated population of about 200,000 at the time of initial white contact, Fijians rapidly declined in numbers. After reaching a low of 82,000, however, they began a slow recovery. Throughout this era their lands were secure, their civil affairs only slightly revised, and their economy still mainly subsistent. When the need arose to supplement native-produced things with trade goods or to raise money for taxes and church offerings, Fijians made copra from their own groves and sold it to traders. Copra production in Fiji increased steadily until the depression of the thirties, and natives consistently produced from one half to two thirds of the total amount exported. At one point, under government stimulus, they undertook the growing of bananas for export, an enterprise particularly well suited to their way of life. But many of these nice adjustments were violently and permanently disturbed by new alien enterprises.

The first economic boom in Fiji came about during the American Civil War, when British textile manufacturers encouraged the production of cotton. Men from many lands flocked to Fiji and started plantations, and the local industry flourished for a few years, until Dixie cotton regained its markets. Coffee and cocoa were also attempted by white planters, but did not meet with much success. Copra has not played the dominant role in the white community of Fiji that it has elsewhere in Melanesia. Although it was the earliest plantation crop and continues first in importance in Vanua Levu and on many of the smaller islands, copra has never been produced in any quantity on the main island of Viti Levu, owing to the presence there of a pest, a destructive purple moth.

The sugar industry, established in 1872, has been the decisive factor in Fiji's transformation. Within seventy years the annual sugar production had risen to over 125,000 tons, five times the quantity and seven times the value of copra; but this feat was not accomplished with native labor. Fijians were not temperamentally suited to the steady work pace required for cane growing; and since they possessed other resources, they did not need or wish to work in the white master's cane fields and sugar mills. For a time the planters were able to make up this deficiency by importing laborers from the Solomons and New Hebrides, but all these workers were repatriated shortly after Fiji's annexation so that planters had to turn to another source. Through an arrangement with the government of India, Indian laborers were then brought in under contract with guaranty for repatriation at the end of ten years. By 1916, when the indenture system was abolished, over 60,000 Indians had been brought to Fiji, and over half of them had elected to remain in Fiji when their terms of indenture were completed. Meanwhile large numbers of nonindentured Indians arrived and settled down as farmers and field laborers.

A decline in sugar prices in 1884 ruined all but the largest operators, so that eventually one company, the Colonial Sugar Refining Company of Australia (CSR), emerged as the sole sugar producer and the largest enterprise in Fiji, representing an investment of over £4,000,000. In 1939 the industry was still entirely dependent upon Indian labor.

The first Indian immigrants served as field workers and mill hands on white plantations, living in rough barracks and enjoying no family life because of the absence of Indian women. When free of indenture, many of them continued to raise sugar in small leased plots, and others became servants, traders, or craftsmen. Later, wives began to accompany their men, and Indian families were established. By 1939 there were about 94,000 Indians living in Fiji, nearly as many as there were native Fijians and five times the number of all other nonnatives, including whites; three quarters of these Indians were born in Fiji. Two thirds of the wage-earning Indians continued to work at sugar, while the other third had established themselves in almost every other kind of enterprise in the islands.

The Colonial Sugar Refining Company solved the labor problem created by abolition of the indenture system by leasing small plots of cane land to Indian farmers; the company purchased all cane and advanced capital, at the same time retaining control over land use and crop practices. Of the 80,000 acres in cane, about 70 per cent was cultivated by Indians working as independent farmers or as tenants of the company.

Most Indian immigrants were Hindus and came from the Ganges plain or from southern India, but a few thousand were Punjabi and Gujarati. Without question, most of them bettered their situations by coming to Fiji. They were industrious and ambitious and generally succeeded in improving their living conditions and increasing their incomes. They monopolized most craft and service industries. They adhered to separate religions—Hindus first in number, then Moslems, then a few Sikhs—but most caste distinctions disappeared in Fiji, along with a number of other social and religious practices disapproved by westerners. Indians regarded Fijians as inferior primitive beings, and the Fijians held Indians in disdain; consequently there was very little mixture of races.

By 1939 Indians were increasing in numbers more rapidly than Fijians. (The annual excess of births over deaths was about 4000 for Indians, 2600 for Fijians.) They were becoming educated and articulate, and events in India encouraged them to demand larger economic and political stakes in Fiji. They regarded themselves as British subjects and therefore entitled to a far larger voice in governing the colony than they actually possessed. Most of all, they wanted land. They looked about and saw Fijians owning nine tenths of all the land in the colony, yet leasing out only a small portion of it and holding idle all the remainder not required for their subsistence. At the same time, they, the Indians, were forced to remain satisfied with small, leased plots held under all manner of restrictions.

Here in the South Pacific the British government faced a dilemma almost as complicated as prewar Palestine or India itself. Pledges had been given to native Fijians to preserve their lands for them; and although the Fijians had not required all this land for actual use, their numbers were increasing as well as their needs for land. Yet, the Indians of Fiji were also British subjects and could not be kept landless and disenfranchised forever. The government's attempts at a decision were not made easier by the personal preferences of colonial officials for Fijians. Moreover, the whole white community shared the sentiments of the officials and in addition feared Indian competition in occupations up to then regarded as the domain of whites.

One attempted solution was to develop Fijians to the point where they could begin to compete more hopefully with Indians in the economic and political rivalry for Fiji. In this enterprise the officials faced the nearly insuperable obstacle of native custom. If Fijians could only be made to become economic individualists, it was reasoned, they would be better able to survive in this age of individualistic capitalistic enterprise. Observers were well aware of the Fijians' disinterest in the gospel of work and save. Even if some unnatural Fijian wished to labor and acquire a surplus of worldly goods, his community would shame him into sharing them. Also, if he spent his energies in working for his own ends, he would not be able to contribute his share of the communal service required by native law and confirmed by government regulation.

One experiment consisted in cutting a Fijian loose from his communal ties and obligations—either by removing him altogether from his community and homesteading him elsewhere or by leaving him in his home village and excusing him from the duty to work for the community. In either case, the government then assisted the native to become a cash-crop farmer, a capitalist working for himself alone and retaining for himself all his profits. One has to admire the boldness of the experiment; those other social reformers, the missionaries, have rarely undertaken so ambitious a transformation.

Most of the Fiji drama took place on the main island of Viti Levu and to a less extent on Vanua Levu, those two islands being the centers of sugar enterprise and of

Indian population. On some of the smaller neighboring islands the copra economy of planter and native still carried on, more or less unaffected by the human crises created by sugar. In large areas of Vanua Levu and in other copra areas like Levuka and Taveuni, planters and natives led existences not unlike those in the New Hebrides, the Solomons, and coastal Papua and New Guinea. Many of them supplemented their incomes by producing bananas for the New Zealand market, which had replaced Australia as the chief market after Queensland protectionists erected tariff barriers.

Dominating all else in the copra areas was the great god Price. The steady rise in the price of copra, which reached its zenith during World War I, brought prosperity to planters and more gadgets to natives. The latter easily survived the price collapse of the thirties, merely giving up trade-store luxuries and returning to the security of subsistence economy and communalism. The planters on the other hand fared badly, just as did their brothers-in-travail in New Guinea and elsewhere. For a time it looked as if the copra planter might disappear altogether from the Fiji scene, leaving the stage to sugar and the new gold industry springing up on the two main islands.

The gold fever which spread through Melanesia as the result of the rich discoveries in New Guinea in the late twenties also gripped Fiji, and a typical rush followed in the wake of discoveries in 1932. As such matters usually go, the individual prospectors were ultimately supplanted by big companies, backed by Australian capital. Two large mines were developed on Viti Levu and one on Vanua Levu. By 1939 over 108,000 ounces of gold were being exported annually. The ultimate effects of this rich new industry on Fiji were hard to predict: it provided an important source of revenue—second only to sugar—for the government, and gave employment to nearly three thousand persons, including the two thou-

sand Fijians who constituted 80 per cent of the unskilled
labor force. Thus, for a time at least, many Fijians reverted to their old-time status of laboring for wages for
the white masters. Yet, gold runs out eventually, and
mining could provide only a respite from the native-In-
dian dilemma born of the sugar industry.

Away to the east of the cane fields, the plantations,
and the gold mines, native life went on fairly evenly in
the smaller, poorer islands of the Lau group. In these
sparsely populated islands natives grew their own food
crops, produced a little copra now and then to exchange
for kerosene and knives at the Chinese trader's, carried on
the affairs of their kinship and community institutions,
and practiced Christian rites blended nicely with native
beliefs. Their most valuable resource was the poverty of
their small islands: nothing in Lau was likely to attract
white or Indian.

By 1939 there were, then, four Fijis. There was the Fiji
of sugar: large, highly rationalized plantations and mills,
producing wealth for its white owners and managers and
subsistence for its Indian workers, and leaving in its train
the basic conflict between Fijian and Indian which dominated political and economic activity in the two main
islands. Then there was the Fiji of copra: dependent for
its continuation upon price factors completely outside
local control. Third, there was the Fiji of gold: highly
profitable to its owners and rich in revenue for the government, but limited in area, in longevity, and in influence upon the course of local events. Last, there was the
Fiji of the Lau Islanders: "Tonganized," and tamed
somewhat by Christianity, but far enough away from the
big islands to escape all but the faintest repercussions of
the caste warfare which went on there.

XVI

SEA HARVEST

Within the cartographer's boundaries of Oceania lie thirty million square miles of sea, but the hungry islander cannot rejoice in this statistic because he does not possess the facilities for harvesting more than a small proportion of these vast stretches of ocean. It is true that food fish and other marine riches abound along the reefs and shores of most islands, enough at least to sustain many native populations and a few foreign enterprises. But beyond the shores, in the great depths and expanses, islanders of yesterday and today have fished only occasionally, either for sport or for sustenance during their long overseas voyages.

Fishing conditions vary enormously from island to island. The waters of some archipelagoes provide bounteously, while others are a despair to fishermen. At volcanic Mer Island in the Torres Strait, a single throw of a small cast net brings in enough food for the whole family. Yet, around the southern shores of equally volcanic Bougainville, a lucky catch is a memorable event.

Wherever there were fish, islanders developed extraordinary ingenuity and skill in catching them. Some were caught with bare hands, others with shell hooks, throw nets, bows and arrows, spears, dragnets, traps, and weirs. At some places tethered suckfish were used to guide fishermen to larger game. Elsewhere fish were captured in a mucilaginous mesh contrived of spider webbing which was trailed along the water's surface from the tail of a flying kite. In quiet waters poisons were often used to stun the fish and bring them to the surface. Even fishponds were constructed at some islands, but no such artificial devices were required at many other places where natural lagoons provided food for the taking.

An event of great importance to many shore communities was the annual appearance of the *palolo*. These reef worms spawn almost exactly one week after the full moon of November; their egg-distended hind portions break off and rise to the surface by the millions, providing a field day for the islanders, who scooped up these delicacies by the ton and feasted to repletion.

Fishing to most natives meant combing the lagoons, reefs, ponds, and streams for daily food—for countless kinds of fish and for shrimps, prawns, crabs, lobsters, clams, mussels, eels, turtles, and octopuses. The exciting and hazardous business of capturing the deep-water tuna and bonito was usually regarded as special sport rather than daily routine.

Food was not the only product of the sea taken by islanders. Shells were universally used as weapons and ornaments, currency and trumpets; on many stoneless atolls they were fashioned into artifacts. Tortoise shell was highly valued for bracelets and pendants; shark teeth were lashed to swords and clubs to render them even more murderous.

The products of the sea brought together beach dwellers and inlanders to trade and sometimes to fraternize. Special items, like giant cowries or nacreous bivalves, were traded far inland to remote areas where even the memory of the sea had been lost.

The bounty of the sea and the ingenuity of man in exploiting it was nowhere better seen than on many of the narrow atolls where islanders developed impressively rich cultures despite their poverty of things of the land. Indeed, a few coconut palms and a coral reef were economic security enough for many communities. Such at least was the case before white and yellow men came to exploit those marine riches with such rapacity that the source of security became an invitation to disaster. Whole archipelagoes were transformed as a result of the search for spermaceti and baleen, for pearl and pearl shell, for tuna and bonito, and for turtle and trepang. From this alien enterprise came necklaces for milady's throat and stays for her corset as well as flavoring for the mandarin's soup and inlay for his caskets. And from it came large profits for shipowners and entrepreneurs of New England, Australia, and Japan. But to the islanders touched by these enterprises came more loss than profit; in return for paltry wages earned as divers and seamen, they had their seas swept clean of whales, their lagoons ransacked of nacre, their numbers reduced by kidnappings and killings, and their health undermined by the occupational dangers of diving.

Whaling proved the greatest disaster. For three quarters of a century Nantucketeers, Sydneymen, and their lesser rivals rollicked through the Pacific in search of cachalot and Bay Right whales, calling at the islands to render their oil and replenish their stores and take their pleasure of brown beauties. Hundreds of vessels used to winter in Hawaii, and miraculously enough the place survived. Less fortunate were the Marquesas, which have never recovered from the onslaught. Other groups espe-

cially hard hit by the melees of whalers and by the rum
and disease left by them were the Societies, Fiji, the
Ellice and Gilbert groups, the Marshalls, and the eastern
Carolines, as earlier chapters described. Later, with the
transfer of whaling to the far northwest Pacific and the
establishment of missions and governments, this scourge,
at least, was removed from Oceania. But then along
came the pearlers.

Pearl fishing is as old as recorded history, and one of
the wonders of the ancient East was the vast fishery
extending from Ceylon to the Gulf of Persia. A second,
more recent fishery was located in the Gulf of California
and was exploited by Spanish masters. The third most
important, the fisheries of Oceania, are known more for
pearl shell than for pearls; on nearly every reef there
can be found specimens of the mother-of-pearl shells
known to commerce: the "gold lip" or "silver lip" pearl
oyster (*Pinctada maxima*) and the smaller "black lip"
(*Pinctada margaritifera*). Prize gold lips grow to nearly
a foot in diameter and may weigh up to twelve pounds
each. Small pearl oysters are also found in Oceania,
but the larger shells, containing fewer pearls and better
mother-of-pearl, have been more profitable over the
years.

The technology of pearl fishing is not complex; the
requirements are a small boat, a diver, a weight for de-
scending, a knife, and a net bag or basket. The diver
descends to the shell bed, tears off the shell, usually by
hand, and places it in the bag, which is then hauled up
to the boat. Shells must then be opened carefully and
cleaned of animal matter and outside coating prior to
being packed for shipment. Before the shallower shell
beds were exhausted, naked divers used to descend and
work in depths of forty to fifty feet until air exhaustion
forced them to surface. This was the pearl diving of
South Seas romance and adventure, and the fictional
pictures have not had to be greatly overdrawn. Dangers

from attack by sharks, giant eels, rays, and other marine terrors were all very real; and lung collapse or paralysis were the usual prices paid for too long or too deep immersion.

The introduction of diving apparatus made it possible to go deeper, stay down longer, and, of course, get more shells. But these technical improvements backfired: the greater volume of shell marketed brought prices down, and many of the best shell beds were exploited beyond recovery. Also, divers' bends and paralysis proved as dangerous as were the hazards from naked diving. A third factor in the decline of pearl fishing was the substitution of other materials for pearl shell in the manufacture of fine buttons, knife handles, and other gewgaws; but good shell was still marketable, and up to 1939 Oceania as a whole continued to export hundreds of tons annually.

Nearly every island group listed pearl shell among its exports, but the three principal fishing areas have been the Tuamotus, the Torres Strait, and Palau. The Tuamotuan atolls were the first to attract attention, and pearl fishing flourished there as the principal industry until companies using diving apparatus cleaned out the beds. The French Colonial Government subsequently installed conservation measures which have permitted some of the beds to recover and provide a regular source of income to native divers. The Torres Strait beds began to be worked in 1868, and their extraordinary wealth in pearl shell precipitated a pearling rush; its full story follows in a few pages. The Palau pearl fishery was systematically developed by the Japanese, who supplemented it with the growing of culture pearls.

During the First World War the marine snail, *Trochus niloticus,* became valuable because of the success of the Japanese in manufacturing buttons from it. The trochus is conical; the best commercial specimens measure three to four inches in base diameter, and about three inches

in height. In nacreous qualities it is not as fine as true
mother-of-pearl, and because of its shape it is not adaptable for use in flat knife handles and inlays, but it possesses other advantages. It matures more quickly than
gold or black lip; in addition, it grows in shallower water
and is consequently easier to collect and more adaptable
to artificial "planting." In short order trochus supplanted
true mother-of-pearl as the source of all but the most
costly "pearl" buttons and flat work. Requiring less
capital investment in boats and complete diving gear,
trochus fishing remained in native hands more than did
pearl fishing, but even so the principal profits usually
went to the nonnative traders and brokers who purchased shell from native divers and disposed of it in the
world's markets.

Trepang, or *bêche-de-mer*, is a sausage-shaped sea
slug found in shallow waters. When dried to a leathery
consistency, it is a favorite ingredient of Chinese soups.
Trepang fishing has been carried out on a large scale
for hundreds of years in the Indies, and early western
traders collected it along with sandalwood when they
ransacked the South Seas for products in demand in
China. Later, Chinese and Japanese traders were the
principals in drying and marketing the trepang, with
the islanders remaining in their usual role of collectors
and laborers. In an average prewar year, several hundred
tons of dried trepang, varying in value up to $1500 a ton,
were exported from Oceania.

Sponges, turtle shell, and dried shark fins have also
entered into the trade statistics of Oceania, but the
amounts exported have always been insignificant.

Much more important have been the large tuna and
bonito fisheries established by the Japanese in their mandated islands. Up to forty thousand tons were caught
annually and the dried product shipped to Japan. As will
be described in a later chapter, this industry remained
entirely in Japanese hands, even to the manning of sam-

pans and the drying of the catch. Its principal effect upon islanders was the way it transformed communities in Palau, Truk, and Ponape into Japanese towns. The influx of Japanese settlers to man the vessels and factories and shipyards, together with their numerous parasitic enterprises, relegated the islanders to marginal roles in the local economy.

The tuna fisheries established by Americans in Hawaii were also manned largely by Japanese, but their only effect upon the few remaining native Hawaiians was to provide them, at typically high Honolulu prices, with the fish most of them had long since lost the skill and incentive to catch. Imagine: Polynesians buying fish caught by Japanese fishermen and sold in American markets! This come-to-pass would however surprise no one who examined prewar trade figures and noted that Oceania, even excluding Australia, New Zealand, and Hawaii, annually imported hundreds of thousands of dollars' worth of canned fish, principally for sale to islanders. Few statistics could be more telling with respect to the changes undergone by native fishing in particular or by island cultures in general.

Summarized, these changes wrought by foreigners' fishing enterprises have served to separate islanders from some of their most valuable resources and, in the process, to subject them to new hazards, new diseases, new limitations, and new ways of life. From these enterprises the islanders' only gains have been financial, if such a term could be used to describe the few shillings or francs or pennies a day natives customarily received for laboring underwater. Nearly every island group has experienced some of the effects of these exploitative fishing enterprises; in one, at least, that enterprise has been the dominant force of change.

TORRES STRAIT

Eons ago the waters liberated by the melting of northern glaciers flooded ancient Sahul Land and thereby separated New Guinea from Australia by a shallow sea. The sea covered all but a few of Sahul's higher peaks, and these mountaintops along with a great complexity of bays and reefs and shoals comprise the ill-fated Torres Strait Islands. Those in the west, including Prince of Wales, Horn, Thursday, Moa, Madu, and Mabuiag, are rocky and almost soilless, in sharp contrast with the lush volcanic Murray Islands situated in the east and constituting the northern tip of the Great Barrier Reef. Between these two groups lie the flat coral and sand cays and reefs known as Tutu, Sasi, Burai, Warabu, Guijas, and their equally euphonious neighbors. But all these islands together are only the small visible summits of far more extensive shoals and reefs which cover much of the bed of this ocean region.

Here in these warm, shallow, coralline seas have flourished a rich marine life unequaled in quantity and variety anywhere in Oceania. There are great submerged pastures of flawless gold lip and silver lip mother-of-pearl, banded trochus, sluggish *bêche-de-mer*, horny-plated turtle, and all manner of edible fish, compensating in some measure for the poverty in land resources of many of these islands, and for the dangerous reefs and boat-devouring currents that rip through the Strait and treacherously change with every season and tide.

Millennia before the Spaniard Luis Vaez de Torres sailed through the Strait bound from Espíritu to the Indies, these waters were a highway for Stone Age men who were pressing through New Guinea toward the south. Whether all natives who reached Australia traveled this route cannot be known, but for paleolithic hunters, with at best only the crudest of rafts and dugouts, these island steppingstones would have provided the safest and easiest approach. Throughout the ages some of the preagricultural migrants may have settled in the Strait Islands and nourished themselves by fishing, but in time new influences and peoples arrived from New Guinea. Tradition has preserved accounts of relatively recent migrations from New Guinea into the eastern islands, and by the time whites arrived Strait Islanders were culturally more New Guinean than Australian, although they kept up a lively commercial intercourse with their neighbors to the south as well as with those to the north.

In fact, Strait Islanders were true middlemen in many ways. Their huge cargo canoes traded far down the Queensland coast and up to the estuary of the Fly River. The fertile volcanic soils of the eastern islands provided ample foodstuffs for any native diet, but this did not weaken the appetites of islanders on Mer, Gaferut, or Erub for things of the sea. And their neighbors in the central coral cays and in the rocky western islands were almost wholly dependent upon the sea for sustenance.

Throughout Oceania the sea has nearly always been a better highway than the land, and Strait Islanders were great travelers for purposes of trade and visiting and warfare. Piracy, plunder-raiding, and head-hunting were favorite pastimes, and under the strong leadership which traditionally obtained, these people developed an organized ferocity and a competence in seagoing savagery exceptional even for Melanesia—a circumstance which came to be grimly known by survivors of early European vessels trapped on the reefs and shoals of the Strait.

No historian has yet undertaken to number the vessels whose ribs lie rotting in the Strait, but it is known that Spanish, Dutch, English, and Malays all contributed their galleons and windjammers and proas. Now and then coins or decidedly non-Negroid skulls turn up in native villages to recall the times when ships were wrecked and looted and survivors massacred. In its wildest era the Strait became a byword for dangerous navigation and even more dangerous inhabitants. Then pearl shell was discovered and Strait Islanders were transformed from hunters to hunted.

The first systematic pearl-shell fishing was undertaken in 1868 by a Sydney vessel. Within ten years over a hundred vessels were thus engaged and the annual take was valued at more than £110,000. Riffraff from every east Australian port flocked to the rich shell beds, and, with no effective government controls in force, white skippers and their mixed crews taught the Strait Islanders new twists in savagery. Many of the divers were signed-on islanders from the New Hebrides and beyond; they and their lighter-skinned masters were turned loose on Strait villages to kidnap males for forced diving and females for diversion. (In describing man's inhumanity to man it should be duly recorded that black and brown islanders have frequently and gleefully followed the lead of their white masters in oppressing fellow islanders, thereby establishing before the world their own claim to civilized status.) From the very beginning the shell-fishing invaders had the advantage over the Strait Islanders by reason of firearms, but their victims did not give up without a fierce struggle, and the blood shed for each season's harvest of mother-of-pearl did not all come from Strait Islanders.

In 1878 the Strait Islands were annexed to Queensland and an administrative center established at Thursday Island. Some of the lawlessness was checked, but for years to come Thursday Island and its neighbors were known as the "Sink of the Pacific." When the shell thinned out, white divers began to be replaced by islanders and Japanese and Malays. Meanwhile fishing methods improved: large schooners served as floating bases and supply depots to the fleets of smaller luggers and dinghies, and diving apparatus replaced naked diving. Depletion of shell beds and price fluctuations rendered pearling a hazardous enterprise, but even so, over a thousand tons of shell, worth over £100 a ton, were sold each year as late as 1899. After that pearling fell off year by year and ceased altogether during World War I; but this had the effect of permitting recuperation of the beds and led to a revival of the industry which persisted throughout the interwar years.

During this latter period pearling became an orderly industry. Government regulations protected the beds against exhaustion by controlling the size of marketable shell and by a strict licensing system. Ownership of large pearling enterprises remained in Australian hands, but fishing operations were carried out on luggers manned largely by Japanese, with a few islanders and Australian aborigines serving as crew. Catches were taken to Thursday Island for cleaning, sorting, and crating, and for shipment to New York and London.

Owing to Japanese initiative, trochus fishing became a very profitable business, with Strait Islanders able to produce on their own about half of the annual catch because of the shallower, more accessible trochus beds in their area. Quantities of *bêche-de-mer* were also landed at Thursday Island and sold to Chinese traders for shipment to the East. Also, Singhalese dealers were on hand to buy turtle shell. Fishing changed this port into one of the most cosmopolitan little outposts in the world, with the ratio of profits following the usual geometric progression from blacks to browns to yellows to whites.

Elsewhere in the Strait area the native islanders secured a better proportion of their marine resources for themselves. Most of the islands were set aside as native reserves, and under governmental and missionary influence the islanders were assisted in transforming themselves into model, law-abiding capitalists. They owned—

and built—their own fishing vessels (no more canoes for these sophisticates!); they conducted their own community affairs according to a strict regimen of blue laws and an exemplary emphasis upon bank savings; they devoted themselves zealously to the rituals of Anglicanism; and they turned out as smart a troop of Boy Scouts as could be seen in any part of the Empire. Should a flinty-eyed old lugger captain of the wild seventies have returned to a native village in the Strait Islands sixty years later, he would have signed the pledge.

Thus, as a result of the excesses of pearlers and the overcompensating efforts of humanitarians, these once fiercely independent masters of the Strait became neither fierce nor independent nor masterful—but of course their world was made a safe and profitable sea garden for the soup-makers and button-traders of other lands.

XVII

MINING

The South Seas planter will be sitting on his veranda watching the palms or cane grow long after most of his mining friends have churned up their claims, spent their quick fortunes, and hied off to other adventures. But while they last, phosphate, gold, nickel, and chrome will continue to exert powerful influences on Oceanic economy and native life. Few generalizations can be made about Oceanic mining enterprises as a whole, except to repeat the familiar statement that the native islanders have profited least from them, save perhaps in the cases of Ocean Island and Nauru.

THE GUANO ISLANDS

The discovery that natural soil can be enriched by fertilizer to grow more and better plants led eventually to the pillage of scores of small islands scattered over the Pacific. The looting is still going on at the phosphate-rock islands of Ocean, Nauru, Angaur, and Makatéa, but the guano islands have been scraped clean.

Millennia were required to accumulate guano (from Peruvian *huanu*, dung), the powder-dry excrement of sea birds, on the barren coral-capped islands, but it took white men only a few years to load it all into ships and transport it to the farms of America, Europe, and Australia. The first Pacific guano islands to be exploited were outside Oceania proper, just off the coast of Peru. A previous chapter described how Peruvian slavers carried away shiploads of Polynesians to work and die on those barren rocks. Exploitation of the Oceanic guano deposits came a little later, after whalers had visited the islands in seach of places for burying their dead.

Guano deposits were found throughout Oceania from one end to the other, wherever sea birds had lived and died and left their remains to dry and accumulate in the sun. Millions of boobies and terns, frigate birds and petrels, curlews and golden plovers—these and many others of intriguing name and graceful flight used these bare islands as permanent homes or temporary resting places, and by their appetites and their skills in fishing converted part of the marine life swarming about the reefs into tens of thousands of tons of valuable phosphates and ammonium compounds, all ready to be assimilated by growing plants. On nearly every island some guano may be found, but the famed "guano islands" of Oceanic history were those coral islands and atolls scattered over some four million square miles of ocean between the Hawaiian, Gilbert, Samoan, Society, and Marquesas Islands. Some of these guano islands are barren treeless rocks—like Canton and Johnston and Howland, of recent memory. Others support dry forests. Still others, such as Fanning, are covered with lush and beautiful vegetation.

Only the southern guano islands became permanent homes for Polynesians and eventually came to play modest roles in the developing copra economy. Many of the northern islands, even the treeless ones, served as resting places for seafaring Polynesians, as attested by the archaeological remains they left behind, but when westerners first visited these islands most of them were populated only by screaming sea birds and voracious land crabs and rats.

Spanish navigators in the sixteenth century and English in the eighteenth sighted many of the guano islands, but accounts by American whalers were principally responsible for focusing attention on their valuable guano deposits. The discoveries were considered so important that the United States Congress, in 1856, passed the Guano Act, allowing Americans to assert the claim of the United States to unoccupied islands for the purpose of taking away guano. Under this act, forty-eight islands were claimed in due course, but few of these claims have survived.

For twenty-five years American companies cleared out the guano from many of the islands and abandoned them to birds and rats. In a few cases the Americans skinned off the surface and left the gleaning to British companies operating out of New Zealand or Australia.

The lot of the guano diggers was hard and lonely. With natives brought in from Hawaii or southern Polynesia to serve as laborers, the company agent and one or two assistants would remain at the job until the island was scraped clean. The richest deposits were located on barren and treeless rocks, with no protection from the painful glare of the sun. Supplies were brought in three or four times a year from Honolulu, Auckland, and Melbourne; everything that came onto the island and everything that left it, including the thousands of tons of bagged guano, had to be transported through the surf which beat against the unprotected beaches. Ship anchorages were poor or altogether lacking, so that the whole business was highly precarious.

Ashore, tramline tracks were laid out from the guano deposits to the landing beach; some of these still remain alongside the shrines of the earlier Polynesian visitors.

With the guano all gone and the bird life decimated, many of the islands were abandoned and forgotten for decades, until the race for cable stations and airports again brought them into world prominence. Other islands, with deeper soil and more rainfall, enjoyed better fates. A few of these were leased to companies and planted in coconuts, the plantations being operated by white managers and by native laborers brought in from Polynesia and near-by Micronesia. Some of the southern guano islands were eventually turned into new homes for permanent settlers from the overcrowded Gilbert Islands.

Meanwhile the quest for fertilizer took a new turn in the islands where, instead of being shoveled off the surface in the form of powdery guano, it had to be crushed out of rock.

NAURU AND OCEAN ISLAND

What Pacific traveler has not watched with fascination the nighttime display of phosphorescence stirred up in his vessel's wake? Phosphorus, held in suspension in sea water and diffused over large areas of the world's oceans, comes principally from decomposed marine organisms. In tropical seas marine life is most plentiful around coral reefs, and there phosphatic matter is concentrated. Shallow submerged reefs were ideal platforms for deposit of phosphorus; and when the reefs were exposed, by emergence of the island or sinking of the coast line, some of the phosphates remained on the surface as deposited and other more soluble phosphates drained down into the softer underlying coral to convert it into tricalcic phosphate.[1] The harder portions of coral limestone were

[1] An alternate theory is that the phosphatic materials came from bird guano deposited on coral islands which subsequently submerged and then emerged.

not affected, so that the usual deposit consists of phosphatic material lodged in pockets—some small, some very extensive—in the harder limestone. When the phosphate is removed, the remaining limestone is a jagged wilderness of pinnacles and crevasses.

The phosphate itself is highly variable, ranging from metallic hardness to crumbly nodules; it may be gray, brown, or even golden in appearance, and contains varying intermixtures of lime and mineral impurities. It can be removed from the larger pockets by power shovels after it has been loosened, but much of the mining has to be carried on by hand methods—chipping away at the small narrowing pockets which sometimes extend tens of feet deep. Then, before shipping and processing, the rock must be broken up and dried.

Raw phosphate has to be made water-soluble in order to become available for plant food, and this is done by grinding it up and treating it with sulphuric acid, the product being the superphosphate now so widely used to fertilize farms and pastures deficient in phosphorus. Soils differ greatly in their phosphate requirements, but in Australia, for example, a ton of raw rock, converted into superphosphate, will supply fifty acres of wheat-producing land.

In the 1930's the world annually consumed between seven and ten million tons of phosphate; without it agriculture as we know it could not exist. America supplied most of its own needs, but Western Europe, Japan, Australia, and New Zealand had to import, and the last three countries came to depend upon Oceania to supply most of their needs.

Australia's great wheat industry could not have developed without phosphate, nor could New Zealand's dairying; and the quest for guano and phosphates sent Britishers prospecting to every lonely atoll and island in the South Seas. But for a while the search was unproductive, and the Pacific Islands Company of London was reduced to scraping up what the American guano diggers had overlooked. Then a company chemist had the curiosity to analyze a doorstop of "fossilized wood" brought home by a company agent as a curio from Nauru, an isolated island in the central Pacific. The rock turned out to be very high-grade tricalcic phosphate, and questioning discovered that both Nauru and near-by Ocean Island were covered with similar material. Ocean Island was still unclaimed, and it was a simple matter to show the Union Jack there and add the island to Her Majesty's Gilbert and Ellice Island Protectorate. But Nauru was German, so the company directors had to proceed cannily to obtain mining rights there from an unsuspecting Germany. The trick came off, however, and the British company started operations in 1900 on Ocean Island, and in 1906 on Nauru. The richness of these deposits turned out to be truly fabulous. The rock was extremely high grade and estimates of reserves ran to twenty million tons on Ocean and a hundred million on Nauru.

Two major problems faced the company: to obtain sufficient manpower for the hand labor predominantly required in mining the rock; and to devise measures for loading the rock into ships.

Local natives were too few, and the rents and royalties paid them for mining leases and for mined rock reduced their incentive to work for wages. At Ocean Island the problem was temporarily solved by utilizing indentured natives from the Gilbert and Ellice Islands and by importing a few hundred Japanese. At Nauru some Melanesians were tried out as laborers but later sent home, and the main reliance was placed upon Carolinians and Japanese.

Ship-loading presented a tougher problem. Both Nauru and Ocean were raised-coral islands which fell away steeply to unfathomed depths save for narrow ledges of fringing reef against which the full force of the Pacific swell broke. There was thus no anchorage or protection for ships, and all cargo that went onto or off the islands had to be boated through a tricky and sometimes impassable surf. Engineers eventually solved this problem by building huge cantilever trestles which swung out over the reef and conveyed rock either directly into the moored ships, as at Nauru, or, as at Ocean Island, into boats which were lightered out to the waiting ships.

While Ocean Island and Nauru were being developed, the same British company discovered similar but less extensive deposits at Makatéa Island, north of Tahiti, and joined with the French in exploiting them. The technical problems were overcome in much the same way as at Nauru and Ocean, and labor was secured locally and by importing Japanese. Germans found phosphate on Angaur Island in the western Carolines and began mining operations there in 1909, with European managers, Chinese artisans, and natives recruited from near-by islands.

World War I marked a change in operation of the deposits at Nauru and Angaur. The former island was taken from Germany and mandated to the United Kingdom, Australia, and New Zealand for the purpose of sharing in the exploitation of phosphate. The three governments set up the British Phosphate Commission (BPC), which acquired ownership of the Pacific Islands Company's interests at Nauru and Ocean and carried on mining as before. The enterprise was financially supported by the participating governments and its output was sold at cost on a quota basis to them, but otherwise it was run like any private corporation. Chinese were recruited at Hong Kong to take the place of Japanese and Carolinians, who no longer were available. Technical improvements in mining, crushing, drying, and loading resulted, by 1939, in a combined exportation of more than a million tons annually, enough to satisfy all phosphate requirements of Australia and New Zealand.

The Japanese government acquired ownership of the German property at Angaur and eventually turned over operations to a corporation in which the government retained large financial interests. Besides working the Angaur deposits intensively, the Japanese branched out to other western Caroline and Mariana Islands where smaller guano and rock deposits were located. Ultimately they were able to ship to Japan about 200,000 tons per annum, thus making a small but highly important contribution to Japan's fertilizer-dependent agriculture. Japanese and Carolinians, the latter under indenture, worked the deposits. In addition, Makatéa maintained an annual production in excess of 100,000 tons and sent most of it to Japan.

All together, the four major Oceanic phosphate islands produced only about 8 per cent of the world's annual output, but their production was vitally important to Japan, Australia, and New Zealand, since these countries needed the fertilizer to sustain their basic economies, had no significant domestic supplies of it, and from the point of view of freight costs were almost prohibitively far removed from other sources of phosphate. Added to this, the Oceanic deposits are among the world's richest in phosphate content, which adds to their freighting advantage. Altogether, the phosphate islands presented a very happy set of circumstances for the British, French, or Japanese miners who removed the ore, for the farmers who spread the refined material over their fields, and for the consumers who assimilated it indirectly in their bread, butter, and rice. But what of the natives who, one could properly assume, originally owned the phosphate?

Ocean Island, or Banaba, which has proved so valuable to its white exploiters, was previously anything but a treasure to its native Banabans. The few hundreds who dwelt there prior to white contact were Micronesians, thought to have come from the near-by Gilbert Islands, whose natives they closely resemble. Ironically enough, the island which has helped to fertilize millions of acres in other lands has itself only meager, infertile soil, and native plant food was limited to pandanus and to coconuts growing in the narrow coastal belt girdling the coralline hump which comprises most of the island. To compensate for their vegetable poverty the Banabans became expert fishermen, but there were no means within their power to increase the paltry supply of fresh water on their too porous and drought-ridden island. Women had to crawl into caves to fill their shell water containers from shallow pools, and, when these too dried up, forced emigration ensued. Droughts started the depopulation and early phosphate operations hastened it along; by 1914 the population had been reduced to four hundred souls, one sixth of the number believed to have been there at the time of first white contact.

Where there had previously been one homogeneous population on Ocean Island, in 1939 there were four crowded together. The phosphate industry, of course, dominated the island. Its managers comprised a staff of several Britishers and the headquarters staff of the Gilbert and Ellice Islands Colony. These whites maintained an entirely separate existence. They lived in comfortable bungalows or bachelors' dormitories and during off-hours energetically performed the British sport and tea rituals.

The eight hundred or so Chinese contract laborers recruited in Hong Kong lived in compounds and had little contact with others when not working. They were not permitted to bring their women with them and did not have access to native women. Free hours were spent in gambling, theatricals, and truck gardening; except for an occasional fracas with Gilbertese laborers, they were industrious and "submissive" workers.

To work for a while on Ocean Island was the Great Adventure for most Gilbertese youths, but since many of them brought along their wives and remained for only a year, the change in their lives was not very profound.

To the remaining Banabans, however, the mining operations proved in time to become quite revolutionary. Their physical survival was no longer precarious: water was assured them from company supplies, and with the money they received from lease of land and phosphate royalties they were able to purchase food and western goods. Instead of living in small dispersed hamlets as they formerly had done, they were concentrated in four large villages. Their own political organization, based on hamlet and district units and upon a complex ritual, was replaced by a government-imposed system involving native police and the usual preoccupation with sanitation and western concepts of welfare.

One element of the old native culture which was retained was the sport of fowling. Man-of-war (frigate) birds, with great wings out of all proportion to their small bodies, were captured and tamed so that they decoyed other birds to within range of their native masters, who then brought the prey down with a kind of bola. In the old days this highly ritualized activity of the adult males was more than a sport, and it added spirit to life on this uninviting island. But like most other zestful things about Banaban culture, this "wanton" aspect of fowling was replaced by mission activities and other watered-down imitations of western civilization.

Nauru, like Ocean Island, was a mass of coral and phosphate, but its fringing coastal belt was wider and the native food supply better. Also, fresh water was more plentiful than at Ocean; and Nauruans supplemented ordinary fishing with sea food from fish-pond reservoirs. The islanders were a strong, fairly healthy branch of Micronesians when first contacted by Europeans.

Nauruans were divided into twelve exogamous, matrilineal lineages, but these lineages were not identified with specific territories; in fact, members of any one lineage might live scattered about in several of the districts which comprised the island. It so happened that one lineage might be able to dominate a district by virtue of the comparatively greater number and influence of its members, but such ascendency was not permanent; interdistrict feuding was common, and political careers fluid. Families usually dwelt in separate units, but sometimes combined with one or two others to form common households.

An unusual feature of Nauru was its emphasis on individual property ownership, including land. Inheritance was ruled largely by primogeniture, with daughters especially favored.

Nauruans distinguished three social strata: nobility (persons of inherited or achieved affluence and their relatives); commoners; and serfs (captured in war or accepted as refugees). Class lines were not rigidly drawn, and it was not unusual for a man of the nobility to marry a commoner.

The old native culture of Nauru, like that of Ocean Island, was only superficially described by early visitors and was so overwhelmingly transformed by events of the last five decades that the past cannot be recovered. Beachcombers and traders started the changes and contributed the advice and arms which encouraged continuous interdistrict feuding during the first century of contact.

Germany extended her Marshall Islands protectorate to include Nauru in 1888, and, following the German pattern, the colonial officials encouraged the Nauruans to increase copra production, there being little else available for trade.

Phosphate mining changed all that. Native landowners were paid for land leased to the phosphate company and received in addition a royalty on all rock removed. In short order Nauruans became very wealthy by Oceanic standards and were able to buy goods at the trade store without having to earn money by manual labor. After the First World War, Nauru was mandated to Great Britain, New Zealand, and Australia, and additional measures were undertaken to safeguard what were believed to be the interests of the natives. The usual British welfare services were installed, school attendance was made compulsory, and many Nauruans were helped to obtain higher education in Australia. They were not encouraged to work with the mining company except in semiskilled jobs. Native standards of living became much "higher," and it was not unusual for affluent Nauruans to own lorries and motor bikes.

Mining operations did not encroach too much on their native food supply or settlements, and they continued to dwell in their villages much as before—except, of course, for the usual sanitary reforms. They were encouraged to elect their own district "chiefs"; and these were not infrequently chosen from among commoners, on the basis of leadership rather than by traditional standards. This represented a marked change in native life, as did the disappearance of polygamy as a result of the mission influence which also wiped out most of the old religious practices.

Nauruans did not have to work very hard to satisfy the new needs, and adaptation to western individualistic economy was easier for them because of their own native concepts of individual property ownership. But, as favored wards, they became increasingly parasitic upon the mandate administration and the phosphate industry, with the inevitable loss of vitality of their old institutions.

Such favored treatment of Nauruans was made possible only by the employment of Chinese laborers to carry out the heavy work of the industry. The coolies at Nauru numbered on an average about one thousand and, like those at Ocean Island, were recruited at Hong Kong for three-year indentures. As at Ocean, they lived in their compound, entirely separated from the white masters and the Nauruans. In their womanless exile they worked industriously and submissively, trading with Nauruans for food now and then, but otherwise keeping to their compounds when off the job, with gambling their major recreation.

Meanwhile the white masters—in government and industry—lived in their bachelors' dormitories or in "married" bungalows, with plenty of sport to keep them fit and plenty of tea and beer to relieve the tedium of their Empire assignment on this dreary hump of coral and phosphate.

INLAND NEW GUINEA

Hope for gold spurred on many of the earliest white South Seas explorers, and substance was added to the dreams when Saavedra discovered traces of it along New Guinea's northern coast in 1528. But after fruitless searching, men turned to the surer profits of sandalwooding, trading, blackbirding, and planting. Planting had become firmly established as the basic commercial economy when gold again entered the picture and overnight created an extraordinary civilization in the heart of Stone Age New Guinea.

A few hopefuls had never given up the search, and as far back as the 1870's there were prospectors strung out along the islands east of New Guinea. Payable alluvial deposits were located on Misima and Woodlark Islands and at isolated places in the interior of the main island, but the indomitables were rewarded for their hardships only enough to keep them hoping. In German New Guinea systematic searches were undertaken, but had to be given up at the outbreak of World War I.

The big strike came during the twenties, when prospectors discovered the incredibly rich pay soil—running as high as £A200 per cubic yard—in the Bulolo River region of northeast New Guinea's Morobe District. For a few years it remained a prospector's show, every man for himself, and a few individual fortunes were made in spite of the difficulties. Supplies had to be portered in from the coast through swamps and over ranges, a journey requiring from ten to fourteen days. The supply track led through territories of wild hostile natives, who added to the miseries of terrain, fever, and dysentery to make this gold adventure a fatal one for many white masters and their native servants. So hard and costly were work and supply conditions that production had to keep above ten ounces a day to pay off the independent miner.

When miners had recovered all the gold they could with their primitive methods, they fanned out into nearly every range and valley in northeast New Guinea. Minor rushes developed in Papua, in the mountains behind Wewak, and even on Bougainville, Guadalcanal, and Fiji; but the Bulolo area retained its lead through the enterprise of the big companies which eventually supplanted the individual miners.

Backed by British capital, some of the more far-sighted miners took over the deposits after crude washing methods had skimmed off the surfaces. Testing proved the existence of deposits which were very extensive but which required modern dredging and crushing methods to exploit. To overcome supply difficulties aerial transport was installed, a plane covering the distance from the coast in thirty minutes as compared with the ten to fourteen days of walking. Everything went by plane: miners and their native employees, lumber, food, heavy mining machinery, cows for a dairy, vehicles, and, of course, beer. In the space of a few years mining centers like Wau and Bulolo became modern towns, complete with hotels, clubs, and cinemas, an entirely airborne civilization in the heart of a neolithic wilderness.

By 1939 these gold-mining communities contained about 700 whites and nearly 7000 native employees, and production, in the peak year, had surpassed 400,000 ounces. Upon the rest of New Guinea the effect of this concentration of population and wealth was revolutionary. Royalties from gold enabled the administration to continue its work energetically throughout the whole Territory during the depression years, when a dependence upon copra economy alone would surely have arrested westernization. So changed was the commercial center of gravity that when a volcanic eruption destroyed the capital town of Rabaul it was decided to shift administrative headquarters to Lae, a coastal town near the gold fields. The air age ushered in by gold mining resulted in scheduled passenger flights to Australia and sliced weeks off ordinary steamship traveling time. The Territory attracted a new type of white man, an individual whose customary tempo was the hustle of western cities rather than the patient planter life.

The effect of all these things on native New Guinea was to speed up the process of opening wild areas to white influence and control, and to provide new experiences for the thousands of natives who worked at the gold fields. The glimpse of white civilization obtained by natives working on plantations was very limited compared to what they saw in the modern, more densely populated mining towns. Also, they received more pay than their copra-making cousins, plus closer contact with more white masters. Altogether, it was a more exciting and profitable way to earn tax money and size up the new white world. It also provided natives with an unprecedented view of their New Guinea compatriots, since thousands of them were concentrated in narrow camps and campgrounds. Feuding developed among workers, and particularly bloody were the fights between those from the Sepik and Markham river areas.

As copra prices continued to tumble, there were few planters who did not yearningly gaze past their forlorn groves and sheds toward the Morobe gold lands, and many made the leap. But the farsighted ones knew that gold would someday give out and that the future of the Territory would continue to depend upon agriculture. Some even suggested that the most worth-while effect of gold business was its opening up of vast new potential farming areas in the temperate highlands.

NEW CALEDONIA

Through a combination of geological accident and French design, almost the only feature New Caledonia shares with the other South Seas Islands is its location. Arriving there direct from the coconut belt, the traveler learned with surprise that this island, so near to Malekula and Fiji, was at one time the world's largest producer of nickel and chromium. Also distinguishing it from the rest of Oceania was its bizarre cultural hodgepodge, compounded of elements of Melanesia, Java, Indochina, and Japan, along with some of the best and worst of France.

New Caledonia extends for 250 miles northwest by southeast and averages about 30 miles wide. The island is extremely rugged; mountain ranges rise to 5400 feet, but are broken in places by deep valleys and large inland plateaus. Erosion has scarred many areas beyond any semblance of orderly topographic pattern, and these areas are practically impassable. The eastern slopes and valleys receive a full measure of rain brought by the prevailing easterlies, with the result that this side has the tropical luxuriance of other Melanesian islands. The western side is drier, however, and is covered with a scrub vegetation so that it resembles Australia's "bush." In climate, also, New Caledonia differs from islands to the north: the hot season is truly hot and humid, but there is enough seasonal change to make it agreeable and healthful for people accustomed to a temperate cli-

mate. The absence of malaria makes the island even
more pleasantly habitable.

In 1939 a stroll through Nouméa, principal town of
New Caledonia and as French as Marseille, made it hard
to realize that one short century before this island was
inhabited only by Stone Age Melanesians. During this
century, it is true, Nouméa's plumbing had not greatly
changed, but everything else had, and the indigenes had
been pushed back into reserves in the less coveted parts
of the island.

The first census of New Caledonia, taken in 1887, recorded about 42,000 of these indigenes, but by that
time the native population had already been considerably reduced through the usual processes. Estimates of
the original size of the population go up to 70,000, but
this number could hardly have been stable in view of the
continuous intertribal warfare which was aggravated by
natives from the east intruding upon the local people.
This eastern influence is most evident in the physical
type and culture found along the eastern coast, which
is nearest the Loyalty Islands.

Some New Caledonian natives share with Australian
aborigines the honors of superlative ugliness, but that, of
course, is mere prejudice based on quaint western notions of beauty. To anthropologists the New Caledonians
are magnificent specimens, so much like the aborigines
in their heavy brow ridges and prognathism there can be
little doubt that these Negroids contain a larger component of the Australoid.

Unlike the aborigines, however, the indigenes were
competent horticulturists and resembled their Melanesian cousins to the north in languages (there were about
twenty languages in use in New Caledonia) and in material culture. The indigenes were grouped into families
and exogamous lineages and, where strong leaders presided, into warring tribes.

Cook's party, the first white men to land in New Caledonia, found the indigenes friendly and hospitable, but it did not require long for the traders and beachcombers to alter that. Marist missionaries landed there in 1840 and began to pave the way for French annexation, which took place in 1853, almost in the presence of a near-by British warship. So slim was the time margin and so great the chagrin of the British naval commander that he committed suicide. And well he might: for there, on Australia's very doorstep, was lost an island almost solidly composed of the ores of nickel, chrome, iron, cobalt, manganese, and many other minerals of rarity and value.

At first, however, the new French masters were less interested in their island's mineral wealth than in its suitability for colonization and penal settlements. Colonists were encouraged to produce the sugar, copra, and coffee needed by France, and land was secured for plantations by engineering native revolts and then stepping in to confiscate their territories. During the pioneer days there was also some prospecting, partly by Australians, but the chief value of the island was its great isolation from France, making it an ideal place of exile for France's undesirables. From 1860 to 1894 New Caledonia played host to over 40,000 prisoners, including common criminals and political exiles. Intellectual leaders of the ill-fated Paris Commune of 1871 and Moroccan Arab nationalist leaders shared exile and punishment alongside the habitual criminals. Although many prisoners died on the island, some of them served out their sentences and returned to France. Still others escaped to Australia or found refuge in beachcombing on neighboring islands. Many remained on New Caledonia, either as free colonists or to serve out their sentences as *libérés*. The government helped the latter group to secure farmlands, and natives were thus pushed back farther and farther. In time thousands of cattle were allowed to graze on the natural pasture, and, with no fences to stop them, they invaded native gardens and increased native resentment. By 1878 this encroachment became unendurable; several tribes revolted and massacred whole settlements of colonists and soldiers. For a time the native campaigns were carried on so efficiently and ruthlessly that it appeared they might recover most of their homelands; peace was finally negotiated, however, and the natives sent back to their reserves. The experience had a sobering effect upon the government, and from that time on there was at least official recognition of "native rights." Among other things, it became clear that natives could not be induced to labor in the mining enterprises which were then being developed; and thereby the colony's chief economic problem was created.

For a while white convicts were farmed out to mine owners and planters, but this practice was neither popular nor profitable; the search for labor consequently turned to Asia. Beginning in 1883 a few hundred Chinese indentured laborers were imported. Japanese were also tried out, but did not prove amenable to the crude working or living conditions. Even a few Hindus were tried; but the hardest working and most docile workers came from Indochina and Java, and hence these places became the primary sources for labor.

At one time New Caledonia was the biggest producer in the world of cobalt, nickel, and chromium. Nickel and chrome mining have remained the economic mainstay of the island, although Canada (in nickel) and Rhodesia (in chrome) took over world leadership in 1905 and 1921, respectively. France and Belgium purchased most of New Caledonia's nickel, and the United States, France, and Australia its chrome. Japan and Germany also took large quantities of crude nickel ore, and during the thirties the Japanese engaged in the actual mining of New Caledonian iron ore to help supply the Japanese market. The Japanese miners, together with compatriots who had earlier settled on the island, became an important element in the commercial life of the colony. In nearly every other respect, however, the economy of the colony was bound to France: the island produced what was needed in France, was more or less reserved as a market for French products, and was governed by a metropolitan bureaucracy.

By 1939 the island had become like none other in the South Seas. From its layout and architecture, Nouméa might have been a coastal town of southern France; and up and down both coasts were sleepy villages reminiscent of Provence. Coffee plantations dotted the landscape, and large tracts of land were set aside for pasturing the colonists' tens of thousands of cattle. Many ore-bearing mountains were scarred by nickel and chrome workings, and sawmills were penetrating the forests where valuable kauri pine timber was being removed.

The composition of the population was transformed even more than the landscape. The 70,000 or so natives who had one time owned the island were reduced to 30,000 in number and pushed back into reserves where most of them subsisted on taro and yams as they had for centuries before. Some of them dived for shell or grew a little coffee and cocoa for export. A few worked for white or Japanese masters, and such experiences, added to mission influence, served to teach them a *patois* French along with other externals of civilization. After it became obvious to the French that natives were unwilling and unsuitable for coolie labor, they were permitted to live their own lives and set their own rate of depopulation. After all, they affected neither one way nor the other the economic life of the colony, which was the concern of the 17,000 whites and 1500 Japanese, and their 14,000 Javanese and Tonkinese laborers.

The economy of New Caledonia was built upon the use of cheap Asiatic labor in the extraction of nickel, chrome, and iron, and it has been an exploitative economy in the classical sense of the term. Chrome ore was mined and shipped direct to its overseas markets. In terms of its chromic oxide content, some 25,000 tons were exported in 1938, comprising about 6 per cent of world production outside the USSR.[2] The New Caledonia mines were owned principally by British capital and were managed locally by British, American, and Australian agents. Except for taxes levied against exported ore, most of the mining proceeds were lost to the colony.

The control over nickel production was also concentrated in the hands of absentee owners, although a few of the nickel mines were owned by local French interests. Since New Caledonian ore is low grade, it must be refined one stage before it can be economically shipped to market. The only refinery and the largest mines were owned by the Société le Nickel, which consequently controlled local production and prices. Some alleged that the Société was owned by the world monopolistic International Nickel Company of Canada; others claimed it was owned primarily by Rothschild and Bank of Indochina interests, and that the Société merely had a cartel agreement with International Nickel in connection with price and quota matters. In either case, controls were vested in outsiders and, except for export taxes on ore, the profits did not contribute to the development of the colony.

Chromium ore was loaded onto freighters at anchorages near the mines, but nickel ore had to be delivered to Nouméa for refining and eventual shipment overseas. In terms of nickel content, some 9600 metric tons were produced in 1938, about 8 per cent of world production outside the USSR.[3]

Mining was largely a matter of makeshift devices and hand labor supplied by indentured Javanese and Tonkinese. Most of the mines were completely isolated and

[2] *Statistical Yearbook of the United Nations,* first issue (Lake Success, New York, 1949).
[3] *Statistical Yearbook of the United Nations.*

afforded only the crudest kind of facilities for the laborers who were compelled by law to serve out their terms of contract. The nickel refining at Nouméa was also a make-shift affair, dependent heavily on hand labor.

Parasitic upon the mining industry was an array of smaller businesses—mercantile, service, food production, and so forth. Ownership of the most important of these firms was concentrated in the hands of a few leading families, whose members also served as "directors" of the foreign-owned mining enterprises because of the French law requiring local representation.

Below the upper class of managers, "directors," proprietors, and big merchants, was a far more numerous category of white small farmers and merchants and white-collar workers. Some of them were children or grandchildren of humble colonists, others of freed convicts. They regarded New Caledonia as their home and fiercely resented the domination of the island resources by absentee owners. They continued to look to France as their cultural fatherland, but wished for more autonomy in economic and political matters. But, however poignant a picture they were used to painting of themselves as the mistreated "little men," they did not fare too poorly. To them physical labor was as abhorrent as it was to the wealthy, and it was a very poor establishment indeed that did not have a few native or Javanese domestics and laborers.

The Japanese were latecomers to New Caledonia, but, like their compatriots elsewhere, they knew what they wanted and proceeded with energy to get it. Of the 1500 Japanese domiciled on the island, the majority were small tradesmen: the "Chinese" of New Caledonia. There was a Japanese store in every village, and in Nouméa they were to be seen smiling behind the counters of most small shops. Few of these tradesmen brought wives along with them, so large numbers of them lived with native women. In an entirely different social class were the

managers of the Japanese iron mine developed during
the thirties. This enterprise mined and shipped ore direct
to Japan and was well advanced toward its annual production goal of a half million tons of ore when World
War II stopped operations. In keeping with French law,
the local "directors" of this Japanese industry were all
good Frenchmen.

The 9000 Javanese and 5000 Tonkinese supplied the
muscle and the sweat to keep the colony solvent. The
Tonkinese worked principally in the mines and at refining; Javanese also worked at the mines, but large numbers of them were indentured to farmers and worked
as field laborers or domestics. Hundreds of them were
free residents of the colony, having served out their
terms of indenture and elected to remain, but the majority were there under three- to five-year contracts. In
return for transportation and guaranteed repatriation
upon conclusion of their indentures, they contracted to
work in the mines or stores or fields for a few francs a
day plus keep. Their employers were backed by government authority, with fines and imprisonment imposed
for disobedience.

Living conditions provided for these contract laborers
were if anything even worse than those provided for
native plantation laborers in the coconut islands to the
north. Perfunctory inspections of Javanese work camps
were carried out by agents of the Netherlands Indies
government; but the Tonkinese, being French subjects,
had no champions and vented their grievances in occasional rather pathetic strikes. Caste barriers were erected
by the white masters against these Asiatics at nearly
every point of potential contact; there was no non-
sense here about "traditional French democracy." Even
the indigenes were ranked higher by the masters.

Over all these factions, with their differing objectives
and resources and needs, was placed a colonial governor
and a staff of career civil servants. The governor en-

joyed autocratic powers and frequently had to use them to discourage tendencies to local autonomy. To advise him and to levy taxes and prepare the budget there was a fifteen-member general council elected by white residents of the island; because of predominant big-company representation on this council, however, it was identified with the interests of overseas owners and consequently had little interest in any "Advance Caledonia" movement. Among other things, this general council saw to it that industry tax levies remained low, and took pains to insure that the contract laborers were not "spoiled."

The governor's task could hardly have been an easy one: to contain the autonomous movements of the white population and to mitigate somewhat, in the name of French democracy, their fierce caste prejudices. And, to make his assignment more difficult, there was growing up under his very nose a colony of energetic and resourceful Japanese, seemingly intent upon adding this French island to the Co-Prosperity Sphere.

XVIII

BASES

Every Pacific Island has at some time or other been coveted by the subjects and agents of foreign powers: some for their land, some for their raw materials, others for the souls or muscles of their inhabitants; and in nearly every case the various manifestations of these forms of alien cupidity have had distinctive effects on island life. Besides the resources just listed, one other motive has led aliens to exploit the islands, and that has been their locations.

Location alone has been an important factor in the annexation and development of a number of island groups: Guam's value to Spain lay in its position athwart the galleon route to Manila; Hawaii's situation along the line to the Far East has had more and more effect on events in that group; and to many Australians who care little about copra or gold, New Guinea's primary function has been her situation as a defensive shield.

It was primarily because of their locations that Great Britain annexed Fanning, Christmas, Penrhyn, and Suvorov Islands in 1888, to serve as possible landing places for the projected Empire Cable (the cable eventually laid ran from Vancouver to New Zealand and Australia via Fanning, Fiji, and Norfolk Islands). Again, the prewar American and British race for central Pacific airfields singled out pin points of land—Johnston, Howland, Canton—that had no other value than that of location. But all these events had little effect on natives; only Penrhyn Island was inhabited, and after annexation no effort was made to utilize it. In three other cases, however, the factor of strategic location has been the dominating influence over the lives of islanders: in Eastern Samoa and Guam, where the presence of United States Navy installations has been the all-important factor; and in the Japanese mandated islands, where strategic far more than straight economic considerations appear to have shaped Nipponese policy.

AMERICAN SAMOA

The Three-Power Convention of 1899 awarded Eastern Samoa (Tutuila and Manua) to the United States, but indifferent Congresses did not act on the matter until 1926, when accession was formerly approved. Since this country's chief interest in the matter was the maintenance of a naval station at the excellent harbor of Pago Pago, the President placed the administration of Samoa in the hands of the Navy Department. Meanwhile there had been the usual inquiries undertaken to define or redefine Samoa's status, and in 1929 a full-dress commission advocated an organic act, with American citizenship and civil government for Samoans; but these proposals were not acted upon.

Administration by the Navy had good and bad consequences for Samoans. The naval governor enjoyed nearly
absolute powers, which usually were exercised benevolently but firmly, thereby giving him a status which
Samoans understand and respect. On the other hand, a
governor's tenure was limited to the Navy's conventional
duty assignment of only two years, and until very recently no governor or his staff came to the job specially
prepared. Nor was it possible to acquire much expert
knowledge in that short period. Thus, the system did not
provide for consistency and continuity in administration.

Throughout the period of naval rule the entire emphasis was upon maintaining a naval station and providing for native welfare. There was no official support for
white man's enterprises; on the contrary, the naval government marketed all native copra (about two hundred
tons annually, the only export), leaving little scope for
the few white traders who had remained.

The administration tended to allow Samoans to run
their own affairs so long as public order was not interfered with. Unfortunately, disturbances to "public order" are inherent in the native polity, and governors on
several occasions have had to interfere violently to "settle" factional quarrels. Under the circumstances opposition was bound to appear sooner or later, and it was only
to be expected that the *Mau* movement should spread
hence from Western Samoa.[1] Some anti-Navy whites
and half-castes added their complaints, and American
newspapers contained letters from "friends of Samoa"
calling attention to the sad plight of the innocent natives
under alleged dictatorial rule by the Navy. There was
then repeated, in miniature, what was taking place in
Western Samoa, and the Navy's solution was similar to
that later adopted by the New Zealand Labour party:
the *Mau* was recognized and the governor even at-

[1] See page 218.

tended their ceremonials as honored guest, but he never permitted any assumption to be made that actual authority rested in anyone but himself.

By 1939 it appeared, on the surface at least, that the experiment in administration had been more successful in Eastern than in Western Samoa, recognizing, of course, the greater complications existing in the western islands. Probing a little deeper, however, it might be argued that paternalistic naval rule had ill prepared the Samoans for participation in the hard competitive world they would have to face unless they were to be kept always as museum pieces. So dependent, in fact, had they become upon Navy facilities in every aspect of living that the *Mau* formally requested of a congressional commission that the United States create a trust fund of ten million dollars for the benefit of American Samoa, asserting that generous handouts of this nature constituted the "practice and policy all over the world by all governments"!

GUAM

The rape of Oceania began with Guam. Two and a half centuries before the unsuspecting savages of Polynesia welcomed white masters to their shores, Guam's fate was already sealed. Magellan led the procession in 1521 and left the usual calling cards. Then came Loaysa, Gaetano, and López de Legaspi, the latter proclaiming Spanish sovereignty in 1564. After 1600 Guam was the official refreshment port for galleons annually sailing between Mexico and the Philippines. But not until 1668 did the Spanish make an effort to civilize their domain in the Marianas; in that year Jesuit missionaries landed and, backed up by soldiers, began mass conversions.

Nearest to Asia in distance, in culture, and in physical type were the Chamorros of the Mariana Islands. At the time of the first continuous European contact there were

between 70,000 and 100,000 of these natives, described
by the first travelers as being taller and fairer than other
natives in Oceania, with long straight black hair, and in-
clined to corpulence—in other words, much like the Polynesians. (Some of the giantism attributed to them may
be discounted: early travelers usually described tallness
and smallness in superlatives, natives having been either
"giants" or "pygmies," with little in between.)

The Chamorros were concentrated on the large southern islands, and Guam appears to have been something
of a native metropolis; for these people were skilled navigators and used to make long interisland voyages in
their fine outrigger sailing canoes. Most of them lived in
villages along the coast and inland and were dependent
upon breadfruit, taro, coconuts, and fish. In addition,
they alone of all Oceanic natives grew rice. Some of the
Chamorros lived in impressively built houses supported
by stone columns, which still stand today, but the majority lived in wood and thatch dwellings like most other
islanders.

Their basic social unit was the family. Marriages were
not difficult to dissolve, but each man had only one wife
at a time; in addition, however, concubines were permitted. The early reports state that the father was the
"legal" head of the family, but that the mother exercised
the true authority. The existing lineage system was
matrilineal; a man thus inherited his estate and titles
from his mother's brother rather than from his father.
The records do not state whether or not the lineages were
totemic, but they were exogamous.

No emphasis whatsoever was placed on premarital
chastity; a virginal bride, in fact, would have been an
embarrassment to her family. The men of a neighborhood banded together in semisecret associations, with
their own clubhouse and ritual festivals. After puberty
young boys dwelt in the clubhouse until marriage, and
it was usual for unmarried girls to be assigned to these

clubs during one period of their lives. There it was customary for them to become sexual partners with the male members; after this sex apprenticeship, girls were usually eagerly sought after as wives.

Social organization was complicated by the existence of a caste system which had economic and political ramifications. About one fourth of the population made up the nobility; most of the remainder were commoners, and between the two were deposed nobility. The nobility were, of course, the political leaders, and also monopolized the activities of warfare, deep-sea fishing, and overseas trading. Commoners made obeisance to them, and paid tribute in food and in farming labor. A nobleman who married or even had sexual intercourse with a commoner would be either slain or degraded to the middle class, in which also belonged nobility deposed owing to other crimes against their caste. There is no credible explanation given of this caste system; the nobility may have been the first settlers and hence land proprietors, or they may have been conquerors. On the other hand, in many Oceanic societies some individuals rise to social eminence and perpetuate their status dynastically; and it is not necessary to account for existence of castes and classes by ethnic racial differences or conquest.

Each Chamorro village, or district comprised of several villages, had its leading man who exercised chiefly authority over his group's activities and estates. Those leaders who distinguished themselves in life became the subjects of cult-worship after death. Their craniums were carefully preserved after burial of the rest of their bodies, and they were supplicated to aid their descendants.

Such are the bare outlines of the life of the Chamorros, who were the first islanders to receive the full impact of white civilization. The complete story is forever lost, for the only descriptions of their culture before they became thoroughly acculturated were made 250 years ago. In one thing nearly all early observers agree: the Chamorros were a strong, vigorous people with a Polynesianlike culture.

In the first year of their systematic enlightenment by Spanish missionaries, about half of the Chamorros were living on Guam. Conversion was rapid, but was handicapped by native revolts. The Spanish, who were pretty good at that sort of thing, eventually brought matters under control by reducing the population to one twentieth of its former size and by concentrating the hardy survivors on Guam for purposes of stricter control. A few natives managed to elude capture by hiding out on near-by Rota, but Saipan, Tinian, and the other Mariana Islands were left for a time to the sea birds. Sixty-five years later the problem of administration had been further simplified, since there remained only 1654 natives to govern. That was the low point, but the population which then began to recover in numbers was no longer pure native. By 1790 there were only 1639 full bloods, but in addition there were 1825 mixbloods: Spanish-native and Filipino-native, the latter deriving from Filipino soldiers and colonists introduced by the Spanish. By 1898, when Guam was captured by the United States and the rest of the Marianas were sold by Spain to Germany, the Chamorro population had recovered in numbers to about 9000 on Guam and about 1100 on Saipan, Tinian, and Rota, but it is doubtful that there was a full-blood native among them. Up to this time all the Marianas had been a cultural unit under Spanish rule; but after this Guam went one way, under the administration of the United States, while the remaining Marianas became linked with the German and later the Japanese dependency comprising the Carolines and the Marshalls.

From 1668 to 1898 the Marianas were ruled by Spanish governors, at first responsible to Mexico and after 1821 to the Philippines administration. The policy—if such existed—appears to have been based on a determina-

tion to win over and hold the natives to Catholicism, to
keep out other imperialisms, and to carry out these objectives as cheaply as possible. (At the beginning there
was also the objective of maintaining a port of refreshment for Spanish vessels.) Save for a few British pirates,
England never displayed much interest in the Marianas,
and the whalers that visited did no great harm, there
having been little left to do. A small colony of Americans and Hawaiians flourished on Saipan from 1810
to 1815, and some Japanese traders established a commercial hegemony toward the end of the nineteenth
century; but otherwise Spanish influence dominated
these islands until 1899, and in fact was, in 1939, still
discernible in the race and culture of the modern Guamanians and their Chamorro cousins on Saipan and Rota.

The Spanish governors of Guam functioned mainly as
Protectors of the Faith. There cannot have been much
incentive in the work for these officials: local revenues
were almost nonexistent, home-government support nominal, and the prestige of the post something less than
brilliant. Actually the islands were isolated for years at
a time, and governors were reduced to supporting themselves and their staffs by levying food and labor and by
monopolizing trade. At times Guam must have more
nearly resembled a sleepy Hispanic-American hacienda
than an Oceanic colony. Meanwhile the Church was supreme: Jesuits, then Augustinians, later Capuchins, and
then Jesuits again.

Two hundred and thirty years of Spanish-Catholic rule
transformed the Mariana Islanders so thoroughly that
their Micronesian heritage was barely discernible. Racially they became hybrids; their language alone resisted
fundamental change, and even it became liberally fla-
vored with Spanish and Filipino (Tagalog) words and
structures.

At the end of the Spanish regime there were about
nine thousand Chamorros living on Guam. Most of them

were dwelling in towns, in itself a radical change from their native manner of dwelling in scattered hamlets near their gardens. The center of their community life was the church and no longer the men's clubhouses. Agaña, the metropolis, was laid out like a Spanish town, with cathedral and plaza and tile-roofed dwellings. Chamorro land holdings were somewhat restricted, although the Spanish governors did restore to them large tracts which had earlier been allotted to Church and Crown; and of course the decrease in population had relieved some pressure on land. In another respect, however, land tenure had changed: with the movement of and decrease in population, the old ties between people and their lineage and district lands were weakened, and the family became the principal landowning group. By 1898 the government owned one half of the land on Guam, and a few families of wealthy *mestizos* owned large portions of the remainder.

The tempo of social life was different. Instead of rhythms based on planting and harvest festivals, upon feuding and overseas expeditions, and upon great co-operative enterprises, the Guamanians piously maintained the Church calendar, with daily prayers, strict Sabbaths, and frequent novenas. On the other hand, the tempo of their horticultural life did not greatly change. Agriculture remained the basis of their economy, but maize, sweet potatoes, and citrus fruits became as important in their diet as native taro, sugar cane, coconuts, rice, and bananas. To the native pigs and fowl were added cows and carabao, the latter being used to pull carts and plows.

In pre-Spanish days each family lived near its cultivations. By 1898 family farmsteads were still a feature of Chamorro life, but many families had a main dwelling in a town and resided at their farms only during the farming week. Formerly the Chamorros were skillful fishermen and supplied most of their protein needs in this

manner. Little of this activity survived the Spanish period; the daring deep-sea fishing, which was monopolized by the native nobility, completely died out, along
with the skill in manufacturing large sailing canoes.

The changes wrought in Chamorro economy went further than subsistence products and tools. In times past,
all save the privileged chiefs produced their own goods
and bartered only for luxuries. Long overseas voyages
were undertaken to obtain choice materials, and not
much importance was attached to currency (shell
"money") as a medium of exchange. Also, nearly all subsistence and commercial activity was carried out by
groups—families, lineages, and neighborhoods. Under
Spanish influence, however, district and lineage enterprises and barter were partly supplemented by family
and individual effort: by wage earning and by the production of things to sell for income in order to buy imported goods. This change was gradual during the first
two centuries of somnolent Spanish rule, but later on it
was greatly accelerated by the development of the copra
industry. In the Marianas copra production never exceeded thirty-six hundred tons a year, but on Guam it
was until World War II the major income-producing industry, and production remained in Chamorro hands.

Early travelers used to remark at the complete nudity
of the Chamorros—a far, far cry from the layers of
Spanish and Filipino garments they later learned to wear.
Spanish-Catholic influence also affected native family
life. Judge the contrast between the unclothed native girl
of pre-white days and her Catholic descendant. The
former, as a prologue to marriage, served a lengthy sex
apprenticeship in a men's clubhouse, becoming all the
more desirable for marriage as a result of her experiences. Her modern counterpart was guarded from all
contact with sex experience and knowledge, always chap-
eroned, never permitted to attend dances or mixed
parties, a pious and virginal member of the local Daugh-

ters of Mary. In most other respects, too, the Catholic concepts of marriage and family relationship supplanted native forms; particularly did the father assume much of the authority formerly exercised by other relatives under the older matrilineal system of lineage membership and inheritance.

Along with these changes there disappeared the matrilineal lineages which had been a regular feature of native society. The settlement patterns and land-tenure concepts associated with lineages were transformed, and the supernatural sanctions behind lineage exogamy were supplanted by other beliefs. The economic factors of common property and co-operative work, which helped hold lineages together, were no longer in force, and the matrilineal principle gave way to the common European emphasis upon patrilineal descent. And finally, the institutions of leadership which integrated a lineage and ranked it in relation to other lineages were changed under the impact of the Spanish regime.

In the pre-Spanish Marianas there existed a wide gulf between nobility and commoners, but much of this was changed under Spanish rule. At first the nobility welcomed foreigners and their unusual new religion, but their sentiments changed when church membership was also opened to commoners and when their own authority over life and property was curbed by the new white rulers. The revolts against Spanish rule which kept the Marianas unsettled for thirty years were inspired and directed by these high-ranking natives, and in the process their numbers were greatly reduced. Meanwhile another class of Chamorro began to emerge as leaders: the natives who had acquired power and influence by supporting and intermarrying with the Spanish. These people gradually emerged as an exclusive *mestizo* class, living Spanish lives and becoming wealthy and influential landholders and officials.

Eventually the Spanish delegated much municipal au-

thority to the semielective Chamorro leaders, so that
there developed a large measure of indirect rule, with, of
course, the Church maintaining its dominance over the
lives of individuals. Chamorro landholders became copra
planters and even imported some Carolinian natives to
work their plantations. Many of them started their own
stores and service enterprises, but the more energetic
Japanese were on the way to domination of commerce
when the Spanish regime ended.

On June 20, 1898, an American cruiser steamed into
Guam's harbor and opened fire on the fort. So isolated
was the island that her Spanish governor believed the
firing to be a salute, and did not learn of the state of
war between the United States and Spain until he sent
out a welcoming delegation to the cruiser. The Spanish
capitulated immediately and were removed to the Philippines. Because of Guam's potentialities as a naval base,
the island was assigned to the Navy Department, and a
naval officer assumed the governorship in 1899.

During the ensuing forty years Guam's history di-
verged from that of the rest of the Marianas. The process
of westernization, which had proceeded so gradually for
two hundred and thirty years under Spanish-Catholic
rule, took some new turnings. On the one hand, naval
administration maintained and even reinforced the regime of discipline and absolutism that had characterized
the Spanish rule; and although the Navy policy was dis-
sociated from the Church, it was paternalistic in other
ways. Countering this influence were the new theories
of Americanism—social democracy and capitalistic enterprise—which reached Guamanians through schools and
through increasing contact with American civilians and
civilian culture. Naturally some strains developed out of
these conflicting influences, but the trend toward the new
was slowed down by the continuing conservatism of the
family system and the Church. Also, the traditional sub-

sistence and barter economy remained entrenched, owing partly to a depression in copra and the scarcity of
money-earning opportunities.

Some of these effects were visible in the settlement pattern. Under the Spanish, Church and State had alienated
about one quarter of Guam's land, and the American administration purchased an additional five thousand hectares. On the other hand, the naval government made it
easy for Guamanians to lease state land and actually encouraged them to resettle in rural areas. As a result, a
smaller percentage of the people lived in Agaña; in addition, the governor supervised all land transfers and
made it next to impossible for nonnatives to secure land.

During Spanish times a few wealthy Guamanian
families were engaged in extending their land holdings:
in six cases, families owned estates exceeding a thousand
hectares. But during the American era this process was
retarded; copra depression, the outlaw of peonage, and
increasing emphasis upon money made land by itself a
poor investment. At the other end of the scale, the new
economy created a class of landless wage earners.

Otherwise, the older settlement patterns did not
change much during American times, except that the
school played more of a role as a community center, and
athletic fields competed with cock-fighting pits as centers
of interest for men.

Americanism went a little further in the field of fashion. Older women maintained their Spanish-Filipino cos-
tumes, but young women turned to American styles in
dress and in coiffures.

In family life the change-over to patriliny was sanc-
tioned by the Navy's rule that children take only the sur-
name of the father; but the mother retained her role as
leader of the family's religious life. American rule also
favored individual property rights: the property of parents dying intestate was by law divided equally among
all legal heirs. In spite of this regulation, however, family

members continued to pool their resources and work as a subsistence unit.

In sex relations the Church-enforced virginal cultism of young women was beginning to be influenced by co-education and contact with Americans. Marriages still involved interfamily contracts, and divorces were rare, but parental arrangements gave way to love matches.

The Church continued to maintain its strong influence over the lives and beliefs of Guamanians, but there were signs of change. Schools were coeducational and compulsory, and in them religious teaching was prohibited. Other contacts with Americans and their irreligious institutions further weakened the authority of the Church. The ultraconservative Spanish padres did not adapt well to the changes, but it appeared that the more recently installed American priests would help rather than hinder in the process.

In the economic field the naval government's policies contained basic inconsistencies. On the one hand, there was an emphasis upon development of money economy; on the other hand, an extreme paternalism. A prosperous copra industry might have resolved these inconsistencies, but between hurricanes, pests, and poor markets, copra exports were never high or very profitable. Official encouragement was given to the development of other income-producing industries, but, with its high-cost labor and its isolation, Guam could not compete successfully in world markets without subsidy, particularly in view of the excise-tax penalty levied against its copra in the United States. Even without the Navy's restrictive regulations against outside industry and commerce, planned as protection for Guamanians, there was little about Guam to attract American or foreign capital to the island. Hence almost the only way most Guamanians could earn money was to work for the naval establishment or its numerous parasitic enterprises, and this did not provide sufficient wage-earning opportunities to absorb all those people attempting to earn the money that was needed to satisfy the newly acquired wants. Under such circumstances, it was inevitable that the old family subsistence and barter economy would prevail, especially in the rural areas. Recognizing this situation, the government sponsored a back-to-the-farm movement and tried to improve agriculture, with new crops and new techniques.

In political as well as economic spheres, Navy rule was benevolently paternalistic but absolute. Whereas in the Spanish era influential Chamorros held high elective and appointive posts, under American rule all high officials were naval officers, and even the municipal authorities were either elected or appointed, according to the discretion of the naval governor of the moment. Democratic reforms might be instituted under one governor and then revoked by his successor, their tours of duty having lasted only two years and their discretionary powers having been wide. A Guam Congress, consisting of some representatives and some appointive officials, was established in 1917, but its function was mainly advisory.

In yet another important respect the Chamorros had enjoyed more political rights under Spanish rule: they were true Spanish subjects and possessed equality with other Spanish subjects before the law. In the American system they were citizens of Guam, and *nationals* but not *citizens* of the United States. Under these circumstances they did not have access to the Federal judiciary system beyond Guam. Citizenship was one of the main reforms desired by an increasingly articulate group of educated Guamanians.

Under Spanish rule the upper class consisted of a few wealthy, landowning Guamanian families, who lived Spanish-Catholic lives and mixed socially with the Spanish officials. Navy officials, however, raised caste barriers against social contact with Guamanians. Through this and the increasing emphasis upon "democracy" and money economy, the land-poor Guamanian aristocracy lost status and a new upper class of energetic money capitalists emerged—but they, of course, likewise did not have access to the society of the Navy ruling caste.

Guam's value to the United States was entirely strategic, a communications point on the way to the Philippines and east Asia. From this point of view it would probably have been desirable if there had been *no* native population to complicate matters. But on behalf of naval rule, it can be said that the Guamanian population increased from 9000 to 22,000 in forty years, and much of that increase was due to public health and medical measures instituted by the Navy. On the other hand, no effective solutions were found for the inconsistencies between a paternalistic autocratic regime and an awakening appreciation of "democratic" institutions; between a subsistence, barter economy and a desire for things only money can buy. What movies described and schoolbooks promised, limitations of the economy and form of government denied. That such frustrations produced so few crimes and neuroses must probably be traced to the moderating influence of the previous two centuries of Spanish-Catholic life.

JAPANESE MANDATED ISLANDS

While Spanish soldiers and priests were transforming Tinian and Saipan into a pious wilderness, the Caroline and the Marshall Islands were left to their Micronesian ways. The Carolines belonged theoretically to the Spanish crown under the world-dividing Treaty of Tordesillas of 1494, but little effort was made by Spain to colonize or Christianize these islands until late in the nineteenth century, after other powers began to display some interest in them. But even Spain did not covet the Marshalls, and these scattered atolls remained unclaimed until German traders induced the Fatherland to establish a protectorate in 1885. Before that time all the islands, from Palau to Majuro, remained vulnerable to the unofficial agents of the West.

It was an ideal situation for the whaling gentry: no irksome governments to restrain their exuberance ashore and no missionaries to spoil their fun. The Marshalls received their quota of disease and disaster, but Kusaie and Ponape were first choice. Kusaie, particularly, became such a resort for scoundrels that missionaries thought it the island most in need of salvation. The natives of Truk solved the tourist problem by inhospitably killing a few eager refreshment-seekers, and thus escaped being overrun. Ponapeans also made some difficulties for a while, but later proved tractable to everything but the raping and kidnapping of wives of the *highest* chiefs. The scourge of whalers lasted until the 1860's, when whaling moved far to the northwest.

Far more persistent were the traders. In the Marshalls they supplied the iron weapons that made it possible for a few ambitious chiefs to extend their domains by bloody conquest of neighboring atolls. In the western Carolines, traders set up their own domains until the natives could suffer them no longer and either killed the interlopers or destroyed their stores.

The first significant proprietary move by westerners in the Marshalls was made by the Jaluit Company, a German trading firm with semiofficial connections. The agents of this company succeeded in making a trade "treaty" with a Marshallese chief; and, following the familiar pattern, it was only a matter of years before Germany established its protectorate.

Germany's interest in the Marshalls was almost entirely economic: the protectorate was valued and administered only as a source of copra and shell and fertilizer. In fact, for many years after the establishment of the protectorate, administration of the group was carried out and financed by the Jaluit Company's local agent. In return for this, the company was granted a virtual trade monopoly and many other substantial concessions.

During these years Marshallese native affairs were not forcibly disturbed, except to the extent that they interfered with orderly trade and production. The Germans preferred to work through the local chiefs and restricted their authority only to the extent of abolishing their feuding and their privilege to inflict the death penalty.

Much more effective in changing Marshallese institutions were the members of the Boston Mission, who set up stations, sent native teachers into nearly every atoll, and succeeded in converting half the population to Protestantism. Jesuits also entered the field near the turn of the century and as usual quickened the race after souls.

The Boston missionaries moved into the eastern Carolines in 1852 and met with spectacular success. They were well along toward their goal of making the islands into native Christian "states" under sovereignty of the United States when Spain tardily became aware of her neglected empire and sent a garrison to set up an outpost on Ponape. By then Ponape was as thoroughly Protestant as a savage community can be made through the singing of hymns and the wearing of Mother Hubbards, so that the ubiquitous padres who accompanied the Spanish soldiers had scant success at first. Their luck changed, however, when some Ponapeans massacred part of the garrison; the Spanish punitive expedition which resulted might have depopulated Ponape had not the padres interceded on behalf of the guilty communities. At this evidence of grace, two whole districts went over en masse to Catholicism, leaving the other three districts to Protestantism. To the forthright American missionaries this defection to Rome was even more bitter than the frustration of their temporal plans, and there was probably some basis for the Spanish charge that the continued hostility of the Protestant districts was due to mission agitation. Anyway, the American missionary allegedly involved was expelled from the islands and re-admitted later only after the usual "vigorous diplomatic representations."

One factor that earlier had led Spain to establish the mark of her sovereignty over the Carolines was the "en-croachment" of German and British traders into the area. The crucial point was reached in 1885, when Spanish and German warships simultaneously raised their flags on one or two islands. The dispute was referred to Pope Leo XIII, who confirmed Spain in her sovereignty but granted free commercial access to the islands to Germany and Britain.

The eastern Carolines continued to prove troublesome to the Spanish throughout their regime, with a black history of intrigue, ambuscade, and bloody reprisal. Mean-while, in the northern and western Carolines, the transi-tion from neolithic to steel-age savagery proceeded more peacefully.

Though Palau and Yap were tacitly under her sover-eignty, Spain did nothing to civilize these islands after the failure of a Catholic mission there in the early eight-eenth century. Neither whalers nor Protestant mission-aries penetrated that far, so that the only early contacts were with traders—British merchants of the East India Company. These adventurers made quixotic attempts to set up little British domains, but their efforts led to noth-ing permanent. Britain displayed only enough interest in the area to dispatch warships on punitive expeditions.

After her sovereignty was confirmed in 1886, Spain made a few halfhearted attempts to keep order—mean-ing, to protect the lives and property of traders—but most of the traders were British or Japanese, with Germans playing secondary roles. The priests, of course, accom-panied the Spanish garrisons, but few souls were saved.

When the Philippines and Guam were wrested from Spain in 1898, Germany promptly purchased Spain's re-

maining island possessions, the Marianas and the Carolines, and added them to her Marshall Islands possessions; these she proceeded to administer as part of her
New Guinea protectorate until they were taken from her
in the First World War. Administrative stations were established at Palau, Yap, Saipan, Truk, Ponape, and
Jaluit, and affairs were conducted in an efficient manner
with very small staffs. Germany's main interest in her
Micronesian islands was in developing them as sources
of raw materials and as markets for German goods. Mission activity was not hampered, but received little positive encouragement; and when all official compulsion
was removed from church attendance, many natives
promptly "reverted." Native institutions were left alone,
except those that obstructed industry and commerce; and
it was in this sense that official pressure was exerted to
transform land ownership from group to individual tenure. Copra was the main economic product, and the supply was increased by the enforcement of regulations
requiring natives to plant new groves. Shell was also an
important trade item, as were handicrafts and guano. In
1909 a syndicate began the mining of phosphate on Angaur, which possessed reserves of an estimated 2,500,000
tons of some of the highest grade phosphate rock in the
world.

The Germans encountered native hostility on turbulent
Ponape, but elsewhere they administered the islands
with considerable insight into native ways and with a
tolerant respect for those native institutions that did not
interfere with all-important commerce.

The instruments of Germany's economic policy were
several large production and mercantile firms, many of
which eventually were merged with the strong Jaluit
Company. With government support, these companies
nearly succeeded in freezing out all foreign competition
from the Marshalls and eastern Carolines, but little headway was made against the strongly entrenched Japanese

and British traders in the Marianas and the western Carolines.

The Marshalls, the Carolines, and the Marianas (except Guam) were "entrusted" to Japan by the Peace Conference following World War I, but to the Japanese these islands were prizes of war. If the gentlemen in Geneva wished to make the matter more palatable to themselves, that was acceptable so long as it did not interfere with Japan's program of integrating the islands into her economic and military empire. The written terms of the mandate were therefore kept idealistic, but Japan's actual objectives were something else. Although not explicitly stated, the islands were viewed by Japan as places to resettle surplus Japanese populations, to produce the things needed by Japan's integrated economy, and to serve as springboards for conquest. Judging by events, one can only believe that Japan's principal native policy was to "Japanize" all who could be so transformed and to allow the rest to die out and so make room for more immigrants: no ruthless policy of extermination or even a calculated program of oppression, but rather a long-range concept of assimilation devoid of the customary sentimental regard for weaker native peoples.

After an initial period of naval rule, Japan placed the administration of the islands in the hands of civilian officials of the South Seas Government, responsible at first to the Prime Minister's office and later to the Ministry of Overseas (colonial, not foreign) Affairs. Headquarters for the islands was established at Palau, with branch stations at Saipan, Yap, Truk, Ponape, and Jaluit. A large and complex bureaucracy was installed, with authority and procedures to cover every phase of life. Officials were civil-service career men, interrelated in a finely graded rank system. Some recognition was accorded native "self-rule" through the appointment of certain natives to the positions of "village chief" and so on, but as more Japanese colonists poured in and officialdom expanded, native chiefs were bypassed and native affairs were assimilated into the life of the colonial communities.

The terms of the mandate provided for freedom of missionary enterprise, and the Japanese did not obviously interfere except to replace German Protestant missionaries with Japanese evangelists. In the case of the few remaining Catholic missionaries, the Japanese even assisted their work with a small subsidy. The Japanese themselves introduced a Buddhist mission, but without much success. The major religious change came about indirectly, as a result of schooling and everyday contacts with Japanese; these influences served to inculcate the religion of the Japanese State through the learning of the Japanese language and public ritual and through propaganda about the glories of Japan. For the rest, the natives were left to their own beliefs.

Economic development went swiftly forward, and before long all foreign interests, including the tenacious Australian firm of Burns Philp, were frozen out of the islands. The entire area was completely integrated into Japan's economy. Saipan and Tinian and subsequently Rota were converted into sugar-cane plantations. Palau, Truk, and Ponape became centers for large fishing industries. Phosphate mining was accelerated on Angaur and later extended to other islands in the western Carolines and Marianas. Bauxite was mined on Palau and manganese on Rota. Trade stores were established throughout the area, and shipping extended to nearly every populated place. But none of this was native; the enterprises were owned and managed by monopolistic Japanese firms, some of them partly owned by the government. Even the labor consisted of immigrant Japanese, Koreans, and Okinawans, except in the mining industries, which did employ some native laborers.

The only commercial enterprise left mainly to natives was copra production, which continued prosperously throughout the Marshalls and Carolines and provided the native producers with their main source of income for buying the civilized things they had become dependent upon. Official encouragement was given to copra production in the form of subsidies for new plantings and the construction of drying sheds.

The greatest change in the life of the islands came about through the mass immigration of Okinawans (the most numerous), Japanese, and Koreans. It is debatable whether the industries were promoted to support colonists or whether colonists were imported to service the industries; in any event, tens of thousands of nonnatives immigrated to the islands and engaged mainly in sugar production, fishing, and mining. As elsewhere in Oceania, the natives were not suited to the kind of labor involved in sugar-cane growing or crushing, so that the employees of that industry were altogether nonnative. In connection with fishing, similar reasons could hardly be put forward to explain why natives were excluded, but it so happened that most of the fishing vessels were manned by nonnatives. Not all the immigrants were directly engaged in production; at each of the main centers there sprang up a rash of small artisan shops, stores, and service establishments. The towns of Garapan on Saipan, Koror on Palau, and Colony on Ponape were particularly thriving and contained most of the amenities of Japanese small town life: cinemas, restaurants, beauty parlors, even geisha establishments. All these enterprises were in the hands of nonnatives, but natives did have access to many of them and thereby acquired new needs and tastes. They were not excluded from participation in the flourishing new life except to the extent that their small incomes limited them. And, although the income-earning opportunities of natives were few, the basic trade goods they needed were reasonably priced and hence available.

By 1939 there were some seventy thousand nonnatives

(Japanese, Koreans, Okinawans) dwelling in the islands, as compared with only fifty thousand natives, and these numbers were diverging rapidly, by increase of non-natives through natural increment and new immigration, and by decline in the native population. By this time, also, great tracts of land had been acquired in one way or another from native owners and set aside as public domain or leased to industries and colonists. So, whether consciously or purposefully directed or not, on the basis of statistics alone the trend was obviously toward the dis-inheritance and extinction of the Micronesians. On the other hand, it must be granted that the Japanese from time to time went to considerable pains to improve na-tive health and education. And, whether as a direct re-sult of government policy or as an incidental by-product of Japanese colonization and commercialism, natives dwelling near the main colonial centers did have access to a higher culture and to a fairly civilized standard of living. Even those living on the out-islands were able to make use of the network of ship and schooner services which linked all parts of the area.

In general, caste lines between natives and nonnatives were not so rigidly drawn here in the Japanese territory as they were in dependencies south of the equator. Whereas in most of the British islands natives were placed in a lower caste and encouraged to survive and remain as picturesque but law-abiding primitives, in the Marianas and Marshalls and Carolines they were *per-mitted* either to die out or to compete in the new order.

Not all these factors applied equally to the 130 in-habited islands and atolls of the Japanese territory. In the Marianas, for example, events took a very special turn. In 1902 there were only 1100 Chamorros living in the Mariana Islands acquired by Germany. These were concentrated on Saipan, Tinian, and Rota, and many of them were but recently returned from "exile" on Guam. In addition, there were some 850 Carolinians dwelling on

Saipan and Tinian, brought there as laborers or as a result of catastrophes on their home islands.

During the German era their Mariana Islands were the least productive of any group in their protectorate. Despite official encouragement, only a few hundred tons of copra were produced each year, with the immigrant Carolinians doing much of the work; the Chamorros themselves were landowners and less amenable to working for others. One result of German influence, however, was the diversification of native subsistence foods and an increased emphasis placed upon individual property ownership.

Saipan was the German seat of administration for the group, but it lapsed into such unimportance after a few years that the German official moved to Yap and visited the Marianas only occasionally. Saipan and the islands north of it were devoted mainly to coconuts, while Tinian was used to pasture cattle. The Marianas proved to be a financial burden to the Germans; nevertheless, the natives increased in number during the German regime. In most respects native institutions were not interfered with; the Hispanized Chamorro and the more primitive Carolinians went their separate ways, and paternalistic German land laws protected both communities from disinheritance.

Even during the German era most of the commerce of the Marianas was in the hands of Japanese traders and overseas trade went almost entirely to Japan. Later, under Japanese administration, the Marianas were transformed from liability to richest asset of all the Micronesian islands. A strongly financed Japanese company moved in and converted Saipan and Tinian into sugar plantations, with the help of subsidies and liberal concessions from the government. Mills were built for processing sugar cane and manufacturing alcohol; ultimately 30,000 acres were placed under cultivation on these two islands and on Rota, with an annual production of 80,000 tons of raw sugar and over 700,000 gallons of alcohol. Thousands of Japanese and Koreans and Okinawans were brought in as laborers. In the beginning the government lent state domain land rent-free to the company, which in turn leased plots to tenant households for cultivation. All cultivations were subject to company controls in the use of land and planning of crops, and all production was sold to the company at fixed prices. Some plots were under even more direct company management, and only a fraction were operated by "independent" planters. Natives participated in this enterprise mainly by leasing land to the government or company.

The Japanese also organized manioc- and coffeegrowing enterprises, which, as in sugar production, were managed by nonnatives. About the only agricultural industry remaining in native hands was copra, which constituted only one half per cent (by value) of agricultural production in the Marianas, and only 4 per cent of all copra produced in the Mandated Territory.

The process of native disinheritance went further in the Marianas than elsewhere in the Territory. There is little direct evidence of calculated mistreatment, but the situation that developed is just another example of a slower, less insatiable native population unable to compete with greedy, better-equipped aliens.

The western Carolines—Palau, Yap, and the southwest islands—also became a center of Japanese industry, but of an entirely different sort. To begin with, the Japanese took over the German phosphate mines on Angaur and expanded them into a very large enterprise. In addition, smaller mines were established on neighboring islands, and exports from all the enterprises eventually reached over 200,000 tons a year. The mining was partly government owned; its management and technical staff was Japanese, but numbers of Chamorros were engaged as skilled workers and supervisors, and hundreds of Carolinians were brought in as laborers, recruited from Yap, Palau, Truk, and other islands under circumstances that smacked of forced labor. Chamorros received better treatment than Carolinians and were even allowed to bring along their wives. The natives on Angaur also worked at the phosphate establishments, but that was hardly adequate compensation for loss of their best garden lands, which had to be skimmed off to remove the phosphate rock underneath. The phosphate from Angaur and other mining sites in the Territory went to Japan, as did the profits, since to pay mining royalties to natives occurred not even to the most softheaded trustee of native welfare.

During the thirties the Japanese also started bauxite mining on Palau and employed local natives as laborers; but fishing, by far the largest industry in the western Carolines, was almost entirely in Japanese hands.

Although the fishing industry was centered at Koror (Palau), fleets roved as far as the Dutch East Indies, and there were smaller establishments at Saipan, Truk, Ponape, and in the Marshalls. Altogether there were some 360 vessels engaged in commercial fishing in the Territory, with an annual catch of from 15,000 to 38,000 tons of bonito, plus large quantities of tuna, trepang, and trochus. Natives engaged in some collecting of trepang and shell, but the deep-sea fishing was carried out by Japanese—a curious reversal for natives once noted for their skillful navigation and daring voyages.

Koror, as administrative center for the whole Territory, became a thriving Japanese town to which natives enjoyed access according to their means. Here in the western Carolines near the seat of government, some effort seems to have been made by officials to help natives in their struggle for survival. Government-sponsored co-operatives were formed to assist them in the production, marketing, and purchase of commodities, and many of these islanders were beginning to make fairly satisfactory adjustments to the new money economy; such, at least, was the case with those dwelling near Koror. But in the southwest islands of Tobi, Pulo Anna, and Sonsorol, only a few had managed to survive the preceding decades of trading and epidemics.

The island of Yap had a peculiar history. Even though it was continuously under the influence of traders, priests, and officials for scores of years, the Yap Islanders clung tenaciously to their old culture—more tenaciously, in fact, than to their lives, because Yap's population continued to decline at a steady and alarming rate.

Yap itself was once the center of diplomatic conflict, but aside from its role as a cable station on the line from Guam to the Far East, it developed very little economically. Copra, the main industry, remained in native hands.

There was a colony of Chamorro settlers on Yap, and these people, like their cousins on Saipan, became rapidly assimilated into the Japanese culture; but the Yap natives themselves remained remarkably conservative. The subsistence economy survived almost intact, and the aboriginal group and class system underwent few major changes. Perhaps one obstacle to change was the native Yap feature of patrilineal land inheritance. Throughout most of Micronesia, property inheritance remained within the matrilineal group, and the Japanese masters, in trying to encourage a transition to the patrilineal system, did violence to many other functionally related native institutions. Hence Yap, with its traditional patrilineal form, provided fewer loopholes for change. In recent years the strongest outside influence to reach Yap came through the indenturing of her young men to work in the phosphate mines on distant islands.

Truk has long excited the imagination of voyagers and naval strategists, but under Spanish, German, and Japanese rule it lagged far behind the other Micronesian centers in economic development. Until it became strategic as a naval base, its only commercial importance came from its fishing industry, smaller than Palau's, and its copra production, which remained in native hands.

Ponape, with its large land mass and extensive, fertile areas, was much better adapted to commercial enterprise. In addition to basing fishing fleets there, the Japanese attempted to make Ponape an agricultural center of their Territory. Its agricultural experiment station worked continually on the development and adaptation of economic plants to island conditions; fibers, pineapples, starches, medicinals, and rice were all tried, but the main cash crop remained copra, with Japanese colonists and natives sharing the production.

Subsistence remained the basis of Ponapeans' economic life, but more and more of them began to participate in the money economy. This was helped along by changes in land tenure which were fostered by both German and Japanese regimes. In the process, many of the corporately held lands were reassigned to individuals, and native chiefs lost much of their former authority over the goods and labor of their subjects. But beyond that, and despite the growth of a large Japanese colony on Ponape, most natives continued with their old forms of prestige-garnering feast exchanges. On the other hand, housing and clothing became increasingly westernized.

Near-by Kusaie was less affected economically by Japanese enterprises, the major transformation to money economy and western concepts having taken place under influence of the early Protestant missionaries, who concentrated their efforts upon this island and changed it from a scoundrel's haven to a Sunday schooler's paradise. One effect of the successive political regimes upon Kusaie was to weaken greatly the power of the local chiefs, once among the most absolute in Micronesia. (It is a noteworthy fact that "democratic" Protestantism has enjoyed its most spectacular successes in those places in

Oceania possessing the most autocratic native governments: in Tonga, Hawaii, and Kusaie!)

The paucity of natural resources in the Marshalls insulated these islands from the foreign influences that destroyed other richer and less fortunate areas. The Germans were content to set up trade stores and to plant coconuts on a few small atolls, and left most production of the main crop, copra, to the Marshallese. The Japanese followed suit, and almost the only nonnatives residing there were a few officials, fishermen, and trade agents of a monopolistic Japanese mercantile firm.

In former days missionaries were very active in the Marshall Islands and converted half the population; that was probably the most important single factor in changing the externals of Marshallese life. Otherwise the most far-reaching changes took place in the institution of leadership. In the old days chiefs had authority over all lands and their products. The Germans reinforced this authority—although weakening the chiefs in other ways —when they levied taxes in the form of copra, depending upon the chiefs to collect the levy and permitting them to retain some of it for themselves. Under the Japanese, however, the chiefs were reduced: all copra was sold direct to the trader, with only a very small part of the proceeds being set aside for the chiefs.

Traders and whalers and missionaries, Spanish and German and Japanese: most of these intruders left their mark on places like Saipan, Palau, Ponape, and Jaluit. In all these, native life was transformed, sometimes beyond recognition. Yet, a few miles away from these centers were islands where natives continued to live much as they had done centuries before, except for iron tools to supplement their shell and stone and for a few new bewilderments about their place in the world. All these out-islands, including Ulithi, Woleai, and Nukuoro, made a little copra, collected some shell, and fashioned a few handicrafts to exchange for goods brought by the trading schooners, but since there was no immediate Japanese need for their lands or their persons they were left for the next alien masters to transform.

XIX

PROFIT AND LOSS

The end of an era was marked by 1939, and that year was a good one for balancing civilization's ledger in Oceania. By that time every exposed volcanic crust and coral outcrop had been seized by alien powers, and every islander had been touched by at least the outer ripples of western or Oriental civilizations: even central New Guinea had seen airplanes overhead. But how assess the changes that had taken place since Magellan? Obviously, simple comparisons were out of the question, for what yardsticks could be used to compare Honolulu and Sydney with the isolated one-trader atoll or the jungle patrol outpost? The alien whites and Asiatics had worked through many kinds of agencies and for varying lengths of time, and the island settings of their exploitations were far from uniform. Nevertheless, in 1939 it was possible to draw up a rough trial balance to cover the four centuries of alien contact and enterprise in the Pacific Islands.

To begin with, it required no great perspicacity to see that white and yellow men had usually profited at the expense of black and brown; but that in itself does not of course condemn all colonial enterprises. Even the most sentimental nativist would have had to agree that Australia and New Zealand provided net gains not only for their own fortunate white settlers, but for the world at large. The great losses sustained by a few hundred thousand aborigines and Maoris could not entirely cancel out the greater gains brought about by the transformation of their lands into good homes for nine million Occidentals. The only pity was that the change had not been accomplished with more humanity and enlightened administration, for there was actually room enough for whites *and* natives. But, leaving aside these special cases, what gains had accrued to the newcomers in the other islands of Oceania?

In 1939 there were some 140,000 whites and 540,000 Asiatics dwelling in the islands (outside of Australia and New Zealand). For a few of these settlers Oceania brought wealth; for many of them it provided satisfactory livelihoods, better than they had had in their native lands. Except in Japanese Micronesia, whites occupied the highest caste positions and usually gained most economically; but Asiatics were beginning to narrow the gap by industry and sheer mass.

The greater profits from Oceanic enterprise went not to the settlers but to owners, shareholders, and directors in Australia, New Zealand, Britain, France, Japan, and the United States; and most of the white "settlers" held to their objective of eventually returning "home" with their earnings.

For mankind at large, Oceania (again excluding Australia and New Zealand) provided only limited economic gains; of all its products only phosphates and, to a less degree, sugar made any significant contribution to world economy. Copra, nickel, chrome, gold, iron, shell, and fruits, however profitable to their individual producers, were not produced cheaply enough or in large enough quantities to influence world markets one way or another. Even the international powers directly concerned regarded the economic products of their island dependencies as supplementary rather than indispensable.

Nor did many of the islands have much value as outlets for surplus populations. In fact, the principal profit derived from owning islands was strategic; and as events were shaping up in the Pacific in 1939, stock in good naval harbors and airplane runways looked definitely bullish.

But turning now to the black and brown peoples, who did not own shares in island companies or compete in international rivalries: What had they gained or lost from all this alien enterprise? Before proceeding, it will be useful to recall that during the centuries before Magellan all inhabited Oceania actually belonged to the forefathers of these islanders, the majority of whom went about their various businesses, neither accumulating great riches nor suffering stern deprivations, increasing their numbers and satisfactorily living out their lives according to their own lights. It is true that from them there came nothing to enrich the rest of the world, but neither came there any harm.

Since 1522, islanders' experiences had varied from place to place—the extinct Tasmanian had little in common with the lively Samoan, and the naked Solomonese had absorbed somewhat less westernism than the dapper Hawaiian—but a few kinds of changes had taken place generally.

The islanders' greatest losses were in their numbers; the population decreased from an estimated 2,500,000 to 3,000,000 in 1522 to 2,000,000 in 1939. Higher death rates accounted for much of this decline: one-sided wars against whites, intertribal feuding made more sanguine by aliens' weapons, and catastrophic new diseases. Lower birth rates were also a factor: disease-induced sterility and infecundity, enforced labor away from home, late marriages, and possibly family instability.

Land and resources were also lost. Even excepting Australia and New Zealand, where the heaviest losses were sustained, islanders lost millions of acres of their best lands, along with guano, phosphates, minerals, and other irreplaceables; at the same time, their forests were stripped of sandalwood and most of their reefs of shell. One can, of course, argue that the lost lands were surplus to their simple requirements and the raw materials of no use in their primitive economies, but that rationalization will have no force so long as title to property is not based on usufruct alone. These things were part of their heritage; preserved in trust, such treasures would have provided islanders with some basis of economic security in the competitive world where they now must struggle.

Many islanders also lost their fine skills: their abilities to turn out pleasing arts and useful crafts, their expert seamanship, their capacities for colorful pageantry. But of course it could be argued that there was no use for these skills any more.

Turning now to the other side. What had islanders gained to compensate them for these losses in natural resources and skills?

For one thing, except in the heart of New Guinea, even the poorest household had acquired a steel knife and an ax or adz to lighten the burden of work which formerly proceeded at a Stone Age pace. Other acquisitions were less useful. Clothes, sewing machines, and other paraphernalia of the mission modesty cult were not required by Oceania's climate and, if anything, were conducive to sickness. Peroxide, lampblack, rouge, powder, pomade, and perfume satisfied the desire to be fashionable, but were not much improvement over indigenous lime, ashes, ocher, coconut oil, and hibiscus. And among the "gains" one must not forget to mention the rum and twist tobacco, the cans of beef and fish, the hurricane lamp (with or without kerosene), the flashlight with dead batteries, the gramophone with one record, the galvanized roof under a blistering sun.

Then, too, there were new skills to replace the old lost ones: motor driving (but in their masters' trucks and launches); copra cutting, shell diving, cattle herding; work for the sake of wages to pay taxes, decorate missions, and buy knickknacks. And, of course, there was cricket or baseball or soccer—tame though healthful substitutes for savage pastimes. But most prideful of all acquisitions were reading and writing and calculating, western or Japanese style: splendid new skills, even though they were hardly relevant to their lives of peasant subsistence and caste subordination.

Institutional losses and gains were less apparent, harder to measure; notwithstanding this, the changes that took place in human relations were far more significant than any mere substituting of calico for bark cloth.

From the point of view of mission reformers, gains were scored in the apparently improved status of women, in the "legalizing" of matrimony, the "outlawing" of polygamy and adultery, the establishing of virginity cultism, that is, in a general westernizing of sexual and family relations. Granting for the sake of argument that those changes *might* constitute gains and that they *may* have generally taken place, it could also be shown that men away from home, working in plantations and mines and ships, cannot beget offspring or train children or do their share of family work, no matter how westernized their morals. And families inevitably lost cohesion when the traditional divisions of labor were disturbed or when mission-trained and commerce-hardened youths challenged their elders' authority.

Yet, with all these modifications, the family as an institution suffered far fewer changes than did the larger social and tribal groupings. The outlawing of warfare took away much of the cohesion of native political groupings, and rule by alien officials frequently resulted in usurpation of tribal authority by native opportunists who counted for little among their fellows but who were wise in the ways of the new masters. Lineage, clan, and tribe were weakened by the trend from communalism toward individualism and lost their very essence when their supernatural sanctions began to be questioned.

All these changes and their attendant losses in group morale did not necessarily lead directly to mass hypochondria and a general will to die, as some anthropological Cassandras like to report, but the weakening of traditional ties did create bewildering and unsettling conditions until new equilibriums were established.

In addition to these specific kinds of losses and gains, there were the more comprehensive ones. Islanders in general gained some security of person with the outlawing of feuding. And, although the immediate advantages could not be ascertained, they were given every opportunity to acquire "eternal life." Also, they were brought out of their isolation into contact with larger polities; in the process, however, they were invariably placed in subordinate caste roles, and the more they became assimilated into the new economies, the more vulnerable they were to world price fluctuations.

But however serious the losses suffered by pureblooded islanders under alien rule, their lot was easier than that of the mixbloods. Most of these latter lived in a caste limbo. Their western or Oriental fathers would not recognize them and colonial society would not accept them; many could and did "revert" to native status, but that too produced its dilemmas.

If the dateline of this audit were 1899, it would have to end on this recital of obvious debits and counterfeit credits, but by 1939 there were beginning to appear some genuine credits as well.

Nearly everywhere energetic efforts were being made to improve islanders' health, to provide for their welfare, to protect their remaining lands from further alienation and their labor from abuses. Some administrations were even making moves to return to the islanders some control over their own affairs. Most hopeful of all, however, was the fact that, save in a few cases, island populations were arresting and even reversing their numerical declines. With protection against the more vicious forms of exploitation and with time for peaceful and gradual assimilation of things alien, it looked as if the islanders might regain some of their savage well-being even in a westernized world. But that, as everyone knows, was not to be.

CATACLYSM AND
AFTERMATH

XX

WORLD WAR II

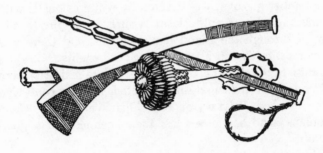

For the whites and Asiatics dwelling or campaigning in
Oceania, World War II was momentous enough; but for
many islanders, who had nothing to do with its inception
and little with its outcome, the war catastrophically disturbed their lives and radically changed their concepts.

Signs of war were evident in Oceania long before Pearl
Harbor. Abrogation of the Washington Naval Treaty in
1934 marked the end of collective security in the Pacific
and turned the western powers to fortifying their island
outposts. The general uneasiness was further excited by
the Sino-Japanese War and by Japan's repeated references to *her* South Seas; and Nazi Germany kept the
rumors flying by demanding return of her former colonies. Meanwhile the race for island air bases, the search
for oil in New Guinea, and Japan's purposeful economic

expansion throughout Oceania gave the coconut strategists plenty to discuss over their beer.

The three main regions of Oceania—American Hawaii, Japanese Micronesia, and the Franco-British South Pacific—responded differently to the outbreak of World War II. In Hawaii and Guam there were few visible reactions other than an increasing tempo in military preparations. In Micronesia we can only speculate about how the news was received. In the South Pacific, however, September 3, 1939, was greeted by white colonials with something akin to enthusiasm. A surge of empire loyalty swept through the island dependencies, and there was an almost festive air about the various benefits and rallies to raise funds and enlist volunteers. White residents were of course the principal ones affected, but the contagion also reached Polynesians and Fijians and New Caledonians, who had never lost their keenness for a good scrap.

Local volunteer defense units were formed on some islands, and many whites left plantations and mines and government posts for overseas duty. It was a festival of solidarity and good fellowship—until the hangover set in. The exodus of volunteers from island enterprises and the mobilization of shipping for war soon had disrupting effects on island economy. Copra prices rose, but copra rotted in warehouses for lack of bottoms to carry it to market; and for the same reasons essential imports had to be reduced. Also, production and commerce and administration suffered for lack of personnel. Co-operative shipping and marketing arrangements helped a little, but such arrangements were hampered by the inevitable bureaucratic weaknesses.

The first severe war crisis came with the fall of France, and the Euro-African drama was repeated on a small scale in the French possessions in Oceania. The Free French movement finally won out in both New Caledonia and Tahiti, although it was a case of principles rather than men, because De Gaulle's representative, the auto-cratic monk-admiral D'Argenlieu, did anything but en-dear himself to the colonials. Meanwhile Australia and New Zealand assumed responsibility for the defense and economic survival of New Caledonia and French Poly-nesia, respectively, and Japanese mining activities in New Caledonia were neutralized by export restrictions.

As Axis power expanded in Europe and Africa and eastern Asia, some islands were strengthened with gar-risons from New Zealand and Australia, but these meas-ures did not deter German raiders from potting at Allied shipping. Two raiders caught several phosphate freight-ers at Nauru, sank five of them, and then shelled the cantilever.

Otherwise it was a quiet, uneventful war, beginning to be tiresome for everyone except the planters who were able to market their produce. And then the Japanese struck.

The extent and progress of the Japanese attack is shown on the accompanying map; details of the military campaigns need not concern us here except as they af-fected the Oceanic setting against which they were fought.

The principal fact is that for nearly five years hun-dreds of thousands of Japanese, British, and Americans worked and fought on these islands, shifting native popu-lations, sometimes mixing blood with them, introducing new materials and ideas, and in many places upsetting the fine balance of island economy and caste relations. But every part of Oceania was affected differently.

For Australia and New Zealand the war brought home more emphatically than ever before how valuable the islands were to national security and how ornamental to national prestige. The need for American support against the common enemy was clearly recognized, and the presence of overwhelming American forces duly ap-

preciated; but Australian and New Zealand statesmen
hinted that, come the peace, the South Pacific would
revert to being *their* lake. The Anzac pact, concluded
in 1944, contained many fine plans concerning the future
security of Oceania and the welfare of islanders, but it
also made it clear that these islands and peoples were
the concern principally of the two British Dominions.
The war also provided tens of thousands of Australians

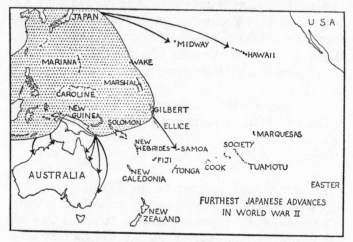

FURTHEST JAPANESE ADVANCES IN WORLD WAR II

and New Zealanders with firsthand knowledge of island
conditions; and while most of them would undoubtedly
have reacted in unprintable language to suggestions that
they remain in the islands as colonists, a few felt otherwise. As for the effect of the war on New Zealand's and
Australia's native peoples, the Maoris participated in no
way different from other patriotic New Zealanders, but
the aborigines on their desert reserves had little or no
contact with the great events.

The first effect of the war on New Guinea was to demonstrate how loose were the ties between the native inhabitants and their white masters. The former remained
in their villages as innocent bystanders, while most of
the latter fled to Papua or Australia. The few whites that

remained were either captured by the Japanese or escaped into the wilderness to serve as intelligence outposts for the Allied Forces. In sharp contrast to the 1914 change-over from German to Australian rule, the Japanese seizure of New Guinea marked a complete break in administration and commerce. Plantations and mines were abandoned and trade ceased. The Japanese attempted to win natives to their side by propaganda, but did not institute any general measures for administration or welfare. For their part, most natives were left to themselves so long as they did not interfere with operations. A few "went over" and a few others evidenced "loyalty" to the cause of their former Australian masters, but most of them took no sides and returned to their pre-European pastimes, including some intertribal fighting and headhunting.

The Japanese, however, changed their practices as their military position reversed; in southern Bougainville, for example, native gardens were systematically pillaged, pigs eaten, and men impressed into labor gangs and women into pleasure houses for the troops. Elsewhere similar things went on, but these occurrences may have resulted from the pique of individual commanders or from supply difficulties rather than from a general policy of ruthlessness. At any rate, such things did not endear the Japanese to natives; on the other hand, New Guinea proved too large and heterogeneous and politically unconscious to permit any universal manifestation either for or against Japanese or Australians.

Papua suffered far fewer changes than the Mandated Territory. Japanese occupation was restricted to the northeast slopes of the central ranges running down the peninsula, and even that occupation was short-lived. Civilian government was supplanted by military, but the administration unit was staffed principally with former territorial officials and residents so that there was a large measure of continuity. Also, an official Production Control Board stationed planters back on their properties and kept copra and rubber production up to prewar levels.

Labor was needed to carry supplies, construct roads and airfields, and man plantations, and natives had to be conscripted by the thousands. At one point the conscript force of Papuan natives numbered two and a half times their normal prewar labor force. As the war moved north, the administrative arrangements functioning in Papua were extended to reconquered New Guinea; the two territories were, in fact, treated as a single unit.

After the main American forces leapfrogged past Rabaul to Manus and Hollandia, it was left to Australians to mop up the bypassed Japanese, and this turned out to be a miserable, tortuous job that was still in process on V-J Day.

Ironically, the Allied "liberators" proved more devastating to native life than the invaders had been. It is likely that the Allies, by virtue of their more massive bombardments, accounted for the larger share of the estimated 15,000 natives killed and 20,000 dwellings destroyed in Papua and New Guinea during the Pacific campaigns. Also, a dysentery epidemic introduced by Allied troops wiped out many hundreds of natives in one area, and the conscription of native labor, which reached a peak of 37,000, severely disorganized many native communities. In some instances the Japanese also resorted to forced labor, but to nothing like the general extent practiced by the Australians. On the other side of the picture, the Australians operated trade stores and hospitals for natives and were not intentionally abusive, and many individual natives made common cause with the Allies and played heroic roles in the conflict.

Copra production and trade came to a standstill in the Solomons soon after Pearl Harbor, and most civilians were evacuated, leaving the few officials and missionaries who chose to remain at their posts. Even after the Japanese closed in on Guadalcanal and Tulagi, some officials managed to avoid capture back of the lines so that a measure of administrative continuity was maintained throughout the occupation. Later, when American forces moved in, control over native affairs remained firmly in British hands, and the British recruited hundreds of Solomonese as laborers for the military forces. Some trade goods were bought by an American government agency and sold to the British for resale to natives, mainly as an incentive for more laborers to work for the military; conscription was not resorted to. Some efforts were also made to revive copra production, but shortages of manpower and shipping interfered, and several plantation areas were used for military installations.

The Solomonese were less affected by the war than were their New Guinea neighbors. Most fighting took place in sparsely populated areas, and only a few thousand natives were in direct contact with either Japanese or Allied troops. Those who worked for whites did so voluntarily; and although the youths who normally would have worked on plantations were denied that source of income, actually they did not require cash incomes.

Certain other changes were inevitable. Those who did work and come in contact with troops learned new ideas about the value of labor and the relations of castes that augured difficulties for their postwar administrators.

The New Hebrides sheltered three major American bases, two on the island of Efate, and one at southeast Espíritu Santo. A few Japanese planes sneaked that far south, but otherwise these islands were spared actual combat, save for the quarreling that went on continually between British and French residents. Administration was not fundamentally disturbed: it couldn't have been! Shipping was somewhat disrupted but copra production flourished, the products going to the United States and

Australia. Although imports were difficult to procure, no real hardships were suffered by white residents, and a few of them made nice profits from the wartime boom. Some natives were recruited to work for the military, and "town" natives on Efate were drawn into the inevitable inflationary spiral; otherwise, most indigenous New Hebrideans were little affected by the war.

For most residents on New Caledonia, on the other hand, war was an experience they were not likely to forget. American troops first landed there in March of 1942 and a few were still there five years later; and during most of that period they dominated island life like an army of occupation. French officials held office, but American admirals and generals decided policy in critical spheres of public order, production, and commerce.

The Japanese residents of New Caledonia were promptly interned and shipped to Australia, but rumors continued to circulate about the presence of Axis sympathizers, and few wealthy residents escaped being branded "Pétainist." In fact, the local political situation was complex to the point of comedy. Americans and local residents succeeded in ousting De Gaulle's unpopular representative, D'Argenlieu, and this started a succession of governors sent out from Free French headquarters with the impossible assignment of satisfying both American military demands and the aspirations of the local French residents. Moreover, the government itself was split into factions favoring the several elements of the population.

Meanwhile the local economy boomed with dollar prosperity. Farmers found a ready local market for their coffee and vegetables and meat. Shops and bars sprang up everywhere, and those who couldn't sell things sold services. Imports were limited and supplies for local residents were short, but this did not curb resales to the free-spending Americans. With France temporarily out of the picture, all imports had to come from Australia and the United States. Australia offered to "assume primary responsibility" for insuring supplies for New Caledonia—and for all other South Pacific areas—but Washington did not go along with this scheme, which contained some all too obvious implications respecting postwar markets. American exporters and their New Caledonian customers also had their private troubles because of Free French "purchasing agents" in the United States who managed to freeze out the private traders through government-to-government transactions.

Far more serious than any of these semicomic little crises were developments in the mining industry. War needs enhanced the strategic value of nickel and chrome, and New Caledonia remained one of the few accessible sources; therefore, the word went out to United States officials to keep production up. Since British proprietors of chromium mines and companies balked at paying the export fees demanded by the New Caledonian government, shipments were held up for a while. Also, coal for the nickel refining had to be brought from Australia and shipping shortages turned this problem into a continuous crisis. Labor, however, proved the worst dilemma.

The New Caledonian mines and refinery were manned with Indo-Chinese and Javanese imported under indenture, and the industries' technical facilities were so primitive that there was heavy dependence on masses of hand laborers. In the midst of the emergency the labor contracts began to expire. Under normal circumstances finish-time laborers would have renewed their contracts voluntarily or have remained as free workers or have been repatriated. With their homelands occupied by the Japanese, they obviously could not be repatriated. And few laborers wished to renew contract when there existed the alternative of earning, literally, ten times as much by working for the troops. On the other hand, mine and refinery managers did not wish to lose their laborers, and in this they were backed by the authorities, both New Caledonian and American. The upshot was that contracts were renewed unilaterally, and the American government, official defender of freedom, was placed in the awkward position of having to support forced labor. Even the Netherlands government had to connive at keeping their own Javanese subjects under indenture, although a consul was sent out to safeguard what few rights remained to them. All these events provoked a series of disturbances all over the island and culminated in a strike centered at the nickel refinery at Nouméa. In the midst of general confusion and rumors about Communist-inspired insurrections, the French government stepped in and vigorously suppressed the disturbance by jailing several leaders and forcing the strikers back to their jobs. Finally, in mid-1945, when the need for nickel and chrome slacked off and enforced labor could no longer be justified as a wartime necessity, laborers were freed and the industries slowed down.

Many New Caledonia indigenes participated in the war by serving as stevedores and construction laborers and garrison troops, and from their whoops of enthusiasm as they careened along the highway in trucks, they seemed to have enjoyed the excitement mightily. Most of them, however, kept to their reserves in the north and saw little of the war save the steady stream of transport planes overhead.

Wartime Fiji was an active military base and a source of critically needed sugar and copra. American and New Zealand troops trained and recuperated there, warships and reserve planes based there, and aircraft refueled there en route to New Caledonia and Australia. Sugar and copra exports remained fairly normal despite shipping and supply difficulties, and some locally produced foods and other supplies were furnished to the forces.

Imports were stringently controlled, but in many other respects life carried on in a most orderly fashion.

In contrast to the other South Pacific bases, there was never any question about who ran *these* islands; top-flight colonial officials were posted there to administrate the mobilization and, one inferred, to see to it that the Yanks be kept reminded that Fiji is *British* territory.

White colonists rallied behind the war effort enthusiastically, and nearly every white male of military age was in service. In addition one of the most picturesque roles in the South Pacific campaign was played by the battalion of Fijian and Tongan jungle scouts, which had a gloriously heroic time harassing the Japanese in the northern Solomons. Fijians at home also supported the war with service and donations, and all this strengthened the ties between whites and Fijians. With the Indians, however, it was a different story. With a few exceptions most Indians were indifferent to the war in which they had so few stakes; nevertheless, except for a strike, their plodding industry kept on producing the sugar that was needed. Meanwhile the Indians' increasing population and wealth, and their more articulate agitation for broader political and economic rights, promised severe headaches for their postwar administrators.

For about a year Tonga was also a supporting base for American troops and an occasional anchorage for warships, but in 1943, New Zealanders took over the garrisoning and Tonga's active military role was reduced. Most war activities were restricted to the area around Nukualofa on the island of Tongatabu and did not greatly disturb the life of the kingdom. Queen Salote reigned, the British consul advised, and church attendance was only slightly affected by the more diverting activities around the camps. Americans found Tongan girls most attractive, but available census figures do not indicate how much.

Soon after Pearl Harbor an enemy submarine tossed a futile shell or two at Pago Pago, and that was the nearest the fighting war came to Samoa; but Tutuila and Upolu Islands were important support and communications bases throughout the first half of the Pacific war, and parts of the central Pacific campaigns were staged through that area.

Tiny Tutuila was overrun by the vastly expanded facilities and forces stationed there. Civil government was subordinated to that of the United States Marines commander, and Samoans responded so enthusiastically to calls for auxiliaries and workers that native community life was thoroughly disorganized.

Western Samoa, with its larger area and population, absorbed the war impact with less disturbance to normal life. Most white wives and children were sent to New Zealand, but plantation life went on, and copra and cocoa were exported in large quantity. There were the usual difficulties in supply, but the New Zealand administration maintained import controls and kept the other reins of government also well in hand. The most serious problem faced by the authorities was the perennial one of trying to govern Samoans made even more ungovernable by dollar prosperity and contact with Americans.

Far, far back of the combat zone were small communications bases—Tongareva, Aitutaki, and Bora Bora —"lost islands,"[1] where GI's were exiled to sit out the war, bored by isolation and made-work, maintaining airstrips and anchorages for planes and ships that rarely came, and wishing to be in Guadalcanal or Tarawa or anywhere but in the deadly beauty and calm of their particular South Sea paradise.

Outside these militarized islands, the war had little

[1] For a poignant and almost documentary description of one of these outposts, see James Norman Hall's *Lost Island* (Boston: Little, Brown and Co., 1944).

effect other than the universal repercussions of shortages in shipping and supply. Great pressure was put
on increase of copra and phosphate production which
brought in dollars and pounds, but that was largely neutralized by restrictions on imports and by rationing. In
fact, some of the outlying islands had to return to subsistence economy. Tahiti's normal tourist trade was interrupted, and the island was insulated, through strict limitations on travel, from "contamination" by Americans
based in near-by Bora Bora. The determined De Gaullist
governor also ruled French Polynesia's economy and
other domestic affairs with the same iron hand, with the
result that his jurisdiction became more French and less
Oceanic. To the booming copra trade, Tahitians—whites
and Polynesians—added the manufacture of curios which
were sold in PX's all over the South Pacific. Even Seabee
artisans were not able to turn out native crafts quite as
"authentic" as those mass-produced in Tahiti.

Up nearer the combat zone a communications base
was maintained at Wallis Island, where the French administrator feuded continually with the British trader,
where copra rotted in the sheds for lack of a vessel to
carry it away, and where GI's sat around and worried
about contracting encephalitis, which a rumor credited
with having emasculating consequences. In the background the yaws-ridden natives kept up their Catholic
routines and did laundry for the Americans.

Further north at Funafuti, Americans and Ellice Islanders lived harmoniously crowded together on a narrow atoll without apparent ill effects on either group save
that of the boredom of the former.

As every Pacific air traveler knew, Canton, Palmyra,
Christmas, and Johnston Islands were transformed into
major air transport stations, but that did not affect any
indigenous populations because there were none there
to affect.

Tarawa and Makin atolls need no recall even to the shallowest of memories. The Japanese invaders took them soon after Pearl Harbor and murdered most of the whites who failed to escape. Throughout the enemy occupation, Gilbertese resisted passively—passivity was their only weapon—and were subjected to mistreatment ranging from confiscation of personal valuables to a Japanese retaliatory bombing raid.

British colonial officials returned to the Gilberts with the American Marines and promptly organized a Gilbertese labor corps which did much useful stevedoring in connection with preparations for the campaign in the Marshalls.

Near-by Ocean Island and Nauru, the phosphate centers, were occupied by Japanese forces early in 1942 and remained in enemy hands up to the end, although American bombers neutralized any value they might have had for the invaders. Some natives from these islands were later discovered by American occupation forces in the Carolines, where they had been taken by the Japanese to work.

Vulnerable Guam, cut off from American aid by Japanese Micronesia, fell into enemy hands soon after Pearl Harbor and was promptly integrated into Japan's South Seas Empire, which by then had become one huge network of bases in support of the southward thrusts.

During the first phase of the Pacific war, before Japan began to be crippled by Allied counterattacks, the Marianas and Carolines and Marshalls were the scene of intensified military and economic activities. Sugar, copra, and phosphate were strategic war materials and their production was kept going. Gardens were planted to help feed the enlarged Japanese garrisons and the gangs of coolie laborers imported for military construction projects. Imports were controlled and carefully rationed, but there appear to have been no serious hardships at first.

In fact, the civilian populations were not seriously inconvenienced during that early victorious period of war enthusiasm.

But later on, when the grim digging-in times came, everything changed. Supplies became scarce even for the Japanese military groups; importation of civilian goods ceased almost altogether. Around the main bases, native lands were confiscated for military purposes and natives were impressed into labor gangs, some being sent to distant islands. Copra making ceased entirely, although sugar growing stalled along.

As Japan's military situation deteriorated, less consideration was paid to natives; but although there were many individual acts of cruelty and injustice, there is little evidence of a general policy of mistreatment, and those islands that were distant from the military bases were simply ignored.

Conditions became much worse after the United States carried the war to the islands. Men dropping bombs on Truk and other strongholds could not very well distinguish between military posts and native houses, and naval bombardments ("Spruance haircuts") unwittingly destroyed some native life and property.

The Marshalls were first to be wrested from the Japanese; then followed Guam, Saipan, Tinian, and Peleliu; and from these centers American planes continued to blast the bypassed islands until V-J Day.

On the staff of each American island commander were several military government officers specially selected and trained to maintain public order and welfare among civilians of liberated and occupied areas. From the very beginning distinctions were made between ethnic groups in these areas. Japanese and Okinawan civilians were herded together and guarded as more or less harmless enemies. Guamanians were greeted as long-suffering friends and were accorded as much freedom and assist-

ance as the military circumstances permitted. Natives—
Marshallese, Carolinians, and Chamorros outside Guam
—were classified as innocent victims of Japanese aggression and prospective wards of the United States. Koreans
presented something of a problem, but were, apparently, defined as rather low-caste allies.

The Marshallese provided good practice for military
government, and it was fortunate all around that these
islanders appeared good-naturedly amenable and charm-
ingly grateful for all the measures taken on their behalf:
the early Yankee missionary efforts paid off here. The
natives were fed, clothed, and doctored, and encouraged
to restore their "democratic" institutions. Soon a trade
program was operating; curios were purchased from natives and goods sold to them, all under close supervision
and controlled prices. An English-language school was
opened, and it was no time at all before the pupils were
lustily harmonizing "Anchors Aweigh."

Circumstances were more complex in the Marianas.
All other requirements were subordinated to building
and supplying the bases for knocking out Japan, and
military government officials had to make-do with supplies they could salvage elsewhere. The result was that
civilians, even Guamanians, had to exist in makeshift
camps on bare rations, and as many as possible were
encouraged to work for the military forces.

Basic policies were laid down by the top command
and were generally humane and sensible, as were most
of the military government officials who administered
the policies. A few officers were overzealous or dictatorial
or temperamentally unsuited to the job of running
others' lives, but as a group they did little harm and
much good.

Hawaii, the place where it all started, witnessed few
shots fired in anger after that first calamitous morning
of December 7, but the war made a permanent impres-

sion upon the land and the people and the institutions of the so-called Paradise of the Pacific.

Hawaii's political separation from the rest of Oceania became even more evident between 1939 and December 7, 1941. While neighbors to the south and west were preoccupied with war, there was little change in Hawaii's serenity, except for a gradual increase in tempo of military construction along with some uneasiness about Japan's potential fifth column. This calm made the sneak attack all the more electrifying.

The immediate effect of the blitz was to shock Hawaii almost into hysteria. Fear and rumor ruled, and the much-advertised interracial harmony gave way to suspicion and strife, punctuated with large-scale arrests of aliens. Civil authorities relinquished control to the military; women, children, and tourists were hustled into ships and sent to the mainland. Total blackouts were instituted and the famed bathing beaches were laced with barbed wire as the population nervously awaited the next blows—which never came.

For four years Hawaii was an armed camp. Its war role during that era has become household knowledge; less well known is the effect the war had on the civilian community. The most editorialized change in island life was the sudden and apparently complete transfer of government from civilian into military hands and the extension of government controls over wide areas of living. Movement was restricted, curfew installed, property commandeered. Prices were fixed, goods rationed, jobs and wages frozen, and shipping controlled. Admirals and generals supplanted civilian officials and mobilization was pushed to a degree quite unrealized on the mainland.

Military construction relegated King Sugar to second rank, but, since sugar was a strategic commodity, its production was officially supported. Pineapple production was also maintained and the pack sold to feed the armed forces. The tourist industry as such no longer catered to holiday seekers, but every tourist facility was overtaxed trying to entertain the tens of thousands of involuntary visitors in uniform. Fishing was one of the few major industries to suffer, since the Japanese-manned sampans were tied up for security reasons or commandeered.

Parts of Oahu's shore lines and cane fields were converted into military installations, but these changes touched only a small proportion of the Territory's land and were much less significant than the changes that took place in the population itself.

In addition to the tremendous influx of soldiers and sailors, the government also imported from the mainland tens of thousands of civilian workers, representing a very large increase in the Territory's total civilian population and an entirely new kind of resident for Hawaii. Local employees were also mobilized. They were "frozen," without appeal, to their pre-Pearl Harbor jobs and permitted to change employment only by directions; their wages were also fixed. This arrangement was eminently satisfactory to employers: for one thing, it kept workers from transferring en masse to the better-paid government jobs. It was also satisfactory to the military, because it enabled the authorities to requisition laborers from plantations for emergency use on military projects. Needless to say, this arrangement was somewhat less than satisfactory to the workers themselves.

After the initial hysteria in Hawaii interethnic hostility became much less apparent. There was a certain amount of trouble between local hoodlums and transient servicemen, but the predicted clash between Filipino and Japanese workers failed to materialize. Local whites and Hawaiians joined up or backed the war as everyone had expected, but it was the Japanese who surprised all the critics. The elders remained on duty and worked doggedly and industriously almost to the man, and their sons enlisted and fought in a manner that should remove forever any suspicion of divided loyalty.

As the war moved farther west, the military authorities returned controls to civilians and things appeared to move back toward normality, or as normal as they could be in the presence of tens of thousands of transient servicemen and mainland workers. But appearances were deceptive; under the surface there were signs of a major change in Hawaii's basic social structure. Under military government the white owners and managers of Hawaii's economy did not lose their control over territorial life; the freezing of men to jobs moved some workers to charge the new military masters and the old owner-managers with collusion to protect the *status quo*. As restrictions were eased, however, there was more and more talk about unionism on the plantations and docks. Resentment against Hawaii's traditional paternalistic system was increased by union-wise mainland workers; and West Coast labor leaders began to turn their attentions to this promising new field with the same zeal shown by those other ideologists, the missionaries, who had preceded them by a century and a quarter.

XXI

AFTER THE BATTLES

World War II unified Oceania to an extent never before realized. For a few hectic years nearly every island and atoll was in some measure brought under the jurisdiction of the Allied Combined Chiefs of Staff and their field commanders. But this unification did not long survive V-J Day. Soon after the cease-fire order, the historic tripartite division re-established itself, with Hawaii moving in one direction, "American" Micronesia in another, and the Franco-British South Pacific in a third. Political and cultural distances between the first two regions were of course shorter than they had been before the war; in fact, the cumulative effects of war served to bring all three regions somewhat closer together than they had been before Pearl Harbor, but not close enough to allow the historian to describe them with the same generalizations.

South Pacific

The sudden ending of hostilities aggravated if anything the South Pacific's wartime dislocations. The rush of military groups to clear out and go home was equaled only by the clamor of the islands' white residents to get back to their plantations and mines. Valuable supplies were left to rot and vast installations to return to jungle. With the military's organization and facilities out of the picture before civil authorities were ready to function, communications and services of all kinds were disrupted. And, of course, everyone but the Japanese was blamed for the confused state of affairs.

Some measure of disorganization, especially in transportation and supplies, obtained throughout the South Pacific, but conditions were progressively worse from southeast to northwest. Tahiti, for example, lacked some of its prewar amenities, but New Guinea's economy was totally wrecked—towns destroyed, plantations overgrown, mines disabled, labor force scattered, and administration confused.

Throughout the islands there was plenty of money but not much to buy, generally favorable world markets but poor shipping facilities; and in few places were the workers content to return to their old jobs for prewar wages. However, none of these stern realities deterred planners from devising fine programs for the hopeful new postwar world.

Implicit in most of the official blueprints were two warring principles: alongside the recurrent theme of native-oriented, internationally minded trusteeship, there incongruously appeared many not so veiled assertions of national sovereignty and empire.

The trusteeship theme was compounded of several things. In the background was the familiar ethic of humanitarianism which had been increasingly in evidence

since the turn of the century. Some memories of the
League of Nations mandate system were also present,
along with echoes of the Atlantic Charter, of Labour
Party socialist policy, and of missionary influence. This
theme was definitely pronative and anticommerce in sentiment, and was based upon the premise that government
alone could implement postwar plans. Probably the first
manifestation of this policy was the Fiji government's
appeal to the Colonial Ministry for a substantial increase in the native welfare subsidy. A little later Australia and New Zealand published their agreement to
co-operate in carrying out similar objectives, and the
theme was again forcefully enunciated by Australia's
Herbert Vere Evatt at San Francisco in 1945. French
officials also made a few tentative pronouncements along
these lines, but American authorities were too preoccupied with their new responsibilities in Micronesia to give
much thought to American Samoa.

The trusteeship principle was applied most vigorously to the planning for New Guinea's future. The Australian Labour Government made it clear that New
Guinea would be administered for the welfare of the
natives, with white residents receiving only secondary
consideration and their enterprises tolerated only to the
extent that they were harmless to native interests. The
usual arrangements were made to pay war damages in-
curred by white residents, but the authorities went even
further and took the unprecedented action of assuming
obligations to pay natives also for their losses in life and
property. Basic wages to natives were increased and the
indenture system of native labor was liberalized, both
pointing to eventual abolition of the system. Also, comprehensive and extremely ambitious plans were formulated for the improvement of native medical service,
education, and self-government; and the program for native economic development envisaged a rising standard
of living based on improved subsistence economy and

supplementary income-earning enterprises for natives. The assumption behind all the planning was that New Guinea natives, given the opportunity, were capable of unlimited "progress."

Similar though less ambitious programs were formulated for the Solomons, and even New Caledonian natives were granted easier access to citizenship privileges. In Fiji native welfare programs simply expanded in the directions already established; and in most other South Pacific dependencies this trend was also evident.

As mentioned above, however, the old signs of national sovereignty and empire also reappeared in the postwar pronouncements and plans. In the dark days of the war, when the colonial powers' resources were thinly spread over such wide areas in the fight for survival, there was much unofficial but not irresponsible talk about jettisoning indefensible island outposts and swapping island territories in the interest of rationalizing measures for security and administrative economy. Suggestions were made, for example, to turn over the Marquesas to the United States, to transfer the Solomons and the New Hebrides to Australia, to amalgamate Eastern and Western Samoa, and to encourage the United States to establish permanent bases at strategic points throughout the South Pacific. The tune changed, however, when the danger passed. It changed so radically, in fact, that responsible American officials had to act with great circumspection to quiet suspicions concerning the intentions of the United States. In numerous acts and statements, the older colonial powers stated their determination to maintain the political *status quo* in the South Pacific, and these sentiments were epitomized in the arrangements made to redistribute the old mandated territories. When the League of Nations expired, the former mandated territories of New Guinea, Western Samoa, and Nauru were left, *de jure* at least, without sovereign ties; but their former mandatory governments lost no time in reasserting claim to them under the new label of United Nations Trust Territories. Even Britain, so scrupulous about giving up India and Burma, showed not the slightest disposition to retire from her South Pacific dependencies.

Trusteeship and internationalism versus strategy and empire make for semantic conflict, but the great powers have never been stopped by a mere paradox. Some effort, however, was made to resolve this one when Australia and New Zealand invited the United Kingdom, France, Holland, and the United States to collaborate in establishing a South Pacific commission "to encourage and strengthen international co-operation in promoting the economic and social welfare and advancement of the peoples of the nonself-governing territories in the South Pacific."[1]

The South Pacific Commission headquarters was established at Nouméa and an international staff was assembled to engage in research and to act as an advisory body to South Pacific administrations. The Commission's functions were restricted to such nonpolitical and nonmilitary matters as economic development, social welfare, education, and health.

While all these policies and plans were being formulated in the rarefied atmosphere of official conference rooms, the nonofficial whites with personal stakes in island production and commerce began to reassert their views on the way islands should be run. Now, with the Japanese threat out of the way, they turned their attention to the new menace of government planners seemingly intent upon destroying the island world they knew before the war. The governments were accused of liquidating white enterprise in favor of giving the natives freedom and help "they could not use and, in fact, did not want." These critics were alarmed at the danger

[1] Excerpt from the Preamble to the intergovernment agreement setting up the South Pacific Commission, drawn up in Canberra in February 1947.

to their personal interests and laid much of the blame to the plotting of leftists in and out of government. And in some instances they believed their fears realized by the rash of native strikes and autonomy movements which broke out after the war.

These outbreaks took many forms. A general restlessness and impatience with prewar living standards and caste institutions was the inevitable result of the disturbances and the flood of new things and ideas brought on by the war. New Guinea natives, for example, were bound to draw conclusions from seeing their white masters flee before the Japanese. And, there and elsewhere, time gaps in administration, contacts with troops, breakdowns in services, and a thousand and one crises affecting every phase of the old life, all contributed to uncertainty and unrest. Then, too, many islanders were becoming aware of events and ideas and standards in the rest of the world through means of education and their increasing literacy.

Nativist manifestations varied from mild cynicism about westerners' superiority to sullen and organized movements against white colonialism. In New Guinea there were some nasty local incidents against the authorities; in the Solomons a few ambitious native leaders managed to organize such a strong and ramified antiwhite movement, the so-called *Marching Rule,* that the authorities had to send a destroyer to "show the flag," and then to round up the ringleaders with police force. This movement followed the familiar pattern of the "Cargo" cults of former days, and there was evidence from some of its slogans that leftists among the Allied troops may have helped to touch it off.

The best publicized of all these movements was the Western Samoans' petition to the United Nations for more self-government and for consideration of the reunion of Western and Eastern Samoa. A United Nations mission duly visited Western Samoa and came back with

a recommendation that the Samoans were not yet prepared for complete autonomy, but should be given
more control over local affairs. Meanwhile the New Zealand government adopted its own plan for changing
Western Samoa from a "Mandate" to a "Trust Territory"; the administrative changes did not go quite as far
as the United Nations plan suggested, but a few reforms
were effected and a few titles changed so that agitation
was quieted for a while.

In the meantime American civilian critics of the Navy's
rule in American Samoa moved the President to set a
date for transferring administrative responsibility to the
Department of the Interior, and to ask Congress to extend citizenship and an organic act of government to the
Eastern Samoans. (The question of union between Eastern and Western Samoa was too intricate for the statesmen to cope with.)

Postwar restlessness showed up in the Cook Islands
in the form of demands for more political rights and for
a larger share in economic gains. The native membership of the Cook Islands Progressive Association became
more aggressive in their tactics to control local industrial
affairs, and they were said to have received encouragement and support from leftist elements in the New Zealand longshore unions. Other factions of native workers
organized an officially sponsored union, and the two op-
posing groups engaged in jurisdictive strife and strikes
against shipping in the best longshore-union tradition.
Even Tahitians organized into "syndicates," but these
were mild affairs and were not taken very seriously.
More significant, for Tahiti, was the action taken by several Tahitians to keep officials from disembarking from
the ship that brought them from France, their object
being to remonstrate against having metropolitan French
colonial officials sent out to fill jobs that Tahitians were
capable of filling. The governor vigorously put down the
"revolt" and demonstrated that France, at least, would

not tolerate any weakening of central authority if she could help it.

In New Caledonia the impatience with prewar ties took a different form. Whites, rather than natives, sought to gain a larger measure of control over local affairs and even pressed for power to subordinate the metropolitan-appointed governor to the will of the locally elected general council. Back of this movement was the wartime experience of managing their own affairs while cut off from France. Back of it also was the desire of the less affluent white residents, who constituted the majority, to nationalize the principal local industries and so ensure that profits from local enterprises did not all end up in the pockets of absentee owners overseas. Another goal was to secure greater freedom to develop beneficial commercial ties with Australia and New Zealand.

Postwar stirrings also ruffled the calm of Fiji's community and there even occurred a mild strike among Fijian mine workers, but Fiji's principal postwar ailment was her chronic Indian problem. Indians continued to outbreed Fijians and whites, and, with their increase in numbers and in political experience and emboldened by events in India, they sharpened their demands for political suffrage. Having alienated whites and Fijians by holding aloof from war activities, they made themselves even more unpopular by carrying off a paralyzing strike against the sugar industry. Even optimists began to despair of a solution to Fiji's perennial problem.

The birth of the United States of Indonesia left temporarily undecided the fate of the Netherlands New Guinea. The Hague Round-Table Conference of 1949 postponed the handling of this knotty problem in an effort to negotiate the larger issues of Indonesian autonomy, meanwhile leaving the Dutch in control pending final settlement, in 1950, of Western New Guinea's sovereignty. Judging from actions and speeches in early 1950 it became evident that neither side would surrender its claims without a fierce political battle. And to the student of Oceania it seemed probable at that time that the natives, unaware of the issues and unable to articulate their own wishes, if, indeed, they had any, would neither be seriously considered nor systematically consulted in this matter of who their masters would be.

While all these more or less local factors were shaping events in the postwar South Seas, world economic conditions were also exerting their influences. Copra and cocoa prices rose, bringing prosperity to those island communities that could market their products. The need for nickel and chrome slacked off, but the renewed demand for gold and oil pressed the operators and explorers to heroic exertions to re-establish mining and test drilling in New Guinea. Interest was awakened in fishing, and American and British experts laid plans for huge ocean-sweeping fishing enterprises. Enthusiasm developed for other industries as well, for growing of tea and rice, and for establishing tourist facilities; and the whole tempo of communications was speeded up by the extension of civil air travel between the principal centers.

In the presence of all this ferment and ungovernable change, of all these clashes of interest and differences in objective, only the most deluded escapist would have chosen the postwar South Seas as a haven of calm and continuity.

American Micronesia

Immediately after V-J Day the new American rulers of Micronesia had to take on the tremendous task of occupying and administering the numerous bypassed and far-flung Caroline Islands in the face of rapid demobilization and general disintegration of all communications and supply facilities. And when the surrender parties put ashore at places like Truk and Ponape and

Koror they found unbelievable want and devastation among both Japanese and natives.

After interning and shipping away all Japanese military personnel, the next significant move undertaken was to repatriate all Japanese and Okinawan civilians, and then to return to their home islands all islanders who had been displaced during the war. This move assuredly simplified the administrative task and removed the cause for probable future difficulties comparable to the Indian problem in Fiji, but the precipitous way the operation was carried out caused many heartbreaks; some Okinawans had spent most of their lives in the islands and had acquired native families which were broken up by the move.

As for the remaining Micronesians, few were starving but most needed medical help; many of their structures and all their boats were destroyed; their life savings, invested in Japanese banks and postal savings, were gone; their standards of living depressed, livestock killed off, lagoons and reefs depopulated of fish by bombardment; their gardens and groves threatened by pests introduced during the war years; their sources of income vanished. And now they were faced with the painful necessity of starting out from scratch to adjust to a new set of masters and rules—their fourth in fifty years.

Unlike the Australians in New Guinea and the British in the Gilberts, the American Naval Command possessed no reserves of precedent and experienced personnel with which to govern their new wards. Guam was administratively separated from the rest of the islands and governed approximately as before, but Saipan, Rota, the Carolines, and the Marshalls posed new and tough problems. Inexperienced officers were stationed on isolated islands and ordered to repair the devastations, heal the sick, rehabilitate the economies, reconstitute and govern native communities, adjudicate quarrels, enforce American-type rules of law and order, and educate their charges for roles in the new age. And, while all this was supposed to be progressing, bases were being dismantled, personnel—including military government personnel —was being shipped home, transport was disrupted, supplies reduced to a trickle, and the whole governing organization demoralized by the lack of any official objective or long-range administrative program for Micronesia. Under these circumstances, Micronesia did not recover stability and prosperity overnight, but that was no fault of the well-meaning but harassed officers who had to cope with these difficulties on the spot.

The world became poignantly acquainted with the exodus of "King" Jude and his Bikini people to make way for Operation Crossroads. The lives of other Micronesians were less dramatically affected than that, but few escaped altogether the consequences of postwar disruptions; and while no one died of hunger, few regained their prewar standards of living during the first two postwar years.

The nadir was reached in the early months of 1946; after that some constructive policies were formulated and gradually implemented. Naval officers were required to attend a university course in colonial administration before undertaking island assignments. Relief goods were sent where critically needed and a start was made in commercial distribution through government-subsidized trade stores which eventually dotted the area. Copra and shell and curios began to trickle in.

All this was done by military government officials working on a day-to-day basis, still waiting for a long-range policy, and understandably reluctant to proceed with any fundamental measures without a green light from Washington.

The turning point for America's captured islands of Micronesia came in April 1947, when the Security Council of the United Nations approved a trusteeship agreement for the Territory and designated the United States as administering authority. In its clauses guaranteeing the rights and welfare of the native inhabitants, this trusteeship agreement was almost identical with those approved for New Guinea, Nauru, and Western Samoa; but, unlike those others, it entitled the United States to close off parts of the area for security reasons.

The trusteeship agreement helped point out the general direction, but it did not set the course. That was left for Washington to quarrel over. The ensuing controversy might have been entertaining had it not involved the welfare of thousands of unconsulted Micronesians. The policy battle lines were drawn between military and civilian departments of the government, specifically between the Navy, which controlled the islands, and the Department of the Interior, which wanted to govern them. The Navy based its claim on the essentially *naval* security and functions of the islands and upon the continuing need to service the islands by naval transport and communications. The Department of the Interior based its claim on the rights of civilian Micronesians to be governed by civilians. Navy defended its ability to govern civilians by pointing to Guam and Samoa; Interior attacked the record of Guam and Samoa. This War of Memoranda was enlivened by shots from the sidelines; both Navy and Interior had their unofficial protagonists who fought the issue back and forth on the editorial pages. Some critics, with little confidence in either Navy's or Interior's capacities for governing, proposed a new executive agency to administer all of the nation's dependent territories.

Various drafts of organic acts were submitted to Congress setting forth charters for governing the Trust Territory, Guam, and Samoa. An Organic Act for Guam was passed by the Congress in 1950, giving Guamanians United States citizenship and some local autonomy, but similar bills for Samoa and the Trust Territory were not acted upon. Without waiting for Congressional decision,

the Executive branch agreed upon a piecemeal transfer
of administration of the islands from the Navy to the Department of the Interior; this transfer began with Guam,
on August 1, 1950, and was in due course followed by
Samoa and the Trust Territory.

Meanwhile, although official indecision may have retarded recovery somewhat in the Trust Territory, the
Micronesians did not sit about and starve while waiting
for Washington to make up its mind. Subsistence living improved and even commerce picked up, with increasing amounts of copra and shell being exported and
more goods being imported. Phosphates were mined and
sent to Japan to stave off a disastrous fertilizer shortage
there, but arrangements were made to reimburse Micronesians in some measure for the loss of this valuable
resource. In general, final objectives were still undecided
but immediate problems were cared for.

Guam's rehabilitation proceeded more swiftly than
Saipan's or Koror's or Ponape's, but, even five years
after Hiroshima, Agaña was still filled with rubble and
many Guamanians continued to dwell in camps far from
their own villages and farms.

Guam also came in for its share of spotlight, and numerous official visitors urged changes in the traditional
order. It was generally recognized that some change was
inevitable if Guamanian economy was to adapt to the
presence of the large defense establishment there. It
looked as if copra economy was out: Guamanians would
in future probably derive most of their income from
working for the military. It also seemed obvious that
their increased contact with mainlanders would sophis-
ticate them to the point where citizenship and more self-
government must be granted.

As in the South Pacific, postwar events in American
Micronesia were influenced by the paradoxical principles
of trusteeship and nationalism; by praiseworthy concern
for native welfare; and by sincere respect for the aspira-

tions of the natives—provided, of course, they did not
conflict with national interests. Otherwise, however, the
South Pacific parallel did not carry through. There were
no white colonials in American Micronesia to criticize
government practices, and from most indications there
would not be any for many years to come. Finally, there
had not yet appeared in Micronesia a protest against
white rule sufficiently organized to be labeled an autonomy movement. Guamanians had their complaints and
expressed them volubly; but even had there been a sentiment of extremism—which was unlikely—Guam's postwar prosperity was not very conducive to demonstrations
of independence. And as for the rest of the natives of
American Micronesia, they had so far had too little opportunity to size up their new white masters. Regarding
this an informed observer of the Oceania of 1950 could
only have predicted: Give them time!

Hawaii

Postwar Hawaii was dominated by the struggle between big business and organized labor. After V-J Day
most of the mainland personnel who had served during
the war returned home, military construction activity
subsided, tourists began to trickle in again, and, on the
surface at least, Hawaii appeared to be returning to normal. It was a slightly altered normalcy, to be sure: the
permanent military establishments were bigger than before the war, and air traffic brought the Territory nearer
to the mainland and gradually quickened the pace of
life; but otherwise life seemed to drift back to *aloha*-
ism. Scratching below the surface, however, revealed
anything but peace and contentment.

The conflict lines between big business and labor were
actually forming before the war, but wartime events
postponed the real battle. In other ways, however, war
provided an advantageous setup for the West Coast

union organizers who appeared in due course to direct labor's campaigns.

Longshoremen and sugar workers were the first to strike, and these initial work stoppages were long and costly affairs; they ended in compromise, however, and did not permanently cripple the Territory's economy, as some observers predicted they would. Even so, for a while it looked as if organized labor were winning; but then there occurred the usual tactical mistake. Union leaders threatened to extend the work stoppage to public utilities, and that threat to the security of everyday life, to ordinary things that affected everybody, aroused the community much more than did the somewhat distant events in the fields and on the wharves. Against a popular indignation, enflamed by a group improbably called "We the Women of Hawaii," the union leaders had little chance, and the tide of labor's popularity and power began to ebb.

Later on, by the time the pineapple workers had got around to demonstrating, big business had the situation well in hand and this strike ended in failure for the unionists. Big business won these first skirmishes by virtue of its superior organization and enormous resources, but it also possessed strong allies in the whole community and in the character and conditions of the workers themselves. No matter how small a stake they may have had in Hawaii's riches, most residents not employed in manual-labor jobs tended to identify themselves with the owning and managing classes. This line-up is certainly not peculiar to Hawaii, but it was strengthened there by the ethnic situation and by the Territory's shortage of intellectuals and disinterested liberals. There is also some possibility that such militant unionism may have been too rich for the blood of the workers, who were mostly Orientals with agelong conditioning in subordinate roles. Also, with boom times past, many workers became concerned for their security, especially when they observed management's increasing interest in mechanization.

At any rate, big business survived successfully the first test of strength, and Hawaii settled back to beautifying its façade for the swelling tourist trade.

XXII

MIDCENTURY: EVENTS AND PROSPECTS

During the decade of the fifties events in the Pacific Islands moved so fast and in so many directions that an anthropological observer, like the writer, must turn over to other specialists most of the task of summary and analysis. It is no longer possible to study a few representative situations—as for instance how a Polynesian village assimilates Christianity, or how some Papuans react to plantation life—and then write about *the* Pacific Islands.

Fortunately more and more specialists are focusing attention upon this vast region. Historians have begun to realize that history is where you find it, and not merely in Europe or North America or the Far East; and the same is true of political scientists, economists, geographers, and demographers, among whom are some scholarly islanders themselves. Until the findings of these specialists are recorded and synthesized one can speak only impressionistically about *patterns* among the innumerable historical events of the 1950's. But underlying these events were certain factors that require no specialized skill to perceive or to appreciate.[1]

Dominating all other circumstances was the quickening rate of population increase in nearly every political unit—both in terms of over-all increase and of changing ratios between co-resident ethnic groups.

Even before World War II Gilbert Islanders were too numerous to be supported on their sparse atolls, and some of them were resettled on the uninhabited central Pacific Phoenix Islands. During the fifties others were transplanted to the northwest Solomons, with more to follow.

Another mass movement took place away from Ocean Island, where phosphate mining removed what was left of the thin soil and rendered agriculture next to impossible. Using some of their large savings from phosphate royalties, the Ocean Islanders purchased an island in the Fiji group and commenced there what appeared to be a highly successful new kind of life.

The reduction of Navy activities and the change-over from naval to civilian (Department of the Interior) administration obliged large numbers of Eastern Samoans to seek their livelihood on Hawaii and the United States mainland. During this same period many hundreds of Polynesians from Western Samoa, Niue, Cook Islands, and Tonga flocked to New Zealand, partly in direct response to economic pressures, partly in search of education or higher wages or adventure. Of these territories Western Samoa presented the most alarmingly rapid rise in population figures, but the hazards implicit in this increase were for the moment glossed over by this territory's continuing prosperity.

[1] With war over it is no longer appropriate to include Australia, New Zealand, and Hawaii with "the Pacific Islands."

Overpopulation appeared more as a threat than an actuality at Tahiti and the other Society Islands, but the promise of higher wages lured hundreds of Tahitians to New Caledonia and the New Hebrides, some apparently with intent to stay. Meanwhile Tahiti's Chinese population continued to increase fast enough to provide politicians with "Tahiti for Tahitians" slogans.

In Fiji, demographic trends continued to complicate the Fijian-Indian issue, with the latter already much more numerous than the former, and the gap steadily widening. Here the immediate problem was not an absolute excess of population over resources but rather the ethnic division of these resources, with Indians clamoring for some of the Fijian-held land.

The specter of expanding population has a different face in every Pacific Island territory and it travels by different timetables, but it is to be found nearly everywhere and ought to be feared.

No population can be called "too large" if there are sufficient resources to support its needs and aspirations, and it is such disparities that occasioned the developments just noted. But *economic* factors were also behind many other kinds of developments in the midcentury Pacific Islands.

On New Guinea most of the richer gold-bearing areas were worked out during the decade, and one of the large enterprises transferred its energies to logging. The search for oil continued, but with so little success that operations began to slacken off—until a dramatic discovery in Papua caused companies to renew their efforts.

On Guadalcanal testing for gold was resumed for a while and then abandoned. Meanwhile on New Caledonia the mining industry continued to boom and to create a demand for labor. Elsewhere, as the supplies of phosphate rock appeared to diminish, the British began a renewed search for other sources, and the French began to worry about how to replace the revenues that

would end with Makatéa's depletion. Some of these circumstances had little immediate consequences for the
islanders themselves, but they all would be felt in time.

World prices for copra fluctuated considerably during
the fifties but remained generally higher than many experts had expected. Also, government-sponsored price-
support programs served to keep producers' incomes
even and fairly high in some territories. A more serious
problem was being created for the future by virtue of
the fact that few new palms were being planted to replace the increasing number past production age. During
this decade cocoa continued to provide Western Samoans with large incomes, but Fiji's fruit industry experienced some market troubles. In Tahiti, vanilla had its
ups and downs but remained a major source of income
for many Tahitians and Chinese.

One of the most novel developments in island agriculture took place in the New Guinea highlands, where a
large and flourishing coffeegrowing industry was established, involving both white and native producers—the
latter just a few years removed from a Stone Age
technology.

Meanwhile agricultural agents of territorial governments and the South Pacific Commission kept up a vigorous search for new income crops, in order to protect
islanders and colonists from the dangers inherent in one-
crop economies.

Shell fishing continued to be a factor in some island
economies during the decade just past—in parts of American Micronesia, in the islands of the Torres Strait, the
Northern Cooks, and the Tuamotus. When Japanese
shell divers reappeared near Australian waters some
white operators were prepared to resume World War II,
but others soberly suggested adding the more skillful
Japanese to their own crews. Pelagic fishing also experienced a revival in the central Pacific, after an unfortunate
start. British enterprise and American capital sought to

establish a large industry in and around Fiji, using Fijians for fishermen—but the fish would not co-operate. Instead, the more experienced Japanese long-line fishermen were called in to supply a cannery built for the purpose at American Samoa, and for a time the business progressed so successfully that other territories began to draw up similar plans.

Economics were also behind many of the changes in transportation which took place during the fifties. Airlines proliferated; by the end of the decade one could fly from Australia or New Zealand or Hawaii to almost any territorial capital within a day or two. At the same time, surface shipping also generally increased, although there were some changes in specific links. The immediate consequences of the acceleration in transport were to bring in more visitors from abroad, mainly as tourists, and to increase movements among residents of different island territories; both of these led inevitably toward smoothing out differences among the islands and between the islands and the rest of the world.

Human reproduction and the tangibles of economics have a way of confounding and frustrating human plans, but in listing the more important factors influencing events in the Pacific Islands during the fifties one cannot ignore the views and objectives of the actors themselves —the people who live in the islands as well as those outside whose positions give them power and influence over island events. There are several classes of these individuals.

First, there are those who look at the islands and envisage orderly groves of coconuts, rich mines, busy highways and wharves. These visionaries are the white settlers, the owners, managers, and shareholders. To them the islands have meaning in terms of colonization, raw materials, and markets. To them, idle lands, unfished waters, and unemployed natives are unnatural, anachronistic, a challenge to enterprise. No one nation holds a monopoly on these philosophers of *free* (*i.e.*, free *white*) enterprise.

But where do natives fit into these plans of colonization and commercial development? In the thoughts of many colonial-minded whites, the indigenous peoples figure principally as labor, useful only so long as it is cheap and tractable. The natives are regarded as inferior beings, inherently and biologically; it is believed that they cannot become assimilated by the superior western culture even were that desirable—which, according to this view, is not the case. Others of this persuasion, more charitably inconsistent, feel that natives deserve a better fate than extinction, and in fact should be encouraged to assimilate as well as they can the inevitably overwhelming colonial culture.

A quite different view of Oceania's future is shared by the officials and politicians who plan island destinies in terms of national interests. To them the islands mean defense outposts, communication bases, spheres of influence. If commerce supports these objectives, then commerce is tolerated, even encouraged: for example, the search for oil is in the interest of national security; gold is important for foreign exchange; phosphate and copra help develop national self-sufficiency.

Toward natives these officials and politicians show more concern and hold out better hopes. Some would create ethnic reserves, draw cordons around the inhabitants, insulate them from alien influence, and leave them alone to remain what they are. Others, somewhat more realistic, look for natives to become more or less self-governing and assimilated into the stronger westernism, in the interest of national stability and of native welfare —just how far this assimilation should go and how it is to come about being matters for debate. Some believe that it can and should be carried only so far that it does not destroy the "genius" of the native cultures, and feel that it should be reached gradually, as a result of long-range planning. At another extreme are those who consider complete and speedy assimilation desirable and inevitable. Between these poles are several shades of opinion, some of which are formalized into official policy; but policy differs from one colonial administration to another and usually changes with successive political parties in power.

Next, there is a vocal but currently uninfluential point of view that envisages an island world freed from specific national ties and from all exploitative types of colonial enterprise. Most proponents of this view would like to see all the islands placed under an international organization having considerably more direct authority than the present Trusteeship Council; some individuals entertain hopes that the islanders will eventually become self-governing within the framework of the international system.

All persons of this persuasion can be described as "pro-native" in sentiment, but there is disagreement among them about what is best for the natives. Some hold to the "ethnic zoo" theory of insulation. Others hope that islanders will ultimately become a species of South Seas peasantry and small entrepreneurs, protected from all forms of alien exploitation and permitted to make their own decisions about what to accept or reject about westernism.

There is still another point of view which values the relatively underpopulated islands as inviting destinations for some of Asia's surplus people. Needless to say, this proposal is not very popular in the islands or among the nations owning or "protecting" the islands.

Last of all, there are the views of the native islanders themselves.

Western Samoans have already expressed their views in no uncertain terms. After forty-five years they succeeded in convincing their New Zealand rulers that they cannot be ruled by outsiders. Whether they succeed in convincing the world that they can rule themselves is another matter, but during 1960 they organized their own government, began writing their own constitution, and cast off all but the slenderest ties with New Zealand. The separation from New Zealand was carried out in a spirit of mutual congeniality, but it remained to be seen whether this lively new nation would choose to remain within the British Commonwealth. As everyone expected, the Samoan government was "democratic"—democratic, that is, by Samoan standards. Only chiefs (*matais*) could vote, and the "elected" leaders of the state were none other than those *matais* whose family titles rank highest in Samoa's ancient social-political hierarchy.

During Western Samoa's move toward independence many individuals suggested inviting their ethnic cousins in Eastern Samoa to throw in with them, but evidently neither the United States government nor their Samoan wards valued this suggestion. Despite Eastern Samoa's drawbacks it seemed less than wise to cast aside Uncle Sam to join in an uncertain enterprise, especially since the Eastern Samoans would undoubtedly be outranked and outvoted by their western neighbors in the management of the new state.

In appraising the Eastern Samoans' wish to stay as they are one must credit them with large reserves of patience. Under Navy administration they became accustomed to inexperienced and short-term naval governors. The first five years under civilian control were harder if anything: a rapid turnover in governors and a radical reduction in jobs. Finally, however, in 1956 there arrived a governor, himself part-Samoan and raised on Samoa, who appeared intent on fulfilling his term of office.

While the more unified and voluble Western Samoans

were demanding and receiving their independence, the near-by Cook Islanders drifted along in their dependency upon New Zealand. The labor strife of the forties subsided, thus contributing to an atmosphere of official smugness and native apathy. When a team of experts reported on the distressing plight of the islands' economy, health, and educational system, their report was tabled. Later, however, New Zealand newspapers drummed up public interest so that officialdom was moved to institute reforms, and these were supplemented by the islanders' own efforts in organizing co-operatives. By 1961 it is too early to predict what effect on the islands will result from the presence in New Zealand of several hundred Cook Islanders, but some radical effects there will surely be.

Many Niue Islanders also migrated to New Zealand during the decade, but that island's most dramatic occurrence was the murder, by Niueans, of the New Zealand resident commissioner. The crucial question raised by this event was whether it happened to be an isolated impetuosity or the manifestation of a general mood.

The Kingdom of Tonga continued almost unchanged during the fifties, except for the activities of its energetic premier, Prince Tungi, who traveled around the world in search of new ways to strengthen Tonga's economy.

Surprisingly enough it was the Crown Colony of Fiji that dismayed most observers of island affairs during the decade under review. The well-known "Fijian problem" continued to aggravate: Indians continued to increase faster than Fijians and to demand land and votes, most Fijians continued to remain Fijian, and so on. Experts agreed that the economy, the society, and the body politic would have to be reshaped to stave off racial conflict and economic disaster, but it took a violent strike to create a general sense of urgency, which was all the more alarming to the whites and the more conservative Fijians in that many Fijians made common cause with

Indians. Plainly the Fijian problem had acquired another complication.

During the decade just passed the Administration of Britain's Western Pacific territories (Solomons, Gilberts, Ellice) was divorced from Fiji and moved to Guadalcanal, but it remained to be seen whether this move would alter things in the Solomons. From the point of view of white enterprise these islands were the slowest to recover from wartime devastation and dislocation. Also, to the disgust of white critics the Administration persisted in maintaining a tight control over commerce and in acceding to the demands of some native groups (mainly on Malaita) for larger shares of self-rule. For some Australians the solution to the problem created by the Solomons' large and "underdeveloped" land area, relatively small population, and minute colonial subsidy, was to turn the islands over to Australia, or to include them in a federation of *British* Pacific Islands, or at least into a union of British Melanesian Islands.

A similar answer was proposed by some Australians to the perennial question, "What to do about the New Hebrides?" But it appeared quite unlikely that any French government or colonist would consent to this solution. The fifties brought few changes to the Condominium, or to the shape of its complex conundrum, involving two wholly different Administrations, two colonial populations, its large and enterprising Indo-Chinese community, and a native population ranging in culture from Stone Age savagery to Presbyterian prudery.

Throughout this decade the economy of New Caledonia continued to be based on mining, and maintained a generally high level of prosperity; but the political structure of the territory underwent radical change. By gaining Paris' consent for "common role" voting, a pro-native faction among the colonists succeeded in wresting local political power from the European industrial and commercial leaders; and this move was lent weight by the metropolitan government's apparent sympathy for more local self-rule. During the short interregnum following the fall of the Fourth Republic the conservative faction regained power in Nouméa, but eventually President de Gaulle re-established the legitimate pronative officials, and was later rewarded for his action, when during the world-wide French referendum of 1958 over 96 per cent of the island's electorate voted to remain linked with France.

French Polynesia also voted in 1958 to remain French, but by the much smaller margin of 62 per cent. As such places go, Tahiti and its surrounding islands were anything but paradisiacally calm during the past decade. Some observers believed that the native discontent with French rule developed during the late war, when a De Gaullist governor acted too autocratically to keep the islands beyond American temptation. Actually much of the anti-French sentiment was a heritage of English missionary days; and it may also have been encouraged by the uninformed and irresponsible chatter of American servicemen and, more recently, of American tourists. In any event, there emerged in due course a popular "nationalist" hero, who might have succeeded in creating an independent *ex*-French Polynesia, but for some tactical political errors and some characteristically *Polynesian* factional strife. The hero was eventually imprisoned and exiled, when some of his more exuberent followers were caught allegedly trying to burn down Papeete; but at the end of the decade his sympathizers were still numerous enough to elect his son to the office vacated by his arrest. Meanwhile some Tahitians continued to brood over the increasing numbers and affluence of the Chinese in their midst, while others prepared for—or at least *awaited*—the streams of tourists which seemed to be heading their way.

Australia continued to administer Papua and the Trust Territory of New Guinea as a single territory during the decade; and although changes in the Commonwealth government resulted in some changes in colonial policy, the march was always toward more native welfare and more native control over native affairs. At the same time the government showed signs of yielding to the demands of white settlers for more land, so that—without actually announcing it—Australian New Guinea seemed to be heading in the direction of a dual, native *and* European society—a dualism made even sharper by the extension of Australian citizenship to New Guinea-born Chinese, which left only the increasing white-native half-castes in a social and political limbo.

No one attempted to poll the New Guineans concerning *their* views on their islands' future. Many of them continued to prosper and to assimilate European political ideas—even to the point of refusing to pay taxes. If "Cargo cults" can be interpreted as being incipient nationalism, then such nationalism remained a lively issue; but at the close of the decade there had not yet appeared any widespread *directed* sentiment of "New Guinea for New Guineans."

One suspects that western statesmen would like to have West New Guinea simply disappear. For the Dutch, it is a financial and a political liability, uncompensated by any strategic return. For Australia, it is strategically valuable—but, according to the popular view, only if it remains out of Indonesia's hands, a sentiment which stands in the way of vitally important relations with Indonesia. And for the United States, strategic worries over New Guinea versus political worries over Indonesia are complicated by political and military ties with the Netherlands. In Indonesia the "Irian question" is kept flamingly alive by politicians, some of whom promise to fight to "regain" it. Dutch authorities accuse Indonesia of military infiltration; Indonesians protest against Dutch defensive measures—and so it goes. Meanwhile the Dutch appear to have embarked upon a course of action designed to westernize their native wards as rapidly as possible, with the apparent objective of encouraging them to *choose* to govern themselves and thereby frustrate Indonesia's claim to govern them. The birth of Freedom has been attended by an odd assortment of midwives in recent years, but by none more unlikely than this.

What does the future hold for these ethnic and political mosaics of the South Pacific Islands?

One factor which must be considered when predicting the future of the South Pacific Islands is the potential influence of the South Pacific Commission. That organization could become a powerful agency for unifying the dependencies as well as for solving some of their economic, social, and health problems. And, of course, another world war would result in more political consolidation, whoever won.

However, external political events and economic conditions, important though they are, will not be all-decisive; the islanders themselves will help determine the shape of things to come in the South Pacific. For one thing, prophets and planners must take into account the native population increases that are occurring in all but a few hopelessly blighted areas. New Guinea can, of course, accommodate large native increases, but many of the atolls and smaller islands are already overflowing to a point requiring emigration and resettlement of their surplus people.

Another native factor to be reckoned with is the variable capacity of the islanders to adapt to the westernism that will beat with increasing force against their shores. This is not a question of racial, of biological, capacity; it has yet to be demonstrated that racial factors have anything to do with cultural *potential*. It is rather a question of specific cultural patterning; and although research in this field is still undeveloped, there is evidence that in-

dividuals shaped in some cultural molds are better prepared to adapt to westernism than those shaped in some
others. Consider, for example, the different fates of the
Maoris and the Australian aborigines: some, at least, of
the Maoris' present survival value, and of the aborigines'
seemingly unarrestable decline, is due to the nature of
the cultures of these two groups.

Then, too, this matter is complicated by the fact that
westernism itself is not a single cultural entity. The de-
fenseless islander is expected to adapt to several varieties
of westernism: the planters', the missionaries', and so on.

With these two sets of cultural variables—the varying
capacities of native groups to adjust to alien influence,
and the differences in the alien influences themselves—
likely to persist for years to come, it may be assumed
that the future of the islands will be checkered with
cases of ruinous maladjustments as well as with some
cases of fairly successful adjustment. In any event, native
cultures will not remain unchanged nor will they revert
to their pre-European patterns.

Mindful of the several hypothetical alternatives and
the inescapable facts of political trends, of economic conditions, and of cultural dynamics, I will now indulge in
some predictions of my own:

The alternative of the official will predominate for the
immediate future; considerations of national security will
outweigh those of commerce and internationalism and
world population. During this era there will be sporadic
instances of resurgent colonial enterprise, as in Australian
New Guinea, but the general trend elsewhere will be toward subsistence-cash crop economies managed for or
by natives.

Increased westernization through education will create appetites for western goods, modern services, and
political independence, and there will be much anger and
strife before islanders learn that these costly commodities cannot be bought or sustained by a few bags of

copra and a fervent wish. Some favored places will like Western Samoa achieve a large measure of autonomy, but most island groups lack the resources required for the fiscal self-support which is a condition of true autonomy. Some, in fact, like the Cook Islands, will become integral parts of the parent nation.

If it suits their convenience and serves their international purposes, the colonial powers may permit the island dependencies to evolve into federated semiautonomous states. But even in that event the South Pacific Islands will inevitably be drawn closer under the economic and cultural hegemony of Australia and New Zealand.

During the fifties American Micronesia proved to be no *political* problem at all. At the beginning of the decade the Navy turned over administration of the islands to the Department of the Interior, but later recovered control over the northern Marianas for military purposes. Guam, an outright possession, continued to bustle with activity; but the rest of the Trust Territory—Rota, the Carolines, and the Marshalls—relapsed into a placidity which had probably not been experienced since World War I. When the Navy left the scene it also removed its very extensive transport and health facilities, which the new civilian Administration was only partly able to replace. In consequence, many islanders have been left to their own resources—for the moment at least.

But what does the future hold for these Micronesian Islanders? The Marianas, including Guam, present one kind of picture, the Carolines and Marshalls another.

So long as the United States maintains naval and air bases on Guam and Saipan, the Chamorros will have opportunities to earn and buy some of the goods and services they are learning to want. As they learn more, by formal education and everyday contact with persons and things American, the gap between expectations and realizations will widen. For some peoples this would encourage revolt or cynicism or loss of ethnic identity, but Chamorros, having become shabbily Hispanized for so many generations, will probably relax easily into becoming second-class Americans.

In the Marianas those who administer the native affairs will be impotent to control the process of acculturation; in the Carolines and Marshalls, however, there is theoretically more leeway for planning and guiding: here our government has several choices. First, it could be decided to do nothing, to leave the islanders to their own devices and insure that no individuals or agencies interfere with their ways of life, either for better or for worse. If this transpired the islanders would likely return to a tolerable aboriginal existence after a generation or two of puzzled insecurity and material deprivation. But this, of course, could not happen. It is not in the nature of Americans to leave things alone, and, even if it were, there remains a legal obligation to the United Nations to do something. This being so, three choices of positive action face the planners.

In the first place, it could be decided to Americanize the islanders consistently and thoroughly, not only by teaching them what to want and expect but by insuring that they can satisfy these expectations. A decision of this sort is improbable for two reasons. To begin with, the cost would be too great; local resources are so slim that the islanders themselves could never pay for the goods and services which help constitute the American way of life, and it is unlikely that Congress would agree to supply forevermore every Trukese with television and every Ponapean with a car. Secondly, there is a general feeling, mainly aesthetic, among policy makers of this political generation that total Americanization of simple Pacific Islanders is culturally undesirable even were it economically feasible.

Another course of positive administrative action lies in the direction of controlled cultural change. An administration staffed with experts in human relations and insured against interference and discontinuity might have an even chance of rationing out to the Micronesians assimilable amounts of Americanization without upsetting the fine adjustments between the islanders' cultures and their restrictive environments. But, like total Americanization, this course of action is not feasible. It would not be possible to create the circumstances required for such an experiment: changes in the Federal administration and Congress, as well as pressures from religious, welfare, and economic organizations, would inevitably destroy continuity and let unassimilable factors come in.

A third alternative represents not a choice but rather a lack of choice; it is the course of action that circumstances will probably force upon the harassed administrators of America's Trust Territory. Interest and appropriated money will always be available for keeping the islanders healthy and educating them American-style. And pressure will be exerted continually to transform their mores and their social and political relations into American patterns. Sporadic efforts will also be made toward economic development, but the resources and opportunities are just not there, so that standards of living will render meaningless many of the well-intentioned educational and social reforms. Furthermore, the expected increase in population will place more and more strain on material resources and thus further complicate the lives of islanders who must think in one world and dwell in another—an inglorious fate for a people whose ancestors conquered the Pacific's vast distances in frail canoes and with the crudest of tools fashioned satisfying existences on infertile specks of land. Of course, there remains the possibility that a people whose ancestors were so resourceful will be able to harmonize the cultural dissonances of the modern world into a new and equally satisfying kind of life for themselves. During the long centuries of Oceanic history they have done it before. Perhaps they will do it again.

XXIII

EPILOGUE

Despite their wide differences, all the possibilities just described are based on the assumption that peace, however uneasy, and westernism, however attenuated, will continue to prevail in the islands. But what of the other alternatives that must be realistically faced in this mid-century period of Communist imperialism and Asiatic resurgence: How vulnerable are the islands to these new threats; and what would become of them if they were enveloped in a new global war?

A totally Communist Asia would probably in due course repeat the same kind of attempt that was made in 1941 to capture Oceania. In that event, the ensuing campaigns would undoubtedly make the island battles of World War II look like light skirmishes, and island cultures would become archaeological. However, more immediate is the problem of how exposed the islands are to the more insidious dangers of sabotage and insurrection.

Some jittery colonials consider the following to be potentially active fifth columnists: the Indians of Fiji, the Javanese and Tonkinese workers of New Caledonia, and Chinese wherever they are. In addition, some uneasiness is voiced over the comings and goings of merchant seamen on vessels from metropolitan ports. And there are a few white colonials who regard the native islanders themselves to be grist for the Marxist mill. It is of course possible that individuals in each of these categories would espouse any cause that promised them a larger share of power; but what of the groups as a whole?

The Indians of Fiji have many grievances, real and imagined, but it is doubtful that many of them would take active measures to change one set of colonial masters for another. Most of their leaders and, doubtless, the large majority of their population properly consider themselves to be British subjects; and although they would probably continue to use their most effective weapon, the strike, to secure political and economic concessions—to gain more *British* enfranchisement—it is most unlikely that they would support insurrection or invasion.

World War II events in New Caledonia demonstrated that some of the Asiatics living there were at least susceptible to Communist teachings. The active agitators were whites who were well known to the authorities and duly dealt with; less well known was the actual extent of their following, but it was believed to have been largely made up of Tonkinese. Judging by the importance of the influence of the Communist Ho Chih Minh in Indochina, it would be surprising indeed if the Marxist word had not spread to some of his compatriots in the mines and refinery of New Caledonia. Though hardly capable of arousing and sustaining mass activity, a few such individuals might conceivably be able to sabotage the production of nickel and chrome. Most Javanese, on the other hand, have so far proved quite indifferent to Communist propaganda.

Anthropologists, and, one suspects, officials too, are

better informed about the most *esoteric* practices of the native islanders than they are about the everyday lives of the Chinese immigrants dwelling in Oceania. The lone Chinese trader, tucked away on an isolated beach, causes little speculation, but what goes on in the larger Chinese communities is a major mystery. It is known, of course, that most island Chinese sent very large contributions to the Chinese Nationalist Government during the war against Japan, and it should probably be assumed that their political sentiments have not yet changed. (Surely it would seem that these successful entrepreneurs would not voluntarily support a doctrine bent on doing away with individual property rights.)

But all the above instances are isolated situations, special security problems for officials who are undoubtedly as alert to the dangers of complacency as to the corrosion of suspicion. A more general problem, more appropriate to the subject of this book, is the question about the susceptibility of the islanders themselves to the doctrines of communism.

Some white colonials have rushed almost eagerly to the conclusion that the rash of postwar nativist movements are sinister manifestations of the long arm of Moscow. It is, of course, quite possible that Allied troops stationed in the Solomons may have prompted natives to show their dissatisfaction with caste subordination, thereby lending encouragement to the "Marching Rule" movement. On the other hand, similar movements have been a feature of culture contact in Oceania for a century or more; in fact, they are typical reactions of subordinated peoples whose old values have been destroyed and whose new aspirations cannot be realized. Some of these so-called "Cargo cults" have taken the form of religious cults passively awaiting the millennium; others have resorted to warfare in efforts to oust their colonial masters, the supposed causes of their frustrations. It would be insensitive to dismiss current manifestations of these movements as mere savage goings-on; but it would be equally shortsighted to deal with them as communist-inspired demonstrations.

Still unanswered is the question: Just how susceptible would the islanders be to the doctrines of Marx? There is much talk about "communism" as an element of the culture of primitive peoples; is this an appropriate term to apply to the social and property concepts of Oceanic natives? (Implied in this question is, of course, the suggestion that if natives are already "communistic," then they would be easy prey to the slogans of Marxism.)

The answer to this question lies in the distinction between "communism" and "communalism." Despite the extraordinary diversity in native Oceanic cultures, a fact which was emphasized in earlier pages, nearly all Oceanic peoples were *communalistic*, that is, they belonged to property-owning groups, usually based on ties of kinship; these corporate groups, rather than the individuals themselves, were the important social entities of native life. Most large units of property, including plots of land, big structures, seagoing canoes, and so on, were identified with groups and not with individuals. But in addition, individuals usually inherited or acquired some kinds of property which need not be shared. Moreover, each tribe or community was made up of several groups, and any individual's property rights depended not only upon the groups he belonged to, but upon his status in these groups. Now this is a long way removed from nineteenth-century western concepts of individualism, but it is just as far away from the Marxist concept of society and property. There would seem to be, therefore, little *native* scope for the spread of Marxist doctrine. Some islanders, it is true, might welcome a change of masters for the sake of revenge or novelty, but few of them possess the motives or the means to support large-scale insurrection. On the other hand, if Armageddon does come to the islands, it is unreasonable to expect that the islanders will rise to a man to defend the civilization that has taken so much from them and given them so little in return.

PRINCIPAL SOURCES AND ADDITIONAL
READING

Two earmarks of scholarly respectability are a numerously annotated text and a large bibliography, preferably containing an impressive sprinkling of articles from foreign periodicals. The first manifests the author's caution, the second his erudition. After some twenty-five years of preoccupation with Oceania—one third spent in the area and the rest reading about it—I have accumulated innumerable facts and opinions which I cannot pin down in neat little footnotes. Moreover, a book of this nature does not seem to be an appropriate setting for a display of bibliographic erudition. Hence, footnotes have been kept to a minimum, and the following list of titles is designed only for the general reader and the beginning student. Also, the list contains mainly works written in English; and except for subjects not covered in books, the list does not include articles published in periodicals. For the reader who wishes to go further into the subject, the titles listed contain extensive bibliographies.

GENERAL WORKS

Freeman, O. W. (ed.), *Geography of the Pacific.* New York: J. Wiley, 1951.

Furnas, J. C., *Anatomy of Paradise.* New York: William Sloan Associates, Inc., 1947. (A penetrating and interesting account of the recent history of the eastern part of Oceania, superbly written by a scholarly journalist.)

Great Britain, Naval Intelligence Division. *Pacific Islands* (Geographical Handbook Series), 4 vols., 1945.

Keesing, Felix M., *The South Seas in the Modern World.*

New York: The John Day Co., 1941. (The best book on the effects of colonialism, written by the acknowledged authority.)

Linton, Ralph, and P. S. Wingert, in collaboration with René d'Harnoncourt, *Arts of the South Seas*. New York: The Museum of Modern Art, 1946.

Robson, R. W. (ed.), *The Pacific Islands Year Book, 1956*. Sydney: Pacific Publications Pty., Ltd. (The indispensable reference handbook on the Pacific Islands: dates, statistics, survey of industries and communications, trade.)

Robson, R. W. (publisher), *Pacific Islands Monthly*. Sydney: Pacific Publications Pty., Ltd. (A magazine of news, statistics, shipping timetables, and editorial comment; with particularly good coverage of the British territories.)

ANTHROPOLOGY

Race

Birdsell, Joseph B., "New Data on Racial Stratification in Australasia," *American Journal of Physical Anthropology*, n. s., vol. 5, 1947.

—— "The Racial Origin of the Extinct Tasmanians," *Yearbook of Physical Anthropology*. New York, 1951.

Howells, W. W., "The Racial Elements of Melanesia," *Studies in the Anthropology of Oceania and Asia*, ed. by C. S. Coon and J. M. Andrews. Cambridge, Mass.: Peabody Museum Papers, vol. 20, 1943.

Hunt, Edward E., Jr., "A View of Somatology and Serology in Micronesia," *American Journal of Physical Anthropology*, n. s., vol. 8, 1950.

Marshall, D. S. and C. E. Snow, "An Evaluation of Polynesian Craniology," *American Journal of Physical Anthropology*, n. s., vol. 14, no. 3, September 1956.

Oliver, D. L., *Somatic Variability and Human Ecology*

on Bougainville, Solomon Islands. Cambridge, Mass.: Department of Anthropology, Harvard University, 1954.

Oliver, D. L. and W. W. Howells, "Micro-Evolution: Cultural Elements in Physical Variation," *American Anthropologist,* vol. 59, no. 6, 1957.

Shapiro, Harry L., "Physical Differentiation in Polynesia," *Studies in the Anthropology of Oceania and Asia,* ed. by C. S. Coon and J. M. Andrews. Cambridge, Mass.: Peabody Museum Papers, vol. 20, 1943.

Shapiro, H. L., "The Distribution of Blood Groups in Polynesia," *American Journal of Physical Anthropology,* vol. 26, March 1940.

Language

Benedict, Paul, "Thai, Kadai and Indonesian: A new alignment in Southeast Asia," *American Anthropologist,* vol. 44, 1942.

Biggs, Bruce, "Morphology-Syntax in a Polynesian Language," *The Journal of the Polynesian Society,* vol. 69, no. 4, 1960.

Capell, Arthur E., *A New Approach to Australian Linguistics,* Handbook of Australian Languages, Part 1. Sydney, 1956.

Cowan, H. K. J., "A large Papuan language Phylum in W. New Guinea," *Oceania,* December 1957.

Dyen, Isidore, *Austronesian Lexico-statistics* (mimeographed), 1960.

Elbert, Samuel, "Internal relationships of the Polynesian languages and dialects," *Southwestern Journal of Anthropology,* vol. 9, 1953.

Grace, George, "Subgroupings of Malayo-Polynesian: A report of tentative findings," *American Anthropologist,* vol. 57, 1955.

―― "The position of the Polynesian languages within the Austronesian (Malayo-Polynesian) Language family," *International Journal of American Linguistics,* Memoir 16. Bloomington, Ind., 1959.

Wurm, S. A., "The languages of the Eastern, Western, and Southern Highlands, Territory of Papua and New Guinea," *Linguistic Survey of the South-Western Pacific,* A. Capell, ed. Nouméa, 1960.

Native Cultures: General

Freeman, J. D. and W. R. Geddes, *Anthropology in the South Seas.* New Plymouth, New Zealand: Thomas Avery and Sons Limited, 1959.

The Journal of the Polynesian Society. Wellington, New Zealand.

Journal de la Société des Océanistes. Musée de l'Homme, Paris.

Mankind. Journal of the Anthropological Societies of Australia. Sydney.

Oceania. Quarterly. University of Sydney, New South Wales.

Native Cultures of Australia

Elkin, A. P., *The Australian Aborigines.* Sydney: Angus and Robertson, 1948.

Elkin, A. P. and Trevor A. Jones, *Arnhem Land Music,* Oceania Monographs, no. 9. Sydney, 1953–1958.

McCarthy, F. D., *Australian Aboriginal Decorative Art.* Sydney: Australian Museum, 1938.

Spencer, Baldwin, and F. J. Gillen, *The Arunta; A Study of a Stone Age People,* 2 vols. London: Macmillan and Co., Limited, 1927.

Stanner, W. E. H., "On Aboriginal Religion," *Oceania,* vol. 30, nos. 2, 4; vol. 31, nos. 2, 4; vol. 32, no. 2.

Warner, W. L., *Black Civilization.* New York: Harper & Brothers, 1937.

Native Cultures of Melanesia

Barrau, Jacques, "Subsistence Agriculture in Melanesia." Honolulu: Bernice P. Bishop Museum Bulletin, no. 219, 1958.

Bateson, Gregory, *Naven*. Cambridge, England: University Press, 1936.

Bell, F. L. S., *Primitive Melanesian Economy: An Analysis of the Economic System of the Tanga of New Ireland*, Oceania Monographs, Sydney, 1953.

Blackwood, Beatrice, *Both Sides of the Buka Passage*. Oxford: Clarendon Press, 1935.

Deacon, Arthur, *Malekula, a Vanishing People in the New Hebrides*, ed. by Camilla Wedgewood. London: George Routledge and Sons, Ltd., 1932.

Elkin, A. P., *Social Anthropology in Melanesia*. London and New York: Oxford University Press, 1953.

Fortune, Reo, *Sorcerers of Dobu*. London: George Routledge and Sons, Ltd., 1932.

Guiart, Jean, "Société, Rituels et Mythes du Nord-Ambrym (New Hebrides)," *Journal de la Société des Océanistes*, vol. 7, December 1951.

—— *L'Organisation Sociale et Politique du Nord Malekula*. Paris: Institut Français d'Océanie, 1952.

Lawrence, Peter, *Land Tenure Among the Garia*, Australian National University Social Science Monograph, no. 4. Canberra, 1955.

Malinowski, Bronislaw, *Argonauts of the Western Pacific*. London: George Routledge and Sons, Ltd., 1932.

Mead, Margaret, *Sex and Temperament in Three Primitive Societies*. New York: William Morrow and Co., Inc., 1935.

—— *The Mountain Arapesh*. New York: American Museum of Natural History, 1938–1949.

—— *Kinship in the Admiralty Islands.* New York: American Museum of Natural History, 1934.

Netherlands New Guinea. Anthropological Bibliography. Yale University. Southeast Asia Studies.

Oceania. See this journal for additional articles on Melanesia by Catherine and Ronald Berndt, K. O. C. Burridge, Paula Brown and H. C. Brookfield, M. J. Meggitt, John Nilles, K. E. Read, D'Arcy J. Ryan, Richard Saulsbury, H. I. Hogbin.

Oliver, Douglas, *A Solomon Island Society: Kinship and Leadership Among the Siuai of Bougainville.* Cambridge, Mass.: Harvard University Press, 1955.

Pospisil, Leapold, *Kapauku Papuans and Their Law.* New Haven: Yale University Publications in Anthropology, 1958.

Powdermaker, Hortense, *Life in Lesu.* New York: W. W. Norton and Co., 1938.

Reay, Marie, *The Kuma; Freedom and Conformity in the New Guinea Highlands.* Melbourne: Melbourne University Press, 1959.

Thomson, Basil, *The Fijians.* London: William Heinemann, 1908.

Williams, F. E., *Orokaiva Society.* London: Oxford University Press, 1930.

—— *Drama of Orokolo.* Oxford: Clarendon Press, 1940.

Native Cultures of Polynesia

Barthel, T., "*Grundlagen zur Entzifferung der Osterinseln-schrift,*" *Abhandlung aus dem Gebiete der Auslandskunde,* vol. 64. Hamburg, 1958.

Beaglehole, Ernest and Pearl, *Ethnology of Pukapuka.* Honolulu: Bernice P. Bishop Museum Bulletin, no. 150, 1938.

Buck, Peter H. (Te Rangi Hiroa), *Mangaian Society.* Honolulu: Bernice P. Bishop Museum Bulletin, no. 122, 1934.

—— Vikings of the Sunrise. New York: Frederick A. Stokes Co., 1938.

——— An Introduction to Polynesian Anthropology. Honolulu: Bernice P. Bishop Museum Bulletin, no. 187, 1945.

—— The Coming of the Maori. Wellington, N. Z.: Whitcombe and Tombs, Ltd., 1949.

Burrows, E. G., Ethnology of Futuna. Honolulu: Bernice P. Bishop Museum Bulletin, no. 138, 1936.

——— Ethnology of Uvéa (Wallis Island). Honolulu: Bernice P. Bishop Museum Bulletin, no. 145, 1937.

Danielsson, Bengt, Love in the South Seas. London: Geo. Allen and Unwin, 1956.

Duff, R., The Moa-hunter Period of Maori Culture. Wellington, 1956.

Emory, Kenneth, "Pacific Islands: Area 21," Council for Old World Archaeology Survey. Cambridge, Mass., 1958.

Emory, Kenneth and Y. Sinoto, "Radiocarbon Dates Significant for Pacific Anthropology," Pacific Science Association Information Bulletin, vol. 11, no. 3, 1959.

Firth, Raymond, Economics of the New Zealand Maori. R. E. Owen, Government Printer, Wellington, 1959.

——— We, the Tikopia. London: George Allen and Unwin, Ltd., 1936.

——— Primitive Polynesian Economy. London: Geo. Routledge and Sons, Ltd., 1939.

Gifford, E. W., Tongan Society. Honolulu: Bernice P. Bishop Museum Bulletin, no. 61, 1929.

Goldman, Irving, "The Evolution of Polynesian Societies," Culture in History: Essays in Honor of Paul Radin. New York: Columbia University Press, 1960.

Golson, Jack, "L'Archaéologie du Pacifique Sud, résultats et perspectives," Journal de la Société des Océanistes, vol. 15, no. 15, 1959.

Handy, E. S. C., Polynesian Religion. Honolulu: Bernice P. Bishop Museum Bulletin, no. 34, 1927.

Henry, Teura, *Ancient Tahiti.* Honolulu: Bernice P. Bishop Museum Bulletin, no. 47, 1928.

Heyerdahl, T., *American Indians in the South Pacific.* London: Geo. Allen and Unwin, 1952.

Hogbin, H. I., *Law and Order in Polynesia.* New York: Harcourt, Brace and Co., 1934.

Keesing, Felix M., *Social Anthropology in Polynesia.* London, New York, and Melbourne: Oxford University Press, 1953.

Kennedy, D. G., *Field Notes on the Culture of Vaitupu, Ellice Islands.* New Plymouth, N. Z.: Polynesian Society Memoirs, no. 9, 1931.

Linton, Ralph, "Marquesan Culture," *The Individual and his Society,* by Abram Kardiner. New York: Columbia University Press, 1939.

Malo, David, "Hawaiian Antiquities." Honolulu: Bernice P. Bishop Museum Special Publication, no. 2, 1951.

Mead, Margaret, *Coming of Age in Samoa.* New York: William Morrow and Co., 1928.

Melville, Herman. *Typee.* New York: Harper & Brothers, 1852.

Metraux, Alfred, *Ethnology of Easter Island.* Honolulu: Bernice P. Bishop Museum Bulletin, no. 160, 1940.

Sahlins, Marshall D., *Social Stratification in Polynesia.* Seattle: American Ethnological Society, 1958.

Sharp, Andrew, *Ancient Voyagers in the Pacific.* London: Penguin Books, 1957.

Skinner, H. D., *The Moriori of Chatham Islands.* Honolulu: Bernice P. Bishop Museum Bulletin, no. 9, 1923.

Suggs, Robert C., *The Island Civilizations of Polynesia.* New York: Mentor Books, 1960.

Williamson, R. W., *The Social and Political Systems of Central Polynesia,* 3 vols. New York: Cambridge University Press, 1924.

—— *Religious and Cosmic Beliefs of Central Polynesia,* 2 vols. New York: Cambridge University Press, 1933.

—— (ed. by R. Piddington) *Religion and Social Organi-*

zation in Central Polynesia. New York: Cambridge University Press, 1937.

Williamson, R. W. and Ralph Piddington, *Essays in Polynesian Ethnology.* New York: Cambridge University Press, 1939.

Native Cultures of Micronesia

Barnett, H. G., *Palauan Society.* University of Oregon, 1949.

Burrows, E. G. and M. E. Spiro, *An Atoll Culture: Ethnography of Ifaluk in the Central Carolines.* New Haven: Human Relations Area Files, 1953.

Fischer, John, *The Eastern Carolines.* Behavior Monographs. New Haven: Human Relations Area Files, 1957.

Gladwin, Thomas and S. B. Sarason, *Truk: Man in Paradise.* New York: Viking Fund Publications in Anthropology, no. 20, 1953.

Goodenough, W. H., *Property, Kin, and Community on Truk.* New Haven: Yale University Publications in Anthropology, 1951.

Grimble, Arthur, *We Chose the Islands.* New York: William Morrow and Co., Inc., 1952.

Lessa, William, *The Ethnology of Ulithi Atoll* (mimeographed). Los Angeles: University of California, 1950.

Spoehr, Alexander, *Majuro, a Village in the Marshall Islands,* Fieldiana: Anthropology, vol. 39. Chicago: Chicago Natural History Museum, 1949.

—— "Marianas Prehistory: Archaeological Survey and Excavations on Saipan, Tinian and Rota," Fieldiana: Anthropology, vol. 48. Chicago: Chicago Natural History Museum, 1957.

Tetens, A. F., *Among the Savages of the South Seas; Memoirs of Micronesia, 1862–1868.* London: Oxford University Press, 1958.

Thompson, Laura, *Guam and Its People*. Princeton: Princeton University Press, 1947.

COLONIAL HISTORY AND SOCIOLOGY

General

Beaglehole, J. C., *The Exploration of the Pacific*. London: A. C. Black, Ltd., 1934.

Brookes, Jean I., *International Rivalry in the Pacific Islands*. Berkeley: University of California Press, 1941.

Dulles, Foster R., *America in the Pacific*. Boston: Houghton Mifflin Co., 1932.

Faivre, Jean-Paul, *L'Expansion Française dans le Pacifique: 1800–1842*. Paris: Nouvelles Editions Latines, 1953.

Kuykendall, Ralph S., *A History of Hawaii*. New York: The Macmillan Co., 1926.

Martin, K. L. P., *Missionaries and Annexation in the Pacific*. London: Humphrey Milford, 1924.

Morison, Samuel E., *The Maritime History of Massachusetts, 1783–1860*. Boston: Houghton Mifflin Co., 1921.

Scholefield, G. H., *The Pacific, Its Past and Future*. London: John Murray, 1919.

Australia

Berndt, Ronald and Catherine, *From Black to White in South Australia*. Melbourne: F. W. Cheshire, 1951.

Foxcroft, E. J. B., *Australian Native Policy*. Melbourne: Melbourne University Press, 1941.

Price, A. Grenfell, *White Settlers and Native Peoples*. Melbourne: Georgian House, 1949.

Turnbull, Clive, *Black War; The Extermination of the Tasmanian Aborigines*. Melbourne: F. W. Cheshire, Pty., Ltd., 1948.

Torres Strait

Raven-Hart, Major R., *The Happy Isles*. Melbourne: Georgian House, 1949.

Papua and New Guinea

Belshaw, Cyril, *The Great Village; The economics and social welfare of Hanuabada, an urban community in Papua*. London: Routledge & Kegan Paul, 1957.

—— *In Search of Wealth: a study of the emergence of commercial operations in the Melanesian Society of Southeastern Papua*. Menasha, Wisc.: American Anthropological Association Memoir 80, 1950.

Hogbin, H. I., *Transformation Scene: the changing culture of a New Guinea village*. London: Routledge & Kegan Paul, 1951.

—— *Social Change*. London: Watts, 1958.

Mair, Lucy P., *Australia in New Guinea*. London: Christophers, 1948.

Mead, Margaret, *New Lives for Old: cultural transformation—Manus 1928–1953*. New York: William Morrow and Co., Inc., 1956.

Murray, Hubert, *Papua of Today*. London: P. S. King and Sons, Ltd., 1925.

Reed, Stephen W., *The Making of Modern New Guinea*. Philadelphia: American Philosophical Society, Institute of Pacific Relations, 1943.

Worsley, Peter, *The Trumpet Shall Sound*. London: Macgibbon and Kee, 1957.

Solomon Islands

Belshaw, Cyril. *Changing Melanesia; social-economics of culture contact*. Melbourne and Wellington: Oxford University Press, 1954.

Firth, Raymond, *Social Change on Tikopia*. London: Macmillan and Co., Limited, 1959.

Hogbin, H. I., *Experiments in Civilization*. London: George Routledge and Sons, Ltd., 1939.

New Hebrides

Belshaw, Cyril. (See above.)

Guiart, Jean, "John Frum Movement in Tanna," *Oceania*, vol. 22, 1952.

—— "Forerunners of Melanesian Nationalism," *Oceania*, vol. 22, 1951.

—— *Un siècle et demi de contacts culturels à Tanna* (New Hebrides), Publication de la Société des Océanistes. Paris, 1956.

Harrison, Tom, *Savage Civilization*. New York: Alfred A. Knopf, Inc., 1937.

O'Reilly, Patrick, *Bibliographie méthodique, analytique et critique des Nouvelles-Hébrides*, Société des Océanistes, Publications no. 8. Paris, 1958.

—— *Hébridais; répertoire bio-bibliographique des Nouvelles-Hébrides*. Société des Océanistes, Publications no. 6. Paris, 1957.

New Caledonia

Burchett, W. G., *Pacific Treasure Island: New Caledonia*. Melbourne: F. W. Cheshire Pty., Ltd., 1941.

O'Reilly, Patrick, *Bibliographie méthodique, analytique et critique de la Nouvelle-Calédonie*, Société des Océanistes, Publications no. 4. Paris, 1955.

Fiji

Coulter, J. W., *Fiji, Little India of the Pacific*. Chicago: University of Chicago Press, 1942.

Geddes, W. R., *Deuba: a study of a Fijian village*. Wellington: Polynesian Society Memoir 22, 1945.

Hayden, Howard, *Moturiki; a pilot project in community development*. London and New York: Oxford University Press, 1954.

Roth, G. K. *Fijian Way of Life*. London: Oxford University Press, 1953.

Spate, O. H. K., *The Fijian People: Economic Problems and Prospects*. Suva. Government Press, 1959.

Thompson, Laura, *Fijian Frontier*. New York: American Council, Institute of Pacific Relations, 1940.

New Zealand

Beaglehole, Ernest and Pearl, *Some Modern Maoris*. N. Z. Council for Educational Research, Wellington. Whitcombe and Tombs, 1946.

Sutherland, I. L. G. (ed.), *The Maori People Today*. London: Oxford Press, 1940.

Tonga

Beaglehole, Ernest and Pearl, *Pangai, Village in Tonga*. Wellington, N. Z.: Memoirs of the Polynesian Society, 1946.

Thomson, Basil, *The Diversions of a Prime Minister*. Edinburgh and London: William Blackwood and Sons, 1894.

Samoa

Gray, Capt. J. A. C., USN, *Amerika Samoa: a History of American Samoa and Its U. S. Naval Administration*. Annapolis: U. S. Naval Institute, 1960.

Keesing, Felix M., *Modern Samoa*. London: George Allen and Unwin, Ltd., 1934.

Keesing, F. M. and M. M., *Elite Communication in Samoa: a study in leadership*. Stanford: Stanford University Press, 1956.

Cook Islands

Beaglehole, Ernest, *Social Change in the South Pacific: Rarotonga and Aitutaki*. London: George Allen and Unwin, Ltd., 1957.

French Polynesia

Danielsson, Bengt, *Work and Life on Raroia* (Tuamotus). London: Macmillan and Co., Limited, 1956.

Newbury, C. W., *The Administration of French Oceania, 1842–1906* (mss.).

O'Reilly, Patrick (ed.), *"Tahiti et la Polynésie Française," Journal de la Société des Océanistes*, vol. 15. Paris, 1959.

Russel, Samuel, *Tahiti and French Oceania*. Sydney: Pacific Publications Pty., Ltd., 1935.

Pitcairn

Shapiro, Harry L., *The Heritage of the Bounty*. New York: Doubleday Anchor Books, 1962.

Hawaii

Crawford, David L., *Paradox in Hawaii*. Boston: Stratford Press, 1933.

Lind, Andrew W., *An Island Community: Ecological Succession in Hawaii*. Chicago: University of Chicago Press, 1938.

Michener, J. A., *Hawaii*. New York: Bantam Books, 1961.

Norbeck, Edward, *Pineapple Town, Hawaii.* Berkeley: University of California Press, 1959.

Shoemaker, James H., *Labor in the Territory of Hawaii, 1939.* Washington, D. C.: Government Printing Office, 1940.

Gilbert and Ellice Islands

Maude, H. E., "The Coöperative Movement in the Gilbert and Ellice Islands," *Proceedings of the Pacific Science Congress.* Auckland, 1950.

Nauru and Ocean Island

Ellis, A. F., *Ocean Island and Nauru.* Sydney: Angus and Robertson, Ltd., 1936.

Maude, H. C. and H. E., "The Social Organization of Banaba or Ocean Island, Central Pacific," *Journal of the Polynesian Society* (New Plymouth, N. Z.), vol. 41, 1932.

Wedgewood, Camilla, "Report on Research Work in Nauru Island, Central Pacific," *Oceania,* vol. 6, 1936.

Line Islands

Bryan, E. H., Jr., *American Polynesia.* Honolulu: Tongg Publishing Co., 1941.

WORLD WAR II AND THE ISLANDERS

Belshaw, C. S., *Island Administration in the South West Pacific; Government and Reconstruction in New Caledonia, the New Hebrides, and the British Solomon Islands.* London and New York: Royal Institute of International Affairs, 1950.

Embree, John F., "Military Government in Saipan and

Tinian," *Applied Anthropology,* vol. 5, no. 1, 1946.

Keesing, Felix M. (ed.), *Handbook on the Trust Territory of the Pacific Islands.* Washington, D. C.: United States Navy Department, 1948.

McCarthy, Dudley, *Southwest Pacific Area: First Year.* (Australia in the War of 1939–1945). Canberra, 1959.

Mair, Lucy P., *Australia in New Guinea.* London: Christophers, 1948.

Oliver, Douglas L. (ed.), *Planning Micronesia's Future; A Summary of the United States Commercial Company's Economic Survey of Micronesia, 1946.* Cambridge: Harvard University Press, 1951.

Useem, John, "Governing the Occupied Areas of the South Pacific: Wartime Lessons and Peacetime Proposals," *Applied Anthropology,* vol. 4, no. 3, 1945.

AMERICAN MICRONESIA (POSTWAR)

Force, Roland, *Leadership and Culture Change in Palau,* Fieldiana, vol. 50. Chicago: Chicago Natural History Museum, 1960.

Spoehr, Alexander, *Saipan: the Ethnology of a war-devastated Island,* Fieldiana, vol. 41. Chicago: Chicago Natural History Museum, 1954.

INDEX